ACCOUNTING
TO
ZOOLOGY

Graduate Fields Defined

Amy J. Goldstein, Editor

Peterson's Guides
Princeton, New Jersey

Library of Congress Cataloging-in-Publication Data

Accounting to zoology : graduate fields defined.

 Includes index.
 1. Universities and colleges—United States—Graduate work—Dictionaries.
I. Goldstein, Amy J.
LB2371.A33   1987   378'.1553   86-22612
ISBN 0-87866-537-4

Composition and design by Peterson's Guides

Printed in the United States of America

10 9 8 7 6 5 4 3 2 1

For information about other Peterson's publications, please see the listing at the
back of this volume.

CONTENTS

Contents

Contents

Contents

Contents

Contents

Contents

Contents

INTRODUCTION

Accounting to Zoology is a comprehensive volume of definitions of graduate and professional fields written by graduate educators. It is the only reference work of its kind. Peterson's Guides has been collecting these definitions for years, updating them annually, for its definitive Guides to Graduate Study. All of the nearly 300 fields covered in those Guides, from A to Z, are described here, grouped within the areas of humanities and social sciences; biological, agricultural, and health sciences; physical sciences and mathematics; and engineering and applied sciences. The statements not only define the fields but also discuss types of graduate programs and degrees, research and applied work, employment prospects, and trends, all from the perspective of experts currently teaching in the field at the graduate level.

This book will be of interest to students at all levels, placement counselors, faculty advisers, librarians, and anyone else interested in a picture of graduate study by subject. It is meant primarily for prospective graduate and professional students just beginning to explore their field. With the definitions all in one volume, a reader can easily look into the related areas of business, mathematics, and computer science, for example, without having to consult many different reference sources.

Because of the broad nature of many fields, any system of organization (see the table of contents for a quick look at this book's structure) is bound to involve a certain amount of overlap and arbitrary choice. Readers should be aware of the interdisciplinary nature of some fields and should therefore be sure to consult a number of the definitions presented here. Environmental studies, for example, is a field whose various aspects are studied in several types of departments and schools at the graduate level. Readers interested in such studies might find relevant graduate programs in city and regional planning, environmental policy and resource management, public policy and administration, ecology, environmental and occupational health, environmental biology, environmental sciences, natural resources, energy management and policy, and environmental engineering. In a somewhat different vein, a reader

1

Introduction

interested in biopsychology might have to look in the biology and psychology areas before finding the definition. An alphabetical index (from accounting to zoology) is provided for quick reference.

The 298 field definitions that make up *Accounting to Zoology* were collected by Peterson's Guides in the spring and summer of 1986 for publication in both this book and the 1987 edition of the Annual Guides to Graduate Study. Some are new, and many were updated from the 1986 Guides. The authors are educators at the graduate level, and they represent a diversity of academic institutions—public and private, large and small, nationally known and more regionally oriented. A few of the authors represent professional organizations in their field. All statements are the authors' alone and do not necessarily represent the opinions of Peterson's Guides. We present them with the certainty that anyone interested in higher education and careers will find this book to be of value.

FIELD DEFINITIONS

Humanities and Social Sciences

Applied Arts and Design

Applied Arts and Design   The applied arts and design cover an extremely broad area within the visual arts. In fact, the terms "applied arts and design" encompass virtually all arts activities with the exception of fine arts (painting, sculpture, printmaking, and those areas of photography, film, and video that are the province of the museum and gallery rather than the consumer marketplace). Applied arts and design, however, are endeavors in which many of the same visual skills and sensibilities often associated with the fine artist are brought into play but are placed at the service of specifically delineated problem-solving demands. In some respects, this makes the designer's challenge especially exciting, for it is necessary to find creative solutions to complex problems, often working within limits imposed externally, such as media production, market restrictions, tight budgets, or a client's personal tastes. Typical fields that fall within the applied arts and design include graphic and advertising design (communication design), fashion design, illustration, film and video, photography, architecture and interior design, product and industrial design, jewelry, textiles, and ceramic design.

Applied artists, though often influenced by historical or contemporary trends in the fine arts, have a profound impact on the world around us. Virtually every object in our daily life, from knives and forks to clothes, the houses in which we live, the cars we drive, the books we read, or the advertising we see in print and on television—all the manmade images and objects that virtually define the modern world—bear the designer's stamp. It is clear that our society has a great need for designers, and their professional services are much in demand. In some areas, such as fashion design, there is a "star system" that makes us aware of the latest trends and who creates them. Much more anonymous, however, are the highly skilled

3

Applied Arts and Design (continued)

(and often highly paid) advertising designers who are the creative directors of major agencies or the art directors who produce the multiplicity of images that we see on television, in magazines, in books, and elsewhere. Illustrators, architects, interior designers, and product designers—indeed all who enter the applied arts fields—are usually stable members of the upper middle class.

Graduate work in the applied arts is somewhat limited. A number of schools offer graduate programs in the disciplines noted above, but in general, a master's degree is not as significant for career entry or advancement as is a thorough undergraduate preparation and the development of a first-rate portfolio. Doctoral programs in design are virtually (and appropriately) nonexistent. Unlike many professions, in which job entry is based on academic records or other documented evidence of previous achievement, employment in the applied arts and design fields is frequently based substantially upon the presentation of a portfolio of work. The quality of this work is critical to the employment process. Graduate study can sometimes provide advanced theoretical understanding of problems in the applied arts and design disciplines. It may be most relevant in such areas as architecture, environmental design, and industrial design. However, students considering the design professions should evaluate the comprehensiveness and quality of their undergraduate training carefully before deciding whether to continue their studies at the graduate level or enter directly into the field.

David C. Levy
Executive Dean
Parsons School of Design

Environmental Design The term environmental design is commonly used to describe some rather different types of graduate educational programs. Usually, it is an umbrella term that encompasses the professional disciplines involved with designing the physical environment—architecture, landscape architecture, urban design, interior design, facility planning, apparel design, graphic design, and industrial or product design. Often in this usage, environmental design is the name of the college within which some grouping of the above programs exists. Another pattern of programs that are typically included under the term environmental design involve those that might be termed generic design programs, in which the focus is on the act or process of designing per se. In these programs, students learn to apply the design process to any environmental system ranging in scale and complexity from a chair to a regional public transportation system.

Students considering environmental design should be aware of three distinct types of graduate educational programs. First are the graduate "first professional degree" programs aimed at preparing students with almost any undergraduate background to become licensed or certified practitioners of one of the design professions, such as architecture, landscape architecture, or interior design. For these programs the profession accredits or recognizes the graduate program as meeting the minimum requirements for the "first professional degree," and graduates of accredited programs receive certain advantages in becoming licensed professionals, chief among these being a reduced period of required apprenticeship. In contrast, the second type of graduate program is based upon the student having completed the "first professional degree" at the undergraduate level or, alternately, upon the student having no interest in becoming a licensed professional. The graduate program in this case is designed to enable the student to explore in depth some particular aspect or to develop a specialization within the discipline, such as computer-aided design or behaviorally based programming. This degree, while not essential for professional registration, is often necessary for a person who intends to teach in a professional school. In some cases this degree is recognized as the "second professional degree." The third pattern is a more traditional research-oriented graduate program, often terminating with the Ph.D. This type of program is intended to prepare students for research careers in academia and in the public and private sectors.

In many cases, all three types of graduate programs exist within the same department or college. However, programs vary extensively in their orientation and emphasis. For example, some emphasize aesthetics and form, while others may stress technological factors such as energy conservation, and still others might focus more on human-needs aspects. In some cases, these are integrated in a balanced way in a single program, but students should exercise care in selecting a program that matches their interests.

Given the diversity of program types discussed above and limited space, it is difficult to be specific about employment opportunities. Projections are, however, that employment opportunities in the environmental design area will be good to excellent in the near future for both the public and private sectors

Environmental Design (continued)

and for university positions. It is advisable, however, that students make inquiries about the prospects for their specific area of interest.

William Sims, Chairman
Department of Design and Environmental Analysis
Cornell University

Graphic Design   Graphic design is the problem-solving discipline in which ideas and concepts are translated into visual form. Through analytical thinking and sound aesthetic judgment, the design practitioner presents information in an intelligible, logical, and credible manner. The profession requires designers to understand society, technology, and the arts and sciences and be able to interact with those in professions outside the design field. Designers provide service for government, business, religion, education, and the whole host of clients who must convey a message to an audience.

The designer's responsibility begins with identifying the communication need. He or she then develops a range of effective solutions through systematic approaches. The final design is executed within the constraints of client tastes, time, money, and available production technology.

Certainly the bulk of what designers do results in printed communications, such as posters, brochures, books, magazines, logos, trademarks, and the like. But designers also employ a variety of production and manufacturing processes for packaging, signing systems, displays and exhibitions, and television—any medium in which information is transmitted and visual interest is to be created.

Although it is utilitarian, graphic design embodies the richness of the fine arts. Clear and imaginative visual communications can be enjoyed for their own intrinsic value. The work of graphic designers stimulates and improves our visual and verbal perception.

Bruce Ian Meader
Program in Graphic Design
School of Art
University of Michigan

Illustration   Although illustration techniques have changed throughout the centuries, the basic purpose of illustration is unchanged. Illustration is the art of elucidation and decoration. Illustrations explain and interpret visually a large variety of emotions and concepts. They may stimulate the imagination, arouse curiosity, promote thoughtfulness, and even provide entertainment.

Those who aspire to be illustrators should possess not only a strong artistic inclination but a keen interest in the world around them, as all of life's experiences must become part of their vocabulary of images. Also essential to eventual success in illustration is a firm commitment to the craft and the readiness to give the time and devote the effort to acquire the drawing, painting, design, and conceptual skills necessary. As illustrators are commissioned by editors and art directors to fulfill a specific purpose or need, they must feel not only comfortable but challenged by the problem solving required. Norman Rockwell wrote in describing the role of this challenge in his career, "The only limit to my work, really, was the limit to my imagination." His words hold true as much, or possibly more, to the illustrators of today and of the future.

Much of illustration has changed with the times. It is more diverse. It is visually more colorful, more attention getting, and frequently more design oriented. However, there has occurred a simultaneous renaissance of traditionalism and of realistic painting. Annuals of the best in today's illustration demonstrate that the variety of styles and personal directions is endless and the only common denominator of the work is excellence.

The ways in which the profession is practiced vary. Well-paid staff positions are available, but most illustrators opt for the stimulation and variety of free-lance work. Illustrations are used editorially for books, newspapers, magazines, and trade publications; in innumerable phases of advertising; in animation and animatics; in annual reports, cards and posters, packaging, and record and cassette covers; in storyboards; in point-of-purchase displays in stores; and now in computer graphics. The list is almost as endless as the variety of illustrators.

Graduate programs in illustration provide several functions. Many permit the already professionally competent or accomplished illustrator to study independently and continuously for an extended period with a highly qualified, nationally recognized illustrator, thereby continuing the search for excellence and the development of a personal style that will enable the graduate to enter the job market at a high level. Some programs offer a series of short and very intense courses, providing possibilities of growth and challenge through the stimulation of workshops and lectures by exciting and respected top illustrators. Other programs provide, in addition,

Illustration (continued)

teacher training for those who wish to enhance their professional lives "on the board" with the invigorating enrichment of teaching. Whatever the direction, these graduate programs can be the major factor in allowing the artist to realize his or her full potential in the intense, demanding, exciting, and creative field of illustration.

Barbara L. Bradley, Director
Department of Illustration
Academy of Art College

Industrial Design   Industrial design is the profession that is chiefly concerned with the development of form for consumer and commercial products of all kinds. In addition, industrial designers in recent years have expanded their practices to include visual communications or graphics associated with product development and commercial or contract interiors and furniture systems, commonly referred to as "open office systems." Approximately 20,000 industrial designers currently practice in the United States, occupying positions in private consultation and corporate staff posts.

Programs for the education of industrial designers can be found in all regions of the United States. Historically, industrial design programs burgeoned in small private art colleges in the middle thirties, but during the last two decades there has been a rapid development of programs in major universities. The private art college places a high concentration on development of skills and techniques of design in studio courses. The university programs are more diverse, developing curriculums based on general university offerings and tailored courses generated within the program and from other areas of study external to the program in design. As the field has grown and changed with the demands of industry and the adaptation of new technologies such as computers and robotics, there has been a concurrent change in the education of designers and the skills they are expected to develop and a new emphasis on graduate study.

Prior to the era of the sixties, graduate study in design was an extension of studio arts, and the majority of designers received Master of Fine Arts degrees. While the terminal degree in design is still a master's, there has been a shifting away from the studio arts focus and a higher concentration on the development of expertise in management, education, computer-aided design and computer graphics, human factors, and planning. The need for this content is a reflection of the evolution and progress in design services from a base in applied arts to professional design services. Currently, graduate degrees range from the traditional Master of Arts and Master of Fine Arts to professional "tag" degrees, such as the Master of Industrial Design and Master of Science in Industrial Design.

Over its fifty-year history of professional service in the United States, industrial design has experienced steady growth and increased employment opportunities. The demand for design services may be shifting to new areas of application, but there is no sign of decline in opportunities. Graduate education for industrial designers is gradually becoming a necessity as additional expertise in advanced technologies and professional development are required. In addition, as educational programs have shifted to major universities, there has been an increase in the demand for designers with terminal degrees to fill academic positions. Many opportunities currently exist in the educational field for qualified industrial designers. Recent studies are producing evidence that the field of design consultation is beginning to diversify, moving away from areas of business that are strictly design related. This trend may mean greater opportunities for the broadly educated designer having developed areas of expertise that are either adjunct to design or not directly related to design activity.

Potential graduate students seeking additional career development are advised to seek out industrial design programs that provide a strong methodological, research and development, and extended career base of expertise for their studies in order to prepare for an evolving design profession.

Joseph A. Koncelik
Professor and Chairman
Department of Industrial Design
Ohio State University

Interior Design Interior design as understood today is an emerging profession of specialized competency within the broad spectrum of environmental design. It has strong links with the history of art as well as architecture and planning. The increasingly urban character of modern life has created a substantial demand for highly specialized expertise in advanced design, research, and design education. Programs of study vary widely from those that are largely self-directed to highly structured programs of study at the graduate level. The Master of Fine Arts degree is the accepted terminal degree

Interior Design (continued)

with the most prominent programs located administratively in an art school or department while others are to be found in home economics, human resources, architecture, design, human ecology, or environmental design.

Interior designers generally develop special expertise in residential or contract work. Their technical development includes knowledge of structure with an emphasis on interior construction, building systems, acoustics, lighting, heating, and air-conditioning. Successful designers have a broad understanding of the history of art and design, business skills, and highly developed visual sensitivity.

Employment opportunities are widely available in architect's offices, design studios, space-planning firms, and design departments of larger corporations. Career opportunities may also be found in related fields such as furniture design, facility management, and interior design education. Over the last several years the popularity of interior design as a professional career has grown substantially. The requirements for professional competence have increased steadily, and opportunities for professional practitioners are extensive.

George V. Bayliss, Dean
Tyler School of Art
Temple University

Photography   The study of photography offers a vast range of applications and opportunities. Under the broad heading of photography, one can find disciplines that are quite varied and distinct from each other, yet they are linked together by the tools and techniques that their respective careers require. Because of this diversity, most graduate educational programs head in one of several directions. One pattern of course work concentrates on a fine arts approach, which includes the historical and theoretical aspects of visual communication as it relates to photography. Students are often required to produce a large final body of work that represents the development of both their conceptual aesthetics and technical skills. Background study in other visual arts and related areas, such as painting, drawing, and art history, are often prerequisites that are completed at the undergraduate level.

Another pattern of programs requires students to complete a body of course work within a multidisciplined approach. Such course work may be quite varied. Offerings may range from technical programs emphasizing scientific and industrial applications to fine art and conceptual programs similar to the approach described above. In either case, graduate students will be required to produce a thesis or a project that demonstrates a mastery of their intended field of study or discipline. A thesis involves the production of a major body of written work and requires extensive research and documentation. In contrast, graduate projects often culminate in the production of a major body of photographic work, for which there should also be written documentation.

Potential career opportunities are limited only to the imagination of the individual. Some of the many possibilities are industrial/scientific photography; fashion photography; commercial applications, including advertising; photojournalism; motion pictures and video; work in photo-finishing laboratories; portraiture; underwater photography; fine art photography; museum curatorship; teaching at both the high school and college levels; social research and documentation; and sports photography. These are broad and generalized headings for which there may be many subdivisions.

The number of students interested in both undergraduate and graduate programs in photography has been steadily increasing during the past fifteen years. As a result, programs and departments of photography have been developed and created to meet this demand. The master's degree is usually considered to be the terminal degree for most programs. While there are several Ph.D. programs currently available, these are usually combined with either historical, educational, or scientific course work requirements. Because of the great diversity that an education in photography may offer, it is advisable for students to thoroughly research their specific areas of interest in relation to the various programs that are offered throughout the country.

David Schrader
Director of Graduate Admissions
Brooks Institute of Photography

Textile Design   The designer is a creator, producing and creating new designs and new configurations for today's market.

Students interested in graduate studies in textile design must develop their excellence in conceptual and weaving aspects of design and color—in either surface design or weaving. Graduates must become proficient, versatile, and desirable to potential employers,

Textile Design (continued)

as well as confident enough to pursue independent self-employment. Graduate students have an opportunity to expand their work in one concentration, something that most undergraduate programs do not allow. Graduate school also allows them to develop their knowledge with a particular instructor or instructors and with a new point of view. While they pursue artistic achievement in fabric design, graduate students explore creative thinking and designing and study the chemistry of dyeing, multiharness designing, photographic serigraphy, and computer design and technology. The textile designer must build sensitivity in many areas, including a broad understanding of and interest in technology, the environment, and human needs for fibers, and be able to engage in analysis, research, and development. Holders of graduate degrees are employed in various areas of industry and teaching or develop their own businesses as free-lance designers or small-business operators.

Today the most advanced programs can be found in graduate schools that are developing computer-oriented curricula and are working with graphic designing in color, new software for color separation for the printer, and computer tapes for power loom designing. In today's world, the computer is becoming a very important tool for the textile designer.

There is also a continued need for M.F.A. candidates who are interested in conservation and renovation in the historic and archaeological areas.

Donald Bujnowski, Professor
College of Fine and Applied Arts
Rochester Institute of Technology

Architecture

Architecture Programs in architecture at the graduate level are, in general, intended for the student who wishes to pursue a career as a practicing architect. As in any professional program, a student must cover the fundamentals of the field with courses in design, architectural history, theory, and building technology. The design studio is the primary vehicle for the exploration of the art of architecture. Teaching in the studio occurs both on a one-to-one basis with over-the-board criticism and in the more formal setting of public review and discussion of projects. Students are taught that building design must be based on ideas. The basis of these ideas must involve both formal and social issues, including spatial definition, circulation sequence, response to a site's context, building function, and user's needs.

Upon graduation, most students pursue professional registration by completing a three-year internship in an architectural firm. Following this work experience, the graduate is eligible to take the licensing examination, a rigorous series of tests covering design, site planning, structural systems, heating and ventilating systems, construction methods, and professional practice. As a registered architect, an individual may either open his or her own practice or work for an established firm. Those students who do not pursue this route often become involved in teaching or in the related fields of planning, landscape architecture, interior design, and historic preservation.

Judith Kinnard
Lecturer in Architecture
School of Architecture
Princeton University

Landscape Architecture Landscape architecture generally describes the field of designing and planning the landscape. Wherever human activity alters the environment, it is properly the mission of landscape architecture to engage in the process of determining the best use of the land and in generating plans and designs to meet the needs of people. An interdisciplinary field, landscape architecture borders, if not overlaps, the fields of architecture, engineering, city planning, and resource management and includes such diverse activities as regional planning, urban design, park planning, and garden art. When practiced at its highest levels, landscape architecture creates works of significant cultural value and artistic achievement.

As a discipline that encompasses the realms of both natural and man-made environments, professional preparation builds upon background knowledge in the natural sciences, social sciences, and humanities. Typical professional curricula include basic course work in design, site engineering, plant materials, history, and theory followed by increasingly complex applied studies in design decision making and research methods. Courses are structured to teach design skills and to develop habits of critical thinking and analysis that provide the framework for competent professional activity.

Landscape Architecture (continued)

Graduate study opportunities in landscape architecture are designed for two general categories of students. The first, for those whose undergraduate background is in liberal arts, fine arts, or sciences and who seek a professional design degree for the first time, aims to provide a program of study that prepares the student for entry into the profession. The format for instruction is normally a combination of extensive studio work, lectures, and field studies. The second program type is designed for those who have previously obtained an undergraduate professional design degree, as in landscape architecture or architecture, and is intended to provide opportunity for the student to pursue advanced study in the discipline of landscape architecture or research. Courses of study vary among institutions, depending upon the intentions of the program and the particular relationship the landscape architecture program has with other academic professional degree programs at the school. In many cases, institutions offer more than one type of program of study. Specializations in landscape architecture available in various programs include regional planning, natural resource management, urban design, park design, historic preservation, advocacy planning, behavioral design, garden art, and computer-aided design.

Successful graduates of professional graduate degree programs in landscape architecture can find employment in a variety of settings, including international firms. Practitioners are employed in public agencies at local, regional, and federal levels or engage in various forms of private practice, with small private offices, large multidisciplinary firms, and consulting groups. Teaching and research attracts those interested in academic careers.

Increased public awareness of the limitations of our environment to support human activity and increasing sensitivity to the value of beautiful and orderly surroundings suggest that landscape architecture skills are very much needed if we are to maintain a quality of life consistent with civilized society. The opportunities for students to prepare themselves to contribute in tangible ways to improving the physical environment through landscape architecture are extensive, and they are available in almost every state in the nation.

Harry W. Porter Jr., Professor
Division of Landscape Architecture
School of Architecture
University of Virginia

Urban Design   Urban design as an activity is one of long standing; as a field of professional endeavor it is much newer. Since the earliest settlements of mankind, there have been self-conscious attempts to make cities, neighborhoods, and building complexes more efficient, more functional, and more aesthetically pleasing. The term urban design has, however, come into usage only since World War II to denote the specific concern of architects and others with the three-dimensional character and processes of the physical development of cities. As a professional activity, it answers the need for skills falling between broad land-use and transportation policy concerns and the design of individual buildings.

In the nineteenth century, city planners—mainly architects and engineers—were closely associated with the social and philanthropic movements that sought to make cities more salubrious places in which to live and work. In the first half of this century, the Modern Movement in architecture exhibited a major concern with city design. Within the Western democracies, however, cities are seldom "designed" as single entities. It has also become clear that many social ills cannot be solved through architectural or physical design. Yet the quality of life depends very much on the quality of the built environment, the activities it makes possible, and the pleasures it offers. Urban design is an endeavor to improve the functioning and the physical layout of cities and thus the quality of life of their inhabitants.

There is no universal definition of urban design. To some it is large-scale architecture; to others it focuses primarily on the design of the public environment; to still others it is mostly concerned with public policy issues pertaining to the livability of subareas of cities. Yet all will agree on some basic concerns of the field. Urban designers are concerned with both the public and private realms of the built environment. They are concerned not only with existing cities but also with new urban and suburban developments. They are concerned with establishing general designs, policies, and guidelines affecting the form and characteristics of city centers, mixed-use developments, residential neighborhoods, industrial complexes, and urban infrastructures prior to the detailed design of particular buildings and the spaces between them.

A number of programs of study are available to the architect and city planner wishing to develop his or her knowledge of cities and urban design abilities. Some of these focus on aesthetic issues, while others have a public policy orientation. There is a need and a demand (both in public service and in private practice) for urban designers. A person interested in pursuing a career in urban design needs to have a deep concern with the quality of the built

Urban Design (continued)

environment and a strong empathy for its inhabitants. He or she must be willing to develop new analytical and design skills to deal with a set of technical and philosophical issues that are different from those that arise in the design of individual buildings. Above all, urban design requires the ability to sustain prolonged analytical, synthetical, and evaluative tasks within a politically charged working environment. For a person willing to devote himself or herself to these endeavors, urban design offers a challenging, rewarding, frustrating, fascinating, and joyous career.

Jon T. Lang, Chairman
Urban Design Program
Graduate School of Fine Arts
University of Pennsylvania

Area and Cultural Studies

African Studies   African area studies programs are interdisciplinary programs that offer graduate students the opportunity to engage in intensive study and research on Africa. African area courses are usually offered in a wide range of fields, including the social sciences and humanities as well as the professional fields. Disciplines include African languages, anthropology, architecture and urban planning, dance, economics, education, folklore and mythology, geography, history, ethnomusicology, political science, public health, sociology, and theater arts.

Students in African area studies usually earn a master's degree, which gears them for postgraduate studies or work with international or foreign organizations that have an emphasis on Africa and African affairs. Some students become employed in higher education or in government jobs as well.

Teshome H. Gabriel
Associate Director, African Studies Center
University of California, Los Angeles

Afro-American Studies   Afro-American studies as a field of concentration in colleges and universities owes its present position and importance to the social ferment accompanying the civil rights and black consciousness movements of the 1960s. Its roots as a discipline, however, lie in the teaching and writing of W. E. B. Du Bois at Atlanta University in the period 1897–1910. It was during this period that Du Bois edited the *Atlanta University Studies,* published *The Souls of Black Folk* (1903), and began his Pan-African activity.

The field of Afro-American studies offers an "area" approach to the study of the black American community, which has had a unique history and status throughout its existence, beginning with the arrival of a small group of Africans at Jamestown in 1619. Constituting 10 percent of the total population of the United States for the last half century and an even larger percentage in earlier times, the Afro-American community has its distinctive institutions, speechways, folkways, and expressive culture, which, subjected to normative "melting pot" analyses, were stigmatized as pathological in the past. The stance and methodologies of Afro-American studies redress the balance.

The field of Afro-American studies is by definition cross-disciplinary, and instruction in the field is often organized interdepartmentally. Even where there is a specific department called Afro-American or Black or Africana Studies, members of the department may also hold appointments in a second department, that of their specialty. Graduate work in the field usually emphasizes in varying degrees the following: an overall conception of the Afro-American community in its historical and cultural dimensions, the relationship of this community to its African origins and to its Western Hemisphere counterparts in the Caribbean and Latin America, and specialization in some particular aspect of Afro-American studies, such as history, politics, literature, visual art, music, or sociology.

The volume of research in the Afro-American field has grown enormously in the past two decades, most of it done in the specialized fields listed above. Less research has been done in cross-disciplinary aspects. The recent expansion in research is attributable to the same impulses that originally brought the field of Afro-American studies into prominence.

Richard A. Long
Chair, Afro-American Studies
Atlanta University

American Studies   Graduate programs in American studies focus upon the culture and society of America from its founding to the

17

American Studies (continued)

present. Theories of culture and culture processes inform the field, which also draws upon theories and methods in such other disciplines as anthropology, literature, folklore, history, art, economics, population studies, and architecture. Foci of study include the culture of everyday life, material culture, popular culture, symbolic systems, historical archaeology, belief systems, social history, ethnic group studies, and artistic culture. More than 300 colleges and universities offer courses in American studies, with over 50 offering graduate degrees. Programs vary in the combinations of courses they offer and in core requirements, though those with an anthropological orientation or with a focus on social and intellectual history seem to predominate. Combinations of history and literature have been frequent in the past. Increasingly, both qualitative and quantitative methods are being employed, as fieldwork techniques of participant-observation-interview and computer analysis enter the field. Because material objects and technologies assume such importance in complex society, the field of American studies increasingly cooperates with archaeology, architectural history, museum curatorship, and historic preservation. Field methods and ethnographic interviewing are helpful in journalism, law, psychology, policy studies, and other research areas requiring an in-context knowledge of everyday life.

Specific graduate programs combine these elements and offerings in a number of different ways. They can best be considered individually by examining graduate catalogs, bulletins, and program descriptions. As a whole the field is served by *American Quarterly*, the professional journal published in cooperation with the American Studies Association. Other journals include *American Studies, Prospects, Journal of American Culture,* and *American Studies International.* The field has active professional associations in a large number of nations around the world, and the study of American culture and society by an international corps of scholars continues to grow.

The area of American studies has a tradition of high scholarship in research and teaching careers in American colleges and universities that reaches back to the 1930s. At the same time, a number of people trained in this field have entered careers in government, business, and the media, for which it also offers excellent preparation.

Melvyn Hammarberg
Department of American Civilization
University of Pennsylvania

Asian Studies   Asian studies is the term used to describe the study of one or several of the twenty or so countries starting with Japan in the north and swinging in an arc around to India. Often, though not invariably, this huge region is subdivided: China and Inner Asia; Japan and Korea; Southeast Asia; Australia, New Zealand, and the Pacific Islands; and India and the other nations of the subcontinent. The most recent subdivision to emerge is the study of the Pacific Rim or the Pacific Basin—a study of the international relations between the nations that comprise the island and littoral states of the Pacific Ocean.

Before World War II, the center of Asian studies was in Europe, where the concentration was on classical language, the discipline was in history, and the countries of interest were Japan and China. With the onset of the Pacific War, the center gravitated to the United States as the federal government underwrote Asian programs in many universities to train young military officers for service in intelligence or in government affairs. Starting in 1950, the national foundations, in particular the Ford Foundation, underwrote the costs of international education, spending some $278-million, of which the largest part, some $37-million, went for Asian studies.

In the late fifties, some scholars came to believe that area studies were at odds with theoretical advancement. This belief caused many students to return to disciplinary study. The Vietnam war brought further disenchantment with Asian studies, particularly the study of Southeast Asia. Since 1967, the United States has traded with East Asia more than any other part of the world—a trade that is accelerating as the East Asian nations develop. Economic benefit has stimulated interest in East Asia. Since the early eighties, the Japanese have shown a willingness to invest in high-technology projects and build factories within the United States. This prospect has brought some state governments to make funds available for the study of Japan as evidence of their desire to have such investment.

These vicissitudes have made diverse the manner in which each school deals with Asian studies, though it is safe to say that studies on Japan and China are far more developed than studies on the other nations of East Asia. Many American schools have formal exchange arrangements with institutions in Japan and China, more in the former than in the latter. Many American schools have come together in consortia to establish a presence in one or more of the East Asian countries. Such consortia support advanced language study in Japanese and Chinese. Twenty-two universities publish journals, occasional papers, and monograph series on Asian affairs. Better than fifty schools have libraries capable of sustaining research in one or more of the East Asian languages. More than fifty schools report

Asian Studies (continued)

that they offer graduate degrees and certificates in East Asian studies. In interdisciplinary programs, there are 144 certificates, 104 M.A.'s, and 16 Ph.D.'s. In disciplinary programs there are 67 certificates, 139 M.A.'s, and 83 Ph.D.'s.

Where do students who have studied the culture of a specific Asian country or East Asia as a region find employment? Within the United States, the universities themselves are the single largest employer. Jobs can also be found on the federal level and in some of the state governments, multinational and large industrial corporations, international organizations, and research firms. If a student has mastered an Asian language, he or she can often find employment in the country where that language is spoken, sometimes with an American concern and sometimes with an indigenous concern. Reflecting the size and vitality of the Japanese economy, Tokyo is an especially fertile job-hunting ground, though Japan has, as the other Asian nations often have, laws regarding the employment of foreigners. The growing interdependence between the United States and the Asian nations suggests further opportunities for students with a knowledge of the languages, economics, and politics of the Asian nations.

Nathaniel B. Thayer
Director of Asian Studies
School of Advanced International Studies
Johns Hopkins University

East European and Soviet Studies The intellectual roots of East European and Soviet studies are in Slavic studies, which in turn were the product of the deep interest in Slavic culture of a group of scholars in England and North America, many of whom were of Slavic origin. Prior to World War II, Slavic studies emphasized the languages, literatures, and histories of the Slavic peoples. After the war, however, traditional Slavic studies were inadequate to the study of the entire region, which included such important non-Slavic countries as Hungary and Romania and which had taken on a new character as part of the postwar "Soviet bloc."

In the postwar period, therefore, East European and Soviet area studies have combined a range of interdisciplinary approaches. Social scientists, especially economists and political scientists, have joined historians and linguists to form more broadly based centers of study. Programs focus on the social, political, and economic systems of the region, while languages and literature are studied to acquire essential research tools and to gain additional insights. Among the many important current issues typically covered in these programs are questions of human and minority rights in the Soviet Union and Eastern Europe, problems confronting multinational societies in the area, regional integration, the decline in economic growth and looming energy shortages, problems of succession in one-party systems, the impact of increased imports of Western technology, the arms race and the burden of defense spending, and Soviet and East European policies and activities in the Third World. The problem of the East's and West's perceptions of each other's roles in the world remains important.

Because of its interdisciplinary character and the importance of the area studied, a degree in East European and Soviet studies provides a valuable preparation for a career in government service, at home and abroad. The expansion of East-West relations has also increased the demand for regional specialists in the business and financial communities. Many students find interdisciplinary language and area studies a valuable first step to more specialized training in business or law or in one of the related academic disciplines.

J. L. Black
Director, Institute of Soviet and East
European Studies and Professor of History
Carleton University

Jewish Studies   Graduate programs in Jewish studies seek to train scholars who will be expert in one or more of the fields falling under the rubric of Jewish studies. Broadly conceived, the field includes any and all aspects of Jewish history, religion, and culture. The more traditional categories of study are biblical studies; classical, medieval, and modern Judaism; and Hebrew language and literature. With the proliferation of undergraduate Judaic studies programs, new rubrics and programs have been introduced, such as Holocaust studies, sociology of the Jewish community, and Yiddish language and culture. Emphases differ from one graduate school to another, and the alert student will seek out those schools that specialize in the area of his or her interest. Whereas most graduate programs in Jewish studies are designed to train academics, several offer M.A. programs specifically for students interested in pursuing careers in Jewish communal work. Not all Jewish studies programs are called by that name or exist as independent departments. At some graduate

Jewish Studies (continued)

schools, the Jewish studies program resides in the Oriental or Near Eastern studies department; at others it resides in the religion or religious studies department; at still others it appears in the guise of modern languages and literature or as the department of Hebrew or as Judaic studies or Hebrew studies.

Sid Z. Leiman
Professor of Jewish History and Literature
Chairman, Department of Judaic Studies
Brooklyn College

Latin American Studies   The area of Latin American studies represents the most popular foreign area studies field in American higher education, reflecting the proximity of the Latin American republics in the Western Hemisphere and the popularity of Spanish, the most commonly taught foreign language in the United States. The term Latin America in ordinary usage refers to the nations of Central America, the Caribbean, and South America, including those of non-Iberian colonial heritage.

Students enter graduate work in Latin American studies for a variety of reasons. Some have majored in Latin American studies as undergraduates, receiving a broadly based liberal arts education in the Ibero-American tradition. Others have field experience in Latin America through such means as the Peace Corps, employment with multinational corporations, study abroad, or family connections. Others have majored in Spanish or Portuguese and seek applications for their language skills. Most share a fascination with the diversity of Latin America and an appreciation of its cultural heritage.

M.A. programs in Latin American studies are interdisciplinary, requiring or leading to fluency in Spanish or Portuguese, and stressing broad grounding in the humanities and social sciences. These programs traditionally have been used as entry-level graduate programs that allow students to sample a variety of approaches before choosing to specialize in a single academic discipline for Ph.D. work. The master's is also a common terminal degree for those seeking careers in applied fields such as diplomatic service, career administration in international organizations, and work in travel and tourism. More recently, growing numbers of universities are offering the option of dual-degree programs that allow the student to complete the M.A. in Latin American studies while simultaneously completing a professional degree in such fields as international management, law, education, and planning.

Although some universities offer interdisciplinary Ph.D. programs in Latin American studies, most students who become Latin American specialists in the American higher education system earn the Ph.D. in some academic discipline that can be applied to Latin America. This reflects the structure of most colleges and universities, in which faculty members hold appointments in disciplinary departments. Despite this tradition of disciplinary training at the Ph.D. level, much teaching and research is actively interdisciplinary. This is reflected in more than a dozen journals that deal with Latin America, most of which are interdisciplinary, such as the *Latin American Research Review,* the *Luso-Brazilian Review,* the *Journal of Latin American Studies,* and the *Bulletin of Latin American Research.* Among recent topics of particular interest in the field are the relationship between state and society in Latin America, popular culture, public policy studies, and transitions from military to democratic regimes. Latin American literature and film are considered to be on the forefront of modern trends.

The large base of students in the more than 200 organized Latin American studies programs at American colleges and universities create a steady demand for Latin American specialists. This demand is augmented by the needs of business, government, and international organizations. A recent study prepared for the National Council of Foreign Languages and International Studies predicts a strong job market for Latin American specialists over the next two decades merely to fill expected vacancies. The growing economic, cultural, and geopolitical importance of Latin America suggests that the current vitality of Latin American studies will endure.

Gilbert W. Merkx
Director, Latin American Institute
University of New Mexico

Near and Middle Eastern Studies   Near and Middle Eastern studies is a term that covers two distinct poles, with a large underexplored middle area. At one pole are Ancient Near Eastern studies, divided into three major cultural-geographical areas: the cuneiform area (defined by the writing system used by the major civilizations in the area), comprising Mesopotamia, Northern Syria, Iran, and Anatolia; the Syro-Palestinian area, inhabited mostly by Northwest Semitic

Near and Middle Eastern Studies (continued)

peoples and in which various Northwest Semitic writing systems arose in the course of the second and first millennia B.C. ; and Egypt. The time span is from Neolithic to the end of the Persian Empire in the fourth century B.C. (except for Egypt, which continues as the proper domain of Egyptology until the rise of Islam). The major division of labor is between the archaeologist and, from the moment that texts begin to appear, the philologist-linguist. This division of labor is most accentuated in the cuneiform area, where the archaeologist and philologist are rarely the same person, and is least sharp in Egyptology. Scholars who regard themselves as primarily neither archaeologist nor philologist but as historian are gradually coming on the scene and effecting a certain amount of synthesis. In the Syro-Palestinian area there is naturally a large overlap with Old Testament studies, and there are some archaeologists and philologists in this area who regard themselves primarily as Biblical scholars.

At the other pole is the Islamic Middle East, from the seventh century A.D. to the present. Included under this heading is the study of non-Islamic groups, such as Christians and Jews, who were often important and active elements in a civilization dominated by Islam. The first focus of attention is Islam and the Arabic-speaking world in which it arose. But the Arabian focus quickly expands to the whole territory once under one or another of the Ancient Near Eastern civilizations (Syria, Iran, Egypt, Turkey) and beyond to North Africa, Sudan, Muslim Spain, India, Central Asia, etc. The spectrum of disciplines is more diversified than in Ancient Near Eastern studies; they include language, literature, philosophy, theology, law, religion, art and archaeology, history, and others. The arrival on the scene of the modern state of Israel adds a new dimension of complexity and interest to the study of the area. As the period studied approaches the present century, the methods, goals, and perspectives of the whole range of contemporary social science disciplines are more and more indispensable—furthermore, these are being brought to bear in interesting ways on earlier Middle and Ancient Near Eastern data.

Outside of Egypt, the polar division leaves undefined, and relatively unoccupied, more than a thousand years of Hellenic, Roman, Byzantine, Parthian, Sassanian, Armenian, Jewish, Christian, and pre-Islamic Arabian history in the area (Ethiopia, located in Africa but with strong linguistic and cultural ties with the Near East, is problematic for this as for all periods). The scholarly possibilities in this "middle world" are exciting, but standard departmental spheres of interest make it difficult in practice to find a footing.

Ancient Near Eastern studies generally lead to academic and/ or museum employment, and currently here, as elsewhere, the market is tight. The situation is relatively the same in post–Ancient Middle Eastern studies. However, a number of "classically" trained people have gone on to nonacademic government and international employment. A recent and growing phenomenon is the emergence of programs of study aimed at an M.A. in a language (Arabic, Turkish, Persian, Hebrew) and sociopolitical or economic aspects of the contemporary Middle East, with subsequent nonacademic government or private-sector employment.

Gene Gragg, Professor
Department of Near Eastern Languages
and Civilizations
University of Chicago

Art and Art History

Art/Fine Arts No one definition of the field of art/fine arts commands universal agreement. However, art/fine arts as it pertains to graduate study is used, in most cases, to classify programs that provide advanced training in the visual arts. These range from the time-honored fine art disciplines of painting, drawing, and sculpture to the newer areas of photography, film, and video and to more vanguard areas only now being defined. These latter include art as activity or performance art, intermedia work, and work utilizing new technological innovations. In addition, areas traditionally defined as crafts, such as fiber/textiles or ceramics, may be classified as fine art when the utility of the object produced is subservient to aesthetic expression.

The objective of graduate study in the field of art/fine arts is to lead students ultimately to a mastery of material and to the creation of work limited only by the boundaries of individual imagination and experience. Entrance to a program leading to a Master of Fine Arts degree requires that students demonstrate a level of proficiency in a particular medium and indicate a personal aesthetic direction. Graduate-level entrance is granted most often to pursue work in a particular discipline, e.g., painting, sculpture, printmaking, or photography. However, as intermedia work is becoming more common, inquiry and experimentation into the use of other media is occasionally allowed or encouraged.

Art/Fine Arts (continued)

Graduate students in the fine arts are challenged to build upon the technical facility and conceptual base they acquired as undergraduates. Emphasis is placed on individual aesthetic choices and on the exploration of contemporary critical issues. Many graduate programs, whether offered by a university or college art department or a professional school of art, also require students to elect classes in art history or seminars on particular thematic or critical issues to augment studio work.

Ultimately, it is the activity of the artist in response to society that determines what is included in the field of art. As a result, areas of study in many professional schools of art and in college and university art departments are continually evolving. Work incorporating performances, advanced technologies, and intermedia formats are recent developments. A rapidly emerging division of artistic activity utilizes advancements in telecommunications and information technology. A few graduate programs in the fine arts enable students to pursue advanced study in art and emphasize the development of an awareness of various new materials and equipment as expressive media. Of these programs, a select few provide art students with previous experience in electronics, telecommunications, computer imaging, video lasers/holography, and so on the opportunity to elect in-depth self-directed study into specific ideas and technical areas.

Although the mature artist is considered a professional, the degree to which individual artists depend on the profession as their main source of income varies tremendously. Many develop complementary careers as artist-teachers, administrators, designers, critics, or gallery directors, or they may work in other related professions.

Carol Becker, Chair
Graduate Division
School of the Art Institute of Chicago

Art History Art history is the most wide-ranging of all humanistic disciplines: the objects it investigates have survived from the earliest traces of human culture in Stone Age caves until today and from every continent of the globe. Indeed, many cultures are known to us primarily through these objects, which, whether artifacts of utility or of sheer display, give symbolic form to man's conscious and unconscious feelings and convictions. The art historian pursues a two-way track, penetrating the cultures of the past by studying their works (buildings, two- and three-dimensional images, and other artifacts) and interpreting the works through investigation of the cultures. Because of the subject's great compass in time and space, students and teachers specialize in limited segments while seeking a broad knowledge of at least the cultural tradition into which their specialty fits.

Art history is a relatively young discipline in America; few graduate degrees in the field were offered prior to the 1930s. The graduate training of the first generation of American art historians (greatly aided by the influx of European scholars during World War II) was largely positivist, focusing on practice without much concern for historical theory and tending to examine art in isolation from its social and cultural context (and "high" art to the exclusion of popular/vernacular forms). More recently, the impact of such European philosophical movements as structuralism, phenomenology, neo-Marxism, and semiology has begun to make advanced training more diversified, although the discipline has not, as is the case with literary studies, been overwhelmed by these impulses.

While studio experience can contribute to an understanding of the art of the past, it is not an essential preparation for the discipline. Students planning graduate work in the field should develop proficiency in foreign languages, particularly German and another European language for Western art, ancient languages for Classical art, and the relevant language(s) for Asian art. Travel for the purpose of seeing museums abroad and works of art in situ is an essential element of preparation for the profession; numerous foreign branches of U.S. colleges accept undergraduates from other accredited colleges for a term or a year, and traveling fellowships for dissertation research are awarded through competition by several foundations.

Holders of advanced degrees in the field qualify for careers in higher education and positions in the curatorial, administrative, and educational departments of art museums (for which the M.A. is sometimes sufficient). Because of the growth and popularity of art history as an elective in hundreds of colleges and universities and the relatively small number of graduate programs, the employment prospects for Ph.D. holders are more promising than in most of the other fields in the humanities. The College Art Association, the

Art History (continued)

professional society for teachers of art history and studio art, operates an effective and fair employment center to which virtually all academic job opportunities in the country are referred.

James S. Ackerman
Arthur Kingsley Porter Professor
Department of Fine Arts
Harvard University

Arts Administration   In today's society no one questions the fact that the general level of education is rising. As a result, increased demands for recognized cultural experiences as well as those of a less well-known nature have become evident. One only has to peruse the "arts and leisure" section of any daily newspaper to recognize the cultural explosion in the growth and availability of arts organizations of all types. These include theater and dance companies, community arts centers, and orchestral, opera, and other musical groups, as well as museums and galleries involving the visual arts. Unfortunately, all too many of these organizations that are created flourish for a short period of time but decline rapidly and soon fade into extinction. Fortunately, more such groups are born than die. The early demise of many of these organizations can be attributed not only to the decline of government funding, inflation, and rising costs our economy has experienced within the last decade or two, but also in untold numbers of cases to poor management. Many organizational managers have been well equipped to provide artistic talents but ill equipped to "manage the show."

Among the more promising approaches to solving the management dilemma and overcoming deficit problems and crisis planning is to employ an administrator who is well trained academically and professionally. A graduate degree in arts administration is designed to provide the necessary tools to better equip managers and administrators in the many facets of arts-related organizations. This training generally includes elements of advocacy; accounting; audience development and marketing; finance and fund-raising; interpersonal, organizational, and labor-related issues; law; long-range planning; and public relations. Arts administration programs—particularly at the graduate level—generally insist on admitting students who have developed strong artistic backgrounds in their undergraduate degree programs but who are more interested in the administrative aspects of an organization. The graduate course work provides the necessary training to equip them to perform administrative functions both efficiently and effectively.

Graduate programs in arts administration are few in number and, while each has a somewhat different approach to the field, all recognize that this formal training is not only desirable but also a virtual necessity if arts organizations are to survive. Most programs recognize the value of academic training as well as the more practical aspects of real-world practices and are properly developed to prepare students to meet the increasing challenges of managing arts organizations. Training is usually open to a selected few because of the individualized, one-to-one aspects of the curriculum. Students desiring to enter this field should be academically prepared and possess some practical experience in the field. A willingness to forgo the artistic career, however, does not mean forgetting the artistic techniques. The abilities to communicate with an artist are imperative. The potential arts administrator should not be a person whose "second-best" activity of administration comes about because of frustration. Imagination, aggressiveness, and dedication to managerial functions are paramount.

James E. Suelflow, Professor
Director, Arts Administration Program
Indiana University

Art Therapy   The art therapist works with individuals and groups in milieu and family therapy. The roots of art therapy stem from a psychoanalytically oriented base; however, recent years have seen the rise of a multiplicity of approaches in the mental health field, and art therapy has expanded in ways that are parallel with this diversity.

Art therapy serves to foster nonverbal communication, in which the graphic image is of primary concern. Art therapy can also work in conjunction with verbal associations and interpretations, in which the image serves to help the patient or client and the therapist understand the emotional problem and come to terms with the resolution of it. In concert with these two primary modes of art therapy that were, historically, prominent in the profession's development (i.e., art as therapy and art as an adjunct to psychotherapy), the art therapist of the 1980s also focuses on the creative and expressive aspects of the patient/client, on the emotional, motor, and perceptual dysfunctions of the person in therapy, and on work with a variety of populations. The therapist also understands that art expression can have great personal meaning and

Art Therapy (continued)

can offer the possibility for reshaping lives and giving a focus for troubled, as well as for healthy, people. Art can serve to reconcile conflicting forces, and it serves as a bridge between the person's inner and outer worlds. Art can give shape to, and point directions for, healthy, expressive release through art production. Art can be a motivating force for expression and communication of all people.

Art therapy is practiced with diverse populations—preschool through the aged. It is an important modality in preventive therapy and with persons having various problems, such as the learning-disabled child, the chemically dependent adolescent, the emotionally disturbed adult, the physically impaired young adult, and the hospitalized older adult. Art therapy is an important health service in a variety of settings, such as psychiatric hospitals, mental health centers, schools, prisons, nursing homes, day-care centers, and substance abuse centers and in private practice.

Personal experience with basic art media (drawing, painting, collage, clay, and sculpture) is fundamental to an understanding of the nature of art and its healing and therapeutic aspects. Variations of media and adaptations for specific populations are included in art therapy preparation. Concentrated study of normal life-span development, human behaviors, handicapping conditions, maladaptive behaviors, and therapeutic counseling methods enables the art therapist to combine this knowledge with the personal experience of the art process for a better understanding of the individual. With graphic images reflecting maturity, creativity, and the expression of personal feelings, the art therapist is able to diagnose, plan remedial treatment, and assess initial, ongoing, and follow-up stages of therapy. The artwork leaves a graphic record of the client's or patient's therapeutic progress.

A prospective art therapist may pursue study in undergraduate or graduate programs, although the American Art Therapy Association (AATA) recommends graduate-level study as the preferred entry-level preparation for the professional field. Clinical and institute training programs are also offered for the preparation of art therapists. A national review process is available through the AATA for those graduate, clinical, and institute programs desiring to obtain this approval status. As of summer 1986, fourteen graduate (master's degree) programs had been identified as meeting standards, thus gaining national approval status for training in art therapy. Upon appropriate and required academic and clinical preparation and with subsequent documented clinical practice in a professional setting, an art therapist may submit an application for national registration. This registration (ATR) is also evaluated and awarded by the AATA.

The profession is a growing one, with an active national association, an increasing body of literature, a professional journal (*Art Therapy*), annual conferences, meetings, seminars, and special study groups. Research is expanding and being disseminated within art therapy and to other human service, health-related professions. Active committees within the AATA focus on education and training, research, art for the disabled and handicapped person, women's and men's issues, art therapy in the Third World, legislation, and other important areas of concern.

Gary C. Barlow, Professor and Coordinator
Art Therapy Graduate Program
Wright State University

Business Administration and Management

Business Administration and Management   As a broad definition, business administration and management refer to the decision-making process concerned with the arranging, directing, supervising, and/or implementing of the affairs of organizations in the public and private sectors, including those that are profit making as well as those that are nonprofit.

In an attempt to provide postbaccalaureate students with the professional expertise necessary to accomplish the foregoing, graduate management programs focus on quantitative, qualitative, and behavioral aspects of the field, utilizing case-study methodology combined with lecture recitation. Many colleges and universities have seen that an internship can provide their students with great insight and sharpened abilities and have integrated this experience into their curricula.

Since the role of the manager is critical to the success of all organizations, the field continues to furnish wide-ranging opportunities with upward mobility to qualified professionals whose interests may range from the position of public accountant to that of business-affairs manager in a consulate office abroad.

Dr. Milton Shuch
Director, Prince Program in Retailing
Simmons College

Accounting   Accounting is a system of collecting data (usually in monetary terms) about economic activity, processing those data, and reporting them for the use of interested decision makers. As such, it is an art, for it encompasses alternative methods and procedures, makes behavioral assumptions, and involves the analysis and interpretation of the results. It is theory based, possesses a measurement methodology, and utilizes the scientific method in much of its research but does not possess the immutable laws of a physical science.

Its approach is to record, in a systematic manner, certain economic events or transactions of an entity and to summarize them periodically in a manner to facilitate the decisions of its various users. These users are typically distinguished as being internal to the entity, such as management, or external to the entity, such as customers, creditors, investors, governments, and society itself. In serving management (management and cost accounting), accounting provides a basis for planning as well as a means for appraising performance against that plan. For external parties (financial accounting), it typically provides a status report (statement of financial position or balance sheet) and a record of recent activity (statements of income and of changes in financial position). Some organizations (for example, governments, taxing authorities, and not-for-profit entities) may require special modifications to the accounting measurement and reporting system.

The accounting system is so versatile that a wide variety of special reports is also possible from this systematized pool of data. For this reason, accounting has proved to be an invaluable control device. This control occurs not only through the interpretation of its information by decision makers but also internally through the way in which it is implemented. The ultimate control is provided by accounting experts called auditors. They either work for the entities being audited (internal) or are engaged periodically to review the accounting and related operations of the entity (external).

Accounting as a system of economic information goes back to the origins of history. It is not clear whether the alphabet was developed to write or keep books. The double-entry method at the core of today's accounting has been used to facilitate society's economic affairs for 500 years.

Today the pervasiveness of accounting information is obvious in the economic activity of all types of organizations. Computers and management information systems have served to enhance the availability and timeliness of accounting information and thus opened up a whole new field for accountants.

Frederick L. Neumann
Price Waterhouse Professor of Auditing
Head, Department of Accountancy
University of Illinois at Urbana-Champaign

Advertising and Public Relations   Advertising and public relations have important similarities and differences. Both are concerned with the transmission of informative persuasive messages to audiences through various media to help achieve the objectives of the sponsor. In the case of advertising, the media carrying the messages are paid for by the sponsor and consist of advertisements via television, newspapers, magazines, radio, mail, outdoor boards, transportation vehicles, and miscellaneous other media. In the case of public relations, the media are usually not paid by the sponsor, and the messages consist of news releases, films and tapes, speeches, annual reports, brochures, policy statements, and other materials. The objectives and content of advertising and public relations are often similar and somewhat overlapping in that they are both meant to inform and persuade people and organizations about the sponsor's products, services, activities, or ideas. The advertiser's communications are most likely to be about the products and services being marketed and the advertiser's activities and ideas as an organization. In public relations, the communications are more often about nonmarketing considerations and may be about the activities and ideas of an organization other than the sponsor. However, advertisers usually use public relations as well, while public relations programs frequently include the use of advertising.

Graduate education in advertising generally takes place in colleges of journalism or communications and in colleges of business administration. Both types of programs usually contain a core of study in advertising theory and practice, campaign planning and strategy, creation of advertisements and promotion materials (copy, art/layout, and production), media, and research. Additional study in consumer/audience behavior, general marketing, and sales

Advertising and Public Relations (continued)

promotion is also included. The educational method usually involves a combination of readings, lectures, and hands-on work with realistic advertising cases. In the journalism and communications schools, the emphasis is apt to be somewhat more concentrated on advertising, often with relatively more emphasis on creation of advertisements, advertising media, and public relations aspects. In the business schools, there is usually more emphasis on advertising as part of the broader activity of marketing and hence on advertising's interrelationships with product design and development, pricing, distribution, and personal selling of the organization's products or services. There is also more course work in other business areas, such as management, accounting, and finance. Only a handful of business colleges offer a graduate concentration in advertising. The typical graduate business concentration in marketing offers only one separate specialized advertising course, with many offering none at all. Important aspects of advertising are included as part of a number of different marketing courses, however. Most employers consider this type of concentration in a graduate business school sufficient for work in advertising management and as account executives.

Graduate programs in public relations can be found in only a relatively few colleges, and only in the colleges of journalism or communications. These programs cover public relations theory and practice, campaign strategy and planning, writing, production, media, research, and audience/public behavior and attitudes. Aside from these few programs, graduate concentrations in advertising, communications, journalism, mass media, or other areas may include some limited course work in public relations. Separate public relations courses are rare in business graduate programs, although some aspects are included in advertising and marketing courses and in courses on the societal aspects of business.

People working toward graduate degrees in advertising are trained either as advertising management generalists or as specialists in such activities as (1) planning an advertising campaign and administering its preparation and execution; (2) developing the advertisements (writing, production, or art/layout); (3) planning, negotiating, and arranging for the media carrying the advertising; or (4) researching various aspects of the above. Public relations workers may similarly be generalists or be specialists in strategy, writing, production, media, research, special events, etc. Generally, those interested in writing, art/layout, and production do their graduate work in these fields rather than directly in advertising or public relations, if they do any graduate work. Some of those interested in research do their graduate work in the behavioral sciences, statistics, or computers.

Employment in advertising, in common with most other service industries, has been growing somewhat faster than the American economy as a whole in recent years. This is projected to continue in the future. Employment opportunities in public relations have been growing in recent years as various business, government, and other not-for-profit organizations have recognized the need to explain themselves and their activities to various publics. This trend is consistent with business organizations' increased emphasis on social responsibility, with not-for-profit organizations' expanding work in marketing and fund-raising, and with the growing interest of organizations generally in overcoming the detrimental effects of size and technology in lessening the organizations' personalized contact with various individuals and groups.

People in advertising work mainly as managers, account executives, writers, artists, broadcast and print production people, media planners, media buyers, media analysts, researchers, marketing or sales promotion specialists, and advertising media salespersons. They may be employed by the advertiser sponsoring the advertising, the advertising agency usually hired to help with the advertising effort, the various media organizations (television, newspapers, magazines, radio, etc.), or various facilitating organizations, such as broadcast production organizations, research companies, and direct-mail houses. Similarly, public relations workers may be employed by the sponsoring organization, public relations agencies, or other facilitating groups.

While there seem to be favorable employment opportunities for graduate students in advertising and public relations, like most highly visible, highly paid, and exciting and glamorous fields, advertising and public relations draw more applicants than there are jobs, at least for the more desirable positions. Furthermore, some people end up working, by intention or not, in related fields in the various media, in marketing, or in other business or not-for-profit areas.

Increasingly, graduate degree holders seem to be getting more and more of the jobs that the best undergraduate students were formerly able to get. However, graduate study in advertising and public relations is usually not required for many types of entry-level positions, at least in writing, art, production, and many jobs in media and research. Some advertising and public relations positions are obtained by applicants who have had graduate studies in writing; art; film, broadcast, and print production; mass media; behavioral sciences; statistics; and even liberal arts. Graduate education is,

Advertising and Public Relations (continued)

however, now apparently strongly preferred by the larger advertising agencies for entry-level account executive work and by the larger corporate advertisers for entry-level management positions. These two types of jobs are among the most sought after in the field.

Morton I. Jaffe, Supervisor
Advertising and Public Relations Area
Baruch College

Finance and Banking The field of finance is one of the older segments of business professional programs. Early on it was separated from its root disciplines of accounting and economics because the growing body of finance-related theory proved sufficient for its own area of specialization. Today finance is one of the most dynamic areas in the business school. There are three main branches of finance that students tend to emphasize: (1) money and banking—the study of macro financial issues related to the flow of funds in the economy, the structure of the banking system, and the role of financial institutions; (2) micro finance—the study of corporation finance, investments, and the impact of information on security prices; and (3) international finance—the study of international capital flows and the reactions of firms to multinational environments.

Part of the excitement of finance is that the very way financial institutions (banks, insurance companies, brokerage firms, etc.) and their industries are organized to do business is changing rapidly. All this ferment provides increased opportunities for bright graduates who have been trained in the discipline, but at some increased risk if they are looking for a never-changing job. Of course, evaluating opportunities and their risks is exactly what the field of finance is all about.

M.B.A. students intending to major in finance should recognize three things: (1) Finance is not an end in itself. It is a tool intended to help people manage resources more effectively. (2) Modern financial theory is a bit complex and requires a good basic background in accounting, economic analysis, and quantitative methods. (3) Because finance is one of the most popular program majors, competition for jobs is keen. There are, however, thousands of positions in the finance area—particularly in corporation finance (for example, capital budgeting analysis, project analysis, credit work, pension benefits analysis, etc.) and in the revenue-producing activities of financial institutions (for example, the work of a bank loan officer or a bank trust officer). After gaining some experience, finance graduates find opportunities as security analysts, portfolio managers, or mergers and acquisitions investment bankers more readily.

A student's course work in finance will probably be divided among the three branches described above. One branch, macro finance, will focus on finance-related issues of the economy as a whole—our money and banking systems, the behavior of interest rates, the impact of taxes, and the saving and investment process. These are the "money and banking" and financial institutions courses. The second branch, micro finance, will focus on issues in corporation finance and investments—how does a corporation make capital budgeting decisions? what is the best way to put together a portfolio of securities? do mergers matter? is this stock overvalued? etc. The third branch, international finance, will focus on the international aspects of both macro and micro finance. These are the international trade and finance courses, the international corporation finance electives, etc.

Ph.D. students in finance tend to specialize in one of the three branches. In recent years the majority have been corporation finance or investments majors because this has been an area of exciting developments in theory—the cost of capital, the true value of information, capital asset pricing theory, and the value of options and other complex financial instruments. More recently there has been great demand for theorists who are doing research on financial futures, options, currency transformations, and other matters that tie together some risks for the corporation by developing with banks and others rather complex portfolio strategies for managing cash. There is now, and will likely be for at least the next five years, an acute shortage of research professionals in finance. This is true for all the branches and most emphatically true for money and banking, where there is currently strong demand from both financial institutions and universities.

Michael Keenan, Associate Professor
Ph.D. Advisor in Finance
Graduate School of Business Administration
New York University

Hospitality Administration According to *Webster's Ninth New Collegiate Dictionary,* the word "hospitable" means "given to generous

Hospitality Administration (continued)

and cordial reception of guests" or "offering a pleasant or sustaining environment." Hospitality, then, is defined as "hospitable treatment."

The hospitality industry is composed of many diverse yet interrelated businesses that rely on lodging, food service, and/or entertainment as primary profit-producing activities. The field may be viewed as being divided into two major areas: the operational division, which provides services directly to the public, and the support segment, which provides services and products to the operations.

There is a continuing need in the constantly changing hospitality industry for persons who are equipped with a variety of professional and academic skills. Graduate programs in hospitality administration seek to prepare postbaccalaureate students to meet this need. Students considering this field of study should be aware of the great diversity among hospitality programs offered at the graduate level. A professional or management program provides extensive professional training and emphasizes the application of advanced management theory to the hospitality industry in an interdisciplinary fashion. For those students who plan to teach at the college level or conduct research in the area of hospitality administration, advanced M.S. and Ph.D. programs are also available.

Career opportunities for hospitality administration graduates are as diverse as the industry itself and include positions in restaurant, hotel, club, conference center, and condominium management; food service for airlines, hospitals, life-care facilities, the military, corporate offices, industrial plants, and schools and colleges; franchise and multiunit organizations; finance; the planning, construction, and furnishing of hospitality properties; the design and marketing of institutional equipment and products; advertising, marketing, research, and sales; accounting and management advisory services; the operation of resorts, entertainment parks, lodges, and other recreational facilities; human resources management; and college teaching and administration.

Melinda Codd, Director
Master of Professional Studies Program
School of Hotel Administration
Cornell University

Human Resources Management   Human resources management
has evolved from the field that was formerly known as personnel
management. Personnel management was traditionally viewed as
encompassing the functions of employee selection, compensation,
performance appraisal, training, and labor relations. Individuals
working in the personnel field were generally considered to possess
lower levels of technical qualification than counterparts in other
fields of specialization and to contribute less to the achievement of
organization goals. Senior personnel manager assignments were
frequently awarded to washed-up line managers who were "put to
pasture" in personnel—where they could do no serious harm.

However, the 1960s and 1970s witnessed events that forever
changed the field. What has come to be known as the "Entitlement
Legislation of the 1960s and 1970s" codified the raised expectations
of society with equal opportunity and treatment guaranteed in the
workplace by this nation's legal system. Possibly of even more telling
impact was the realization in 1974 that national productivity had not
only ceased its increase, but had actually declined. When coupled
with dramatic increases in productivity among a number of our
trading partners, American industry had its focus suddenly fixed on
worker productivity. The impact of these developments was to help
American executives recognize that human resources hold the key
to the survival of not only American companies but of the entire
American economic system.

Rather than thinking of the work force as a necessary cost of
production, as was done in earlier times, human resources
management recognizes employees as a company asset representing
a significant investment. Human resources management represents
an evolution of personnel management, which—while still
performing the traditional functions of recruiting and selection,
training and development, employee relations, compensation,
evaluation and improvement of performance, and human resource
planning—represents a systems approach. It recognizes the
interdependence and dynamic interaction of the human resources
management functions with each other and with the objectives of the
firm. Significantly, it recognizes how integral human resource
planning is with strategic planning, and it provides more direct
support for the achievement of the organization's goals.

Therefore, the human resources management function is
increasingly being looked on as a profit center in the organization.
Human resource managers continue to work in the primary
functional areas, and in addition, they function in the role of internal

Human Resources Management (continued)

consultants to line management. One of their key duties is to bring the latest ideas from behavioral science research and theory to line managers and help translate them into very practical and operational terms. Top human resources management specialists tend to combine a general business management education and orientation with advanced study in human resources management or behavioral sciences.

The objectives of human resource management can be most pointedly summed up by the words of Peter Drucker: "In the better use of human resources lies the major opportunity for increasing productivity.... Management of men should be the first and foremost concern of operating management; rather than the management of things."

T. Roger Manley
Professor of Management and
Organizational Psychology and Head, Management Department
Florida Institute of Technology

Industrial Administration As modern society makes increasing use of technology, managers must keep informed to handle their own jobs effectively and to understand and communicate with technical specialists. Industrial administration programs are typically designed for people who desire professional management training to complement their engineering or scientific education and experience but who do not necessarily have business backgrounds. They may want to modify their careers, move from a technical track to a management track in their industry, or simply proceed at a faster pace along a career path they have already chosen. The broad-based but compressed nature of industrial administration programs enables them to fulfill these goals.

Industrial administration students take course work in accounting, finance, marketing, operations management, quantitative methods, management information systems, human resource management and organizational behavior, economics, strategic management, business law, and business communications. For several reasons, this broad training proves very beneficial to a student's future professional life. A business—like any other organization—is a system, and even if you are very firmly and efficiently placed in a particular area in that system, you can be more effective if you understand not only your job but also the challenges and decisions confronting people in other parts of the total system. Another benefit of broad training is the career flexibility it provides. Students frequently enter industrial administration programs with a chosen career path. Once in the program, they may encounter a new and interesting management area of which they were not aware. As a result, their entire career path may be changed. In other instances, industrial administration graduates have started their careers in particular jobs and then, when an attractive opportunity opened up, were able to move from one function to another. Broad training increases the likelihood of such cross-function mobility and promotion. Finally, broad training helps one work toward positions in general management where the challenges and the rewards may be greater.

Another key attribute of industrial administration programs is their quantitative analytical approach to management problem solving. Although students must be able to analyze business problems qualitatively, large amounts of diverse and conflicting information frequently require that solutions be backed up with mathematical analysis. Industrial administration programs develop and refine students' analytical backgrounds, adding quantitative techniques to the students' range of skills and familiarizing them with the computer as a tool for analyzing, interpreting, and solving management problems. Most programs also recognize that quantitative skills must be complemented by well-developed social, interpersonal, and communications skills. Successful managers are not only good decision makers but must also be effective in getting their decisions implemented by working with and through people.

Finally, industrial administration programs teach time management. Students learn quickly what all successful managers know: to be effective, one must also be efficient, be able to prioritize tasks, and be adept at tackling the important things first.

Students who complete industrial administration programs are highly sought by business and industry for a variety of challenging and rewarding positions. These positions include manufacturing management and production and operations management, as well as positions in the traditional functional areas of management.

Gordon P. Wright
Professor of Quantitative Methods and
Director of Doctoral Programs
Krannert Graduate School of Management
Purdue University

Insurance and Actuarial Science   Insurance may be studied at the graduate level as an academic discipline leading to the Ph.D. or D.B.A. degree, and thus to careers in academic teaching and research. Industry-oriented research careers may be an alternative to teaching. The study of insurance may also be pursued as part of professional business education in the form of an insurance concentration within a Master of Business Administration program or as a major in a Master of Science in insurance program.

Regardless of the path pursued, graduate insurance education involves the study of insurance from both the industry standpoint and the consumer standpoint, with the view that both are interrelated in many areas. Industry-oriented portions of the graduate programs are increasingly reflecting the financial services nature of insurance and its place in the emerging integrated financial services industry. Additionally, the programs deal with issues of organization, management, marketing, investments, law, and government regulation. The interdisciplinary nature of insurance studies should be apparent. The consumer-oriented portion concerns individuals, but its focus is mainly on issues vital to business firms as insurance consumers, and as such this focus is part of a related area known as "risk management." The risk management process involves the identification and evaluation of pure risk as well as the application of risk management techniques for risk treatment, including risk control and risk financing. Insurance and risk management studies offer professional career opportunities both in the insurance industry and in insurance or risk management departments of industrial organizations.

Because the scientific treatment of problems of risk and uncertainty requires predictive analysis, the development of statistical and quantitative analytical skills is part of graduate insurance education to a certain degree. A separate but closely related discipline is actuarial science, which may be pursued by students who possess a high level of mathematical skill. Although most students of actuarial science look forward to a career in the insurance industry, they are also valued as consultants in the areas of pension and other employee benefit plans and as consultants to government agencies such as the Social Security Administration and state insurance regulatory agencies.

Youssef I. Kouatly
Professor of Insurance and Risk Management
Barney School of Business and Public Administration
University of Hartford

International Business In the United States, "international business" was included rather late in the fields of study open to graduate students across the land. It became a logical component of the classic Master of Business Administration or of the shorter and rather more flexible Master of Science, now being offered by most schools of business administration. A particular aspect of international business is its interdisciplinary nature, combining the traditional and functional areas of finance, management, and marketing at the international level with such disciplines as anthropology, geography, history, economy, law, and political science. It comes then as no surprise that these studies perhaps allow for less specialization but give a broader understanding of the world at large.

Two schools of thought seem to prevail in the present curricula. First there are those that consider international business a mere extension of or an addition to the existing functional areas of the M.B.A. program and as a way to prepare Americans to deal with an environment that is "foreign" to them. The second view holds that international business *is* the foreign world and cannot be taught on the basis of American values and traditions. Therefore, depending on the scholastic conviction of an individual school, more or less emphasis will be put on programs abroad, studies of foreign languages and cultures, and exchange programs with overseas universities. It can be assumed that the latter trend will increasingly prevail, even if only for the obvious reason that unless they are utterly prepared, American graduates will find themselves at a disadvantage competing with their foreign counterparts.

If it is true that the next decade will be particularly challenging in the international service areas, the graduate who can "serve" abroad in a variety of ways will be much in demand. Prospective employers include, among others, national, foreign, and multinational corporations; international agencies and organizations; and the U.S. government.

Michel Struelens
Professor of International Business and International Relations
and Director, Center for Research and Documentation
on the European Community
American University

Management Information Systems The field of management information systems (MIS) is both a broad and an often

Management Information Systems (continued)

misunderstood discipline. MIS, as its name indicates, contains elements of management and the management decision processes, information and the impact of information on management decisions and organization processing, and systems (computer based) to gather, store, transmit, manipulate, and present data to various users. As generally understood, MIS is an integrated man/machine system for providing information to support the operations, management, and decision-making functions in an organization.

The study of MIS most often takes place in business schools rather than computer science departments since the discipline emphasizes the application of computer-based technology to assist organizations in their management decisions and day-to-day processing requirements. Students pursuing a master's degree in MIS will often combine the graduate degree with undergraduate work in other areas such as accounting, marketing, computer science, and industrial engineering to build a greater understanding of organizational processes. The practical training in a graduate program will often include work in understanding and applying computer technology to organizational problems, the design of computer-based systems for data processing, and the design of decision-support systems for all levels of management. The recognition of organizational vulnerability to the centralization of data in computer systems has also led some institutions to develop courses on security, audit, and control of information systems.

Study of MIS at the doctoral level is relatively new. Two major approaches are found in these programs: the technical approach and the management approach. Schools emphasizing the technical concentrate on problems related to adapting computer technology in a safe and efficient manner to organizational uses. A background in computer programming and math is important in these schools. Schools emphasizing management concentrate on better design of the total system for users and search for factors that distinguish between successful and unsuccessful systems.

Students with master's degrees in MIS are highly sought after to work in the data-processing area as programmer/analysts or in other functional areas where a knowledge of MIS is valuable. There continues to be an exceptionally strong demand for Ph.D.'s in MIS for teaching positions, particularly for individuals who have gained both technical and functional backgrounds.

Larry E. Rittenberg
Associate Professor of Accounting and Information Systems
University of Wisconsin–Madison

Marketing   As a field of study, marketing concerns itself with all the activities that occur between the production and the consumption of goods and services. Specifically, the marketing student learns about product development, product-line management, advertising, personal selling, promotion, pricing, retailing, wholesaling, consumer decision making, buying behavior of organizations, consumerism, legal aspects of marketing, international marketing, marketing research, and information systems.

The significance of marketing appears to be increasing as top policymakers of profit-seeking and not-for-profit organizations are recognizing its vital role in two major interest areas. First, marketing is the arm of the organization that helps to define the opportunities available to the organization and the threats it must face. Second, marketing performs all the work required to sell the goods and services produced by the organization. Consequently, employment opportunities are excellent, including such jobs as product manager, account executive, market research analyst, planning analyst, market analyst, sales representative, and media planner.

Currently, academic research in marketing focuses on consumer behavior, research methodology, sales-force management, the effectiveness of advertising, market segmentation, organizational buying behavior, and the role of marketing in corporate strategy development.

Leon Winer
Chairman, Marketing Department
Lubin Graduate School of Business
Pace University

Quantitative Analysis   Quantitative analysis employs the scientific method to solve managerial problems. The methodological approach to problem solving is through model building that attempts to capture the essence of the business problems and solutions thereof. This approach requires interdisciplinary skills in mathematics, statistics, and computers. Emphasis in these skills is equally weighted in theory and application. In addition, basic knowledge of economics, management, engineering, and psychology is necessary, depending on the problem being addressed. Due to their interdisciplinary nature, most quantitative analysis problems are solved through the team approach.

Graduate degrees in quantitative analysis from business schools are identified as majors in the areas of operations research, management science, econometrics, managerial economics, business

Quantitative Analysis (continued)

statistics, and quantitative methods, as well as quantitative analysis. These majors, generally, are coupled with a basic understanding of the broader areas of business.

In the fifties, the use of quantitative analysis was limited to defining and solving small-scale problems related to production and operations management. The use of quantitative analysis to solve problems in the private and public sectors is diffusing because of (1) the growth of quantitative analysis as an academic discipline in universities during the last twenty years, (2) the evolution of computers and user-friendly software, and (3) a better understanding by decision makers of the place of quantitative analysis in problem solving. The techniques of quantitative analysis are being applied not only broadly in all functional areas of business but also to large-scale economic, socioeconomic, energy, and environmental models. The techniques of quantitative analysis are even being used in the humanities (history, psychology, and sociology), in the arts (music and art), and by professionals (law and medicine).

The market for M.B.A. students with quantitative analysis as a major is excellent in both the private and public sectors. There is a shortage of Ph.D.'s in quantitative analysis, especially in academia; there are currently three academic positions for every doctoral graduate in the field. The forecasted demand for quantitative analysis graduates is expected to exceed supply at all degree levels for the next decade.

Samuel D. Ramenofsky, Chairperson
Management Science Department
Loyola University of Chicago

Real Estate   Graduate education in real estate prepares the student to make rational decisions in the real estate market using tools of analysis derived from economics, finance, and law. Economic principles are used to explain how real estate, which consists of land and its attached improvements, is allocated to competing end users. Here the field draws heavily from topics covered in traditional urban and regional economics courses and treats real estate like other scarce resources allocated in a market-oriented economy. The student will examine various theories of land price determination and will use these models to understand how land is allocated to competing residential, commercial, industrial, and other end users.

In addition, the student will examine how factors influencing the demand for services provided by real estate interact with factors influencing the supply of real estate services available for consumption to produce real estate value. Inflation and the federal income tax are two factors studied in some detail.

The student will study the time value of money and learn how to compute the periodic payment, amortization schedule, and effective borrowing cost (or effective yield to the lender) for a variety of mortgage instruments, including the conventional fixed rate, graduated payment, adjustable rate, wraparound, shared appreciation, reverse annuity, and other instruments that are used in the marketplace. In addition, the student will examine various techniques for structuring real estate transactions, such as equity participations, joint ventures, and real estate syndications.

The relationship between risk and return in real estate investments will also be examined. A discounted cash flow model is first used to project likely future returns provided by a real estate investment and then used to compute the present value of the investment. Uncertainty with respect to future real estate market performance is then incorporated into the discounted cash flow model, and optimal choices among various investment alternatives are modeled using portfolio selection theories developed in economics and finance. The historic performance of real estate investments will be compared to returns provided by common stocks, bonds, and other investment alternatives on a risk-adjusted basis.

Current areas of interest in real estate research include pricing alternative mortgage instruments; pricing mortgage-backed securities; improving techniques used to estimate real estate value; development and estimation of models used to explain variations in real estate prices, both spatially and over time; and development of models capable of predicting the demand for real estate services by the various end-user groups as well as the demand by real estate investors.

Typical entry-level positions for students who successfully complete a graduate program in real estate are a lending officer for a commercial bank or savings and loan association, a real estate investment analyst for a securities firm, a real estate developer, a real estate appraiser, a commercial real estate broker, a real estate educator, and a researcher in real estate in government, academia, or business.

Thomas G. Thibodeau
Assistant Professor of Real Estate and Regional Science
Southern Methodist University

Taxation The study of taxation involves an in-depth analysis of the Internal Revenue Code, U.S. Treasury regulations, Internal Revenue Service rulings, and the various other substantive provisions of tax law. In addition, the typical tax program supplements this analysis of authoritative concepts with a review of the leading judicial doctrines and an evaluation of the impact of the court system on the interpretation of the tax law. The study of taxation might also include investigation of the social, political, and economic rationale underlying the tax law.

During the past ten years, as our tax system has become more complex and the demand for tax specialists has increased, graduate study in taxation has grown at an extremely rapid pace. In 1975 there were only fifteen graduate tax programs offered through the business colleges in the United States, with a combined enrollment of 1,448 students. Currently, there are approximately ninety graduate tax programs, with a combined enrollment well in excess of 8,000. However, despite this extremely rapid rate of growth, the supply of tax professionals has not kept pace with the increasing market demand.

Students considering graduate study in taxation should be aware of two distinct types of graduate tax programs. The "Type I" (academic) programs, which are typically located in college towns or small cities, are designed to complement a broad-based academic program with some graduate tax courses. This type of program would appeal to a student who has worked a few years and would like to return to school on a full-time basis to obtain a balanced master's degree. The tax courses in the Type I programs are typically taught by full-time tenured professors. The primary objective of the "Type II" (professional) programs, which are typically located in the major metropolitan areas, is to produce tax specialists. Accordingly, such programs usually offer an extensive, broad variety of specialized tax courses, taught by professional practitioners serving as adjunct faculty members. Type II programs usually appeal to the part-time evening student.

Myron S. Lubell
Coordinator of Tax Studies
Florida International University
and
Barry C. Broden
Director, Tax Institute
University of Hartford

Communication

Communication   Students of communication join a discipline that is ancient yet still emerging. From the Sophists' time until our scientific age, training in rhetoric—the art of argument and persuasion—was a chief training ground for social success. With the coming of the mass media, there arose the study of propaganda, the scientific analysis of communications content and effects, and research into cultural, organizational, and policy aspects of communication systems.

The new discipline encompasses both interpersonal and mass communication and all modes and media. It can be divided into three interrelated branches. The first is the study of signs and symbols in the different modes—the "languages" of vocal, pictorial, gestural, and digital coding of human significance. In this branch the codes and modes of communication are systematically analyzed and messages and meanings are studied in different social contexts.

The second branch deals with behavior and interaction through messages. Here the social and psychological aspects of encoding and interpreting messages are studied. Sociolinguistics and psycholinguistics, cultural anthropology, and the study of attitude formation and change and of public opinion are relevant to this branch of communication study.

The third branch deals with large-scale communication institutions and systems. The history, management, regulation, and policymaking of mass media belong here, as do theories of communication systems and of the role of communication in business, government, and other organizations.

The study of communication is conducted on many levels. More and more schools offer courses in the analytical and critical use of mass media. Colleges and universities add to such studies the learning of some of the more complex communication and media skills and the aesthetic and sociopolitical analysis of communication practices and policies. The most advanced programs can be found in the graduate schools that offer programs leading to the master's degree and the Ph.D. in communication. These programs develop scholars, researchers, teachers for the other levels of education, and communication executives, as well as practitioners. Communication research, teaching, and theory is one of the fastest-growing areas of attractive career opportunities in academic life.

George Gerbner, Dean
Annenberg School of Communications
University of Pennsylvania

Journalism Journalism is a field broad enough to include practitioners in news companies with print outlets, in broadcasting, and in advertising and public relations. The words "mass communications" are often associated with the more generic term "journalism." Those in the field work to make more sense of the world around us, acquaint publics with the unusual, reveal the fabric of society, and, on the other end of the continuum, influence patterns of consumption and engineer consent. As diverse as the field has become, all these persons work in the information business amidst an information explosion.

Graduate studies in journalism can range from intensive research preparation to the actual practice of journalism in the field. Theory and methodology studies are the core of many graduate journalism curricula. Social science quantitative research tools have become staples in such undertakings. Doctoral work is offered in over twenty recognized programs across the country to stock the future needs of journalism education. Much of the research in the field is done in concert with other social scientists in sociology, psychology, and political science and with those in the disciplines of law and history. Increasing attention is being paid to ethics and management, calling upon the talents of philosophers and business specialists.

A person trained in graduate journalism is trained generally. Job opportunities extend beyond the field of journalism into such markets as government and corporate service. A number of prospective employers still indicate that they would hire a person out of a liberal arts college with no previous journalism experience, but the growing reality is that journalism majors now form the majority of hires. Journalism graduate school is a place where students with no prior journalism experience can be exposed to the field and practice some of the skills needed to be a success. The research-oriented person can find a niche in survey work, time buying, and myriad other opportunities in journalism. The returning professional can acquire specific skills and academic preparation so that he or she can return to the field with improved options for advancement.

Student numbers are holding up in graduate journalism education and suggest a market for future educators. Given the number of mergers and acquisitions by group owners now occurring in the editorial and advertising agency worlds, the short-run job picture is one of selective entry; however, given the breadth of the field, the longer-term prospects for employment in journalism are very good. The challenge of professional accomplishment remains; the promise of strong vocational opportunities should be an incentive for those who are qualified and have a natural curiosity and a willingness to work hard. An accomplished journalist today can find an increasing number of ways to seek and find reward and satisfaction.

Edward P. Bassett, Dean
Medill School of Journalism
Northwestern University

Mass and Organizational Communication Mass communication consists of study of the media by which information and entertainment are delivered in society, the processes by which this content is shaped, and the effects that content and form exert on people and groups. These fields of inquiry have been enriched by approaches from many disciplines in the social sciences, humanities, and physical sciences.

Some students of mass communication aim for careers in which they write or portray ideas in other ways for distribution through the media. Others seek to manage media or communication services or help establish communication policy in government. Still others become researchers in academic settings, the private sector, or government. Job opportunities in media production—journalism, advertising, broadcasting, and elsewhere—are tight; student interest outstrips the number of entry-level openings. By contrast, demands for people prepared to enter communications management and policy positions are increasing rapidly, as are careers in research. Even the number of academic positions is greater than the supply of qualified entrants.

Degree programs in mass communication differ widely. Some emphasize job skills. Others integrate the understanding of communication institutions, processes, and effects with other fields—history, sociology, literature, the arts, philosophy, engineering, mathematics, and more. Current research in the field includes the social impact of new telecommunications media; the effects of mass media on politics, health behavior, education, consumer activity, and other areas; economic structure in the communication industries; communications law, policy, and regulation; international trade in communication services; and communication and national development, among other subjects.

Mass and Organizational Communication (continued)

Students who are considering graduate study should look closely at the statements of aims describing different programs and at the content of core courses. They should ask also about the careers or professional destinations of recent graduates.

Peter Clarke, Dean
and Susan H. Evans, Director of Academic Development
Annenberg School of Communications
University of Southern California

Radio, Television, and Film   The study of radio, television, and film involves many subfields, including radio and television production, broadcast management, broadcast journalism, mass-media law, information technologies, film production, film history, media criticism, aesthetics, writing, instructional television, and similar media-related disciplines. In addition to departments of radio-TV-film, programs can also be found in departments and schools of communication, speech, mass communication, and telecommunication. Students interested in graduate study should consult the college catalog or professional guide under each of these listings and seek in-depth information from the specific graduate program.

Many students concentrate in radio-TV-film to study television or film production. Students who want this type of training should thoroughly research a graduate program before making application. Many departments, while offering some courses in television and film production, must restrict entry to a small percentage of students. Some programs deliberately avoid stressing production courses at the graduate level. Correspondence with the department's director of graduate study is sometimes necessary to get a clear picture of a program's orientation.

Depending on the orientation of the graduate program, different paths of study are offered. For example, a preprofessional program that primarily trains people to enter the radio and television industry will ordinarily have different courses and a different emphasis than liberal arts curricula, which provide a broad-based foundation for many career choices or additional graduate study. Moreover, it may not be the curriculum but rather the initiative of students to locate internships and other professional experiences that will determine employment opportunities and direction after the graduate program is completed. For students who broaden their horizons beyond specific radio and television stations or specific geographic areas, career opportunities in media are plentiful.

John R. Bittner, Chair
Department of Radio-Television and Motion Pictures
University of North Carolina at Chapel Hill

Speech and Interpersonal Communication The study of human communication as the creation of shared meaning through symbolic transaction is a complex enterprise that evokes interest among scholars in several academic disciplines. These interests converge in the field of speech communication.

Speech communication brings together two important traditions in the study of human actions and values. The first of these is a tradition of rhetorical scholarship on human discourse. This tradition dates back more than 2,500 years, with origins and variations that reflect the range of historical and contemporary themes in systems of Western philosophy. The second is a twentieth-century tradition of sociobehavioral science scholarship on human interaction. This tradition is concerned primarily with description and explanation of the features of human communication processes and relationships among factors relevant to these processes. Each of these traditions subsumes various methodologies and theoretical frameworks for understanding human communication. They are unified by a common concern for the study of human discourse through symbolic forms: by central themes such as language, meaning, social influence, and the qualities of interaction in intercultural, interpersonal, group, organizational, public, and mass communication contexts.

Graduate programs in speech communication are structured according to several different models of theoretical and applied instruction. Doctoral programs customarily focus on research and scholarship. These programs generally rely on discovery-based approaches to learning and mentor-protégé relationships between graduate faculty members and students. Some employ variations such as the research team concept, in which new students are integrated with a working group of faculty and more established peers. Doctoral programs in speech communication are designed generally for students who wish to pursue academic careers, but these programs frequently accommodate the interests of persons who elect to enter nonacademic professions such as training, human resources, and organization development in business, industrial, and institutional settings.

Master's degree programs typically offer both thesis and nonthesis options. Study under the thesis option is roughly analogous to work in a doctoral program, but of less intensity and shorter duration. A master's degree with a thesis often is expected for admission to doctoral programs in speech communication. Nonthesis master's programs usually require more course work or some form of project in lieu of a thesis. Sometimes, nonthesis study is associated with programs in applied communication designed primarily for nonacademic professionals. It is possible to enter graduate study in speech communication from bachelor's and master's programs in other disciplines, for example, psychology, sociology, linguistics, philosophy, education, and nursing.

Employment opportunities continue to be available for qualified graduates in both academic and nonacademic sectors. At this time, availability of academic positions balances approximately with the supply of doctoral recipients interested in such positions, but the supply/demand ratio varies across specializations within the field. Some academic opportunities are available for the master's degree recipient. Although speech communication generally does not offer the type of training found in career-oriented professional schools, nonacademic opportunities for graduate degree holders in speech communication have increased substantially in the 1980s.

Tom D. Daniels
School of Interpersonal Communication
Ohio University

Criminology

Criminology has existed as a field of study for about a century. Recently, the term "criminal justice" has emerged to cover much of the same ground of inquiry but with special focus on the operation of the criminal justice system. While there are some who argue forcefully for a distinction between the two terms, nearly all would agree that there is considerable overlap in meaning and that the terms are often used interchangeably. In any case, criminology is the senior term with an international tradition of usage.

In its broadest definition, criminology encompasses the scientific study of offenders, of crime as a social phenomenon, and of the criminal justice system. As an interdisciplinary science, it draws on the knowledge and methods of a large number of disciplines, including psychology, sociology, biology, political science, and economics. It serves to integrate and focus these several disciplines around the multifaceted problem of crime. Thus, criminologists are concerned with the causes of crime, the costs of crime, and the control of crime. Criminology has both practical aspects involving the operation of the criminal justice system and theoretical aspects ranging from the explanations of human behavior to the design of crime-reducing environments. Whether in the nature of such public policy issues as capital punishment, gun control, and drug abuse or in the nature of treatment issues regarding the individual offender, the scope of criminological investigation seems virtually limitless. The police, the courts, and the various corrections agencies are the chief components of the criminal justice system examined by criminology, and they plainly suggest the kinds of occupations the graduates of criminology programs enter. In addition, criminological study leads to careers in criminal justice planning, criminological research, teaching, and public policy analysis. Juvenile delinquency, juvenile justice, and juvenile treatment are also subsumed under criminology. Recently, a new dimension has been added to the field of criminology through the privatization of criminal justice. Private enterprise has made a major thrust into the area, notably in security and in corrections.

The field is a rich one and has experienced an extraordinary growth rate in the past decade or so. The social issues that characterized the ferment of the 1960s—questions of individual liberty, social order, equality, and the power of the state—are deeply woven within the fabric of criminological study and perhaps help to account for the immense increase of criminology students in recent years. Because of its scope, criminology holds the interest of those seeking a humanistic, liberal education as well as those seeking an exciting professional career. At present, criminology is in a very dynamic phase and offers a fascinating time for student entry.

Eugene H. Czajkoski, Professor
Dean, School of Criminology
Florida State University

Demography and Population Studies

Populations are studied with a combination of formal demography, on the one hand, and substantive inquiry from the orientation of one or another scientific discipline, on the other. Formal demography is a special kind of applied mathematics, concerned with properties of the population model, and particularly the relationships between the state of population elements, and changes in that state, in abstraction from other phenomena. The model is inherently dynamic because the central question is the change in population size through time, and the answers ordinarily involve the change through time in relevant characteristics of the individual members of the population.

The substantive discipline of population studies is focused on phenomena defined in concrete terms (minimally in space and time), and in this sense it is closely akin to history and geography, as distinct from the sciences (which focus on particular analytic aspects of phenomena, defined abstractly and viewed from one frame of reference). The distinction has various consequences. Most demographers are also specialists with competence in some particular science, as well as demography. Most demographic research tends to be interdisciplinary or nondisciplinary in character. In most graduate schools, demography is not an autonomous department of university instruction; the typical training program requires fulfillment of the academic obligations of some department, such as sociology or economics, in addition to specialized instruction in demography.

Demographers concern themselves with both the determinants and the consequences of population change. The study of determinants is subdivided into the four processes by which a change in population size can occur: fertility, mortality, immigration, and emigration. Research on the determinants of migration (and urbanization) is likely to emphasize the economic and political conditions that circumscribe these processes. Research on the determinants of fertility and mortality, to the contrary, requires models incorporating a range of biological and sociocultural parameters to define the questions sharply and delineate useful directions of inquiry. As a particular example, concern about high fertility has led in recent decades to a vast expansion of inquiries into the detailed reproductive process and the ways in which the incidence and efficacy of individual fertility regulation may be improved. In this respect, and more broadly, demography has always been inherently cross-cultural and international in its perspective.

The consequences of population change are manifold, since they concern changes in the numbers of individuals distributed over many characteristics, such as age, education, labor force status, and geographic location. Literally no socioeconomic problem facing a nation is without its demographic dimension. Because of the ubiquity of population considerations in answering practical questions, because the demographer is trained to deal with concrete rather than abstract elements of problems, and because of the power of the population model in such work, the student trained in population studies is favored for employment by governments at every level and by industry and business (such as in the field of marketing, where "demographics" has become well established), as well as in traditional academic pursuits.

Norman B. Ryder
Office of Population Research
Princeton University

Economics

Agricultural Economics and Agribusiness   The primary emphasis of agricultural economics and agribusiness is on the application of economic and business principles to the solution of problems related to agriculture and the rural economy. Conceptual frameworks employed in agricultural economics come largely from economics. Because several research and educational activities frequently involve implications for public policy at local, state, national, and international levels, other social science disciplines are also relied upon in analyzing and evaluating policy alternatives. Widespread use is made of quantitative techniques, such as statistics and mathematics, in analytical processes.

Research programs are oriented toward the solution of emerging and prospective problems in the organization, growth, efficiency, and management of the food and fiber sector and toward the evaluation of alternative public policies that bear on the operation and performance of the agricultural economy. International trade and development activities are carried on as useful opportunities are seen to contribute to the solution of problems with an international dimension.

Agricultural Economics and Agribusiness (continued)

Major continuing programs administered by academic institutions are in farm management, farm finance, marketing, agribusiness, economic outlook, public policy, and rural economic and community development. Various other topics, such as energy and natural resources, are dealt with according to their importance and the current interest in them. In extension teaching, emphasis is placed on the incorporation of new knowledge and the development of innovative approaches to meeting various educational needs. Clientele groups served range from decision makers at the individual farm, firm, and industry levels to state and national government officials.

Instructional programs lead to baccalaureate and advanced degrees. Graduates find employment in diverse fields of farming, finance, and agribusiness; in academic institutions; in government at local, state, and national levels; and in international activities.

Paul L. Farris, Professor
Department of Agricultural Economics
Purdue University

Economics Economics is the study of the allocation of scarce resources among competing uses, either through conscious public policy or through market forces. The analytical skills of economists are useful in evaluating alternative methods of achieving society's goals and objectives and in formulating strategies and policies that will help to achieve these objectives.

Graduate study is a necessary prerequisite for those who wish to pursue careers as economists. The master's degree is typically sufficient preparation for those who wish to work as government economists at the state or local level or as research assistants in consulting firms or the federal government. The Ph.D. is normally required for teaching positions at the university level and for economic staff positions with industry, consulting firms, or the federal government. Employment prospects are currently reasonably good for economists, especially those with Ph.D.'s.

For selecting a graduate program, students should consider the fields of specialization offered, the political predilections of the faculty, and the size and reputation of the program. There is a growing tendency for economists to specialize in rather narrow subfields within the discipline. Among the possibilities are labor economics, econometrics, environmental economics, international economics, urban and regional economics, money and banking, industrial organization, public finance, health economics, and economic history. Each graduate program has a different mix of specializations and course offerings, which should be noted by the prospective student. The applicant should also be aware of the differences in language, mathematics, thesis, and qualifying examination requirements for the graduate degree.

Economics programs also vary in general emphasis. Some are effectively limited to the study of microeconomic problems from a neoclassical perspective. Others offer a strong macroeconomic option with either a monetarist or Keynesian focus. A few programs are strong in nontraditional analysis from an institutionalist, post-Keynesian, or Marxian perspective. These different schools of thought have a somewhat subtle political component. Neoclassical and monetarist economists support the free market, oppose government involvement in the economy, and align themselves with conservative political groups. Keynesian, institutionalist, and post-Keynesian economists support government involvement in the economy to correct imperfections (such as pollution and poverty) and are often affiliated with liberal political movements. Marxian economists believe that the market economy is inherently unstable, unequal, and degrading to workers and should be replaced by economic planning and socialism. These political differences should be considered by students searching for the appropriate graduate program.

Richard W. Hurd, Associate Professor
Whittemore School of Business and Economics
University of New Hampshire

Mineral Economics   Mineral economics applies the principles of economic analysis to the problems of finding, extracting, processing, and using minerals. As practiced, the field seeks to accommodate a wide variety of approaches to the problem. Historically, almost all the students had backgrounds in mineral science or technology and an interest in moving on to the business or public policy side of the mineral industries. More recently, students with backgrounds in the social sciences have increasingly found the applications orientation of the field to be an attractive alternative.

Mineral Economics (continued)

These differences in backgrounds and in interests, combined with an emphasis on flexible curriculums and different career orientations, lead to considerable differences in the characteristics of mineral economists. Some stress the economics. Others engage in activities in which their previously acquired skills in mineral science and technology are combined with the economics. The field was designed for people interested in industry, government, or consulting. Graduates have assumed important roles in leading firms engaged in the production, processing, and use of minerals; major financial institutions; government and international organizations with mineral concerns; and consulting firms. Many have found academic positions in mineral economics programs throughout the world and in economics and business programs for technically oriented students.

Training tends to concentrate upon economics and related areas such as business, statistics, and operations research. It is impractical to also include substantial training in mineral science and technology. Thus, only those with substantial prior training in science and technology can undertake work that combines those fields with economics. The field also has long encouraged the appropriate use of computers and quantitative methods. However, the stress is on problem solving and encourages use of a wide variety of techniques. Still another variation is in the relative emphasis of market and public policy influences. Both the curriculums and the students' approaches differ considerably. Some schools stress that the persistent influence of public policy requires that mineral economists understand the role of politics; other departments are more concerned with the business administration aspects of the field.

Formal programs in the field exist at only four American universities, but several others try to tailor programs within existing mineral science or technology curriculums. Each of the universities maintains modest enrollments so that only a few mineral economists graduate each year. Thus, while the demand for skilled mineral analysts in different sectors has fluctuated considerably, positions have always been available for graduates. The field should continue to be an interesting and rewarding one for able, ambitious people interested in a broad-gauged approach to mineral problems.

Richard L. Gordon
Department of Mineral Economics
Pennsylvania State University

Education

Education   One of the purposes of education is to help individuals develop an approach to living that will enable them to function effectively in a society and world that is culturally diverse and in a constant state of change. Colleges of education have the responsibility for preparing professionals to assist students in acquiring the knowledge and skills needed for a successful living career. These skills are more than the ability to read, write, and compute; they include the abilities to develop a scientific approach toward work and life, to create, to enjoy the creations and expressions of others, and to contribute solutions to the problems of the universe. Within the next decade, the need for teachers will be great. For those not already in education, a way of satisfying this need is through graduate study at the master's level. Graduate study at the doctoral level is also important, for it is at this stage that the writer, the researcher, the scholar, the policymaker, and the leader are developed.

Graduate study is encouraged for those who have liberal arts degrees as well as for those who have already had some education in the field. Most graduate schools and colleges plan their master's degree programs to accommodate the needs of the profession. Many educational institutions today have identified the need to expose educators to the impact of technology on learning, and they therefore offer education in this area. Attention is also given to local and state certification and credentialing requirements. Most master's degree programs require 30 to 52 credit hours. Depending on the student and the requirement of the degree, one to two years of study may be involved.

Students who have majored in education or who have become certified at the undergraduate level often find it necessary to pursue additional study in the field of education. Advanced study can help teachers become more effective in the teaching and learning arena. Through graduate study at the master's level, teachers begin to learn how to combine theory and practice in educational settings. Research on teaching and learning begins to take on new meanings and contributes to a better understanding of children's behavior, as well as providing a clearer definition of the needs of the profession. Graduate study for those interested in administration, counseling, and bilingual education and for those who are eager to provide services to the exceptional child through special education can be the route to a more intense and rigorous exploration of all forces that impact on schools and schooling. This study often combines

Education (continued)

supervised fieldwork, internships, and opportunities to observe and to record with a variety of courses all grounded on research. Theory and practice are thus interwoven.

Graduate study at the doctoral level provides opportunities for those individuals who are more keenly interested in making a contribution in the field through a combination of field experience, knowledge, and research. Most graduate schools that offer doctoral degrees have structured programs that accommodate a variety of interests, such as educational psychology, administration, counseling, curriculum and instruction, anthropology and education, and educational policy. Requirements for doctoral degrees vary by program and institution. Generally, most programs require a minimum of 50 to 60 hours above the master's degree plus a dissertation. The time needed to complete the study also varies but usually takes a minimum of three to four years, depending on the type of research project that is involved as well as the amount of time the student is able to invest.

Graduate study in education at the master's and doctoral levels can help provide what is needed for improving the quality of schools in the United States.

Gwendolyn C. Baker
Graduate School
Bank Street College of Education

Adult Education   The professional field of adult and continuing education is centrally concerned with fostering the process of adult learning and extending the capacity of adults to become increasingly self-directed learners. There is recent recognition of the importance of helping learners become conscious of psychocultural assumptions constraining their development. Adult education has been defined as "a process whereby persons who no longer attend school on a regular and full-time basis (unless full-time programs are especially designed for adults) undertake sequential and organized activities with conscious intention of bringing about changes in information, knowledge, understanding or skills, appreciation and attitudes; or for the purpose of identifying and solving personal or community problems." (Liveright and Haygood, eds., *The Exeter Papers.*)

Graduate programs frequently include courses in adult learning and development, program development, instructional dynamics and group process, administration and organization of adult programs, history and philosophy of adult education and lifelong learning, social context of adult education, community education and development, and comparative adult education. Fields of practice in which instruction is frequently given include adult basic and secondary education, higher adult education, continuing professional education, educational gerontology, occupational and vocational education, labor education, staff and organizational development, consultation, and community development.

Graduate programs prepare students for professional careers in adult and continuing education in colleges and universities; public schools; proprietary schools; training and organizational development programs in business and industry, government, the military, and unions; cooperative extension; community organizations such as libraries, museums, churches and religious organizations, youth organizations, social action groups, associations of older adults, and other groups concerned with specific public issues; and nonformal educational programs in international development.

Jack Mezirow
Teachers College/Columbia University

Agricultural Education   Graduate programs in agricultural education are designed to provide for the continuing professional development of persons engaged in the various areas of the agricultural education profession. Graduate curricula at the master's and doctoral degree levels vary among universities, although programs characteristically provide the flexibility and content necessary to meet the specific needs and interests of the candidate. Fields of specialization include teacher education, supervision and administration, secondary and postsecondary teaching, extension education, education in business and industry, research, state supervision, or a combination of these areas. Programs may also be planned with emphasis on international agricultural development and other related areas, such as curriculum and instruction.

Degree candidates typically receive guidance from a structured committee of 2 to 5 graduate faculty members representing discipline areas of the students' interest. The graduate committee provides direction in developing a program of study and specific plans for meeting degree requirements.

Agricultural Education (continued)

Universities offer various master's and doctoral programs designed to develop competencies in areas of research, teaching, and scholarly writing that serve primary career paths. Internships, independent study, and special projects are frequently incorporated into graduate programs in order to provide experiences not available in existing university courses. The diverse nature of agriculture and its related support services provide numerous career opportunities for agricultural educators with graduate credentials in education.

Persons interested in graduate study in agricultural education should consult with appropriate personnel at various universities for specific information regarding admission standards and graduate curricula.

William E. Drake, Professor
Agricultural and Occupational Education
Department of Education
Cornell University

Art Education Art education usually refers to the training of teachers of the visual arts, to the preparation of public school art administrators, and to the education of the college and university faculty members who train art teachers. This rather conventional definition of the field focuses on schools and schooling. A new and broader definition of art education has also come into usage that includes art instruction in social and cultural agencies other than schools—in museums or art councils, for example, or in health and custodial-care institutions or recreation and retirement centers.

Graduate study in art education may involve four separate and distinct tracks: three at the master's level and one at the doctoral level. For those students who possess an undergraduate degree in art education, the master's degree represents a second level of professional training. Such a degree (or its equivalent) is a requirement for permanent teacher certification in many states. Many in-service teachers complete their master's degree by attending summer sessions or evening classes while they continue to teach full-time at an elementary or secondary school. Another group of candidates for the master's degree in art education can be seen in those students who have earned a B.A. or B.F.A. in studio art (or more rarely in art history) and who are concurrently working toward meeting state certification requirements. For them, the master's degree is an entry-level professional degree, and most such students pursue their studies on a full-time basis. A third avenue toward the master's degree in art education prepares students who have baccalaureate degrees in studio art or art history and who are preparing for careers in museums or other nonschool settings. Such students need not meet state teacher certification requirements, but they are usually expected to complete an internship in a museum, an arts council, or a similar cultural agency.

At the doctoral level, students may pursue either the Ph.D. or the D.Ed. in art education. In theory, the Ph.D. concentrates on original research or scholarship and the D.Ed. emphasizes the practical applications of research. Such distinctions are increasingly difficult to sustain, however, and while some universities offer both the Ph.D. and the D.Ed., others offer only one or the other. In either event, the scholarly requirements of the two degrees are almost indistinguishable, and the capabilities of graduates are rarely a function of whether they hold a Ph.D. or a D.Ed. Most doctoral students in art education are well established in the field before they begin their studies, though some may have earned their M.A. or M.F.A. in art, in art history, or in a related field, such as aesthetics or perceptual and developmental psychology. An increasing number of doctoral students in art education combine summer study with a leave of absence from a college or a public school system. For most such students, the doctorate is the third level of professional education, though for some it may also provide the opportunity to change careers. The scholarly focus of doctoral research in art education is wide and varied, ranging from studies of artistic behavior and aesthetic education to computer-based art instruction and arts administration. Research methodology at the doctoral level is also highly diverse and often draws upon related disciplines, such as history, philosophy, sociology, anthropology, and political science.

Employment opportunities in art education are fairly stable but, at the same time, they are now subject to variables that did not previously apply. In the past, most art educators were employed by educational institutions—in public or private schools for holders of bachelor's and master's degrees and in colleges or universities for those with the doctorate. The so-called "culture explosion" has now created new opportunities for art educators in nonschool settings even though, strictly speaking, the primary purpose of such institutions is not teaching and learning. At the same time, seemingly unrelated phenomena such as declining birthrates, the feminist movement, taxpayer revolts, and student materialism have combined

Art Education (continued)

to restrict employment opportunities in schools and colleges. Such conditions do not apply in every region of the country, however, though it can probably be said that there are more in-school opportunities for art educators in the rapidly growing Sun Belt and more nonschool opportunities in "smokestack" cities, where the cultural base has been a century or more in the making.

Harlan Hoffa
Associate Dean for Research and Graduate Studies
College of Arts and Architecture
Pennsylvania State University

Bilingual and Bicultural Education   Bilingual and bicultural education is the field of study that aims to prepare personnel for working with the bilingual child and/or designing a curriculum in such a way that a bilingual child is the eventual product. At the college level, bilingual education involves the preparation of teachers who will work with the bilingual child. The preparation of the bilingual teacher requires work at both the undergraduate and graduate levels. It also involves acquiring an academic degree determined by the university offering the program and certification in one form or other as determined by the appropriate state education agency.

Often the degree is in education and involves such courses as curriculum, psychology, administration, supervision, methodology, and testing. The same holds true of the certification program; however, the preparation of the bilingual education teacher should also include the appropriate competence in and knowledge of language, linguistics, cultural anthropology, psycholinguistics, sociolinguistics, culture, etc.

There is currently great demand for bilingual education teachers, particularly at the elementary school level. This is especially true in areas where multilingual or bilingual societies occur, such as in the Northeast, along the West Coast, and in the southwestern part of the United States. There are some aspects of bilingual education that are controversial, but that is not surprising since many aspects of monolingual education, which has a longer history, are just as controversial. However, given the continuous immigration of foreign language speakers into the United States and the increased travel and commerce throughout the world, one can safely predict that bilingual education will be in demand for a long time to come. Moreover, new areas of demand are opening up, such as the instruction of the migrant child and work in adult education with the monolingual person and with the adult illiterate.

Sound research in bilingual education and in second language teaching and learning has increased significantly in the last twenty years. However, there are many areas still needing sound basic research.

Students pursuing bilingual education enter a field that is alive with interest and very much in need of highly prepared personnel.

Joseph Michel
Division of Bicultural-Bilingual Studies
College of Social and Behavioral Sciences
University of Texas at San Antonio

Business Education   Business education is an ambiguous term that encompasses at least four common focuses:

(1) The most common use of the term at the graduate level refers to the advanced preparation of teachers of business subjects for instruction at middle school through graduate institutions (with the latter often requiring a doctorate) and, more recently, with the advent of microcomputers, even at the elementary school level. Students generally have an undergraduate major in business education or in one of the business fields. Instructional areas in which a graduate might teach include typewriting and keyboarding, general business, economics, shorthand, accounting and bookkeeping, business communications, information processing and word processing, records management, microcomputers and data processing, and management. In some institutions, graduates would also teach marketing and distribution. Students in this first category tend to be instructors seeking professional development for their current job setting or for movement to a different level of instruction. Demand in this category is beginning to exceed supply, especially in some areas of the United States. Teacher shortages are expected within the next five years.

(2) The next most common application of the term is to programs in business administration and management, particularly when offered through continuing education. In these cases, students are being prepared to function in managerial levels within the business world. Graduate students in these categories come from a wide diversity of undergraduate programs. The high demand for

Business Education (continued)

graduates of such programs has generally fallen off from the peak of a few years ago, though it continues to be strong.

(3) A third meaning of "business education"—the preparation of individuals to function specifically in offices in supervisory or administrative positions—is quite common at the undergraduate level and is used infrequently at present for graduate programs, though some growth in this area is anticipated. Titles of such programs are Administrative Systems, Office Systems Administration, Office Management, and many others. Graduate students typically have an undergraduate major in this field or a related secretarial field. Demand for employees with graduate degrees emphasizing both technical and interpersonal skills is growing.

(4) A final usage of the term is for those preparing primarily to enter the private sector as business training and development personnel. This appears to be a rapidly growing market, with businesses looking for persons with graduate degrees concentrating on both business and training. Several sources have identified this category as the major growth area within business education during the current decade. Students entering programs with this focus come from a wide variety of backgrounds, typically emphasizing education or business; attempts are made to strengthen the student's background in areas of weakness.

Gary N. McLean, Professor
Business Education
University of Minnesota

Community College Education   Commitment to accessibility and equal educational opportunity, responsiveness to emerging community needs, low-cost programs, and a comprehensive curriculum make the community college an attractive environment for those interested in continuing education. The community college currently enrolls 53 percent of all freshmen and sophomores in the country. Both public and private two-year colleges offer broad-based programs that enable students to obtain associate degrees, occupational credentials and certification, job training, remedial education, enrichment courses, and an opportunity to progress to four-year senior institutions. However, with the pull of the job market, the role played by the college's traditional transfer program has been diminishing. Presently, career education continues to maintain an ascendant position as a vehicle for upward mobility, training, and employment.

The nature of the community college, in large part, depends upon the changes that are occurring in society. Thus, with the burgeoning growth of the adult population, the need for recurring education programs, lifelong learning, academic remediation, and occupational training has increased. As the community college continues to enroll proportionately more minority group members and older undergraduates, the challenge will be to offer programs and services to meet the unique needs of diverse constituencies. Based on the increased number of part-time and nontraditional students, combined with the rapid rate of technological growth in this country, a variety of community college positions will be available in order to keep pace with the demands of the changing educational marketplace.

A master's degree, obtained in a traditional academic department, is the typical preparation for community college instructors. However, in recent years an increasing number of faculty members and administrators have pursued doctorates. For those interested in becoming instructors in occupational programs, professional experience in a specialty area, along with some pedagogical training, is considered equivalent to a graduate degree.

Master's and doctoral programs, geared to preparing professionals for positions in administration, student affairs and services, and other allied service roles, are available at a number of major universities. While some programs focus specifically on community college education and grant degrees within that specialty, most departments offer an emphasis in the community college as part of a more broadly defined program, such as higher education or educational leadership.

Linda H. Lewis, Assistant Professor
Department of Educational Leadership
University of Connecticut

Computer Education   Computer education, a comparatively new field of research, currently presents two primary areas for study: (1) the roles of the computer in educational settings and (2) the development of appropriate strategies for teaching and implementing computer applications in a business environment. The first deals primarily with the computer in formal instructional

Computer Education (continued)

environments such as the school or university; the second, with the computer in administrative or corporate functions. A graduate program in computer education has its foundations in instructional theory but draws from related disciplines, namely, artificial intelligence, cognitive and behavioral psychology, and computer science. Thus, while the field is primarily educational, it has a strong base in philosophy, psychology, and technology. Most graduate programs in computer education require readings in these related fields as well as in educational theory.

Early research in computers in formal educational settings was done primarily by the military. Most of these studies reflect the tutorial/drill-and-practice mode of learning. This orientation to the use of computers has continued to grow and can be found in those university programs specializing in experimental research, wherein learning is measured in a computer versus a traditional setting. However, other programs feature alternative approaches. These are usually characterized by a holistic approach, which integrates elements of societal concerns into an instructional program featuring a developmental and/or reconceptualist philosophy of education. These concerns might include such topics as the historical and philosophical roots of technology, implications of a technocratic society, its impact on the workplace, and related ethical questions. This second type of program frequently emphasizes the creation of a computer environment and the preferred role of the computer as tool rather than tutor. Research in these programs generally tends to be of an ethnographic or descriptive nature. At the root of the controversies over the role of the computer in education lie conflicting definitions of intelligence, human thought, and the nature of the person, thus the importance of foundations in philosophy, psychology, and technology.

Computer educators are in demand at every level of society, but nowhere has this need been more in evidence than in the school. Consequently, most current programs reflect the concerns and demands of the formal educational setting. Foremost among these demands is an understanding of microcomputer technology, its challenge and limitations, and its potential roles in a classroom. Although computer education students are not expected to achieve the proficiency of a professional programmer, they are required to develop programming skill in several languages and to be prepared to teach programming in an appropriate context. As a prerequisite to programming skills, most specializations require that the student develop an understanding of and facility in problem solving. Another major area of endeavor for the degree candidate is applications software. Computer educators must not only become "hands-on" experts in word processing, data files, and spreadsheet software, but they must also research the literature in these and related areas and develop a repertoire of applications for a given educational context. Finally, most programs place a heavy emphasis on the design and/ or evaluation of software and its integration into the curriculum. Thus, while philosophies and instructional theories differ from one program to the next, there exists a more or less stable body of skills, understandings, and research required by all.

Research in modes of instruction in computer technology at the corporate level is in its infancy. Whereas the computer in the school has been an object of research over a number of years, universities are only now beginning to apply their resources to this area of critical need. Prospective students of computer education with primary interests in corporate education should investigate the potential for pursuing this interest when applying to a given program.

Louise A. Mayock
Assistant Professor of Computer Science
Chestnut Hill College

Counselor Education   Counseling can be defined as a therapeutic relationship between a professionally trained and credentialed counselor and an individual or individuals attempting to maximize their human potential. The focus is upon helping clients to gain greater self-understanding, improve decision-making abilities, and implement behavior-change skills for resolution of problematic or developmental concerns. The field of counseling was built upon the philosophical belief in human worth and dignity and the practical notion of helping people understand themselves and eliminate self-defeating behaviors. It is a facilitative process that encourages the learning of new behavior and attitudes.

Preparation for counseling involves interdisciplinary study; some course work may be taken in psychology, sociology, or education. Much of the time it involves two years of graduate work leading to a master's degree, but several colleges and universities offer undergraduate majors in counseling, human services, or human resource development.

Students with degrees in counseling work in many settings with diverse groups of clientele. These settings include schools, employment and rehabilitation agencies, churches, and business and

Counselor Education (continued)

industry. It appears that in the immediate future the demand for counselors in schools and public agencies will decline consistent with the decreased federal and state support provided to education and social service. On the other hand, counselors will find increased job opportunities in the industrial sector and, as national licensure proceeds, private practice.

The demand by out-of-school youth and adults for counselors to address specialized counseling concerns has grown considerably. New areas of attention include marital and family counseling, alcoholism counseling, drug counseling, suicide prevention, counseling the older individual, sex counseling, and holistic counseling for health. Essentially, then, counseling situations in the future will continue to fall into three broad types: crisis, preventive, and developmental.

John J. Pietrofesa, Professor
Counselor Education
Division of Theoretical and Behavioral Foundations
Wayne State University

Curriculum and Instruction   Conveying the essence of the field of curriculum and instruction in a few paragraphs is not an easy task. Indeed, the extent to which curriculum and instruction should be linked together is one of the primary issues of the field. Curriculum work is more likely to be perceived as content oriented—the subject matter of what elementary and secondary schools (and colleges and universities, for that matter) teach—while instruction is more likely to be viewed as process oriented—how the subject matter is actually offered to students. But neither of these distinctions holds up well in practice since one of the most commonly used definitions of curriculum includes all of the experiences that young people have under the auspices of the school, an orientation that integrates subject matter and process in one operational definition.

There are three common uses of the word "curriculum." The first is to speak of the curriculum of a school. This usage refers to the subject matter or content dimension of the field. A second usage is of curriculum as a field of practice—what curriculum workers actually do. Depending upon position, practitioners may teach (usually in higher education); supervise elementary and secondary teachers; coordinate curriculum planning, implementation, and evaluation; or be involved in the design and development of instructional material. The third usage of the word "curriculum" is as a field of study. This use includes, of course, the study of curriculum as content and curriculum as practice, but it also includes empirical research and theorizing. Most of the latter work is done in higher education.

Graduate programs, available in most of the major public and private universities, offer the master's degree, the Ed.D., and the Ph.D. Master's degree graduates are usually employed in central office positions, as supervisors, curriculum coordinators, and directors of curriculum in public school systems. Those who complete a doctoral program most often are employed to teach and conduct research in colleges and universities. Some go into public school work in the same positions already mentioned, and others are employed by research and development agencies and the publishing industry to design and develop instructional materials. Increasingly greater numbers are finding work in industrial training programs, adult education, community centers, trade unions, and religious and secular publishing houses.

The historical distinction between the Ed.D. and the Ph.D. programs (the Ed.D. as a practitioner's degree and the Ph.D. as a research degree) has all but disappeared in most institutions. As a result of their historical development, some institutions offer one of these degrees and some the other, while many offer both.

Recent interests in the reform of education may open up additional opportunities for practitioners in this field. To take but one example, many states are requiring greater study in areas such as English, mathematics, science, and foreign language, and these new standards will require a considerable effort in curriculum development for proper implementation. As a result, this field, like many in education, is beginning to hold more promise for those who are interested in it.

Gerald R. Smith, Chair
Department of Curriculum and Instruction
Indiana University Bloomington

Early Childhood Education   Graduate study in early childhood education can be defined by the age of the children and the curriculum specialization. In the past, early childhood education has been divided between preschool (nursery school and kindergarten) and primary school (kindergarten through grade 3). This division,

Early Childhood Education (continued)

arbitrary though it may have been, was also reflected in graduate study; preschool training was heavily influenced by concerns for child development, and primary school education was informed more by learning theory and curriculum design. Over the past two decades this distinction has gradually disappeared. More and more early childhood educators consider the child from birth through age 8 as the appropriate focus of research and training. However, students must be aware that graduate programs are not always prepared to offer equal emphasis to the major educational and developmental epochs along this broad spectrum. Some schools offer particular competence in infancy, others on the child from 3 to 5, still others the child from 5 to 9. Such emphases as these are also apt to signal particular strengths among the faculty as regards pedagogical, curricular, and developmental issues.

Graduate study in early childhood education may be further divided into three major curriculum specializations: development and learning, curriculum and teaching, and equity. Students who specialize in the first of these generally concentrate on the explication and extension of theory and knowledge of child development and learning to the practice of child care and education. Typically, students in this specialization are highly interested in research practice, either basic (e.g., studies of egocentrism) or applied (e.g., children's use of the microcomputer). In the second specialty, curriculum and teaching, students tend to develop expertise in one or another of the curriculum areas commonly found in the preschool or primary grades, such as reading, the arts, children's literature, writing, and mathematics. These students tend to look for a career in teacher education or school administration. The third specialization, equity, is a new but growing field. Issues ranging from the education of minority and handicapped children to policy studies on day care are appropriate foci.

Students who complete master's-level study usually have little difficulty gaining employment as master teachers, day-care directors, or supervisors or administrators. Early childhood students who complete doctoral studies can be employed as teacher educators in two- and four-year colleges and in universities offering graduate study in early childhood education. There is substantial growth in state regulatory and consultative agencies for graduates of both levels of study. The increase in day-care use, the growing population of young children, and the continued emphasis on early childhood education suggest that a fairly healthy employment picture is likely to get even better.

David E. Day
Professor, Early Childhood Education
School of Education
University of Massachusetts

Educational Administration Educational administration as a graduate-level program of studies is aimed at generating knowledge about the organizational life of school systems and preparing individuals to manage educational enterprises so that clients receive designated services in the most effective and efficient manner possible. Hence, most departments of educational administration have two major missions: (1) an academic/research purpose, that is, examining the various elements of the practice of administration, the conditions influencing governance and policy formation, and the structure and processes of formal organizations; and (2) a professional purpose of training, that is, the teaching of students so that they may assume administrative roles and be able to make decisions, plan, organize, motivate, coordinate, and appraise people, resources, and events. Theoretical constructs and models of inquiry are drawn from many other disciplines, such as economics, sociology, political science, business management, and psychology. The implementation of administration is mostly grounded in technical, human, and conceptual skills.

Departments of educational administration vary not only in the balance between research and training but in their perspective on the practice of educational administration. For example, some departments will stress the systems approach to management, others will base their view on instructional leadership, and still others will interpret administration as a human process of interaction. Consistent with department interpretation and state education department requirements, programs of work will vary with regard to number, types, and content of courses (i.e., internships, practicums, theory courses, methodology and research courses, and courses within the department vs. electives within education and in other disciplines outside the field of education). Moreover, the number of faculty members and their specializations, such as higher education and community college education, will determine programs offered. Therefore, the prospective student is encouraged to inquire about

Educational Administration (continued)

various departments in order to make a selection that matches his or her interests and needs.

The pursuit of research falls into several domains that for the most part have been constant for the past fifteen years. These are organizational dynamics, policy analysis, the federal government's involvement and its implication for school management, school finance, leadership behavior, governance and decision making, and evaluation of instructional programs and personnel (these should not be considered all-encompassing). Specific studies within each of these domains are usually influenced by current educational issues attracting national attention. For example, the public attention of improving schools has resulted in effective school studies (evaluation domain), and the recent passage of federal legislation on the implementation of special education (federal involvement) has brought activity in mainstreaming.

Graduates of educational administration programs have several options to choose from to practice as administrators. Those acquiring a master's degree and a state certificate can take positions as assistant principals, principals, or directors of programs at local school districts; middle-management positions with state departments of education; or supervisory positions with regional educational service centers or the county superintendent's offices. With additional course work beyond the master's degree, students can receive a superintendent certificate permitting them to become assistant superintendents or superintendents of public school districts or to hold executive positions, such as commissioners with state departments of education. Parochial and private schools are other marketplaces open to graduates. Students with a doctoral degree have the options listed above plus the opportunity to pursue research-based roles, such as teaching at the university or college level, conducting research at research centers and labs, working for federal organizations such as the National Institute of Education or the U.S. Department of Education, and becoming deans, vice presidents, and presidents at community colleges.

Employment opportunities for the next five to seven years appear to be very good. Student enrollments are likely to increase again, causing more schools to open and existing schools to grow, thus creating a demand for more principals and assistant principals. Community college enrollments are expanding as well. Retirement of professors of educational administration and superintendents will continue to necessitate replacement. State departments of education and federal agencies will be needing new personnel in emerging areas, such as vocational education and technology. Other markets will develop for administrators as new programs, such as corporate businesses establishing their own in-house educational unit for employee training, continue to emerge.

Leonard A. Valverde
Department of Educational Administration
University of Texas at Austin

Educational Measurement and Evaluation   Educational measurement and evaluation are related fields of training found in many graduate colleges of education. The measurement field is concerned with processes for assigning numbers or labels to represent aspects of reality. In doing so, an individual (i.e., educator, psychologist, or businessperson) can then utilize these numbers or labels to develop theory, make predictions, make decisions, or just be better informed about a person, a place, an issue, some behavior, etc. Popular examples of this work are the development of tests to assess knowledge, the use of rating systems to observe a child's behavior, and the development of a categorization system to classify people into personality types. In other words, the measurement field is an attempt to scientifically approach the problem of providing valuable data for subsequent use.

Evaluation concerns the assessment of the worth of a program. Its purpose can be dichotomized into formative evaluation (program improvement) and summative evaluation (program rating). An evaluator tries to determine strengths and weaknesses of a program and often will recommend actions that the program may take to make it more effective in various settings. Training in this field usually involves considerable background in measurement and in statistics, although there are training programs that emphasize an approach that relies more upon evaluation as an art rather than as a science. These programs encourage their students to obtain training in philosophy, history, and anthropological techniques for formulating approaches to collecting information and drawing conclusions. Graduate training in measurement is much more similar across the country than is training in evaluation. The interested student needs to assess carefully the orientation of the programs that are available for graduate work to ensure consistency with what is desired.

Employment opportunities in these areas are excellent, particularly for those who have received training in the more

Educational Measurement and Evaluation (continued)

quantitative applications of the field (e.g., statistics, measurement theory, and computer skills). This approach provides the graduate with skills that apply to a wide range of problems. Graduates find employment in consulting firms, educational agencies, the federal government, and industry. Each of these employers, and others as well, need people skilled in the collection of information, the analysis of such information, and the drawing of conclusions and implications for practice. For example, personnel departments, programs providing continuing education, and city planning units all have a need for such skills and often hire persons to perform measurement and evaluation functions for the organization.

The two fields have active research programs that upgrade the profession and keep its members well informed with useful solutions to important problems. The development of theories relating to computer-based measurement and evaluation techniques, particularly as they apply to instructional programs, is but one of the more exciting new areas. Several other areas of research have developed in response to considerable public interest in the effects of coaching for the Scholastic Aptitude Tests (SAT), possible biases in using tests to select persons into employment and training programs, and the degree of effectiveness of compensatory education programs (Head Start, Upward Bound, etc.).

Educational measurement and evaluation require both strong quantitative and verbal skills. Most employment settings involve planning for data collection and analysis, research supervision, and drawing inferences from results. There is a need to communicate with others during all phases of these activities. Individuals who possess these skills and have a strong educational background in measurement and evaluation are in a good position to seek employment in a variety of interesting settings with goals ranging from the highly theoretical to the highly practical.

Robert W. Lissitz, Chairman
Department of Measurement, Statistics, and Evaluation
University of Maryland College Park

Educational Media/Instructional Technology　　The terms "educational media" and "instructional technology" are used interchangeably by some professionals, but they have unique and quite different meanings to others. Educational media are generally defined to include a variety of electromechanical, photographic, and digital devices and the educational materials they display. Some examples are television, film, slides, audiotapes, and, more recently, computers and their accompanying "courseware." In some cases, print materials (books, journals, newspapers, etc.) are also included as educational media. For example, it is common at the public school level to employ media specialists who are expected to be knowledgeable about both print and nonprint media.

There is much less agreement on what constitutes instructional technology. Some use the term interchangeably with educational media as defined above. When this is done, print media are usually excluded. Others define instructional technology not as devices or materials but as "a systematic way of designing, carrying out, and evaluating the total process of learning and teaching in terms of specific objectives, based on research in human learning and communication and employing a combination of human and nonhuman resources to bring about more effective instruction" (Presidential Commission on Instructional Technology, 1970). Other terms sometimes used synonymously with instructional technology are instructional development, instructional design, and systems approach.

Due to the disparate definitions that exist, two distinct lines of research have emerged. One focuses on the devices themselves and their capacity and effectiveness in varied situations. The second focus is on the design of instruction that may or may not be delivered by a hardware device. The first line of research typically asks such questions as, "Which device is more effective?" or "Can this device be used to teach this objective?" The second line of research shifts the focus to the learner, asking, "What is the most effective sequence of instructional events?" or "What instructional strategy is appropriate for this type of objective?"

Programs of graduate study are available at over 100 colleges and universities. A limited number of locations have recently instituted undergraduate programs. Master's, specialist, and doctoral degree studies are all available, but not at every institution. Graduate programs usually have one of three different emphases: (1) generalist studies in selection, acquisition, storage, retrieval, and circulation of existing print and nonprint instructional resources, (2) production of one or more media formats, or (3) systematic design of instruction to achieve specific learner objectives. Thus, potential students should inquire closely about the programs they are considering.

Employment opportunities vary widely depending on the graduate's skills. In the public school sector, opportunities are quite limited due to reduced enrollments and tighter school finances.

Educational Media/Instructional Technology (continued)

Many states require school media personnel to be certified. This may be accomplished by completing an approved program or by taking the required courses and applying directly to the state. Positions in higher education as faculty members are similarly limited in number, the single exception being a high demand for faculty to teach computer-related courses. In contrast, positions in business, industry, government, and the military are relatively plentiful for graduates with instructional design skills. There is less, but still some, demand for production specialists and a limited demand for instructional resources specialists. Prospective students should inquire about the placement rate and types of positions filled by graduates of programs they are considering.

Kent L. Gustafson
Professor of Instructional Technology
University of Georgia

Educational Psychology   Educational psychology is an applied area of the general field of psychology. It incorporates elements of such other areas in psychology as social, developmental, school, and experimental psychology. Its major focus is on the application of psychological principles to the teaching and learning process, and it is concerned principally with the identification of factors and implementation of procedures that help to maximize the benefits of education.

Programs in educational psychology invariably include courses that may be subsumed under the major areas of learning, human growth and development, research and statistics, and evaluation. The area of learning includes major learning theories (classical, instrumental, cognitive, social learning, and gestalt) and describes the application of learning principles to the management of human behavior. It also includes extensive consideration of important constructs, including motivation, perception, memory, learning styles, teaching styles, problem solving, concept formation, intelligence, aptitude, attitudes toward learning, cognition, creativity, and giftedness. The area of human growth and development includes such topics as moral development, social development, cognitive development, nature vs. nurture effects on growth and development, and personality differences. The area of research and statistics includes research designs; parametric and nonparametric statistical procedures, including multivariate techniques; and computer application, including the use of statistical packages. The area of evaluation includes the development and standardization of tests, reliability, validity, norm-referenced tests vs. criterion-referenced tests, bias in testing, and evaluation models.

For students who major in educational psychology, job opportunities are possible in a number of different areas. For instance, they may work as researchers in public or private institutions, administrators in school systems, college professors, consultants, mental health specialists in clinics and hospitals, and in some instances as licensed psychologists in private practice. Since programs in educational psychology differ in structure and emphasis, preparing graduates for varying kinds of work experiences, it is important for prospective students to select a program in which the course of study will prepare them so that they may satisfy their career objectives.

Norris M. Haynes, Associate Professor
Coordinator of Educational Psychology
School of Education
Howard University

Education of the Gifted   Education of the gifted encompasses a field of research, theory development, and practical application. There has been a great increase in interest in gifted and talented youth since 1972. Programs of research, graduate study, and teacher training have sprung up at a number of colleges and universities throughout the United States. New journals (e.g., the *Gifted Child Quarterly,* the *Roeper Review,* and the *Journal for the Education of the Gifted*) have been developed to report theory, research, and practice in this field. Several professional organizations (e.g., the National Association for Gifted Children and the TAG Division of the Council for Exceptional Children) have also developed large memberships and active programs to serve the needs of researchers, theorists, and practitioners in the field.

Major areas of concern are the definition and identification of giftedness and talent. A report from the U.S. Office of Education in 1972 proposed six categories of giftedness or talent: general intellectual ability, specific academic talents, creative talent, talent in the visual and performing arts, leadership, and psychomotor ability. With this definition came an increase in the percentage of potentially gifted youth. Thus, schools now often identify 5–10 percent of their students as gifted or talented. Other theoretical conceptions have

Education of the Gifted (continued)

stressed the role of motivation and personality factors in determining giftedness.

Intelligence and achievement tests are widely used in identifying the gifted and talented, along with rating scales and nomination instruments completed by teachers, parents, and potentially gifted youth themselves. Practitioners frequently use specific cutoff levels of test scores or combinations of scores in identifying youth for programs, but there is little agreement among researchers as to the precise levels that define giftedness or talent.

Programs of educational activities for gifted and talented youth can now be found at all age levels, from preschool through college. The most popular form of program at the elementary level is the resource room/pull-out model. In this approach gifted youth leave their regular classrooms for as much as one full day per week for special studies stressing thinking skills, independent research, and affective experiences. Some elementary schools organize full-time self-contained classes for the gifted.

At the middle school level, special high ability or honors sections in mathematics, science, English, and social studies are often used. Special seminars for the gifted are also common. These classes place great stress on inquiry methods, problem solving, and independent research. Many middle school programs also provide opportunities for gifted youth to be accelerated in their courses. Thus, three years of middle school may be condensed to two years, or students may be allowed to take high school courses one or two years ahead of time.

High school programs may offer a variety of special services for the gifted and talented, including honors classes, College Board Advanced Placement classes, seminars, opportunities to work with mentors, field trips, and career education classes. A number of schools also use Individual Educational Plans (IEPs) with gifted and talented youth.

Full-time residential schools for the gifted and talented have been opened in a number of American cities. National talent searches are conducted regionally using the Scholastic Aptitude Test with seventh- and eighth-grade youth. Several universities are now major research and development centers (e.g., Connecticut, North Carolina at Chapel Hill, Teachers College at Columbia University, South Florida, Purdue, Virginia, Washington in Seattle, Georgia, Texas A&M, Johns Hopkins, and Northwestern). Generally, programs for the gifted and talented are growing all over the country with funding from state educational agencies. There seems to be an increasing recognition in the United States and throughout the world that the identification and nurturance of talent is vital to the future development of all nations.

Dr. John F. Feldhusen, Director
Gifted Education Resource Institute
Purdue University

Education of the Multiply Handicapped The education of the multiply handicapped is the area of special education concerned with children who have more than one disability. Multihandicapped children are those having any combination of disabilities, such as those who are deaf–mentally retarded, deaf-blind, or mentally retarded–physically handicapped. The knowledge and skills necessary for educating such children are much more than the ability to educate children with the same handicaps appearing singly. For example, a teacher qualified to teach both deaf children and blind children is not necessarily qualified to teach deaf-blind children. There are two related reasons for this: (1) the etiologies that cause more than one handicap (e.g., maternal rubella) often affect the child in several or all areas of development so that they have the effect of more than two handicaps, and (2) the handicaps interact with each other so that their effects are multiplicative rather than additive.

Multihandicapped students as a group are remarkably heterogeneous. The combinations of handicaps they have as well as their overall developmental levels vary widely. This group heterogeneity, as well as the individual complexity imposed by each child's combination of disabilities, poses problems in assessment, classification, educational placement, and service delivery. Probably more than for other handicapped children, education of the multihandicapped requires the support of ancillary services such as physical and occupational therapy, audiology, and speech pathology.

Since the mid-1970s, public school systems have provided education for multihandicapped students in a variety of educational settings. These are (1) special classes in regular elementary or secondary schools; (2) special classes in special schools, such as a multihandicapped class in a special day school for the physically handicapped or a state residential school for the deaf; and (3) resource services in a special school, such as a teacher of the multihandicapped who provides tutoring, manual-sign training, and interpreting in a special day school for the mentally retarded. Many multihandicapped children have been placed in state institutions or

Education of the Multiply Handicapped (continued)

hospitals for the mentally retarded, but the trend today is to educate them in settings as similar as possible to those of nonhandicapped children of the same age.

Training for teachers of multihandicapped students is generally provided at the graduate level. In most states today, prior undergraduate training in general or special education is necessary to enter the graduate training programs and to receive certification by the state. Some states offer a teaching certificate in the general area of education of the multihandicapped, while others certify teachers in each specific area of disability in which they have been trained.

Persons with graduate training in education of the multihandicapped may obtain employment not only as teachers, but also as diagnosticians, consultants, and program supervisors. Compared with other areas of general and special education, employment prospects in the education of the multihandicapped today are fairly good. This is partially due to the expansion of educational services to these students. The attrition rate for teachers in this area is also fairly high, but this is less true when teachers have been appropriately trained.

Thomas W. Jones, Associate Professor
Coordinator, Multihandicapped Specialization
Department of Education
Gallaudet College

Elementary Education Elementary education most commonly refers to the teaching of children in kindergarten through grade 6. State teacher certification laws follow various patterns, however, and adherence to them may mean that an institution has included concerns that elsewhere would come under early childhood or middle school education. Graduate work may involve attention to all subject areas as well as classroom management, educational media, counseling, foundations, and evaluations, or it may stress concentration in a more limited field. Reading is often treated as a separate area of study, as are music, art, and physical education.

Richard T. Salzer
Department of Learning and Instruction
State University of New York at Buffalo

English Education   English education is an interdisciplinary field of study encompassing a diversity of graduate programs that deal with the education of teachers of English. Graduate programs in English education are located either in schools or colleges of education or in departments of English. Although programs vary extensively, students can expect to study areas such as literature, linguistics, composition, communication, speech and theater, curriculum theory, learning theory, and research methodology. The degree of emphasis in these areas will depend on the institution and the particular career goals of the individual students. At the Ph.D. level, students generally specialize in one area of interest— composition theory or literary study, for example—but still take a diversity of courses to provide the necessary breadth of knowledge about English education.

At the M.A. or M.Ed. level, English education programs provide classroom teachers and other educators with current theories and research results in English education so that they can become more effective practitioners. Ph.D. programs prepare individuals to become teachers or researchers at the college or university level. Graduate programs in English education also prepare individuals to become supervisors, teacher consultants, and curriculum coordinators and developers. Increasingly, individuals interested in educational publishing, editing, or curriculum development study in English education. Some individuals become trainers in private industry. Because of the teacher shortage projected for the 1990s, those with a Ph.D. in English education should find it easier to obtain employment as teacher educators at the university level. Also, with increasing numbers of teachers going into the field, the need for consultants and supervisors should continue to grow.

Maia Pank Mertz, Professor
English Education
Ohio State University

Foreign Languages Education   Students in a foreign language education program pursue an exciting blend of interdisciplinary studies. These programs involve research and study in first- and second-language acquisition, in comparative and contrastive linguistics, in the psychology of learning (both in the affective and cognitive domains), in the methodology of second-language

Foreign Languages Education (continued)

instruction, and in cross-cultural studies. Students in typical programs also continue to develop their own linguistic skills and cultural backgrounds in two or more foreign languages. Housed in foreign language departments or in schools of education, these programs are available at both the master's and doctoral levels.

Graduates of a program in foreign language education may pursue a variety of career options. If they have experience and background in teaching at the secondary level, they may choose to investigate positions in large school districts as curriculum specialists, supervisors of foreign language teachers, or heads of foreign language departments. If their interests focus on postsecondary education, they will find opportunities available as coordinators of language programs at universities and colleges, as trainers and supervisors of teaching assistants at such institutions, or as professors teaching courses in methods of teaching second languages, which prepare teachers for middle school or secondary school instruction. A third career alternative involves writing, editing, or consulting on foreign language textbooks, as publishers seek authors who are fluent in foreign languages and who are also well versed in up-to-date methodology. A fourth option, which encompasses all the preceding ones, is continued research in the complex field of second-language acquisition and second-language instruction.

Constance K. Knop
Professor, Curriculum and Instruction/French and Italian
University of Wisconsin–Madison

Foundations and Philosophy of Education   The foundations of education encompass a wide variety of specialty areas devoted to the study of the institution of education as well as to training professionals in academic and nonacademic settings. These areas include the history, philosophy, politics, and sociology of education and comparative-international education; educational statistics; educational psychology; tests and measurements; and, at times, special education. While these diverse areas are viewed as individual specialties, they are usually included within the general area of foundations of education since they are all directed toward the theoretical understanding of how education as an institution functions in this and other societies. Foundations specialists are concerned with both basic and applied research. Thus, for example, the philosopher of education may do basic research in such traditional philosophical areas as epistemology and ethics but also be concerned with transmitting skills to prospective teachers that will enable them to deal with such issues as the meaning of learning, the use of logical tools, and the equitable treatment of students. Foundations of education specialists usually have substantial training in those disciplines that relate most closely to their particular expertise, for instance, in philosophy, sociology, psychology, and political science. This training, however, is viewed as supportive rather than central to their professional identity, which lies in teaching and research within the field of education.

Students may enter into the study of the foundations of education in several ways. At the bachelor's level, students who are in teacher training programs ordinarily take a sequence of courses in the history, philosophy, and psychology of education as well as work in tests and measurements and in child development. These courses constitute a core that introduces the student into the basics of professional education. At the master's level, students specialize in one of the foundations specialties but ordinarily take additional course work in one or more related areas. Students have the option of working toward either the M.A. or M.Ed. degree. Doctoral work in the foundations of education is directed toward producing competent specialists who teach and do research at the college or university level or to obtain training that complements other fields. For example, nursing professionals may obtain a doctoral degree in educational psychology as a means of increasing their teaching competency, as well as taking courses and doing research in the human delivery service aspects of nursing. At this level, both the Ph.D. and Ed.D. degrees are generally offered in most foundations areas. The Ph.D. has traditionally been geared toward training professionals to assume teaching and research positions at the university level. The Ed.D. degree has traditionally been taken by individuals whose professional identity is more closely aligned with work in educational systems as superintendents, principals, and curriculum and special education specialists. Recently, however, both Ph.D. and Ed.D. recipients have found positions in such varied occupations as hospital administration, training programs in industry, library administration, and government service. While the job market at the doctoral level has been fair to good, because of the wide diversity of areas within the foundations of education,

Foundations and Philosophy of Education (continued)

individuals have been able to structure their programs of study to best meet their individual needs and future career goals.

Steven I. Miller, Chair
Department of Foundations of Education
Loyola University of Chicago

Higher Education   Since its full emergence on the education scene over two decades ago, higher education as a field of study at the master's degree level and particularly at the doctoral degree level has made a positive impact on American higher education far out of proportion to the number of departments or programs of higher education in the nation's colleges and universities.

Students majoring in higher education have traditionally prepared themselves for leadership positions in higher education administration at the public and private college and university level as well as at the community college level. These positions involve academic administration; business and finance management; institutional planning; management and analytic studies; state, regional, and national higher education policies; student personnel administration; comparative higher education; urban higher education; and research related to all aspects of higher education.

Individuals with master's degrees in higher education are more likely to hold middle-management positions in the areas cited above, while persons with Ed.D. and Ph.D. degrees in higher education are today occupying every type of top-level leadership position existing in American higher education as well as the higher education systems of a number of foreign countries. These include chancellors, presidents, state commissioners of higher education, deans, vice presidents, provosts, and university professors of higher education.

In recent years the Ed.D. and Ph.D. in higher education have played a unique role as the "umbrella" doctoral degrees for a multitude of academic disciplines, especially in the fastest-growing segment of American higher education—the community and junior colleges. Today many instructors who earned their doctorates in higher education teach general education courses in English, the natural and social sciences, humanities, math, and almost all other subjects at the freshman and sophomore levels in at least 90 percent of the nation's community colleges that enroll more than 1,000 students. A considerably smaller percentage of the faculty teaching in the academic disciplines in four-year colleges also hold doctorates in higher education, but they do exist in numbers that are surprising to academic traditionalists.

For the majority of these faculty members, most of whom specialized in a higher education college teaching track, the doctorate in higher education, whether Ph.D. or Ed.D., was an alternative choice to the Ph.D. in English, math, biology, political science, etc. Many of them, primarily in the community-junior colleges, were even encouraged by their presidents and deans to pursue the higher education doctorate in lieu of the traditional doctorate because the master's degree in a teaching discipline, with a minimum of 18 semester hours at the graduate level in that discipline, is considered to be the standard teaching degree in community colleges throughout the country.

Internships in college and university administration or college teaching are generally included in the programs of individuals majoring in higher education.

Dayton Y. Roberts, Professor
Chairman, Higher Education
Texas Tech University

Home Economics Education   Home economics has been defined by the American Home Economics Association as the field of knowledge and service primarily concerned with strengthening family life through educating the individual for family living, improving the services and goods used by families, conducting research to discover the changing needs of individuals and families and the means of satisfying these needs, and furthering community, national, and world conditions favorable to family living. Home economics education has stood as one member of a large family of educational programs designed to serve the occupational education and training needs of a major segment of our society.

Responding to the needs and changes in society as well as to federal mandates, home economics education currently has a dual role. In the consumer and homemaking role, individuals and families are assisted in improving their home environments and the quality of personal and family life. In the occupational home economics role, students are given employable skills in occupational areas identified with home economics. The number of skills and employment opportunities relating to these skills are increasing to meet the needs of society in the areas of caring for children and the aging. There

Home Economics Education (continued)

is also a growing need for services in business and industry to meet the changed life-styles in today's society.

Ralph G. Field, Head
Department of Adult and Occupational Education
Kansas State University

Mathematics Education Mathematics education is a term used to cover any and all facets of mathematical training, from preschool through college. It includes many topics from the field of education as they are specifically applied to mathematics. Some of these are patterns of instruction used in the classroom, such as individualized, activity based, problem centered, or interdisciplinary; methods of instruction, that is, lecture, discovery, computer assisted, programmed, or other; the psychology behind the patterns and methods of instruction; and the content, when it is taught, and the conditions under which it is taught. Another major concern of mathematics education is evaluation. This includes the evaluation of the student, the teacher, the mathematics program, and the school and the means by which these evaluations are done. Perhaps the richest field of mathematics education research for now and the immediate future relates to the use of high technology in the teaching of mathematics. The use of calculators and computers in the classroom should bring about significant changes in the content and approaches used to teach mathematics and in the amount of time devoted to problem solving.

Mathematics education also involves human factors: the student and the teacher. Research and information on brain hemispheric specialization and its impact on the teaching of mathematics is now coming to the forefront. Much work has been done, but more is needed, on teaching mathematics to various types of students, such as the gifted, slow, learning disabled, physically handicapped, environmentally handicapped, and math anxious. The works of developmental psychologists, such as Piaget and Bruner, are beginning to have impact upon the curriculum. The teachers and their training, attitudes, and competence also play a major role in a child's learning of mathematics. Another field that mathematics educators are investigating more is mathematics education in foreign countries, such as Japan, China, England, and the Soviet Union.

Today there is a significant shortage of teachers of mathematics, and this is perhaps the most serious problem to be faced in mathematics education. The number of people receiving a bachelor's degree in mathematics education decreased over 60 percent from 1971 to 1981. In 1981, over 50 percent of the new teachers of mathematics were not certified to teach mathematics. In the 1970s, raises for faculty at institutions of higher learning did not keep pace with the annual rate of inflation, thus producing a loss of earnings. Many well-qualified teachers of mathematics are taking positions outside the field of education at significant salary increases. So while the prospects for employment in the field of mathematics education are good, a shortage will continue until economic conditions are changed. Graduates in the field of mathematics education are employed as teachers, mathematics supervisors, mathematics program directors, college professors, mathematics consultants to publishing companies, and authors.

Richard Evans
Mathematics Department
Plymouth State College

Middle School Education   The middle school movement began in the 1960s as a replacement for the junior high school, which had failed to achieve its promise. Like the Roman god Janus, the exemplary middle school looks backward to build on the child-centered elementary grades and forward to prepare the student for the more subject-centered high school. More important, the middle school looks inward to develop a program that is unique but appropriate for the youngsters it serves.

The middle school program is designed for youngsters who are in transition from childhood to adolescence, a period characterized by swift, turbulent, and uneven changes in physical, socioemotional, and intellectual development. Its grade structure ranges from 4 to 9, although grades 6–8 constitute the most generally accepted pattern. Because youngsters are maturing earlier, the grade structure of the middle school is more compatible with the preadolescent period than is the junior high school.

The greatest obstacle toward improving middle schools is the lack of personnel who have specialized training for middle school education. Middle schools require teachers who are flexible and humanistic; who are skilled in such areas as personalization, individualization, interdisciplinary learning, and team teaching; and

Middle School Education (continued)

who view the nature of preadolescents as an opportunity for learning rather than an obstacle to learning.

States have begun to offer middle school certification, but exceptions are allowed. The most common exception is to permit elementary-certified teachers to teach the lower grades and high school teachers the upper grades of the middle schools. Such practices, without requiring appropriate in-service or graduate training, are not conducive to improving middle schools.

As the number of middle schools continues to increase and as administrators become more aware of the crucial need for specialized training, the demand for certified middle school teachers, administrators, and supervisors will continue to grow. Graduate training in middle school education offers the most immediate and practical way to meet the expanding job opportunities in this field.

Adolph Crew, Chairperson
Program in Middle School Education
University of Alabama

Music Education Music is a universal language of ordered sounds and silence—a purveyor of human expression of intellect and emotion in an aesthetic context. Its legacy can be traced through all ages of human existence. Education in music has graced the stages of time from civilization to civilization and permeates the social environment to this day.

Music education can generally be defined in two broad categories. In the one, the primary thrust pertains to music instruction in such areas as performance, theory of music, music history, composition, and conducting. The second category is an amalgamation of all the above, but in the context of the teaching of music primarily in the elementary and secondary schools, though not necessarily precluding the preschool, college and university, and adult education levels.

In the first category of education in music—whether performance, theory, history, composition, or conducting—the emphasis intensifies a focus on generally one or two specific professional disciplines. The performer studies the theory and history of music, but the concentration is on the development of a professional level of performing competence in voice or instrument, or possibly in the conducting of music ensembles. A composition major will study theory, history, and performance of music but will emphasize the writing and arranging of original music for a variety of performing media from solo works to those encompassing multiples of performance categories and personnel, not excluding electronic media. The composer of music will also be a master of theory, history, and orchestration, and may perform and conduct, but the primary professional scope will be in composition. Many combinations of expertise and tangential careers can be developed from the study of various components of education in music, including music criticism, musicology, ethnomusicology, and other derivations.

The second category, music education, is commonly the designation given to the area of study in which one is broadly prepared to be a teacher of music in areas with variable labels, such as elementary music, general music, vocal music, instrumental music, music appreciation, music theory, music history, music in the humanities, music in special education, music therapy, and many other comparable appellations. Practitioners of music education are expected to be thoroughly grounded in the performance of music skills as well as in the history and theory of music and conducting and composition. In addition, study in this professional category includes a thorough preparation in the pedagogy and psychology of instruction—a complete assessment of a philosophy and the principles and objectives of the teaching of music to all ages and levels of students. Preparation for this professional thrust also requires a background in general education, music, and professional pedagogical training, including apprentice teaching and ultimate certification as an authorized teacher of music. Certification is usually obtained at the undergraduate level, but it is often possible and practical to earn certification while pursuing graduate studies. Graduate students who gain a thorough knowledge of the theory and practice of music education as advocated by noted foreign pedagogues Orff, Kodály, Dalcroze, and Suzuki will augment employability attractiveness. Also not to be overlooked in disciplinary preparation for the last two decades of the twentieth century are the operational skills, knowledge, and understanding of the scope and promise of computers, microcomputers, synthesizers, and other technological media in the realm of education in general and in the field of music education in particular.

Although historically professional qualifications were based essentially on performance skill in instrument, voice, composition, conducting, or teaching, it is now imperative to hold a graduate degree, especially in higher education and in music supervision. A

Music Education (continued)

master's degree is mandatory in most instances, with a Ph.D. or its equivalent highly recommended for those who wish to secure a position in higher education or public school supervision and administration. Salaries of teachers of music are often affected by the law of supply and demand, but traditionally music teachers—especially those in secondary schools and colleges and universities who have conducting responsibilities—find compensation at levels that are above average. Salaries of supervisors and administrators of music programs are comparable to those of similar positions in other disciplines.

James A. Middleton, Professor
Director of Graduate Studies
Department of Music
University of Missouri–Columbia

Reading   Reading as a discipline is generally considered to have originated with the publication in 1910 of *The Psychology and Pedagogy of Reading* by Edmund Burke Huey, although research in the late nineteenth century by psychologists created the climate for Huey's book.

Reading is usually considered to mean the process of constructing meaning from written texts. There are three major theoretical models explaining how this occurs: bottom up, top down, and interactive.

Bottom-up theorists assert that comprehension is dependent upon the reader's ability to process lower-order units of print such as letters, letter clusters, and individual words before they are able to process higher-order structures such as sentences and paragraphs. This process is frequently referred to as decoding. The assumption is that the reader must decode each word in a selection in order to comprehend the selection and that once the reader has decoded letters and words, meaning is automatic.

The top-down theory of reading asserts that comprehension is dependent on the reader's background knowledge of the world, including language and its usage, concepts, ideas, beliefs, experiences, and attitudes. The reader uses this prior knowledge stored in memory to make predictions about the meaning conveyed by the printed text. Therefore, each reader constructs his or her own meaning in light of his or her own stored prior knowledge. It is believed that readers use sentence-structure clues and meaning clues to recognize words and that these higher levels of processing influence the lower levels.

The interactive theory of reading holds that neither a top-down nor a bottom-up theory alone explains the reading process. Interactive theorists believe that it is the interaction between the two processes, that is, processing lower-order units of print while simultaneously making predictions based upon stored knowledge, that allows the reader to construct comprehension.

Research in the area of reading covers a wide spectrum, including investigations into teacher preparation and practice, the sociology of reading, the physiology and psychology of reading, the teaching of reading, and reading for atypical learners.

Graduate studies in reading education generally focus on preparing reading professionals for a variety of positions as classroom teachers, reading teachers, remedial reading teachers, reading specialists, consultants, college professors, and researchers. The job market for reading professionals with a master's degree is considered to be good to excellent for positions in school systems. Prospects for those with a Ph.D. or Ed.D. are considered to be fair to good for positions in school systems as program administrators or consultants and at colleges and universities as instructors and researchers.

Gary W. Bates
School of Curriculum and Instruction
College of Education
Ohio University

Rehabilitation Counseling　　The professional rehabilitation counselor works with people who have physical, mental, and social disabilities in order to help them understand their limitations and capabilities and use this knowledge to build vocationally and socially productive lives.

In addition to conducting individual and group counseling sessions, rehabilitation counselors may perform a variety of other tasks, depending on their employment setting. They collect and analyze vocational, educational, social, psychological, and medical data to form a basis for understanding the client's current problems. They administer tests and interpret the results. They help clients develop vocational plans and secure employment, and they work with employers to develop job opportunities. When clients have problems that interfere with their rehabilitation goals, rehabilitation counselors assist them in finding proper help from other

Rehabilitation Counseling (continued)

professionals or agencies. In order to determine if the methods and techniques they are using to accomplish these tasks are effective, they conduct follow-up studies and other research.

Rehabilitation counselors also serve as advocates for disabled persons to create public awareness and acceptance of their needs and rights. They promote the development of service programs and new or revised legislation to meet these needs.

Over eighty institutions nationwide offer graduate programs in rehabilitation counseling. Many are accredited by the Council on Rehabilitation Education (CORE), a national accrediting body. There are thirty-three programs at the doctoral level.

Rehabilitation is a field in which the current need for skilled personnel exceeds the numbers available. This need will continue, for many more professionals will be required to provide care for the thousands of persons newly disabled each year. The scope of rehabilitation continues to expand, and the private for-profit sector is expected to be the largest growth area in rehabilitation in the next decade, adding to the already considerable demand for personnel in the public and private nonprofit sectors. Business and industry are also providing a new frontier for employment of rehabilitation counselors, who can provide the expertise to contain costs associated with work disabilities. Job prospects generally are very good, especially for the nationally certified rehabilitation counselor.

Patricia Dvonch, Chairperson
Department of Rehabilitation Counseling
New York University

Religious Education   Religious education is understood in several ways. As a generic term it includes a variety of pedagogical activities associated in one way or another with religion, e.g., formal and informal instruction, Bible study, moral education, socialization, and theological education. In recent years it has acquired a specific meaning as a particular focus of academic study designed to investigate the theory and practice of these activities. In this latter sense religious education is perceived as an academic field with its own literature, guiding principles, and focus on the act or process whereby individuals acquire religious identity and religious groups socialize new members. As the process of religious education has come to be understood as an intentional activity carried out in families, schools, churches, and synagogues, the need to reflect on its nature and methods has generated research and a corpus of knowledge that professionals in the field are expected to master.

Students selecting a graduate program in religious education should be attentive to the existence of two distinct approaches in the field. Each begins with particular assumptions and operates in its own theoretical framework. The first approach puts the emphasis on education, the second on the religious dimension. The first frames the goals and objectives of religious education in terms of learning theory, developmental psychology, curriculum design, and teaching methods. The second, while not excluding pedagogical issues, is more "cultural specific" in that it studies sacred texts, belief systems, and theologies of particular faith traditions. It is common that the same school or department while giving greater prominence to one or the other incorporates both approaches. Some graduate programs do this by encouraging interdisciplinary study.

The variety of degrees in the field reflects the differences in approach and orientation; for example, in many places the M.S., M.Ed., and M.R.E. stress educational and pastoral aims and objectives, while the M.A. and M.A.R. put greater emphasis on the teachings of one or more religious traditions. The master's degree is regarded by many as the "first professional degree," aimed at preparing teachers and administrators. Some students who have no intention of pursuing a professional career in religious education enroll in master's degree programs to acquire familiarity with religious studies as a complement to their work in such other fields as social science, literature, the arts, and library science. A number of institutions offer doctoral degrees in religious education. They are research oriented, generally terminating with the Ph.D. or Ed.D. The doctoral degree is necessary for a person who intends to teach in a college or university and more often than not desirable for someone who wishes to pursue a career in research in the public or private sector.

Employment opportunities open to individuals with graduate degrees in religious education are most often in church settings or in agencies and institutions with some church affiliation. Job descriptions vary greatly. They include classroom teaching, adult education, informal instruction, program design, curriculum planning, administration, editing, and full-time research. Some opportunities, especially for researchers, are available in the private sector. Because of this diversity, graduate programs in religious education in colleges and universities stress breadth of vision, critical

Religious Education (continued)

thinking, and the acquisition of communication skills. It is the kind of background that also stands one in good stead in secular pursuits, management, and civic leadership.

Berard L. Marthaler
Department of Religion and Religious Education
Catholic University of America

Science Education   As the term implies, science education is a hybridization of two fields, science and education. A person entering science education is expected to study and have experience in both fields. College and university programs are generally administered by an academic unit either in science or education. The more common situation is for the program to be administered in a college or school of education, either as a department or a program within the secondary or curriculum department. In a few instances, science education is a program or department that is jointly administered by science and education.

Science education at the graduate level has as its primary goal the enhancement of science teaching. Usually this goal is directed toward teaching at the elementary and secondary school levels, although some programs include it at the community college, college, and university levels. Science education programs are designed to achieve this goal in a variety of ways. At the master's degree level, the emphasis is usually on the preparation of master teachers by providing preservice science teachers with greater depth and breadth in subject matter and professional studies, including planning, learning theory, teaching methodology, evaluation, curriculum theory and design, and research analysis. Master's degree programs may also be directed toward the preparation of curriculum specialists, science supervisors, directors of instruction, and department chairpersons. A few programs, however, are directed toward preparing persons who have degrees in science to become beginning science teachers. A majority of the master's degree programs either have an optional thesis requirement or do not require a thesis.

At the doctoral degree level, emphasis is usually on the preparation of science educators, or those who will be responsible for the professional studies component of science teacher preparation. Most programs require additional course work in science and provide the opportunity for specialization in areas such as curriculum, evaluation, supervision, research, and instruction. Nearly all programs include preparation in designing, conducting, interpreting, and directing research in science education. Selected doctoral programs include preparation for science teaching at the community college, college, and university levels.

Research topics in science education are varied, but all relate either directly or indirectly to the teaching and learning of science. A majority of the research is conducted using an experimental design, but designs involving questionnaires and library research are not uncommon. Research utilizing naturalistic inquiry is growing in acceptability.

Employment opportunities for master science teachers at the secondary school level are excellent and, as a result of a number of factors, including more science credits being required by most states for high school graduation, they are predicted to be even better in the future. Employment for science educators is slowly improving and is predicted to be very good in the future as a result of increasing demands for the preparation of greater numbers of science teachers for elementary and secondary school classrooms.

Thomas P. Evans, Chairperson
Department of Science, Mathematics,
and Computer Science Education
Oregon State University

Secondary Education Graduate study in the field of secondary education serves several potential populations. Students may choose to pursue continued study in this field in order to accomplish one of the following: (1) to improve their effectiveness as secondary school teachers through continued formal study (several states require continued graduate study as a basis for maintaining valid teaching licenses); (2) to enhance their possibilities for leadership positions in supervision of other faculty members, instructional areas, or curriculum development; (3) to prepare for positions in institutions of higher education where advanced expertise may be applied to the field of secondary education and/or to teacher preparation assignments; or (4) to prepare for a career in basic research and/or applied research.

Typical areas included in graduate study in secondary education are organization and structure of secondary schools; curriculum development; instructional dynamics and strategies; cocurricular activities; methodology; essential professional foundations studies related to history, philosophy, sociology, and

Secondary Education (continued)

psychology; international education; and advanced study in the teaching area of specialization.

Master's degrees are commonly offered to assist teachers in maintaining instructional skills and to provide opportunities for initial advanced work in this field. Specialist degrees and doctoral-level degrees are also available at numerous colleges and universities. Students should take considerable care to determine the primary focus and emphasis provided at various institutions when considering the pursuit of graduate work in secondary education. Congruence of goals is an important element.

Selected institutions continue to offer special master's degrees (often designated as M.A.T. degrees). These programs are designed to provide basic, initial license requirements for holders of bachelor's degrees not in the field of education.

Most students pursuing graduate work in the field of secondary education, however, will already have achieved initial preparation for teaching. Therefore, the pursuit of graduate work is most frequently viewed as a means of affirming professional decisions and as a vehicle for maintaining certification and licensure. Employment opportunities are certainly enhanced by continued professional development gained through graduate study. Students who have completed advanced degrees at the doctoral level continue to find employment opportunities in institutions of higher education, as central administrators in public and private schools, in state-level educational agencies, in federal educational agencies, and in industrial and business positions related to personnel development and program development. There currently exists a critical shortage of teachers in the fields of mathematics and science. Also evident are regional shortages in such teaching areas as industrial education/ technology and foreign languages. Individuals with undergraduate preparation in these fields are advised to consider the possibility of gaining certification and graduate credit through specially designed programs. Other employment opportunities in research and/or publication agencies are available as well.

An increased concern for elevating the quality of practicing teachers throughout the nation and an increased expectation that present teachers must seek renewal and constant updating of skills and knowledge contribute to the need for many to select graduate study in secondary education. As secondary schools are expected to change and improve, classroom teachers will be expected to lead the way and to carry the burden for improvement. Many graduate programs in secondary education combine expectations of scholarship with desire for improved practice. It is apparent that the expectations of the profession and of the public both demand greater scholarship in the teaching specialty and increased teaching skills. Graduate study in secondary education can help practicing professionals reach such increased expectations.

Donald W. Jones
Coordinator, Secondary Teacher Education
Ball State University

Social Studies Education   Social studies education is undoubtedly one of the most diverse and diffuse fields of study in education. This diversity is reflected both in the perspectives of study on the field and in the practice of social studies education. Central to most definitions is the ideal of education for citizenship. That is, it is generally accepted that within the public school curriculum the social studies have the special responsibility of developing in students the knowledge, dispositions, and behaviors that prepare youth to effectively carry out the duties of a citizen in a constitutional democracy. However, once one moves beyond general statements concerning the goals of social studies education, one finds considerable diversity. Many social studies educators see the focus of citizenship education as developing in students a critical perspective on contemporary social problems. Others emphasize the uncritical transmission of our culture as the proper focus. Still others place the proper emphasis on developing social action skills to influence public policy. Another major theme governing the teaching of social studies is to develop in students inquiry skills and knowledge in the various subdisciplines of the field. Finally, as the title of the journal of the National Council for the Social Studies (*Social Education*) suggests, there is, particularly at the elementary level, a focus on the social development and integration of youth into society.

Research into social studies education is as diverse as the goals of the field suggest. Much of the research takes place in schools within the traditional social studies course framework: family, neighborhood, and community studies (primary grades); state, U.S., and world history; geography; economics; civics or government; psychology; and sociology. Research typically looks into the impact of new innovative curricula in these areas. Variations in instructional technique within these content areas have also received considerable research attention. Social studies researchers study the influence of special curricular experiences designed to achieve goals in areas such

Social Studies Education (continued)

as multicultural education, global education, law-related education, peace studies, future studies, values or moral education, reduction of sexism and racism, science-related social issues, analysis of public issues, and development of critical thinking skills. Researchers also analyze curriculum and textbooks for bias and explore the impact of noncurricular factors (hidden curriculum) on students' social development. In addition to the above, there exists a rich tradition of historical and philosophical inquiries into the nature of social studies past and present. Recently two new trends in social studies research have emerged. Ethnographic research techniques are increasingly being applied to the study of social studies classrooms and the lives of social studies teachers in schools. Also, radical critiques of the practice of social studies education have begun to appear regularly in the literature. These critiques frequently rely on Marxian analyses and attempt to show that the current practice of social studies education legitimizes dominant political and economic interests in society, and it thereby restrains the emancipation of all peoples from domination and exploitation.

Students completing graduate studies in social studies education face a variety of career options. Many choose to return to the public schools to assume teaching, curriculum development, and/or supervisory responsibilities. Positions are also found within regional and state departments of education. People in these positions are primarily responsible for implementing statewide programs, providing in-service education, and exercising leadership for the field at the state level. In addition, a wide range of private and government-funded organizations offer employment for individuals with a background in social studies education. These organizations develop curricula and provide leadership in such areas as economic education, law-related education, peace studies, and constitutional rights studies. Opportunities also exist for curriculum and textbook development work for independent foundations and textbook publishing houses. Finally, there exist career opportunities within higher education for the teaching of social studies methods, supervision of student teachers, and graduate study of social studies education. At the present time, the number of these jobs is few due to the limited number of students selecting study in these areas.

James S. Leming, Associate Professor
Department of Curriculum, Instruction and Media
Southern Illinois University at Carbondale

Special Education   The field of special education is multidisciplinary, drawing from such disciplines as psychology, sociology, public studies, education content (e.g., reading), and computer science. Each graduate program may have its own individual strengths within one or more of those disciplines, but all focus on training personnel to serve exceptional people in educational settings.

Master's-level programs generally train students as master teachers of exceptional persons, consulting teachers who aid other teachers in planning programs for exceptional persons, educational diagnosticians, and supervising teachers in special education. Often the course work is categorically organized (e.g., course work in mental retardation, behavior disorders, learning disabilities, physical handicaps, vision handicaps, hearing handicaps, speech and language, multiple handicaps, and the gifted). Other graduate programs are organized in such a way as to train personnel to deal in more generic areas. Course work in generic programs is focused on educational problems associated with a wide variety of handicapping conditions. Often the courses are defined as education for the mildly handicapped and education for the severe and profoundly handicapped. Other programs offer specialty areas in early education, elementary education, and secondary education. Recently a few graduate programs have begun offering course work related to infancy. Most programs that offer comprehensive special education training programs at the master's level teach students to be competent to work with handicapped or gifted individuals from birth through adulthood, with most trained to serve in elementary education programs. Master's degree program graduates find employment in public and private schools, day-care facilities, vocational education facilities, human service clinics, mental health centers, hospitals, and other institutions.

Many state and private universities have special education programs that offer advanced training leading to the Doctor of Education (Ed.D.) and/or Doctor of Philosophy (Ph.D.). At many institutions the requirements for the two degrees differ very little. However, at other institutions the Ed.D. is considered the professional degree that is designed for those who will assume practical leadership roles, such as in school administration, whereas the Ph.D. is viewed as the research degree. Those who fulfill the requirements for the Ph.D. generally have a strong background in research design and issues in special education that may be resolved through research. The Ed.D. program often trains students to utilize research in developing and evaluating educational programs and

Special Education (continued)

provides course work and practical experiences in school finance, educational policy, and administration. Many institutions view Ed.D. programs as the training of "change agents," i.e., those administrators and leaders in education who provide leadership in improving the services offered to handicapped and gifted persons.

Employment opportunities are similar for holders of the Ph.D. and holders of the Ed.D. degrees. Positions are available in universities and colleges, public and private schools, clinics, hospitals, research centers, and other institutions.

Richard E. Shores, Professor
Department of Special Education
George Peabody College for Teachers
Vanderbilt University

Teaching English as a Second Language   TESL is a growing area, full of questions that begin with its very name, teaching English as a second language: Why "second"? Many of the students in ESL programs are learning English as a third or fourth language. Does "second" suggest "secondary"? Any language is primary or secondary depending on the needs of the speaker and listener, as well as the requirements of the context. Responding to these and other concerns, the profession has suggested another name, teaching English to speakers of other languages (TESOL), which affirms one certainty—that the students are indeed speakers of other languages. Outside the United States, TEFL, teaching English as a foreign language, is the title most often used.

Whatever the acronym, those in TESL are concerned with the development of English language skills by students whose native language is not English. In the United States, these students may be immigrants, refugees, American citizens whose home language is not English, exchange students, and visiting professors or businesspeople and their families.

ESL is taught in many contexts. In kindergarten through twelfth-grade programs, common models include (1) "pullout," in which students leave their regular classroom for special ESL instruction; (2) intensive ESL programs, which may or may not include instruction in content areas; (3) immersion programs, which present all school subjects in understandable English; and (4) special English classes within a bilingual program, in which students maintain their native language and study in two languages. For adults, the contexts are equally diverse and may include a special content-area focus, ESP (English for special purposes).

Current research and discussion includes such topics as the degree to which the learning of a second language is like that of the first, the effectiveness of rule learning (as opposed to the more natural "acquisition" process), and the students' need to develop cognitive-academic language proficiency (CALP) as well as basic interpersonal communication skills (BICS).

A prospective ESL teacher should have an excellent command of all aspects of the English language and a fascination for language in general. Personal skills are equally important and include an intense interest in people from other cultures, an ability to convey that interest and respect to students, and a critical understanding of North American culture. In addition, ESL teachers in the United States must be able to guide students through their individual accommodation to a new language and culture. Most ESL teachers become advocates for their students, either within schools or in the community at large.

These personal and academic skills are recognized in course requirements for TESOL certification. Though requirements vary from state to state, TESOL, the professional association of ESL teachers, sets the highest standard. It recommends work in three areas: (1) academic specialization (general linguistics, English linguistics, first- and second-language acquisition theory, and culture and society), (2) pedagogy (theory and practice of teaching ESL, including evaluation), and (3) a language and culture other than English.

Graduates of ESL programs work in the United States or abroad, at levels from preschool through university and adult education programs, and in business and community organizations. The demand for ESL teachers appears to be increasing as more people recognize that ESL is a subject that students need and that must be provided by qualified professionals.

Barbara Jacobs Agor
Graduate School of Education and Human Development
University of Rochester

Urban Education   Graduate studies in urban education focus on the delivery of relevant high-quality educational systems for children living in the inner city. For the student wishing to teach in the public

Urban Education (continued)

schools, the study of urban education relies heavily on a curriculum specifically directed to minority and poor youth. A graduate student may take courses examining the psychology, sociology, and history of the Hispanic-American child, the black American child, and the Asian-American child. Students not wishing to enter into public school teaching also explore these areas with additional study typically including educational administration, counseling, school finance, politics, and basic and applied research.

Current research trends in the area have centered on the analysis of effective elements of the urban school. These include examinations of reading programs, early intervention programs such as Head Start, issues related to teacher competence, and bilingual education. Public school financing is another topic for research in the field. Methods of research are usually a combination of both quantitative and qualitative models.

With the school-age population expected to increase dramatically in the 1990s, especially in the urban centers, the demand for teachers, administrators, counselors, and teacher educators will be great. The current societal emphasis on educational improvement, the prospect of funding from governmental sources, and the necessity for addressing an increasingly pluralistic school population are factors that contribute to a favorable employment picture for the prospective urban education graduate.

Richard K. Gordon
Department of Educational Foundations
California State University, Los Angeles

Vocational and Technical Education   Graduate study in vocational and technical education is designed to prepare individuals with a broad, comprehensive knowledge of the field. Programs at the master's and doctoral levels provide students with qualifications needed for leadership positions in vocational and technical education in both the public and private sectors. Many programs require a core of common courses, with options for specialization in functional areas such as administration, research, curriculum development, and program evaluation. Applied courses in related fields such as business or engineering are required in most programs of study.

Vocational and technical education programs are found in various public and private organizations and serve students at the secondary, postsecondary, and adult levels. Graduate programs prepare individuals to assume administrative and supervisory positions in local school divisions, state departments of education, technical and community colleges, military training programs, and private business or industry. Another option for students graduating from a comprehensive program at the doctoral level is vocational teacher education. Graduate programs are also available with an emphasis on preparing vocational teacher educators to serve in four-year institutions of higher education.

Graduates with advanced degrees from comprehensive vocational and technical education programs will find numerous opportunities for employment. The need for persons with a broad knowledge of the field will continue in this country. The increase in vocational and technical education programs in developing nations of the world is creating a demand for additional administrative and instructional personnel. Those with the qualifications needed to plan, deliver, and evaluate comprehensive programs of vocational and technical education in various settings will be in demand during the foreseeable future.

Nevin R. Frantz Jr., Director
Division of Vocational and Technical Education
Virginia Polytechnic Institute and State University

Environmental Policy and Resource Management

The area of policy studies is a comparatively new field with roots in political science, law, sociology, economics, and psychology as well as other social sciences. Some researchers and graduate programs focus on the process by which policy is made; students are taught to fit knowledge of a specific policy area (environment or housing, for example) into a general understanding of the process by which policy is made. Others emphasize the substantive problems in a given policy area, trying to help their students understand these problems in all of their depth and complexity. Well-educated students must have knowledge of both process and substance, but graduate programs will differ in emphasis.

The generalizations just made about policy studies in general apply as well to environmental policy and resource management. Substantive knowledge is doubly important in the environmental field because of its inherent complexity. Environmental policy

Environmental Policy and Resource Management (continued)

scholars must have, or acquire, a broad and solid understanding of how the world works physically. Over the past thirty years modern society has learned again and again how the activities of humans are limited by the realities of the physical workings of the earth on which they live. All policymaking in the environmental and resource management field must be based on thorough knowledge of the physical world.

Building on that base, environmental policy scholars also need to acquire knowledge of the process by which policy is made. The economic model, used so widely, is far from being sufficiently comprehensive to be satisfactory. It is particularly important to develop a thorough understanding of the role of citizens in policymaking. Many "rational" or "sensible" schemes for resource management have been overturned by an angry and aroused citizenry.

Environmental policy and resource management inevitably carry the scholar and the practitioner into the realm of values. It is no longer valid, if it ever was, for policymakers to assume that they know what people's values are. It also is unrealistic to expect to develop a value-free science in this area. Environmental policy makers must self-consciously incorporate value investigations and value analysis into their procedures. This is doubly important for resource management since most natural resources have the potential to serve a number of values. Value analysis is the least developed of the knowledge areas needed for wise environmental policy making.

Having stated the ideals for graduate training in this area, it is necessary to report that most institutions offering such training fall short of the ideal. Many schools of forestry or natural resources are strong on understanding how the world works physically but weak on the policy process and even weaker on value analysis. The natural scientists who dominate their faculties may disparage sociopolitical-philosophical analysis. Other institutions may be strong on the latter but weak on knowledge of ecosystems and how they work. Typical subfields in this general area of inquiry are resource management, wildlife management, pollution control, and social science (policy). Potential graduate students should investigate carefully the strengths and weaknesses of the institutions they are considering. Schools with strong faculties imparting knowledge as to how the world works physically as well as socially and politically can provide suitable training even though all these talents may not be available in the same professional school, given that students have the freedom to put their own program together to acquire the main knowledge thrusts identified above.

Students graduating in this field have good job prospects. Environmental problems will continue to be prominent on the public agenda in the foreseeable future and may even escalate in importance. The societal need will be present, but the field is so new that many institutions requiring environmental policy advisers will not have this category of employee in their lexicon. Students should expect to be quite entrepreneurial in convincing potential employers that they need someone with their talents. Graduates of these programs often find employment in governmental agencies. A growing number find employment in consulting firms, many of which have developed specialities relating to one or another set of environmental problems. In quite recent times we are also seeing many business firms creating positions requiring environmental knowledge for successful fulfillment. An applicant who combines specialization in some physical science or engineering area with solid knowledge of how the world works politically, socially, and economically has a special advantage in seeking employment and in being advanced to a responsible position.

Lester W. Milbrath
Director, Environmental Studies Center
State University of New York at Buffalo

Folklore

Folklorists study culture, particularly those aspects that are both traditional and expressive. "Traditional" refers to those forms, processes, and concepts that favor continuity and that are learned informally by word of mouth or by imitation. "Expressive" suggests the symbolic and iconographic means by which groups express their sense of themselves, their place in the world, and much of what is significant to them. Thus the folklorist is drawn to a wide range of traditional expressive forms, such as song and story, festival and pageant, handicraft and art, foodways and costume, custom and religion, architecture and workplace skill, and dance and play. We examine those forms and the processes and meanings that undergird them in a variety of social settings, including ethnic and regional cultures and occupational, familial, and sectarian groups. Fundamentally cultural pluralists, folklorists share the conviction that only through understanding the diversity of folk cultural means

Folklore (continued)

of expression and the many textures of everyday life can we appreciate the depth and vitality of the human experience.

Folklore is an interdisciplinary field that shares subject and method with such disciplines as anthropology, literature, ethnomusicology, history, museology, linguistics, and historic preservation. A modern folklorist is apt to specialize in both group and genre. He or she is likely to have a variety of research skills, ranging from the use of standard bibliographical materials to familiarity with the tools of ethnographic fieldwork. In addition to traditional academic research, many folklorists also involve themselves in public programs sponsored by arts and culture agencies and institutions. Although the academic job market in the mid-1980s is tight for many fields in the humanities and social sciences, most folklorists find employment, either in academia or in the public sector. Folklorists who teach generally end up in departments of English, anthropology, history, or American studies. Folklorists working in the public sector are likely to be employed by state or regional arts agencies, museums, or preservation programs, particularly those stressing cultural conservation.

The discipline's vision has widened considerably in the past decade. For example, folklorists have been in the vanguard of material culture studies, a recent pandisciplinary movement. Once oriented toward texts and artifacts, folklorists are now also considering context, performance, style, aesthetics, and meaning. They are also beginning to explore the applications of their research to matters of social policy. Although the study of folklore and folklife has burgeoned since the late 1960s and its scope has broadened, most folklorists would agree that the discipline has not lost sight of its goal to understand that which is simultaneously commonplace and extraordinary, the role of tradition in everyday life.

Burt Feintuch, Coordinator
Programs in Folk Studies
Western Kentucky University

Geography

Since the first department of geography was established in an American university in 1903, geography has developed as a specialized field of knowledge concerned with the ways people live in different regional environments; with the manner in which territory is organized for social, political, and economic purposes; with the uses of natural resources and the ends toward which those uses are directed; and with the relations between these considerations on the one hand and domestic and international policies on the other. These interests transcend a more traditional division of the field into physical and human geographies, and they reflect the fact that environments, however defined, are composed of elements of both natural and cultural origin. The range of inquiry by geographers, then, like that of historians, is extremely broad.

To a considerable degree, geography functions in as nearly an interdisciplinary manner as is possible for any given discipline. Like history, geography intersects with all of the social sciences. Students of geography are expected to have a sound general education in the social sciences and even, depending on their interests, in certain of the humanities. They may also need a background in statistical methods. Nonetheless, the ecological focus of the discipline in both human and natural terms remains distinctive among the social sciences.

Although many departments have clear-cut formal programs of study leading to advanced degrees, programs in many universities are tailored to the individual needs of students, depending on their interests, and the resultant flexibility may prove attractive to many. Degree programs at the master's level normally can be completed in a little over a year. Programs leading to the doctorate, however, may be assumed to require at least three years, but this period will vary with each university concerned and with the extent to which extended field investigation is incorporated into the student's program.

Recipients of advanced degrees in geography find employment in colleges and universities, in a variety of government agencies, in both public and private planning agencies, and in private industry where the location of industry and of other economic activities is a continuing problem for investigation, clarification, and policy determination.

Norton Ginsburg
Department of Geography
University of Hawaii
and
Environment and Policy Institute
East-West Center, Honolulu

Gerontology

Gerontology is the study of the phenomena of the aging process from maturity to old age. It includes concern for the elderly, which is implemented through planning and delivering services to them. Gerontology is a relatively young subject, dating from the 1920s, when the first biological and psychological studies of age were conducted.

Graduate instruction in gerontology is currently offered in one of two ways. It can be approached as an emphasis within one of the disciplines such as sociology, psychology, biology, political science, or the humanities. From this perspective, instructional programs concentrate on scientific rigor and methodological approaches to describe and understand the causes and results of aging. Frequently the instruction is done at the doctoral level and leads to careers in research and college teaching.

The second approach emphasizes the current problems and potential of older people and seeks means by which the problems can be alleviated and the potential can be optimized. This is a professional orientation to the field and is evident in instruction that prepares students for employment in social service, health, government, planning, and educational agencies and for jobs in the corporate and business sectors of society. This instruction is frequently offered through professional schools of such fields as social work, public administration, education, planning, public health, medicine, law, and allied health. However, at approximately 500 community colleges, colleges, and universities, gerontology instruction results in the award of a certificate, degree, or other credential in aging.

Over the past two decades research in gerontology has developed rapidly, and a much better understanding of the phenomenon has been obtained. This knowledge is currently being applied in both the public and private sectors, and job opportunities for graduates have increased substantially over the past decade. These positions have occurred as a result of the rapid expansion of government programs for the elderly, but nonprofit corporations and proprietary organizations have also begun offering many services to the elderly. It would appear that job prospects for professional school graduates will continue to increase as the human service system is professionalized and that research and teaching positions for doctoral graduates will also grow. The older population has expanded at a rapid rate during this century and will continue to do so in the foreseeable future; thus the prospects for the field are extremely bright.

David A. Peterson, Director
Leonard Davis School of Gerontology
University of Southern California

Health, Physical Education, and Recreation

Health Education   The term health education is used variously to refer to a program, a field of study, a goal, or a process. The field of study usage embodies the other meanings of the term. As such, health education is the study of various combinations of programs, methods, and procedures designed to support voluntary adaptations of behavior conducive to physical, mental, or social well-being. It is generally seen as a field of professional preparation, as distinct from academic study, because the health education specialist is prepared to apply—not just study—educational methods and procedures in the service of health programs or goals.

Another dimension of health education that makes it a professional field of study is the ethical or philosophical commitment implied by the notion of supporting "voluntary adaptations of behavior conducive to health." Many social and behavioral science disciplines study behavior, but most are not primarily concerned with its relation to health and few place emphasis on voluntary adaptations. Health education combines with health promotion to influence environmental, organizational, and economic supports for behavior conducive to health.

The recent emergence of health education and health promotion as a centerpiece in national and international health policies and in commercial and employee "wellness" products and programs has been attributed to two trends. One is the growing awareness that behavior or life-style factors such as smoking, alcohol misuse, stress, and poor diet, exercise, and safety practices account for a large proportion of the leading causes of death and disability. Health education and voluntary self-management of these life-style behaviors are essential to the success of national and international efforts to reduce morbidity and mortality. The second trend is the growing cost of medical care, which has made policy analysts and others more conscious of the need for prevention and health

Health Education (continued)

education. As a result of these trends, the demand for health educators has spawned some 250 graduate degree programs in school and community health education.

The community health education track has been added in colleges and universities where previously the health education training was limited to teacher training for school health education. In addition, about fifteen graduate schools of public health offer Master of Public Health or Master of Science and Doctor of Public Health or Doctor of Science degrees in health education. Most of these include a major emphasis on behavioral sciences, communications, community organization, epidemiology, biostatistics, environmental health, or health administration. School health education specializations continue in many universities. Other subspecializations such as patient education, occupational health education, and international health education have been added at a few.

Employment opportunities vary widely according to geographic region and settings for the practice of health education. The subspecializations in school, work site, community, patient, and international health education are giving way to an emphasis on generic health educator skills. Breadth of training prepares the student to work in any setting. Employment depends on the job market, which changes markedly from one decade to the next.

Lawrence W. Green, Director
Center for Health Promotion Research and Development
University of Texas Health Science Center at Houston

Physical Education and Human Movement Studies   Students who undertake graduate study in physical education join a profession and a discipline that are as old as humankind itself but that are continually taking on new forms. What motivated the early leaders of physical education to investigate the phenomenon was the recognition that exercise and wholesome health practices had the potential to contribute to a better life. The acceptance of physical education in the school systems of the nation was prompted by the recognition that a healthy body and possession of athletic skills are coveted by our society. Undergraduate study of physical education focused initially on health and exercise and eventually became oriented toward teacher training. Graduate programs grew out of this orientation. Over the years, the concerns of some graduate programs have broadened so that directions other than service delivery have emerged.

Today, physical education as a phenomenon is considered to be both broad and varied. Physical education represents expressions of aesthetic values; reflects humankind's physical, competitive, and cooperative nature; involves both physical and cultural aspects of society; and affects both our physiological and psychological dimensions. In order to study the above areas, departments have typically utilized a multidisciplinary approach, applying concepts from such parent disciplines as biochemistry, physiology, mechanics, psychology, sociology, anthropology, and philosophy. But departments have one or two general thrusts at the graduate level, and it is well to be aware of these.

Most graduate programs of physical education emphasize the professional and applied thrust, and many of these programs are found within colleges of education on university campuses. These graduate programs subscribe to the belief that physical education practitioners have the responsibility of conducting suitable programs of activity for various publics, and they conduct research and scholarly activities that are designed to improve the practice of conducting such service-delivery programs. This approach is particularly characteristic of master's-level programs.

The second approach regards physical education from the point of view of a discipline. Departments adopting this view consider that the conceptual undergirding of physical education is the study of human movement and that they are studying man in motion and those factors governing man in motion. Many such departments have adopted names such as kinesiology, human movement studies, or human kinetics. These departments tend to specialize, especially at the Ph.D. level, in programs such as exercise science, biomechanics, motor behavior, and the like. Typically, these programs emphasize in-depth knowledge in these specific areas, and graduate students are expected to conduct basic research even though many of these programs have strong applied research emphases.

In the next decade, the field of physical education and movement science is expected to undergo much change. There is a growing concern with health, and more people are recognizing that exercise is a valued commodity. But more than a simple expansion of the exercise and health-related fields is in evidence. Fields such as sports medicine, sports biomechanics, motor learning, sports psychology, and sports sociology are also expanding. Taking the

Physical Education and Human Movement Studies (continued)

place of the "old" physical education is a lively and expanding interest in the exercise and movement sciences. To those students who find this attractive, welcome to a discipline that promises to be an exciting and worthwhile endeavor in the years ahead.

Glyn C. Roberts
Director of Graduate Studies
Department of Physical Education
University of Illinois at Urbana-Champaign

Recreation, Parks, and Leisure Studies Graduate work in recreation, parks, and leisure studies is available at both the master's and doctoral level. Most master's degree programs are of a professional nature and tend to emphasize one or more of the traditional specializations in park and recreation administration. They are recreation resource management, therapeutic recreation services, and general recreation and parks administration. Within each of these are additional subspecialties such as resource planning (recreation resource management), pediatric recreation (therapeutic recreation services), and program supervision (general recreation and parks administration). A fourth specialization has emerged. Its focus is recreation and the private sector, with considerable attention being given to the formation and management of recreation businesses and services, including resort management, employee services, fitness centers, and tourism and travel.

All four specializations tend to emphasize the development of supervisory and management competencies rather than research skills with internships and concurrent practicums as part of the curriculum. Within those institutions where leisure studies is a graduate option, the focus is research and the development of conceptual skills. Generally, the leisure studies component is found at the doctoral rather than at the master's level.

An undergraduate degree in recreation and parks administration is generally required for graduate study. This is especially true for those programs leading to a master's in therapeutic recreation services or in general recreation and parks administration. The recreation resource management programs tend to admit students who have had an undergraduate major in geography, forestry, or some related natural resource specialty, as well as those who have an undergraduate degree in recreation and parks. Where there is a strong leisure studies component, an undergraduate major in one of the social or behavioral sciences is generally acceptable. Reflecting the specialties offered, recreation and park curricula may be domiciled in any one of several academic or professional degree programs such as forestry, natural resources, recreation and parks, arts and sciences, education, physical education, and allied health.

Whereas the master's degree programs emphasize the professional preparation of practitioners who can administer a park and recreation service, function as a therapeutic recreation clinician, or manage a private recreation enterprise, the doctoral programs are devoted almost exclusively to the preparation of recreation and park educators and researchers. These programs follow the more traditional patterns of the Ph.D. and Ed.D. degrees, although there are a limited number of universities that offer a professional doctoral degree (Re.D.) in parks and recreation.

Work experience as a recreation practitioner is generally required of those candidates who are in a doctoral program in parks and recreation. A master's degree in recreation and parks is desirable but not always required. Three content areas tend to characterize the doctoral program. They are (1) research methods, especially quantitative methodologies, (2) the application of behavioral and social science theories or ecological and natural science theories to leisure behaviors, and (3) concepts and issues of professionalism. The latter subject area is often also included in master's degree programs.

Recreation, parks, and leisure studies is a growing specialty in which management and administrative concepts and skills are applied to the problems and delivery of recreation and park services, both public and private. Graduates may be employed by government agencies, private recreation interests and firms, planning and consulting organizations, as well as in institutional and educational settings.

H. Douglas Sessoms, Professor
Chairman, Curriculum in Recreation Administration
University of North Carolina at Chapel Hill

Health Services Management and Hospital Administration

Increasingly, society has come to recognize and value the contributions of the field of health services management to health

Health Services Management and Hospital Administration (continued)

status. Much of the significant progress in improved health status has resulted from the managerial ability to make medical and health advances widely available to the population. The field of health services management (also often called health services administration and, when applied specifically to hospitals, hospital administration) is concerned with the process, which has both interpersonal and technical aspects, through which the objectives of health services organizations are specified and accomplished by utilizing human, financial, and physical resources and technology. Health services managers are the professionals who carry out this process. There is a wide variety of health services organizations, all of which require the skills of managers. These organizations are located in both the private and public sectors. They may be institutions, the most prominent of which are hospitals, or they may be programs or agencies, such as public health departments, visiting nurse associations, and planning agencies.

Graduate education in this field has taken place since 1934; today, a master's degree is the most widely recognized professional credential for entry into middle and upper levels of health services management. Most graduate programs require two years of full-time study with a period of field experience (often in the summer between the two didactic years) under the preceptorship of a practicing health services manager. Graduate programs in health services management in the United States and Canada may be accredited by the Accrediting Commission on Education for Health Services Administration (ACEHSA), and this serves as a hallmark of quality in that accredited programs have met certain academic standards. Within broad parameters, the curricula of the programs show considerable variation, but students in accredited graduate programs can expect the focus to be on the disciplines of management and of administrative and analytical skills and on their application to health services organizations.

Underpinning graduate education in health services management, there is an extensive base of health services research addressing myriad issues within the general areas of cost, quality, and accessibility of health services. Graduate programs in this field contribute significantly to this research effort through the work of their faculty and students. A number of graduate programs, particularly those with a strong research focus, provide opportunities for doctoral study in health services management or for students in other disciplinary areas, such as economics or sociology, to apply their disciplinary interests to health services issues.

Because of an aging population, with concomitant increases in the need for health services; advancing medical technology; and increasing complexity of the health-care delivery system, which places greater emphasis on the need for effective management, the demand for health services managers is expected to continue to grow. However, in recent years there has been a significant increase in the supply of health services managers due in large part to the relative attractiveness of this field. While the health-care sector will continue to grow, students would be well advised to explore recent placement experience for graduates of the programs in which they are interested.

Beaufort B. Longest Jr.
Professor and Director, Health Administration Program
University of Pittsburgh

Historic Preservation and Museum Studies

Historic Preservation   Historic preservation is a very broad term used to describe the activities that promote the protection and continued use of the built environment. The scale of the problems considered within this field may be large (e.g., a plan for preserving an agricultural region, an island, or a city), or they may be small (e.g., the disassembly, storage, and reuse of an architectural detail). The range of disciplines with which the preservationist should become familiar includes architecture, architectural history, planning, landscape architecture, art conservation, history, cultural geography, law, economics, real estate and development, tax accounting, public administration, sociology, personnel management, and political science.

The interdisciplinary nature of the field is generally recognized by graduate preservation programs and, indeed, permits a great variety of emphases among them. Some programs attempt to synthesize most, if not all, of these disciplines, leading to a graduate degree in historic preservation per se. Other programs are rooted in one of the disciplines, from which vantage point the others may be considered. Obviously contributions may be made by both the "preservation generalist" and the "preservation specialist."

Graduate programs in historic preservation vary in length. A few require only one year, although two years have become commonplace at the master's level. The requirements also vary. The number of required courses is generally small, allowing students to develop their interests, and the requirements for internships and/or theses differ, to some degree depending upon the expectations of the college or department(s) through which the programs are administered. Some programs are involved with community-based projects, sponsor courses in primary and secondary schools, and/or hold short courses and training sessions lasting from one day to a few weeks.

Upon completing graduate study, preservationists are employed in a variety of private and public positions in nonprofit organizations, professional firms, and business enterprises, as well as federal, regional, state, and local governmental units and agencies.

Michael A. Tomlan, Assistant Professor
Graduate Program in Historic Preservation Planning
College of Architecture, Art, and Planning
Cornell University

Museum Studies   Museum studies is the term used to describe both museology—the "science" of museums, their history and theory—and museography—the techniques employed in museum work and study. Both are directed to standardizing and codifying the body of knowledge and practice that has been developing since the eighteenth and, particularly, the nineteenth and twentieth centuries with regard to museums.

Museums have been defined by the American Association of Museums as permanent, nonprofit places dedicated to the collection, preservation, and interpretation of specimens from the natural world and of artifacts made or used by human beings. Museums should be open to the public on a regular basis and employ at least some professionally trained and paid staff members. These may include not only museums of art, science, natural history, and history, but also science centers, arboretums, zoological parks, and other institutions and places that meet the criteria established through national and international accord.

Of special interest to the museum professional is ICOM (International Council of Museums) and its U.S. national committee, AAM/ICOM. They offer membership to institutions and individuals on staff and participation in deliberation and decision making affecting museums worldwide. International committees (fine arts, archaeology and history, documentation, ethnography, museology, etc.) meet yearly in selected world capitals, as does ICOM, every three years, to discuss objectives and strategies for promoting and improving museums. Issues of governance, illicit traffic in antiquities, development, exhibitions, and ethics, as well as special events and exchange of personnel, assistance, and exhibitions are given priority. ICOM sponsors publications, partnerships, seminars, and cultural assistance programs in all parts of the world. It is administered in Paris by the secretary-general, Patrick Cardon.

There is disagreement in the field as to whether museum studies can properly be called a "science," and experts have differed, describing museology as everything from an "art" itself, to a social science, to just practical work, to a science. This debate rages on, and interested persons can consult the *Museological Working Papers*, published by the ICOM Committee on Museology (Paris and Stockholm), for detailed opinions and comments; they may also wish to consult *Museum News* and *Curator*, as well as other professional publications. There is little disagreement, however, that museography, the techniques employed in museums, is very specialized, requiring training in the documentation of collections and registration procedures, as well as a knowledge of conservation and its practices, administration, development and funding, security, publications, public affairs, education, exhibitions, research, connoisseurship, and acquisitions. Museum professionals may be expected to have a knowledge of several of the preceding, though in major museums each area may be headed by separate specialists. It is generally agreed that a knowledge of the parts of a museum makes for smoother functioning of the whole. And the history of museums, as well as their function and role in society, is being given increasing attention.

The trends and future of America's museums are assessed in the report of the American Association of Museums Commission, *Museums for a New Century* (1984). Current social, economic, political, and scientific trends that will affect the future of museums are explored; changes in the needs and operations of museums are identified. Museums are viewed as centers of research and learning that supplement universities. The report anticipates greater support from business and notes the unique blend of public, government, and private museum support that is characteristic of the United States. It contains sixteen recommendations for museums to meet the twenty-first century.

Museum studies programs can take a wide range of forms: some of these are essentially an internship at local institutions or

Museum Studies (continued)

college museums and represent the learning-by-doing approach; some comprise one or more courses as part of an undergraduate major in another field or as part of a graduate degree, usually a master's. There are also individual workshops, seminars, and training sessions of short duration, lasting from one day to one week and more, given by professional associations, organizations, and others outside the academic field. Some museum studies programs are master's degree programs, and still others lead to postgraduate certificate and degree awards. The type of study chosen should reflect long-range objectives in the field. While some museums and universities think training in a discipline is sufficient, most are finding additional work in museum studies valuable for increasing specialization and responsibilities. More and more positions are requiring museum studies as preparation for professional work in the field.

Flora S. Kaplan, Associate Professor
Director, Museum Studies Program
Faculty of Arts and Science
New York University

History

History History, the study of change over time, is a way of thinking. The discipline seeks to imbue its practitioners with a sense of a usable past that can render the present both meaningful and relevant. Despite its vast chronological, methodological, and conceptual range, the field is united by this core belief that the present is intelligible only in terms of what preceded it. To study the past is not to live in the past but rather to gain a fundamental and humanistic perspective on the present.

Graduate studies in history are most often limited only by one's imagination. A methodological focus in areas as diverse as quantitative techniques or the history of ideas; thematic concentration in political, economic, or social history; and chronological specialization are among the options offered by leading graduate institutions. Although most schools still emphasize a graduate degree in history as essential training for research and teaching positions in colleges and universities, a growing minority are now shaping their graduate programs around the option of nonacademic careers in such fields as public administration, government service, community development, and archival and museum work.

In the 1970s, the job market for traditional, academically related positions in history was very tight, and very likely it will remain so in the foreseeable future. However, employment opportunities for graduate degree holders in history have improved from the trough of the mid-1970s, when there were 1.8 new Ph.D.'s for every history job opening. By 1980 that figure was down to 1.1.

The number of students entering American schools will increase by about 18 percent in the next two decades, and by the 1990s this increase will enhance demand for college faculty in general. More specifically, the number of doctorates granted in history has been steadily declining since 1971, and an increasing number of job candidates with graduate history degrees have been seeking and finding nonacademic employment; over 20 percent in recent job markets accepted positions outside academia. These two trends promise a positive need in the future for graduate degree holders in history who are equipped with the skills of critical reasoning that can be applied to both academic and civic leadership.

William L. Barney
Department of History
University of North Carolina at Chapel Hill

History of Science   The history of science is a discipline in which the methods of historical research are employed to explore and analyze the genesis and evolution of the sciences and the growth of science as part of the intellectual and social experiences of mankind—from the time of the earliest known records and artifacts to the present.

A wide variety of approaches, perspectives, special knowledge, and skills characterize this discipline, which comprises the history of the natural and social sciences, technology, mathematics, medicine, and the health sciences.

While science is its subject and history its method, the field is closely related to various allied fields such as philosophy, religion, government, sociology, law, and public policy.

Persons planning to enter the field—depending on the area of concentration chosen—are advised to secure a sound foundation in history, one of the sciences, language skills, philosophy, and social

History of Science (continued)

analysis. At the professional level it is expected that scholars not only master some special area of concentration but also acquire a general knowledge of the major scientific events and their consequences over the entire field.

Barbara Gutmann Rosenkrantz, Professor
Chairman, Department of the History of Science
Harvard University

Public History The terms public history and applied history have evolved in the last ten years to describe the development and application of historical skills in nonacademic settings. Although initially perceived as a solution to the job crisis of the 1970s, public and applied history is now considered a viable way to educate a new generation of broadly trained and flexible professional historians. Public and applied history also represents a realization that historians can make a contribution to society not only as teachers, but also as archivists, publishers and historical editors, preservationists, museum curators, historical agency and public administrators, corporate and government policy analysts, and oral historians.

Public historians generally apply their historical skills in five different career areas: (1) private nonprofit organizations, such as historical societies, museums, and research institutions; (2) individual or small-firm consulting in such areas as cultural resource management and historical and policy research for government agencies and corporations; (3) public agencies, such as executive, legislative, and judicial branches of state and federal governments; military services; planning agencies; and public archives, libraries, preservation offices, and museums; (4) private-sector corporations in areas such as banking, communications media, marketing and advertising, publishing, public relations, and utilities; and (5) educational institutions that offer courses and/or programs in public and applied history.

Graduate programs in public and applied history generally offer an M.A. degree, although some provide Ph.D. degrees as well. Programs vary in their orientation and, in addition to subject-matter history courses, they offer training in one or more of the following fields: archival management, cultural resource management, historic preservation, historical editing, museum studies, policy studies, public administration, and publishing. Some programs are generalist in nature, requiring an introductory knowledge of several of the above fields, while other programs provide more specialized and intensive training in one or more areas of public and applied history. A common thread of all the programs is that an internship, an on-the-job learning experience, is the culmination of graduate training. The variety of graduate programs should enable a student to match his or her career and professional interests.

Employment opportunities have remained strong in all areas of public and applied history that do not solely depend on grant money for support. Most program directors continue to report high employment rates for their graduates.

Michael C. Scardaville
Director, Applied History Program
Department of History
University of South Carolina

Home Economics and Human Development

Home Economics and Human Development Home economics includes a number of disciplines from the natural and social sciences, all with one major focus—the improvement of individual and family well-being. Home economics was defined at the 1902 Lake Placid Conference as "the study of the laws, conditions, principles, and ideals which are concerned on the one hand with man's immediate physical environment and on the other hand with his nature as a social being, and is the study especially of the relation between these two factors...." This definition has served to define the scope and direction of home economics for over eighty years. Today it is commonly accepted that the focus of home economics is the study of interactions between individuals and their near environment, with the ultimate aim of improving individual and family well-being. Home economics programs typically include study of the child, the family, the consumer, nutrition, food science, textile science, clothing and apparel, merchandising, and tourism, food, and lodging administration. Home economists have conducted both basic and applied research in various areas since the field's beginnings, including food consumption patterns of individuals and families, composition of foods, nutritional requirements of individuals at each stage of the life span, family economics and resource management, physiological and psychological development of children and adults, family interaction, adaptation of clothing for special needs, social and

Home Economics and Human Development (continued)

psychological importance of clothing, and home design for contemporary families.

Home economists recognize that understanding the interaction between and among various subject matter areas concerned with the individual and the family is just as important as the study of the basic interaction. For example, chemists study protein and psychologists study child behavior, but it is within home economics that nutrient needs of the growing child are considered along with factors that affect the child's acceptance of a variety of foods.

Recently, there has been an expansion of home economics involvement beyond the home. The basic concern continues to be ensuring individual and family well-being, but this concern is no longer limited just to the home setting. The reason for this is attributed to major changes in family functions. Traditionally, the family assumed responsibility for providing food, clothing, and shelter for its members, and thus the home was the primary source of goods and services. As society became increasingly large, diverse, and complex, duties traditionally carried out by the family moved to other institutions. Concern for such things as design of the workplace, the quality of food and lodging away from home, the management of market activities that contribute to the quality of consumer choice, and laboratory research that tests the permeability of protective clothing for pesticides are all now well within the focus of home economics and individual and family well-being.

Future generations will ask home economics researchers to deal with many diverse problems, opening the way for them to play a greater advocacy role. As our population grows and expands, the policies adopted by federal, state, and local governments will have increasing significance in everyday lives. In one way or another, the decisions of government will impinge upon individual and family well-being. The need for home economics and the potential for its contribution has never been greater.

Jay Stauss
Associate Dean for Graduate Studies and Research
College of Human Ecology
University of Tennessee, Knoxville

Clothing and Textiles Clothing and textiles is a career field that offers many broad employment opportunities. The career title itself shows that the field is very broad, with job potential ranging from the basic formation of fibers and fabrics to the final end use of apparel and home furnishings and other uses, including industrial applications. Areas of subspecialization in this field include textile science; textile management; textile sales; clothing and apparel design; clothing and fashion merchandising; apparel wholesale and retail marketing; retail sales of apparel; operation of privately owned design and specialty shops; academic careers in high schools, colleges, and universities; and various careers that are directly related to home economics.

Employment opportunities in fields related to clothing and textiles are plentiful and are in great demand now. Positions are continually being advertised for all degree levels, and advertisements for persons with Ph.D. degrees for university and college teaching positions appear in the trade literature very frequently.

Jack T. Gill
Chairman, Department of Fashion and Textiles
College of Nutrition, Textiles, and Human Development
Texas Woman's University

Consumer Economics   Consumer economics at the graduate level is an emerging field and thus somewhat varied. Regardless of the particular program, its focus is on consumers and families as they interact with private markets and on how public programs and policies affect the interactions. Both the effects of consumer and family behavior on markets and the effects of market behavior and public programs on consumers and families are studied.

Because it is a small and emerging field, consumer economics is usually found in association with closely allied areas of study such as family economics. Depending on the university, either the sociological and psychological or the economic underpinnings are stressed. Universally the field is characterized by a focus on applied, empirical, and policy issues rather than on the theoretical.

Students with degrees in consumer economics find positions in university teaching; government service, such as with regulatory agencies like the FTC; and research agencies focusing on consumer and family behavior and on consumer affairs in the private sector.

W. Keith Bryant, Professor
Consumer Economics and Housing
Cornell University

Family Science Family science, the discovery and application of knowledge about the family, is a new field in the social sciences. There are two rather different processes in the discovery part of the field. One of these is integrating knowledge that already exists. There is a great deal of knowledge about families that has been discovered in older disciplines, such as psychology, anthropology, economics, sociology, biology, and history, and before family science emerged as a separate field this information was fragmented and disconnected. Family science integrates these fragments into a coherent body of knowledge. The other process in discovering is that family scientists use the body of knowledge that has already been acquired as a springboard for discovering new information. The new research is primarily a search for information about the internal dynamics of families and the way families interact with their ecosystems.

The application part of family science transforms abstract and technical knowledge into information that can improve the quality of family life. A number of different professions have emerged to carry out this application function. One of the most widely known is marriage and family therapy. This is a clinical or counseling approach to help people who are having serious difficulties coping with their life situations. Family life educators work in school settings to teach principles and skills that can help students understand the family and be effective in their own families. Family extension agents work with extension programs to promote healthy family life, and divorce mediators work with lawyers and judges in helping couples cope with the challenges of managing and adjusting to divorce. Marriage and family enrichment is a recent development in the field, in which leaders conduct retreats or workshops with structured family facilitation programs that help families avoid difficulties and create home environments that optimize human development, fulfillment, and actualization.

Family scientists are employed in a variety of settings. A large number teach in universities and colleges, and an increasing number are being employed in public schools. Many are in research positions in universities and private settings. There is still a large demand for marriage and family therapists in organizations such as hospitals and mental health clinics, and many therapists set up a private practice. Marriage and family enrichment is usually an avocation, or it is done as a supplement to a primary profession rather than as a primary profession.

Wesley R. Burr, Director
Family Living Center
Brigham Young University

Industrial and Labor Relations

Industrial and labor relations is a broad field encompassing all aspects of the employment relationship. Institutes, schools, or departments, usually with interdisciplinary faculties, are organized at a number of universities to engage in research and offer instruction on the many and complex topics that relate to the search for ways of achieving workable and equitable balance among the often common but sometimes conflicting goals of employees, employers, and the larger society. Faculty members in industrial relations units are specialists in labor relations, personnel or human resources management, labor economics, labor law, industrial sociology, industrial psychology, and organizational behavior. Increasing international competition, changes in the nature of work and the composition of the labor force, extensive governmental regulation of the employment relationship, and industrial reorganization and deregulation have made modern organizations increasingly aware of the importance of effectively utilizing and developing human resources for the success of the enterprise and to the need for broadly trained industrial relations specialists.

Graduate work at the master's degree level leads to professional careers in business, government agencies, and labor unions. In business, industrial relations opportunities are available in labor relations and in personnel or human resources management. Personnel or human resources management includes generalist positions in which the objective is the recruitment, development, and retention of a qualified and satisfied work force and specialized areas such as compensation, employee benefits, health and safety, education and training, and affirmative action. Labor relations includes collective bargaining, grievance processing, arbitration, and mediation. Both union and nonunion settings offer opportunities for employment. Similar positions in the management of labor relations and personnel are available in both government agencies and nonprofit organizations. Many industrial relations graduates are also employed by specialized federal and state agencies that administer labor relations, equal employment opportunity, and similar laws regulating the employment relationship. Employment with labor unions is commonly found in their research and education departments.

Graduate work at the Ph.D. level leads primarily to university and college teaching and research and secondarily to research-oriented careers outside the academic world. Industrial relations schools or institutes and industrial relations departments in business schools have been the major employers.

Industrial and Labor Relations (continued)

Job opportunities for graduates in industrial and labor relations have been excellent in recent years. The U.S. Department of Labor projects that the number of jobs in this field will increase through the mid-1990s. Women are entering graduate work in industrial relations in increasing numbers and finding the job market receptive. Only small numbers of minority group members are currently pursuing graduate-level work, and employer demand for them greatly exceeds the supply.

Undergraduate degrees in one of the social sciences, such as economics, psychology, sociology, and political science, provide particularly appropriate preparation for graduate work in industrial and labor relations. Backgrounds in business administration, communications, and social work are also appropriate.

Walter Franke, Director and Professor
Institute of Labor and Industrial Relations
University of Illinois at Urbana-Champaign

International Affairs

The study of international relations at the graduate level takes two rather sharply different paths these days. One is much more "academic" than the other. It draws upon the mainstream social science disciplines of political science and economics, with some sociology and psychology and perhaps some humanities—notably history and regional cultural studies—as well. This path leads to the Ph.D. degree and, for the most part, to careers in university-level teaching and scholarship. But some who follow it find employment as analysts with research organizations, government or private, or in the whole range of policy-oriented practitioner careers. These might be in government agencies, private firms, or international intergovernmental and nongovernmental organizations.

The second path aims directly at preparing students for the "real world" of practice. Most students who follow it seek only a master's degree; a few continue for doctorates. Some of the graduate programs focus on the study of particular countries or geographic regions, such as China, Western Europe, or Africa. But most of the programs within this second path have more in common with graduate programs in business and organizational management than they do with the programs of the first path. This variant emphasizes training in the systematic analysis of policy problems. It is based upon the premise that problems in the international sphere differ only superficially from those in the domestic and that both types are susceptible to the same—often heavily quantitative—analytical techniques.

All of these graduate programs have been affected by the widely shared perception that the phenomena of international life are more complicated than they were a generation ago and that economic relationships in particular should be better understood by both academics and practitioners. Global and regional problems of economic security—not only for nation-states but for groups within them—are receiving some of the attention that was once largely focused on questions of military security. And international relations are increasingly understood to consist of relationships not only among the sovereign collectivities called states and their governments but also among nongovernmental organizations of all sorts, business firms, and even individual intellectual and professional persons. During the last few years, however, with the increase of tensions in relations between the United States and the Soviet Union, there has been a resurgence of interest in the military aspects of national security. In response, many academic institutions have added to their course offerings and programs that deal with strategy, with the allocation of military resources, and with issues relating to arms control and disarmament.

Richard H. Ullman, Professor
Woodrow Wilson School of Public and International Affairs
Princeton University

Languages, Literatures, and Linguistics

Asian Languages   The older Asian languages departments have historically been modeled on classical languages departments, which means that the philological study of the premodern, written languages forms the core of the department, and teaching and research include linguistics, literature, ancient history, and philosophy. That broad range is sometimes indicated by the inclusion of such terms as "cultures" or "civilizations" in the titles of the departments. In such cases, early modern and modern history are usually taught by members of the history department, while

Asian Languages (continued)

specialists on contemporary history are usually located in the political science department. After World War II, there was a rapid expansion of the field as training in the modern languages became more important. Many of the newer departments took as their model European language departments, thus focusing more narrowly on literature and leaving the teaching of other aspects of the Asian cultures to the other disciplinary departments. These departments are usually entitled Asian Languages and Literatures, or some such. At the same time, there was a growing awareness at the national level that American expertise in East Asia and other parts of the world was sadly lacking and that the training of such specialists was relatively expensive because of the difficult languages involved. As a result, foundations (chiefly the Ford Foundation) and then the government, under the National Defense Education Act, funded a number of language and area centers across the country. The U.S. Department of Education still provides such funds to a number of National Resource Centers, as they are now called. Many of these language and area centers house interdisciplinary degree programs, primarily at the M.A. level. Earlier, in the 1960s and 1970s, these interdisciplinary programs primarily provided training for students planning on entering doctoral programs; either the students had adequate language training (probably from military service) but had not yet selected a discipline, or they had a grounding in a discipline but because their interest in Asia was a late one, they did not yet have enough language study to be accepted into an advanced degree program. This has gradually changed, and fewer such M.A. graduates now go into doctoral programs. Instead, these students are more frequently preparing for careers in government or private business, and, increasingly, these interdisciplinary degrees are being combined with degrees in such professions as law, business, and education. Asian languages departments usually provide language training in the classical and modern languages, as well as more specialized courses geared for these professions, as a service to the whole university community, while providing advanced training for their own graduate students, primarily in literature but also in linguistics, early history, and so forth, depending on the range of offerings in that department. There is at least one case in which the language pedagogical function was made into a separate department, but it does not seem to have been a successful experiment.

It should be clear to a prospective student that by itself ability with language is not normally considered an adequate recommendation for acceptance into an Asian language department. The department will want to see evidence that the student has some sense of how the language training will be used. If the goal is only to improve language ability, the student ordinarily will not be admitted into a department for advanced study and will certainly not be given financial assistance. Asian languages department students, upon receipt of a doctoral degree, normally expect to obtain a position teaching language and some courses in their specialty. Near-native facility in the spoken modern language is often required, and so an extended stay (two or more years) overseas is often necessary preparation. Contrary to expectations, enrollments in Chinese language classes have not responded to the increased interest in China. Rather, enrollments in Japanese classes have shown a sharp increase and so there have been more job openings on the Japanese side. Korean is represented in the larger Asian language programs, as well as such languages as Mongolian, Tibetan, and Manchu, but these are offered in very few universities, and job opportunities are accordingly even rarer.

Albert E. Dien, Director
Center for East Asian Studies
Stanford University

Celtic Studies   Celtic studies in the broad sense embraces the whole range of cultural activities of the Celtic-speaking peoples from earliest accessible times to the present. More narrowly, it focuses on the various individual Celtic languages and literatures. The Celtic languages fall into three groups: Continental, including above all Gaulish; Goidelic, including Irish, Scottish Gaelic, and Manx; and Brittonic, including Welsh, Cornish, and Breton. The literature of Continental Celtic offers two or three short texts that one may count as literature, and beyond that only bare inscriptions. The other two groups, however, can boast the two single longest-lived vernacular literatures in Western Europe, mainly in Irish and Welsh but to varying degrees in the other languages as well, spanning every century from the sixth to the twentieth. Modern study of these literatures has been proceeding steadily for well over 100 years, but there is an enormous amount still to be done, even at the most basic levels of first-time edition and translation. Opportunities for making major, even pioneering, contributions are extraordinarily good.

An individual program of study in Celtic studies inevitably reflects a balance between the interests of the student and the

Celtic Studies (continued)

resources of the institution. Typically, the student will be working in a department of something other than Celtic studies, and the program will combine Celtic studies and a (presumably more widespread) sister discipline. The non-Celtic component of the program may involve almost anything in the humanities, but especially English (the likeliest possibility), comparative literature, history, linguistics, Irish studies, medieval studies, folklore, sociology, music, and perhaps other fields. The Celtic component will normally involve—at the Ph.D. level, at least—the following: mastery of some significant form of either the Irish or the Welsh language, extensive study of some range of materials existent in that form of the language, and lesser work in other forms of the same language as well as in a second Celtic language and perhaps others beyond that—for example, mastery of Middle Welsh and extensive study of Medieval Welsh tales and romances together with work in Modern Welsh and Old and Middle Irish, or mastery of Modern Irish language and extensive work in the syntax of contemporary spoken Irish together with work in Middle and Old Irish and in Modern Welsh and Modern Breton. The exact amount of language work will vary, but there will always be a significant amount for the simple reason that original research in the field almost inevitably involves exploration of raw primary materials. It is an advantage to begin graduate study with reasonable knowledge of at least one Celtic language, though it is certainly not a necessity. Either way, prospective students should be thoroughly confident of their ability to learn foreign languages of both the "living" and "dead" varieties. Whether to learn languages, to gain access to primary materials, or simply to study under the ranking experts in the field, everyone coming into Celtic studies should anticipate finding a way to spend time—the more the better—in modern Celtic territory, in Ireland, Wales, Scotland, or Brittany, as appropriate to their program.

The availability of support for study in Celtic studies appears to be as good as in any humanities field, especially as pertains to travel abroad. Opportunities for long-term employment, however, are very limited. Outside of the major universities of Ireland, Scotland, Wales, and (to a lesser extent) Brittany, academic positions wholly committed to Celtic studies are *extremely* few, probably less than fifteen in all, junior and senior together. Significantly less rare, though still by no means common, are those that combine Celtic studies and one of its sister fields. Beyond academia, the Celtic studies graduate can offer more than anything else experience working and contributing at the forefront of a wide-open scholarly field.

Gregory Nagy, Professor
Chairman, Department of Celtic Languages and Literatures
Harvard University

Classics Classicists study the civilizations of ancient Greece and Rome. All departments of classics are devoted to the languages and literatures of the Greeks and Romans; many also embrace the study of their histories and philosophy; some include classical art and archaeology. Classics is an area study, and it is difficult to set a limit—geographical, temporal, or conceptual—to its domain. Traditionally the primary focus of many departments has been on Greece during its classical period, from about 700 to 300 B.C., and on Rome from about 200 B.C. to 400 A.D. Some departments cover earlier periods, and others extend their interest to medieval Latin and Byzantine Greek. A few treat modern Greek language and literature.

Classicists study both the written and the material remains of antiquity. The former study is known as classical philology broadly defined, and it includes as its main branches literature, history, linguistics, and philosophy, while epigraphy, paleography, and papyrology constitute ancillary disciplines. Those trained in classical philology have a thorough knowledge of Greek and Latin languages and literatures and generally have a good knowledge of one of the special disciplines within the field. The career goal of most is college teaching.

Classical archaeology treats of the material culture of the ancients and is again divided into Greek and Roman, though here a new classification of prehistoric is frequently added. Archaeologists generally command both languages but concentrate their interest on archaeological method as well as on ancient art and topography. Many study particularly architecture, painting, sculpture, or numismatics. Archaeologists utilize scientific methods more widely than they did in the past, and this requires an expertise in technical procedures heretofore unimagined. College teaching, excavation, and museum work are traditional career goals of those with doctorates in classical archaeology. Rescue work against road building and other construction provides a new area of employment.

Fewer students nowadays receive the kind of early training in Latin and Greek that was the norm even thirty years ago. Because classical authors are fundamental constituents of a liberal arts

Classics (continued)

education, however, most departments of classics have turned to the teaching of courses in English translation, such as mythology and literature in translation. This trend will continue, and commentaries on translations of ancient authors are beginning to appear to serve the languageless student. More and more departments will be engaging in these kinds of activity, and it may be one day that students of classics will routinely be trained not only in Greek and Latin but in translation, theories of translation, and literature in translation.

At the same time, teaching and research in the classical languages are being immeasurably aided by the use of computers. Classicists have been among the leaders in the field of computers in the humanities, and thanks to the Thesaurus Linguae Graecae, almost all of Greek literature can now be accessed by computer; work is under way to prepare a similar corpus of Latin authors. When these two projects are complete, classicists will be able to study ancient texts in the original with a speed, efficiency, and understanding unimagined by our predecessors of the nineteenth century. The best is yet to come.

All classicists are area specialists and apply to the ancient world scholarly methods shared by other disciplines. Because of common theoretical interests, classicists often find fruitful areas of collaboration with philosophers, political scientists, historians, and anthropologists; archaeologists generally find themselves conceptually allied with art historians, but they now share interests even with chemists and metallurgists. Classics is a broad and demanding field, but it rewards its devotees with years of intellectual challenge and fulfillment.

William F. Wyatt Jr., Professor
Department of Classics
Brown University

Comparative Literature In essence, comparative literature designates the general study of literature in all its aspects. Historically the term "comparative" was taken over from nineteenth-century linguistic philology and anatomy and applied to literature with the ambition of comparing national literatures in their international relations of influence, translation, and use of the classical and medieval heritage. Since the 1950s, many departments and programs of comparative literature have been founded in North America. Most of them have as their purpose the study and teaching of literature irrespective of frontiers and linguistic medium. The use of translation is a practical necessity, but at the same time students are required to have competence in at least two or three foreign languages and are encouraged to learn even more. While most departments and programs center mainly on the literatures of Europe and the Americas, there are some that are quite open to the study of literatures elsewhere, for example, those of the Orient, the Middle East, and Africa. A topic such as "oral literature" or the emergence of literature in new nations would require special linguistic competence and also reliance on translation.

There are great advantages to comparative literature as currently conceived in most places. It studies the "reality" of literature in the sense that movements, currents of ideas, subject matter, technique, and fashion have always, since the Romans, traversed the boundaries of nations and language communities. The various versions of neoclassicism, the baroque, the Enlightenment, romanticism, realism, symbolism, and modernism are all international phenomena. Latin remained through the Middle Ages, the Renaissance, and into the seventeenth century as a prime language of literary expression. Besides, any theory of literature should properly take into account a great range of literatures and periods in order to assure its validity. Likewise the study of literature as an "institution" or pursuit among other human activities must have some comparative international scope when it deals with the relations between literature and the other arts, psychology, social ideologies, and philosophy (including aesthetics).

Many of those who take a degree in comparative literature go on with a secure foundation to study and teach in language departments, programs in the humanities or general education, or in some capacity in the private sector. At present there is great emphasis on theory in a number of institutions, yet the durable perspectives of critical and historical study continue in force. There are undeniably fashions in literary study that come and go. Comparative literature is capacious enough to accommodate them and to make them too a subject of study.

Lowry Nelson Jr.
Professor of Comparative Literature
Yale University

English   English as an academic subject first defined itself about a century ago with the aid of philology, as methods developed for the study of the European languages were applied to the native tongue. The new discipline subsequently formed alliances with history, notably cultural history, and turned itself toward what could be learned of the English-speaking peoples through study of their linguistic artifacts, especially the imaginative ones. With the emergence in the late 1930s of literary criticism as an autonomous discipline, questions of poetics came to the fore: efforts to discern the modes of organization by which a play or a poem differs from some other kind of good writing. And very recently, under French auspices, attention has been turning to the role of the reader in creating what is read, even to the question of whether any controlling "meaning," independent of what readers bring, inheres in a text at all.

In graduate departments all four of these emphases are apt to be found operating in various proportions, the oldest—the philological—being at present on the whole the least vigorous. (It remains a key discipline for medieval studies.) By nearly universal consensus, no one enjoys competence for research and teaching in English in the absence of a comprehensive acquaintance with English literature from at least Chaucer's time until ours and with American literature of the nineteenth and twentieth centuries. The historical disciplines are therefore active, and most departments organize their curricula with the aid of agreed notions of "periods": medieval, Renaissance, eighteenth century, romantic, Victorian, and modern, with American studies a separate category. Interest in the fourth emphasis, modern and postmodern literary theory, is concentrated at a small number of institutions but represented at most.

Most English Ph.D. holders expect to teach in colleges and universities, and in many programs supervised teaching of undergraduate sections is considered an important part of the candidates' experience. Jobs for some years have been scarce but appear to be growing less so, the fact that fewer advanced degrees were granted in the seventies than in the sixties having eased the market somewhat. Beginning instructors and assistant professors may expect to be called on to teach in areas outside their field of doctoral concentration, in many cases composition courses. Seminar and course work during the advanced degree program is thus normally selected to equip the young scholar with as broad a range of literary and historical experience as possible.

Hugh Kenner
Department of English
Johns Hopkins University

French   French, like other languages and literatures, is part of the humanities, and French departments are concerned with the study of texts and their interpretation and meaning; their historical, social, and cultural contexts; their transmission across time; and the relationship of individual works to the tradition. French literature has the distinction of remaining remarkably vital, and also central to the Western literary tradition, throughout its long history, and more than most other literatures, it has often entertained close relationships with philosophy, politics, and social thought. Accompanying the study of French literature is the study of its medium, the French language, including linguistics and the history of the language, and the means to train future generations of students in language skills.

Traditional fields within the study of French literature have tended to be the Middle Ages, the Renaissance, the baroque and classical period (the seventeenth century), the Enlightenment (eighteenth-century literature and philosophical thought), the nineteenth century, and the twentieth century. Most of these fields have been the object of lively reassessments and reevaluations in recent years. One notes in particular a distinct revival of interest in medieval studies, including medieval theories of language and interpretation, and in renaissance studies, often with an interdisciplinary focus (giving attention to developments in other art forms). New work is being done in such once-neglected subjects as the eighteenth-century novel, the interrelationships of literature and society in the nineteenth century, feminist literature and theory, and the place of popular literature and culture.

Along with renewed scholarship in certain historical areas, there has been a new vitality imparted to French studies over the past two decades by new forms of thinking in what the French call "the sciences of man"—linguistics, anthropology, psychoanalysis, and historiography. French departments have often been the American port of entry for the movements loosely known as structuralism, semiotics, and poststructuralism, which have generated new approaches to interpretation and programs of research and in general a ferment of ideas. While at times the debate on these ideas appears to have the effect of making academic departments into battlegrounds of different methods and ideologies, one senses that exclusive claims to truth in approach are now a thing of the past, that most French departments currently represent a variety of approaches to literary analysis and literary history, and that they encourage intellectual and methodological pluralism.

Most graduate programs in French remain oriented toward careers in college and university teaching, though a few programs have sought to explore other fields in which a knowledge of French

French (continued)

culture can be useful. Most programs give an opportunity for—or indeed require—the teaching of French to undergraduates and include some work in methods and materials of language teaching. Such apprentice teaching has come to be seen as a necessary part of graduate school training by prospective employers, since most beginning teaching positions entail a considerable portion of language teaching. The job market for Ph.D.'s in French has improved markedly in the past few years, in part as a result of a renewed commitment to foreign languages in the undergraduate curriculum in many colleges, some of which have reinstated foreign language proficiency requirements. Opportunities for initial employment can now be rated as good. While the tenure hurdle remains difficult in many institutions, large numbers of retirements in the coming decade suggest that there will be an increased need for qualified senior faculty. The younger generation of scholars-teachers-critics is currently the liveliest in decades. As they move into senior positions, they promise continuing intellectual vigor for French studies.

Peter Brooks
Chairman, Department of French
Yale University

German   German is the only language spoken on both sides of the Great Political Divide, and it is used in the two neutral countries of Austria and Switzerland. The two Germanies exemplify both the division and the cohesion of Europe, and they exert decisive influence on their economic communities (the EEC and Comecon). German is also one of the great literary languages, the home of major artistic and intellectual legacies, and the medium of such influential figures as Luther and Marx. With little regard to the social, political, military, and economic significance of German-speaking Europe, American graduate programs in German are oriented toward literary studies first, with a secondary role assigned to linguistics and the history of language. Where the curriculum has been broadened to include general studies of German culture, it usually reflects its origin in intellectual history. Students interested in current affairs will find few opportunities for concentrated study; a few additional programs support some course work in other disciplines related to the German-speaking area.

Literary studies commonly are structured according to historical categories, with primary attention given to works from the high Middle Ages, from the baroque period, and from the middle of the eighteenth century to the present. The popularity of recent theoretical innovations in sister fields, notably English and French, is facilitating the entry into the American academic community of major developments in German criticism and literary theory that had heretofore received relatively little notice. The curricula of many departments now show the influence of this discourse and of culture and area studies on traditional literary-historical instruction, but the changes are gradual and do not cause much controversy.

Some schools also offer concentrations or degrees in other living Germanic languages and cultures: Netherlandic, Danish, Swedish, Norwegian, or Icelandic.

Only persons holding the Ph.D. can expect to teach German at the college level, and the secondary schools usually require state certification and a master's degree, at least after a few years of teaching. Employment of German instructors at the college level will remain restricted in this decade; an improved market is likely to await those completing the doctorate in the early nineties. At present, graduate study often eventually leads to a nonteaching career drawing on the skills acquired in the degree program. In the secondary schools, change is coming more quickly: a surge in public demand for expanded foreign language instruction is causing teacher shortages in parts of the United States.

Most graduate students will find financial support spanning at least four years toward the doctorate, usually in the form of a teaching assistantship. Many departments actually require one year of teaching as an assistant, with a stipend. In addition, some almost expect one year of study in a German-speaking country and may be able to supply fellowship support to that end. However, not every program can accommodate all its qualified applicants, whereas others may not be able to fill all support slots. For this reason, and because of keen competition for superior applicants and an uneven geographic distribution, multiple applications are strongly recommended. Offers of financial support vary not only in level, but also in composition, duration, amount of service required, and even in terminology. One institution's tuition remission may be another's fellowship. Applicants should study offers of support carefully and weigh them against their professional goals and the quality and scope of degree programs. Differences of financial packages may be small

German (continued)

when compared to those in later professional competence in research and in teaching.

Albrecht Holschuh
Department of Germanic Studies
Indiana University Bloomington

Italian   Graduate students in Italian are interested in pursuing the study of one of the richest literary traditions of the West, primarily with the intention of teaching the language and its literature on the college level. Opportunities to do so are at present somewhat more numerous than in other language and literature areas because Italian has been a latecomer as a subject of study in higher education. In almost all programs opportunities exist for study or research abroad, usually after the M.A. is earned. Frequently teaching is an integral part of the graduate student's training; for the most part, he or she is entrusted with language courses, benefiting from varying degrees of guidance and supervision in class preparation and actual performance. American students often find themselves in programs with students born and educated in Italy, but this need not result in a feeling of unequal competition, as a distinction is always made between mere linguistic competence and the ability to engage in original and independent intellectual work—*the* standard by which achievement in graduate school is judged.

While specialization in contemporary Italian literature, both poetry and prose, is particularly popular, the Middle Ages and the Renaissance—with such world figures as Dante, Petrarch, Boccaccio, Machiavelli, and Ariosto—are not far behind. All literary approaches are practiced, from the philological establishing of texts to the application of aesthetic and historiographical, structuralist, and semiotic theories and techniques. The study of Italian literature is no longer considered along purely national lines; boundaries are constantly crossed in interdepartmental and interdisciplinary programs. The Italian component plays an important part in comparative literature studies because of Italy's historical role as a link between antiquity and the modern world.

A genuine interest in literature and ideas; a command of other languages, especially Latin; possibly the experience of travel in

Europe; and curiosity about and receptiveness to other cultures are some of the desirable prerequisites for graduate work in Italian.

Olga Ragusa
Da Ponte Professor of Italian
Chairman, Department of Italian
Columbia University

Linguistics   Linguistics, the science of language, is perhaps the oldest topic of investigation and speculation, from the biblical accounts of divinity to the amazingly precise and rule-governed grammar of Panini, to Aristotle, the medieval philosophers, the seventeenth-century rationalists, the nineteenth-century linguists, neogrammarians and behaviorists, the structuralists in the twentieth century, and the revolutionary revival of mentalism in the 1950s. Because of the nature and role of language throughout the history of humanity, linguistics has remained a dynamic and vital science or art, depending on one's disposition.

These days linguistics is generally treated as a science—a natural science, inasmuch as it deals with formal, abstract, and discrete objects and with empirical observation of those objects' properties and behaviors. It also deals with the psychology of cognition and learning. It could equally be (and has been) regarded as a discipline in arts and humanities because of the inevitable interconnection of language with other human activities, including art, communication, the media, literature, and other cultural creations. The place of linguistics as a social science is also well attested, as can be seen in its close affinity with anthropology and its perhaps not so obvious impingement on education, history, philosophy, and other fields of study.

Graduate linguistics departments and programs, which are often in humanities divisions, have traditionally trained students for academic careers. In recent years, however, there has been a surge of demands for competent linguists from industries. This is due to the developments in artificial intelligence, communication sciences, computer applications in natural-language processing and understanding, information sciences, and other high-technology activities. There are also developing fields in bilingualism, teaching English as a second language, literacy, linguistic problems of ethnic minorities, and other topics in applied linguistics. As a result, graduate programs are offering an increasing number of courses in computational as well as urban and applied linguistics.

Linguistics (continued)

There is a marked trend in the last few years of increasing numbers of applicants for both undergraduate and graduate programs in linguistics.

John Moyne, Executive Officer
Ph.D. Program in Linguistics
Graduate School and University Center
of the City University of New York

Near and Middle Eastern Languages   The study of the languages of the Near and Middle East has traditionally been divided into two major areas: the premodern literary languages, some long dead, and those of the modern period, which include both literary and spoken languages and dialects. Hebrew and Arabic are the most widely studied Near and Middle Eastern languages in the United States, with emphases varying between literary and spoken skills. There is no uniformity in departments in terms of the range of languages taught; some teach only Hebrew—ancient, modern, or both—while others teach only Arabic or Qur'anic, modern standard literary and spoken dialects. In some departments Turkish, Persian, and Urdu may also be found. To these must be added the ancient Near Eastern languages written in cuneiform scripts (Sumerian, Akkadian, Eblaite, Ugaritic, Hurrian Hittite, and Elamite and Urartian Persian) and those in alphabetic scripts (Aramaic, Phoenician, Hebrew, Syriac, Ethiopic, and others).

The study of these languages, ancient and modern, may be pursued in departments of Near or Middle Eastern studies, Judaic or Islamic studies, modern languages and linguistics, and occasionally classics and other related programs of study. Approaches vary from the purely philological and linguistic to the literary and dialectical (spoken). Graduate research opportunities vary according to departmental resources, library facilities, and field-research potential.

It is difficult to define the field of Near and Middle Eastern languages in general terms, since each language or family of languages is the subject of a number of specialties and subspecialties. Furthermore, each of these languages represents a complex literary and historical legacy whose importance cannot be overemphasized for our understanding of the history, politics, culture, and religions of a strategic area of the world. The study of Near and Middle Eastern languages provides a basis for academic careers, governmental service, and business careers, as well as simple humanistic value, i.e., the ability to speak non-Western languages and to read a vast and often otherwise untranslated literary corpus.

Opportunities for graduate work lie in the areas of modern language teaching, which nowadays is utilizing computer and video technology to enhance the study of spoken language in environments where native speakers are often not available. Archival research in the vast library holdings of the countries of the Middle East and in the files of Western governmental agencies offers special opportunities but requires advanced language skills. Linguistic and dialect research requires fieldwork in the countries of the Middle East. The study of documents from ancient times, cuneiform records and manuscripts, and their relationship to ancient history, literary and biblical studies, and linguistics also necessitates the study of a number of these ancient and modern languages.

The study of Near and Middle Eastern languages thus offers a wide range of opportunities to the student. Prospects for employment for individuals with such language abilities will vary according to the area or areas of specialization. In the long term, the need for scholars, language teachers, and translators will surely increase, but students should check carefully into those areas where their respective interests lie.

David I. Owen
Department of Near Eastern Studies
Cornell University

Portuguese   Portuguese, the sixth most spoken language in the world, is used on every continent, either as a result of the Portuguese discoveries in the fifteenth and sixteenth centuries or of the considerable number of emigrants who in recent times have sought improved economic opportunities in northern Europe, the United States, Canada, Venezuela, Brazil, South Africa, and Australia. Portuguese is, of course, the language of Portugal and Brazil, but it is also an official language of Angola, Mozambique, Guinea-Bissau, and Cape Verde in Africa, and it is spoken as well in many areas of the Orient, where the Portuguese have left the indelible imprint of their presence.

Graduate studies in Portuguese can lead to the M.A. and Ph.D. degrees. The most frequent specialization is in literature. Traditional philology now shares the field with research in applied and

Portuguese (continued)

theoretical linguistics. African literature written in Portuguese has recently been receiving increased attention. In some programs, certain aspects of Spanish linguistics and literature may be included. Many graduate programs offer some formal training in foreign language teaching methodology.

The M.A. in Portuguese usually includes general preparation in Portuguese literature, Brazilian literature, and Portuguese linguistics. The first two emphasize literary analysis; the third deals principally with phonetics, phonology, syntax, and historical linguistics. At the Ph.D. level, the student normally chooses either Brazilian literature, Portuguese literature, or Portuguese linguistics as a field of specialization. Linguistics study emphasizes its research and theoretical implications, while literary study leads to research involving knowledge of the latest critical methods.

Employment for those with advanced degrees in Portuguese is largely to be found in teaching, where opportunities are usually enhanced when Portuguese has been combined with a strong minor in another commonly taught European language, preferably Spanish. In addition to selected universities, Portuguese is taught in some primary and secondary schools and community colleges on the East Coast and in California. For the former, the Ph.D. is required; for the latter, the M.A. and appropriate teaching credentials are necessary. Outside the teaching profession, it is wise for the graduate to have acquired expertise in an auxiliary, nonlanguage field and to consider language proficiency as a supplement. The language component of one's career is very useful and can increase employment opportunities in business, industry, government, private research and development firms, and multinational corporations, but language competence in and of itself leads to relatively few jobs purely on the basis of an advanced degree, inasmuch as the principal interest of such organizations is usually preparation and skills in other than a foreign language field.

Claude L. Hulet, Professor
Department of Spanish and Portuguese
University of California, Los Angeles

Romance Languages and Literatures The field of Romance languages and literatures includes the language, literature, and culture of the countries whose languages are derived from Latin.

Departments in American universities are variously organized; the most common organizations are into an entire department encompassing all these fields or into two departments with the traditional division of French-Italian and Spanish-Portuguese. Less frequently taught languages, such as Catalan and Rumanian, may be included in these departments. The organization is often due to administrative and historical reasons rather than intellectual ones.

Within these fields, it is possible to take an M.A. or a Ph.D. degree in a national language or literature. Depending on the administrative flexibility of a particular department, one can take a degree with a double concentration. Degrees in Romance linguistics are also normally earned within a Romance department, although some universities place this discipline in a general linguistics department.

In this field, the thesis subject, both in terms of period and subfield, normally establishes the area in which the candidate will be working. The areas of interest open to a candidate are too many to mention but they include the following: medieval, Renaissance, baroque, romanticism, realism, naturalism, modernism, avant-garde literature, history of ideas, intellectual history, critical edition, poststructuralist criticism, semiotics, pedagogy, second language acquisition, theoretical linguistics, historical linguistics, and biography.

Students interested in this field should acquire a strong background in both the culture and language of their areas of study. To this end, they should take every opportunity to live and study abroad.

Frank P. Casa, Professor
Department of Romance Languages and Literatures
University of Michigan

Russian   Most, though not all, graduate programs in Russian are part of a program in Slavic languages and literatures. In some institutions, the graduate curriculum in Russian is affiliated with a Russian area studies program. In most but not in all instances, a graduate course of study in Russian has a linguistics and a literature branch.

Graduate programs in Russian linguistics are geared to a Ph.D. degree in most institutions. They will include course work in historical and comparative Slavic linguistics, in the structure of modern Russian (phonology, morphology, syntax, and stylistics), in

Russian (continued)

the history and dialectology of the Russian language, and in general linguistic theory. Course work in Old Church Slavonic and in at least one other Slavic language is generally required. Most programs will also require proficiency in one or two major foreign languages, normally French and German. Most curricula in Russian linguistics also involve some work in Russian literature, literary criticism, and poetics. The dissertation may be a synchronic or diachronic investigation of any aspect of Russian grammar, stylistics, or poetics. A dissertation may also deal with language acquisition, language pedagogy, sociolinguistics, and other such topics. Editions, textual criticism, and linguistic analysis of texts of linguistic interest are further possibilities. Graduate students will usually be given an opportunity to develop and practice their language teaching skills in the classroom.

A graduate program in Russian literature will, in most institutions, lead to either an M.A. or a Ph.D. It involves in both instances course work covering the whole range of Russian literature from the eleventh century to our own day, literary criticism, and literary theory. Most programs will encourage students to also take courses in Russian civilization, Russian history, and related disciplines. Some institutions will require graduate students to acquaint themselves with at least one other Slavic literature, and some will require course work in Old Church Slavonic and/or the history of the Russian language. Most programs will also require proficiency in at least one major foreign language, normally French or German. A Ph.D. dissertation may deal with any scholarly topic defined by genre, formal structure, period, school, or author. In some instances a scholarly edition or an annotated translation of a major work of literature will serve as a dissertation. Most institutions will give their graduate students an opportunity to develop their teaching skills in language classes and in sections of Russian literature courses taught in translation.

Victor Terras
Professor of Slavic Languages and Literatures
Brown University

Scandinavian Languages and Literatures   In a firm belief that all aspects of Scandinavian culture, past and present, constitute a viable area of academic pursuit, the Scandinavian departments throughout the United States contribute to a strong liberal arts education.

Scandinavia's cultural, scientific, social, and political achievements have long attracted worldwide attention and admiration. Its impact on other postindustrial societies is considerable, when one takes into account its relatively small population. An increasing number of students recognize that to study Scandinavian culture is no longer an esoteric undertaking but that to do so is to focus on some of the most important issues facing the Western world today, including social welfare, ethnic mobility, economic equality, and support for the arts. The steady growth in student enrollment in Scandinavian graduate programs is related to an awareness of Scandinavia as a social laboratory and a contributor to world culture.

The Master of Arts student is trained in the methods of language pedagogy, philology, folklore and mythology, and literary theory and analysis or can choose an area studies degree emphasizing modern history and politics. All students are required to display broad knowledge of the literature and literary history of Scandinavia with a focus on the student's major language area, usually Danish, Norwegian, or Swedish. The M.A. degree qualifies the student either to pursue a Ph.D. degree, teach at the high school or college level, or pursue a career in a number of other professions, such as international business, journalism, and translation.

The Doctor of Philosophy student is trained for a scholarly career on either the college or university level. Training is also given in writing publishable papers in order to prepare for dissertation work. To the degree that finances permit, students are encourged to participate in conferences and to present papers as another element to help in preparing for an academic career.

Generally the Scandinavian departments in the United States do not have any problems in placing their graduates in teaching positions throughout the country, frequently in tenure track positions, of which an amazing number open up at regular intervals.

Sven H. Rossel, Chairman
Department of Scandinavian Languages and Literature
University of Washington

Slavic Languages and Literatures   Graduate programs in Slavic languages and literatures normally offer two specializations: literature and linguistics. These fields potentially include study of any of the fifteen living Slavic languages (as well as Old Church Slavonic) and their literatures, but American university programs in practice have concentrated their resources on a few of these, and primarily on Russian. Polish, Czech, Serbo-Croatian, and in a few

Slavic Languages and Literatures (continued)

institutions Bulgarian, Ukrainian, or others are sometimes offered, either as minors or in certain larger departments as major concentrations for graduate degrees. Some Ph.D. programs in Russian also admit minors outside the Slavic field, for example, in other literatures, history, or philosophy.

Ph.D. programs in Slavic languages and literatures continue to be oriented toward preparing candidates for college and university teaching and research. Candidates in Slavic linguistics usually master at least three modern Slavic languages in the course of their program in order to study linguistic structure and historical development. They will study modern linguistic theories, structuralism, historical grammar, and other topics and may pursue research in any of a large variety of subfields. Ph.D. candidates in Slavic literatures acquaint themselves thoroughly with the major periods, works, and authors that constitute their chosen literatures, and in studying the literary process will be expected to study also literary theory and criticism relevant to their fields. There is a recent trend toward convergence in linguistic and literary analysis, with dual competence becoming an increasingly popular orientation. Functional reading knowledge of French and German are required by most Slavic departments for Ph.D. candidates, with one or the other language required for the M.A.

The M.A. curriculum is usually designed to lead to the Ph.D. program, but the degree may be combined usefully with training in other fields, e.g., the social sciences, business administration, law, library science, and education. It can also serve to prepare for such other careers as government work, journalism, translation, and high school teaching (though opportunities in the last are slight at present). Special programs in translating are available in some institutions. Moreover, a number of schools offer Soviet and East European area programs. Students interested in these should be aware that they are distinct from Slavic languages and literatures, and admission to them may require separate application. These programs often take the form of a certificate in area studies, which may be combined with a graduate degree in any one of a number of disciplines: Slavic languages and literatures, history, economics, political science, and others. Specific information about this, as well as other features of a given university's offerings, should be obtained before application is made.

Johanna Nichols, Professor
Chairman, Department of Slavic Languages and Literatures
University of California, Berkeley

Spanish   Graduate study in Spanish encompasses three major components: (1) language/linguistics, (2) literature, and (3) culture/ civilization. Programs of study at both the M.A. and Ph.D. levels usually require some general work in each of these areas, together with more specialized concentration in one. The most frequent specialization in most departments is literary study, with both geographical and chronological subdivisions available: peninsular Spanish literature (medieval, Golden Age, eighteenth and nineteenth century, twentieth century) and Spanish-American literature (colonial, nineteenth century, twentieth century). A specialization in language/linguistics, often with strong supporting work in general linguistics, is increasingly frequent within Hispanic studies and can range from a more traditional philological focus to the application of the most recent methods in theoretical or applied research. Culture/civilization is less often selected as a specialization and draws necessarily on parallel study in history and/or anthropology.

There is a growing interest in linguistic and literary theory across the discipline, and significant numbers of courses make it possible and advisable for students to acquaint themselves with both traditional and innovative theoretical approaches. In addition, most graduate departments carry out a modicum of formal training in foreign language teaching methodology and see as desirable a substantial period of residence in a Spanish-speaking country.

Employment opportunities for holders of advanced degrees in Spanish are to be found mainly in teaching. The M.A. degree (and often formal certification as well) is necessary for high school and junior college teaching; the Ph.D. is required for university and senior college positions in which research and publication might be expected in addition to teaching. Employment can also be secured, though less frequently, in government agencies, with private research and development firms, or with multinational corporations, all of which may have on occasion a need for expertise in the language and culture of Spanish-speaking countries.

Merlin H. Forster, Chairman
Department of Spanish and Portuguese
University of Texas at Austin

Translation and Interpretation   Persons interested in translation and interpretation, two related yet completely separate professions, must realize that language skills are only a small part of the overall requirements to enter these professions. Both require exceptionally

Translation and Interpretation (continued)

well-rounded individuals who are able to comprehend, analyze, and reexpress either orally (interpretation) or in writing (translation), according to the rules of a different cultural setting, any kind of general, scientific, and technical material. A perfect understanding of all shades of meaning within a given cultural pattern, as expressed in the foreign language, must therefore be taken for granted.

Interpreting may be practiced in courts, hospitals, and the armed forces and by escort interpreters. Conference interpretation, however, is the most difficult form. It can be performed in two modes: consecutive and simultaneous interpretation. In consecutive interpretation, the interpreter takes notes during a speech and delivers the same speech in the target language after the speaker has ended. This is usually done in segments of no more than 10 to 15 minutes. In the simultaneous mode, the interpreter sits in a soundproof booth and receives the original speech through earphones. As the speaker talks, the interpreter simultaneously interprets into his or her native language. The interpretation is received by the participants through earphones over the desired language channel.

Conference interpretation requires graduate university training of at least four years' duration, including extensive studies abroad. Conference interpreters usually know a minimum of two foreign languages but only work into their native language. Most conference interpreters work on a free-lance basis. Positions on the staff of large organizations such as the United Nations or the U.S. Department of State are rare and well paid and require exceptional qualities. Most conference interpreters belong to the International Association of Conference Interpreters, based in Geneva, Switzerland, the only worldwide association of conference interpreters. The association guarantees the professional quality of its members and their respect of the rules of professional ethics.

Translators must possess exceptionally good writing skills in their native language along with, obviously, an outstanding knowledge of their foreign languages. They may occasionally be required to translate into their strongest foreign language but must always have a native speaker check their work. As is true for conference interpreters, graduate study in several countries is a must for the translator.

Translators must be well read and have a vast general background in order to be able to cope with the large variety of materials that they are exposed to in their professional activities. In the United States, most translators belong to the American

Translators' Association. Most translators work for the translation agencies, which get most of their work from corporations and the government. Some government agencies, such as the Joint Publication and Research Service, deal directly with translators.

Wilhelm Weber, Dean
Graduate Division in Translation and Conference Interpretation
Monterey Institute of International Studies

Writing   Just as there are worse and better ways to say things, so too are there worse and better ways to write them down. Serious students of writing believe that it is important to write as well as one can and that improvement is possible. While some programs offer training in playwriting, the writing of screenplays, technical writing, and journalism, this description addresses the writing of fiction and poetry since it is principally on these two forms that the study of writing at the graduate level focuses.

Learning how to write the best stories and poems one can write is largely a matter of trial and error, of learning to tell whether successive revisions and new work are pointing in a good and promising direction. Specific skills can be learned, certainly, each skill contributing to the student's gradually becoming his or her own least forgiving and most trusted editor. Programs in writing teach these skills. They also provide the student with the incentive to excel in front of an audience of competent instructors and peers.

The central course in any writing program is the workshop, a weekly or biweekly meeting in which recent writing by the students themselves is discussed and evaluated. Ground rules for the meeting will vary from instructor to instructor, as will the terms each instructor emphasizes within his or her workshop. Each piece of writing is scrutinized for its clarity, interest, range, and grace, though judgments of its strengths and weaknesses in these general categories will necessarily vary too. The student is usually left not with a consensus opinion on how to improve the work in question but rather with individual readings of it, readings which he or she must then sort out and put to use. In programs with a favorable ratio of faculty members to students, tutorial work is often of special help to the student whose work can profit by even more detailed attention than it receives in workshop.

Compared with the number of students enrolled in graduate writing programs at any one time, very few writers of fiction and still fewer poets manage to support themselves solely by their writing. The limited market for the best stories and poems therefore compels

Writing (continued)

many graduates to consider teaching as the career most complementary to their continuing interest in writing. But while the number of writing programs at both the undergraduate and graduate level has increased dramatically in the past ten years, thereby opening up many positions for writers, academic budgets remain so tight that the holder of a Master of Fine Arts or Doctor of Philosophy degree in writing will not easily find a job as a teacher.

James McMichael
Director for Poetry
Program in Writing
University of California, Irvine

Law

Students thinking of law study soon discover that the programs of most law schools have a great deal in common. The choice of one school over another is not easily made on the basis of catalog descriptions of the teaching methods, course offerings, and formal requirements. The similarity is natural, since most American law schools share the aim of educating lawyers for careers that may take many paths and that will frequently not be limited to any particular state or region. Although many lawyers eventually find themselves practicing within some special branch of the law, American legal education is still fundamentally an education for generalists. It emphasizes the acquisition of broad and basic knowledge of law, an understanding of the functioning of the legal system, and, perhaps even more important, the development of analytical abilities of a high order. This common emphasis reflects the conviction that such an education is the best kind of preparation for the diverse roles that law school graduates occupy in American life and for the changing nature of the problems any individual lawyer is likely to encounter over a long career.

Within this tradition some schools combine an emphasis on technical legal knowledge and professional skills with a concern for illuminating the connections between law and the social forces with which it interacts. To promote the first, schools provide students with opportunities for the application of formal knowledge to specific professional tasks, such as intensive instruction in legal research and writing during the first year, clinical education, and courses or seminars focusing on concrete problems of counseling, drafting, and litigation. The second concern is reflected in curricular offerings that devote substantial attention to relevant aspects of economics, legal history, philosophy, comparative law, psychiatry, statistics, and other disciplines. Almost all law schools offer some students the opportunity to work on law reviews that are published by them but are student run and edited. The law reviews, of varying quality and influence, publish scholarly work as well as work done by law students. Most schools have a moot court program that uses simulated cases for training in brief writing and advocacy.

Prudent applicants should consider the quality of a school's faculty and student body, how a school's view of legal education and its course offerings relate to their own interests and future plans (as to course offerings, "more" is not necessarily "better"), the predominantly "national" or "local" character of a school, formal and informal opportunities for joint degrees in the case of law schools that are part of a university, library facilities, and placement record. All of these elements, in addition to more individual preferences, should be carefully weighed, but no single factor should ever be considered decisive.

Gerhard Casper
William B. Graham Professor and Dean of the Law School
University of Chicago

Liberal Studies

Graduate programs in liberal studies are a relatively recent phenomenon in American higher education. The first such program was inaugurated at Wesleyan University in 1953. Since that year, growth and expansion have been most dramatic. As recently as 1979, the *New York Times* reported the existence of nineteen master's programs in liberal studies. Seven years later, in 1986, the Association of Graduate Liberal Studies Programs listed among its membership seventy-one institutions offering or about to launch programs in the field.

Though curricula vary among the liberal studies programs, they share common ground in terms of purpose. All are dedicated to promoting the values inherent in liberal arts study. The programs are interdisciplinary in nature and are designed to be terminal rather than to be stepping-stones to further graduate work. The primary difference among the several college and university programs in the

Liberal Studies (continued)

liberal studies is in the degree of elective choices available to students. Some institutions, for example, offer the opportunity to specialize in an interdisciplinary subject area or cluster such as the humanities, social sciences, or natural sciences while electing a required minimum number of courses from the remaining areas or clusters. Other programs have students follow a required sequence of interdisciplinary courses, supplemented with elective courses selected from among the school's graduate offerings. Whatever the approach, all emphasize breadth of study rather than single-discipline specialization. The degrees most commonly granted by liberal studies programs are the Master of Arts in Liberal Studies (M.A.L.S.), Master of Liberal Studies (M.L.S.), and Master of Liberal Arts (M.L.A.).

Students enrolling in liberal studies programs represent a wide variety of educational and experiential backgrounds. There are those whose love for learning grew out of a strong liberal arts background and who wish to study on a higher level in a stimulating environment. There are those whose undergraduate degree was career or professionally oriented and who now desire to attain the benefits of liberal arts study. It is not unusual to find among the entering class of a liberal studies program teachers, librarians, businesspeople, physicians, social workers, people in publishing, and retirees. They are there to pursue a graduate degree designed to enrich their lives and to develop in them valuable critical skills.

Frederick M. Binder
Professor of History
Coordinator, M.A.L.S. Program
College of Staten Island
of the City University of New York

Library Science

Library science (or librarianship) is a discipline centrally concerned with methods and problems of acquiring, organizing, and providing effective access to recorded information. It includes the study of the purpose, functions, management, operations, history, and problems of libraries, library systems and networks and related information services. In addition, the study of children's literature, with respect to content as well as to problems of access, is widely accepted as an important component of librarianship.

The study of library science can be approached from two somewhat different perspectives. The first of these stresses the practice of librarianship and the goal of preparing students to work at various professional levels in libraries. The second viewpoint treats librarianship more as an academic discipline; it places emphasis on understanding basic problems of access to recorded knowledge, the problems that libraries are intended to solve, and the forces that are changing current concepts of library services. It encourages a critical view of present libraries and library practices and holds that educational programs should look more toward career-long professional development than just toward the student's first professional position. Library schools differ in their relative emphases on these various goals and viewpoints. Though all objectives stated above are important, it is difficult to do justice to all of them in a program that lasts only one academic year, as is the case with most master's degree programs. A few schools, however, offer master's programs that are longer than one year; two-year programs seem to be attracting increasing attention. Some library schools offer the Ph.D. degree and/or a Certificate of Advanced Studies in addition to the master's degree.

Automation and computer technology have become of critical importance to libraries and to librarianship; most schools have introduced some aspect of computer studies into their curriculum. Some schools have developed information science programs either as integral or as somewhat independent parts of the study of librarianship. These programs usually include computer-related studies. A few schools have adopted the name "information science," while others with similar commitments have considered librarianship sufficiently broad to include such newer studies without a change in name.

Irrespective of the particular approach taken, or the name given it, the emphasis and depth of these programs vary widely among different library schools. This variability, together with variability in the more basic views of librarianship mentioned above, underscores the importance that each prospective student should attach to a study of the catalogs or announcements of the schools under consideration and the importance of choosing a school that has goals in harmony with the student's own.

Don R. Swanson, Professor
Graduate Library School
University of Chicago

Medieval and Renaissance Studies

Medieval and Renaissance studies have emerged as coherent graduate programs over the last generation or two. Each originated with a tendency to focus in a particular area, medieval more on philosophical and religious traditions, Renaissance more on literature and the arts. But both have now become genuinely cross-disciplinary, drawing upon all of the traditional disciplines (history, literature, art history, philosophy, etc.) while making some additions of their own, such as paleography and manuscript studies.

Programs are of essentially two types. A few programs (particularly Toronto's Pontifical Institute and Notre Dame's Medieval Institute) offer graduate degrees in "medieval studies," meaning that the student must do course work and demonstrate competence across an entire range of disciplines. Most others (those at Toronto's Centre, SUNY at Binghamton, UCLA, and many more) coordinate cross-disciplinary study for degrees offered within specific departments. Such programs act as facilitators for students who wish to extend their medieval or Renaissance course work into complementary disciplines. There are advantages and disadvantages to each approach. The first is most genuinely interdisciplinary, but it could possibly put students at a disadvantage in academic institutions if no concentration in a particular area develops. The second places students firmly in a given department or discipline but may reduce the cross-disciplinary aspects in some instances to little more than "filler." The key is to find the right combination of integration and specialization.

In an age when emphasis upon the humanities as essential to the educated citizen is once again receiving attention, graduates with an interdisciplinary understanding of the foundational periods in European civilization should be in demand. In practice, demand depends much upon the existence of suitable humanities programs or of departments with an eye for the enrichment brought by historians, philosophers, and others with interdisciplinary training.

John Van Engen, Director
Medieval Institute
University of Notre Dame

Music, Dance, and Drama

Creative Arts Therapies Art therapy, dance therapy, drama therapy, and music therapy are different specializations within the creative arts therapy profession. All of the specializations share common theoretical and operational principles relating to the use of the creative process in therapy. Each specialization is represented by different national professional associations. There is a coalition of creative arts therapy associations that is working to develop the shared interests of all creative arts therapists.

Art, dance, drama, and music therapy are perceived by some graduate programs as a single field integrating different art modalities in therapeutic practice and by others as distinct disciplines. All programs, whether integrated or specialized, perceive creativity and the artistic process as inherently therapeutic. The arts, in that they involve all of the senses and different modes of expression, augment the scope of clinical programs both in terms of diagnosis and therapy. Training programs universally support the interdependent relationship of the creative arts therapist with other mental health professionals. Although individual training programs may emphasize a particular psychological theory, the field as a whole relates to the wide range of theoretical constructs that characterize the mental health field; psychoanalytic, humanistic, behavioral, holistic, etc. The clinical use of the arts in therapy is applied to all age groups, from preschoolers to the elderly, within individual, group, family, and milieu-oriented treatment programs. An increasing number of creative arts therapists are working in private practice. Clinical programs address a variety of client problems, ranging from emotional disturbance to physical and mental handicaps. The arts are also being applied to stress reduction programs and to the treatment of physical illnesses.

At the present time, there are approximately 200 institutions of higher education in the United States offering educational opportunities in creative arts therapies. Art therapy, dance therapy, and drama therapy have professional entry-level requirements for the master's degree, whereas music therapy has historically conducted professional training at the baccalaureate level. Master's-level training is available for graduates of undergraduate music therapy programs. A small number of schools will admit graduate students who do not have previous music therapy training into music therapy programs. Art therapy, dance therapy, and drama therapy place more emphasis on the importance of liberal education at the bachelor's level. Creative arts therapy course work is often included in degree programs in related clinical and educational disciplines. Psychodrama is also included in the creative arts therapies and is unique in that it has a single conceptual and philosophical structure, and training generally takes place in nonacademic institutes. Psychodrama students often receive graduate degrees in other

Creative Arts Therapies (continued)

professional disciplines. Course work in psychodrama is, however, offered in a number of creative arts therapy master's degree programs.

All programs emphasize practical clinical training, usually over the course of two years of full-time study. Most programs require undergraduate preparation in one or more artistic modalities and psychology and also require clinical experience. Although not necessary in all graduate programs, the master's thesis is emphasized in some. The field as a whole values research, which is considered to be essential for the further development of the profession. Historically, the arts in therapy have been developed in this century by people trained in the fields of art, medicine, psychology, social work, education, and religion. Ph.D.-level research has been done in the arts and therapy in these related fields, and in the future, creative arts therapy doctoral programs will be developed to serve the profession, which is in need of advanced graduate training and research.

Since the profession is in the developing stages, most creative arts therapists have created their jobs within the various sectors of health and education delivery systems in the United States and Canada and many foreign countries. This pioneering work continues today. There are opportunities for job development, especially within regions where the profession has not been established. Many find employment by first applying for positions in related disciplines and then educating employers in the clinical use of the arts.

Shaun McNiff, Professor and Dean
Institute for the Arts and Human Development
Lesley College Graduate School

Dance Dance in higher education is a relatively recent phenomenon. Consequently the majority of graduate degree programs have been established in the last fifteen years. Existing programs continue to be refined, and new programs emerge yearly. This relative newness makes the study of dance a rich, fresh, and vital experience. Programs are expanding; new career directions are being explored and defined; faculty members tend to be committed, energetic, and imaginative; and today's graduate students will be tomorrow's pioneers in dance scholarship and creative investigation. Although the prospective student must consider alternatives more carefully in a rapidly changing discipline, the intellectual opportunities and the creative rewards in this vital field more than compensate for this. Each institution represents unique values, and specific programs vary greatly, yet at the core of all programs remains the study and exploration of dance as art. Dance is a kinesthetic medium with physical, emotional, spiritual, and intellectual overtones, thus the study of dance must remain connected to visual and motional experiences. For this reason most graduate programs in dance have requirements that encourage the student to remain connected with the studio. In the exceptional programs where this is not possible, students are usually expected to enter these programs with extensive studio experience.

Graduate degree programs in dance can be clustered into two groups: those programs designed for the future artist and those designed for the future scholar, researcher, educator, or therapist. In the first cluster, the curriculum will usually focus on the development of technical skill, choreographic craft, and aesthetic point of view. Additional courses will often be available in such areas as Labanotation, teaching methodology, dance history, criticism, and dance therapy, and the course of study will usually culminate in a performance project. These programs most often grant the Master of Fine Arts degree. In the second general cluster, dance is studied as a phenomenon. The curriculum will focus either on teaching, therapy, production, or administration as applied disciplines or on research methodology and subject-intensive courses that will lead to investigative questioning about the nature of dance. This program cluster will usually emphasize courses in dance theory and culminate in a project, thesis, or dissertation. The Master of Arts, Master of Science, Master of Education, Doctor of Philosophy, and Doctor of Education are the most commonly offered degrees for this second group of programs. It should be noted that the Master of Arts, Master of Science, and Master of Education are considered initial graduate degrees, indicating that further study is expected at the M.F.A. or doctoral level. These initial graduate programs take one to two years to complete. The Master of Fine Arts is considered a terminal degree with no expectation of further study within the university context. M.F.A. programs usually take two to three years to complete, and doctoral programs take three to five years.

Since university dance programs have historically been associated with other disciplines—most often physical education, music, or theater—dance is still often housed administratively within one or more of these programs. The location of the dance program in a school of fine and performing arts, in a school of music, or in a college of health, physical education, recreation, and dance does

Dance (continued)

not necessarily indicate the nature of the program. It is vital that the prospective student inquire about the type of degree or degrees that are offered, the curriculum that leads to that degree, and the project or thesis that will be required to complete the degree. Only with this complete information can one program be accurately compared to another. Since some programs are generalized and others are specific, it is important for the student to clarify his or her goals for graduate study and to compare those goals with the available curricula and other resources. Some important questions to ask are: Who are the faculty, and what are their strengths and areas of special expertise? How many graduate students are enrolled, and how many graduate faculty members are there? What are the library resources for dance, and what facilities are available for rehearsal and production? How vital is the dance community at the university or in the community? What are the curriculum requirements?

Dance is a growing field with career opportunities in higher education, dance therapy, dance scholarship, and performance, but the development of any career in dance requires motivation, perseverance, and talent. Few careers in dance will generate a high salary, and many jobs must be largely self-created. Dance is pursued as a profession out of a commitment to and an appreciation of the art.

John Gamble
Chair, Department of Dance
University of North Carolina at Greensboro

Drama/Theater Arts   The play, as an example of the human experience expressed through the language of the theater, is the focus of all drama/theater arts graduate programs. Equally common pedagogically is the recognition that the play, of itself, is an incomplete artistic endeavor. It was written to be performed, and that requires of the student an understanding of the crafts of theater and some skill in at least one of those crafts to be an educated person of the theater. Consequently, all graduate programs produce plays as a laboratory experience. This also serves a cultural purpose for the entire campus, but the primary reason for performing plays is to give graduate students practical experience in how to put on plays.

Programs that emphasize text analysis, criticism, theater history, theory, standard research procedures, and aesthetics while at the same time requiring some degree of competence in one of the theater crafts make up the majority of graduate departments in the United States. They are aligned with the academic approach of most other disciplines in the humanities. A research thesis is usually required, and two years of study will earn an M.A. degree. Another year of course work, usually in theater history and criticism; at least one foreign language; and a substantial research dissertation will culminate in the Ph.D. Neither the M.A. nor the Ph.D. will lead to employment as professional theater practitioners. Also, neither degree will equip a person with the skills needed to pass exams required by certain theater unions, such as the Scenic Artists.

There are other graduate programs designed to train students in the skills and crafts of the theater disciplines in an effort to prepare them for professional careers. A student is usually required to specialize in one of the following areas: acting, directing and/or stage managing, design (scenery, costumes, or lighting), playwriting, and technical production. The curriculum for each area of training is prescribed and is made up of a sequence of comprehensive courses designed to equip the student with the techniques necessary to express talent as a theater artist. Admission to such training programs is based on an audition or samples of theater work in an effort to measure talent and potential for growth as a practitioner. The course of study in such programs is two or three years and culminates in the M.F.A., which is considered a terminal degree in the areas cited above. A small number of schools also provide training in theater administration as a specialization. Study in this field involves economics, accounting, and other business practices as applied to theater. Still another area of specialization is dramatic criticism and literature for careers as critics or literary managers (also as dramaturgs) in the resident, regional theaters. This area of study emphasizes theory, criticism, aesthetics, theater history, and text analysis and is heavily focused on research, but as applied to performance needs. An offshoot of this concentration, with added training in acting or directing, is an area of study called "performance arts." Students of dramatic criticism and literature can continue for another year or two beyond the M.F.A. and earn a D.F.A. or Ph.D.

Graduates of the training programs can enter the teaching field, where the M.F.A. is often a better credential than the M.A. But most seek employment in the professional theater. Students of design are prepared to pass the union exams. Many training schools have arranged to provide Equity candidacy weeks for their acting students, allowing them to take the Equity exam. Stage managers and technicians can usually find jobs in the regional, professional theaters as can dramaturgs with less frequency. No training program,

Drama/Theater Arts (continued)

however, can guarantee employment, and this is especially the case for actors, directors, and playwrights.

> *Earle R. Gister, Associate Dean*
> *School of Drama*
> *Yale University*

Music   Those embarking on graduate study in music can normally be placed in one of two categories: students for whom a master's degree represents a polishing and completion of undergraduate studies and students for whom a master's degree is an introduction to doctoral work.

Many young performing musicians see the master's degree as an opportunity to continue their work with a valued mentor for a fifth or sixth year of collegiate study. Others take advantage of the master's degree to gain a new point of view about instrumental or vocal study by moving on to another institution (and different teachers). All young performers are aware that the jury of the Tchaikovsky competition cares as little about the academic degrees held by a candidate as does the auditioning committee of a major orchestra.

Those instrumentalists and singers who aim toward the doctoral degree in musical performance (D.M.A.) normally have a college or university teaching or administrative post as their objective. To accomplish this such musicians will, of course, wish to improve their powers as executant performers. But they will wish in addition to develop their knowledge of musical history and theory, partly because they may themselves be called upon to teach such subjects at the undergraduate level and partly because there are growing numbers who believe that "academic" and "applied" studies in music are at their best synergistic. To receive a doctoral degree in musical performance, a student will normally perform a variety of recitals and lecture recitals and will complete a series of formal papers (at some institutions a dissertation). In increasing numbers, students involved in such programs are better integrating their academic studies in performances that are different as a result. While improving their performance skills, doctoral students in performance will acquire not only the pedagogic ability to teach their performance specialty on the undergraduate level, but also a knowledge of musical coherence that will be helpful in developing the broader audience so vital for music in the balance of this century. Students who set out upon doctoral programs in composition should reflect not only on the quality of the faculty or on the situation of electronic music studios at the institutions where they matriculate, but also on the on-campus availability of skilled and interested performers willing to concern themselves with new music. Students embarking on doctoral programs in music history and theory should bring to their work a broad knowledge of and interest in music, good ears, high intelligence, and a good working knowledge of the principal Western European languages, especially German. Such students will certainly wish to take into account the availability both of a rich musical environment and of fine library facilities at the schools they attend. Students interested in pursuing graduate work in music education should be inspired not only by the love of music but by the possibility of passing along a lifelong dedication to music to those in a K–12 setting.

Robert Freeman
Director, Eastman School of Music
University of Rochester

Philosophy and Religion

Missions and Missiology Missiology is an emerging academic discipline and science that researches, records, and applies data relating to the biblical origin, history, anthropological principles and techniques, and theological base of the Christian mission. Thus missiology is a theological discipline on the one hand, involving the study of the salvation activities throughout the world geared toward bringing the kingdom of God into existence, and a social science discipline on the other, involving the impact of the Gospel message on individual men and their communities. Its task is to investigate scientifically and critically the presuppositions, motives, structures, methods, patterns of cooperation, and leadership that churches bring to their mandate.

The student involved in missiological studies must deal with such areas as the biblical perspective; the historical perspective of the expansion of Christianity worldwide; the cultural and cross-cultural perspective; the strategic perspective of world evangelization, church planting, church growth, leadership, and discipleship; linguistics and

Missions and Missiology (continued)

Bible translation; and cross-cultural education. At present, research is being carried out in all these fields of missiology. Efforts are concentrated in three primary areas: the so-called primitive areas of the world and areas where one encounters traditional societies, areas of rapid church growth, and the urban areas of the world.

Graduate study usually leads to the Master of Arts for both new recruits to missions and seasoned missionaries. The M.A. is primarily designed for basic training in mission approach and strategy as well as principles of cross-cultural communication. The Doctor of Missiology degree is designed for the field technician and international educator. The Ph.D. in intercultural studies is intended for the research professional, the mission administrator, and the university and seminary educator.

Job opportunities abound within traditional mission and Bible translation organizations. Generally speaking, apart from denominational missions, one is required to recruit backers to support fieldwork. In church-related schools, Bible institutes, Christian colleges and universities, and seminaries, teaching opportunities are open to people with credentials who are experienced in the field. Missiological preparation is useful for all kinds of cross-cultural ministries and pastoral service in cross-cultural communities.

Marvin K. Mayers, Dean
School of Intercultural Studies
Biola University

Pastoral Ministry and Counseling   This past decade has seen an unprecedented growth in the study of pastoral ministry. The major reason for this rests with a renewed impetus to understand the nature and function of pastoral ministry as belonging to every Christian by reason of baptism. Students wishing to prepare for pastoral ministry within the churches are confronted with the major issues of vocation and spiritual formation as essential factors in determining one's readiness for ministry.

Training programs are numerous and include the traditional model of seminary education, which until recently emphasized a curriculum of studies for ordained ministry. In addition to this model, there are the university-based graduate programs that offer a Master of Arts degree with a choice of emphasis in the area of pastoral ministry studies. The opportunity for this emphasis recognizes (1) the significance of the "charisms" of ministry as plural and (2) that these charisms do not exist uniquely in ordained ministry. The pluralism of charisms in the New Testament and early church history stands in strong contrast to the historical development that has tended to limit the function of "charism" to the ordained ministry.

This shift in understanding has brought with it a renewed recognition and interest in the charism of ministry recognized as service to the people of God and to human need. It includes both service to the individual in need and attention to the structures through which oppression creates human distress. This charism has been recognized in our contemporary language as the ministry of pastoral care and counseling. The ideal of pastoral counseling is central to the church's ministry of healing. It is rooted in a strong theological tradition of what it means to be church.

Graduate studies include a core of theological and biblical studies in dialogue with the field of psychology and the other social sciences. This emphasis in psychology includes an ongoing dialogue with theology so that the practice of pastoral counseling will include more than a psychoanalytic framework. Some of the contemporary writings in the field of pastoral counseling have tended to emphasize a psychological approach over a pastoral or "ecclesial" approach to pastoral counseling. At present there is a growing emphasis to restore the practice of pastoral counseling to its roots within the church's tradition of pastoral ministry.

In addition to graduate studies, students must participate in a supervised practicum that will provide them with a clinical, pastoral education experience. The practicum training programs for pastoral counseling have been certified and provide students with onging opportunities for continued growth and development in this field.

At the present time, positions in pastoral ministry and counseling appear to be dependent upon the geographical and cultural needs of the churches. Students have found positions as chaplains or pastoral counselors in church-sponsored social agencies, campus ministry programs, hospitals, outreach and care programs for the elderly, hospice work, or the many other areas where the churches seek to respond to human need.

Claire E. Lowery
Coordinator, Pastoral Ministry Program
Boston College

Philosophy   Broadly speaking, philosophy might be described as the critical study of ideas and issues. As traditionally conceived, philosophy is thought to differ from the sciences chiefly because it approaches its questions using nonempirical methods in which reflection is primary and observation and experiment are at most secondary. A number of philosophers believe, however, that there is no basic methodological or conceptual difference between philosophy and science, and that the distinction between them is to be drawn in terms of either the greater generality of philosophical questions or the relatively indirect way in which empirical data bear on them, or both. As different as these two conceptions of philosophy are, philosophers who hold one of them usually have little difficulty communicating with philosophers who hold the other; certain methods and standards, including the use of arguments to establish positions, the attempt to distinguish differences without overlooking similarities, and the appeal to principles of logic in assessing reasoning, are standard among philosophers of virtually every sort. The prevalence of these and other philosophical methods and standards does not imply, however, that there is a generally accepted definition of what philosophy is, and no definition is offered here. It is preferable, in a short space, to provide appropriate description rather than definition.

  Philosophy might also be characterized in relation to some of its typical aims. It seeks to establish standards of evidence, to create techniques for evaluating ideas and arguments, and to provide rational methods of resolving conflicts. Philosophy attempts to develop the capacity to see the world from the perspective of other individuals and other cultures, to enhance one's ability to perceive the relationships among the various fields of study, and to deepen one's sense of the meaning and varieties of human experience. As the critical study of ideas and issues, philosophy may examine concepts and views drawn from science, art, religion, politics, or any other realm. Philosophical appraisal of ideas and issues takes many forms, but philosophical studies often focus on the meaning of an idea and on its basis, coherence, and relations to other ideas. To provide a sense of the wide scope of the discipline, the traditional subfields and some of the less general fields of philosophy are sketched below.

  The broadest subfields of philosophy are most commonly taken to be logic, ethics, metaphysics, epistemology, and the history of philosophy. Logic is concerned with providing sound methods for distinguishing good from bad reasoning. Ethics takes up the meaning of our moral concepts—such as right action, obligation, and justice—and formulates principles to guide moral decisions, whether in private or public life. Metaphysics seeks basic criteria for determining what sorts of things are real and whether there are, for example, mental, physical, and abstract things (such as numbers), or just matter and energy. Epistemology is concerned with the nature and scope of knowledge: what is it to know, and what sorts of things can be known or, at least, be the objects of justified beliefs? The history of philosophy ranges over both major philosophers and entire periods in philosophy, such as the ancient, medieval, modern, nineteenth-century, and twentieth-century periods; it seeks to understand great figures, their influences, and their importance for contemporary issues.

Many branches of philosophy have grown from the traditional core areas. Philosophy of mind addresses not only the possible relations of the mental to the physical (e.g., to the brain) but also the many concepts having an essential mental element: belief, desire, emotion, feeling, sensation, passion, will, personality, and so on. Philosophy of religion attempts to understand the concept of God, including special attributes such as omniscience, omnipotence, and omnibenevolence, and to assess the various grounds people have offered to justify believing in God. Philosophy of science clarifies both the quest for scientific knowledge and the results yielded by the quest; it explores the logic of scientific evidence and the nature of scientific laws, explanations, and theories. Philosophy of art concerns the nature, appreciation, and assessment of art, including both the performing arts and painting, sculpture, and literature. Philosophy of language treats a broad spectrum of questions about language: the nature of meaning, the relations between words and things, and the various theories of language learning. Subfields related to ethics are numerous. There is, for example, political philosophy, which concerns the justification and limits of governmental control of individuals; social philosophy, which treats moral problems with large-scale social dimensions; philosophy of law, which explores what law is, what kinds of law there are, how law is or should be related to morality, and what sorts of principles should govern punishment and criminal justice in general; medical ethics, which addresses many problems arising in medical practice and medical science; and business ethics, which treats such questions as how moral obligations may conflict with the profit motive and how these conflicts may be resolved.

There are many other subfields of philosophy, and it is in the nature of philosophy as critical inquiry to develop new subfields when new directions in the quest for knowledge, or in any other area of human activity, raise new intellectual problems. Among the subfields not yet mentioned, but often taught at least as a part of

Philosophy (continued)

other courses, are inductive logic, philosophy of logic, philosophy of history, philosophy of mathematics, philosophy of medicine, philosophy of education, philosophy of feminism, philosophy of linguistics, philosophy of criticism, philosophy of culture, and philosophy of film. It should be apparent, then, that philosophy pursues questions in every dimension of inquiry. Many of these questions are not only intellectually interesting but also important in nonacademic pursuits. Moreover, the methods of critical and integrative thinking that philosophy teaches are applicable to countless problems in business, in government, in law, and in other nonteaching professions. Graduate study in philosophy, then, is not and should not be limited to those whose aim is to teach in the field.

Robert Audi
Professor of Philosophy
University of Nebraska–Lincoln

Religion   Academic programs in religion involve the study of religion and/or religious traditions in human life and culture from the perspective of the humanistic disciplines. Specific religious traditions studied include native African religions as well as the commonly known religions of the Far East and the West. Most major religion departments offer courses of study in Buddhism, Christianity, Confucianism, Hinduism, Islam, Judaism, and Taoism. Multiple methodologies learned from other humanities are employed in the study of these religious phenomena. These disciplines include anthropology, the arts, history, linguistics, phenomenology, philosophy, psychology, and sociology. All of them are brought to bear on the study of intrareligious topics that arise in such specializations as comparative religion and the history of religions or in specific foci of concerns in religion and society or religion and personality or religion and cultures as well as the study of holy scriptures and religious law, literature, liturgy, mysticism, or theory. No student can become a scholar in every topic and method of the study of religion, but most major programs will expose their students to the breadth of the field.

Norbert M. Samuelson
Associate Professor of Religion
Department of Religion
Temple University

Theology   In the broadest terms, theology is the study of religious doctrines and practices from the intramural viewpoint of the adherents of a particular religious tradition. In contrast to the academic study of religion, which admits of a neutral stance, theology is usually studied from the perspective of those committed to a particular religious belief; however, the contrast between "theology" and "religious studies" is variously understood and is sometimes more a matter of theoretical emphasis than an actual distinction.

In the United States, the study of theology tends to be primarily concerned with the Judeo-Christian religious tradition; however, attention is also given to the theological teachings of other world religions, such as Islam, Hinduism, and Buddhism. Historically, most departments of theology were originally sponsored by a particular church or religious group for the training of clergy and other ministers. In some institutions, such an affiliation and purpose continue to predominate; other departments have become interdenominational and prepare students for a variety of occupations. While the theological orientation of academic programs may vary considerably from one institution to another, most departments of theology presently include a spectrum of theological perspectives, including ecumenical and interreligious dimensions.

As an academic discipline, theology customarily includes a number of subfields. Biblical studies are concerned with the literary analysis and theological interpretation of scripture; as an academic pursuit, biblical studies require proficiency in the original biblical languages and utilize the findings of such other disciplines as archaeology, philology, and ancient history. Systematic theology is concerned with the analysis and critique of the historical development and contemporary understanding of religious doctrines; systematic theology pays special attention to such issues as the philosophical presuppositions and warrants for religious belief, the methodology employed in expressing religious doctrines, the interaction of religion and culture in doctrinal formulations, and the interpretation of religious ideas and insights within different historical-cultural contexts. Ethics or moral theology is concerned with evaluating the personal and social responsibilities that arise from religious belief; currently, the investigation of ethical issues involves a diversity of moral viewpoints and values, as well as a broad spectrum of questions—ranging from traditional concerns about personal conduct and human relations to recent problems in such diverse areas as medicine, politics, ecology, economics, technology, and nuclear disarmament. Pastoral or applied theology is concerned with the practical dimensions of religious belief; this branch of theology usually includes theological reflection and training in such

Theology (continued)

areas as pastoral counseling, ministerial leadership, group dynamics, communication arts, liturgical celebration, and community organization. In addition, departments of theology frequently offer distinctive courses that appeal to specific groups; for example, black theology considers the Afro-American religious experience, feminist theology examines the religious experience of women, and liberation theology focuses on the religious perspective of the oppressed.

In any program of theological studies, the emphasis placed on these subfields varies with the career goals of students. Some programs emphasize the more theoretical aspects of theology; students enrolled in such programs (e.g., M.A., Ph.D., and S.T.D.) usually intend to prepare themselves for positions involving teaching, research, and writing. Other programs have a more pastoral orientation; students in these programs (e.g., M.R.E., M.Div., and D.Min.) are usually preparing for ministerial positions in churches or synagogues. Such positions generally require a graduate-level degree in theology. Both types of programs are available in larger departments of theology.

John T. Ford
Associate Professor of Theology
School of Religious Studies
Catholic University of America

Political Science and Public Policy

City and Regional Planning City and regional planning is the formal process with which cities and regions determine what needs to be done for their physical growth and welfare and how they must proceed in implementing the plans and programs they choose. The field of modern city and regional planning is a rather new one in the area of professional disciplines. It developed primarily from three movements and incorporated a fourth one that came about in the field around the same time. The three movements were the efforts of social reformers in the late part of the nineteenth century to provide decent housing for the growing multitudes of low-income urban residents; the efforts of many civic leadership groups to provide more green spaces, more play areas, and some order in the physical development of cities; and the efforts of people in many professional fields to introduce to the urban conglomerations the new utility systems, reduce congestion in the streets, and increase the mobility of urban populations. The fourth movement was centered on the efforts of many city reformers to introduce a form of urban government that is characterized by accountability, sensitivity to the needs of the population, and effectiveness in achieving stated objectives.

City and regional planning has evolved from the early parts of the twentieth century primarily in response to what were perceived to be the crucial problems of the urban areas in each period. From its early emphasis on low-income housing, the field moved to an emphasis on parks and playgrounds, to another emphasis on efficient streets and utility systems, and then to an emphasis on producing a master plan of all the needs of urbanized areas. Comprehensiveness in considering the needs and all the pertinent factors and cooperation in considering all the actors involved became the trademark of American city and regional planning after World War II. In the 1960s the emphasis in the field was on increasing the scale of the operation so that entire urbanized regions were included in each case and all the actors in each action were also included. In the 1970s the emphasis returned to the enlargement of the concept of comprehensiveness by including more elements of environmental planning and an extensive array of social programs promulgated by the federal, state, or local government. In the 1980s the city and regional planners are intensively involved with all aspects of urban development, and while there is still a preponderance of public-sector positions in city and regional planning, there is also a growing utilization of planning in the private sector for both key planning and managerial tasks. Large banking enterprises, land development companies, and corporations that plan and manage large hospitals, schools, and research institutions employ planners in increasing numbers.

Although there are differences of emphasis in the field of city and regional planning concerning the most appropriate subject matter of concern in each case, there seems to be a unanimity within the field of American city and regional planning that the planning process itself should remain comprehensive in its approach, cooperative in its attitude, and continuous in its operation so that it can shift and evolve as is called for in each case. For the remaining years of this century it seems almost certain that city and regional planning will forge ahead, preparing for cities and regions the plans

City and Regional Planning (continued)

and programs they need to meet the needs of the people and the activities within their boundaries.

Dr. Anthony R. Tomazinis
Professor of City and Regional Planning
Chairman, Curriculum Committee
University of Pennsylvania

Government/Political Science The role of the state and the centrality of politics in determining that role are the concerns of the discipline of government/political science. It attempts to comprehend the ideas, behaviors, movements, institutions, processes, and policies that characterize governments and political systems.

Research in this discipline promotes an understanding of the origins and the content of political thought; the foundations of individual and mass political behavior; the organization, powers, and interrelationships of the major branches of government; and the formulation, administration, and impact of public policies. To this work political scientists bring the skills of content analysis, elite interviewing, aggregate data analysis, survey research, and a variety of quantitative methods. Their analyses draw from work in the other social sciences, including history, economics, sociology, philosophy, and psychology. On the frontier is research by scholars engaged in positive political theory, policy analysis, and public choice.

Employment following graduate education in this discipline can be both scholarly and applied. Teaching at either the secondary or the college level remains a popular occupation for political scientists. College-level teaching often includes research. Many political scientists have pursued their research beyond academe into both private and public sectors. Businesses and consulting groups recognize the value of the skills generally acquired by political scientists, particularly when their work involves government contracting. Various levels of government—local, regional, state, federal, and international—are major employers of persons with graduate education in this discipline.

Current developments indicate that strong methodological training is advisable for those who contemplate graduate study in political science/government. As questions regarding the efficacy of government activity increase, the technical skills of the policy analyst will be in greater demand. Prospective employers will seek individuals who possess both a firm grasp of the substantive elements of the discipline—political ideas, institutions, and policies—and the skills to measure the impact of government on human life.

Bruce F. Norton
Director of Political Science Programs
American University

Public Policy and Administration   The field of public policy and administration is broadly concerned with the formulation, implementation, and analysis of policies at all levels of government. As the role and functions of government continue to grow in size and complexity, the skills required to make the system function smoothly also increase. The purpose of most graduate programs in public policy and administration is to provide these skills—which include systems analysis, political economics, organization theory, statistics, and public management—in the context of the issues, problems, and institutions of the public sector. Programs are roughly divided into those that provide intensive, specialized study in a particular policy area—for example, urban policy or political economy—and those that offer a broad-based interdisciplinary curriculum. Because the structure and objectives of programs vary widely, even within each of the two broad areas, students contemplating graduate study in this field should examine their career aims before selecting a program.

The career paths of those with graduate degrees in public policy and administration (more broadly labeled "public affairs") also vary widely, ranging from elective politics to program evaluation, from support positions in the federal government to administrative positions in city government. Many students, especially those entering the job market for the first time, may expect to be "in-and-outers," moving periodically among departments, agencies, or levels of government or between public-sector and policy-relevant private-sector jobs. This flexibility stems from the fact that graduate programs in public affairs are designed to prepare graduates to function effectively in a variety of professional environments. Most curricula—especially those of interdisciplinary programs—include not only a core of problem-solving and managerial skills, but also practical application of skills and information through field research, case studies, and agency internships. This continuous exposure to the realities of government is accompanied by seminars on specific policy issues: welfare reform, toxic-waste regulation, energy conservation, national security,

Public Policy and Administration (continued)

political values and ethics, local government reform, international migration, and other topics of current interest.

Although education in public affairs is distinguished by its broadness of scope, most programs, even the most general, provide opportunities for specialization. There are, for example, numerous cooperative degree options that combine course work in public affairs with course work in law, engineering, business, foreign studies, political science, and other areas with public policy applications. Also, because most policy issues tend to fall into one of several broad categories—energy and environment, health and human services, international affairs, intergovernmental relations, foreign policy, and urban affairs—students who wish to specialize can often concentrate their course work and field experiences in their chosen areas.

The demand for professionals in the field of public policy and administration is strong, not only because government is growing but, more importantly, because the public demand for accountability and efficiency in its government is growing. In this sense, educational programs in this field play an important public service role, improving the responsiveness of government to its people and thereby improving the quality of life itself.

Max Sherman, Dean
Lyndon B. Johnson School of Public Affairs
University of Texas at Austin

Urban Studies   Since the beginning of recorded history, cities have served as breeding grounds for civilizations and have always influenced the shaping of political, economic, and social institutions. It was only during the last part of the nineteenth century, however, that urbanization as a process became a matter of social concern. The urban way of life became dominant in the developed countries and is rapidly becoming so in most other countries. While the significance of cities in relation to the development of social, economic, and political institutions has not been altered, the growing numbers and diversity of their populations as well as the liberalization of the sociopolitical systems led to a situation in which cities became more visible, not only because of their contribution to culture and civilization but also because of the nature and magnitude of their problems. In addition, in developed countries the urban way of life has become predominant in nonurbanized areas. Urban systems became complex, and, as their problems appeared to be unmanageable, the need for specialists trained to cope with the situation emerged. Therefore, the field or science of urban studies attempts to examine the nature of urban systems and the problems plaguing them. It also identifies appropriate methodologies for their management. Research in this field promotes the understanding of the origins of urban institutions and their functioning or malfunctioning, and it produces a body of knowledge and theories on urban systems.

Urban studies researchers bring to the field a diversity of backgrounds and specializations. Primarily, urban studies is an interdisciplinary field requiring knowledge and expertise in the study and management of social and physical systems. Therefore, there is a recognition that urban studies should emphasize the study of the relationship between the individual and his or her physical environment as well as the relationship to other individuals and groups. Programs offering degrees in urban studies normally reflect disciplinary origins in social sciences, but eventually their emphasis is shaped by their faculty and teaching and research resources. While many programs tend to approach the field from a generalist point of view, in reality none cover, or could cover, its breadth and depth. Therefore, curricula, while emphasizing a basic general knowledge, move rapidly to stress one or more areas of specialization. These specializations vary depending on the institution but, generally speaking, are of three categories. The first emphasizes management and administration of urban and public institutions, and the emphasis is clearly on the administration. Other programs branch into the areas of problem solving, and the emphasis is on methodologies and planning techniques. The third category stresses the study of the nature and origin of current problems, and the emphasis is clearly on theory of growth interactions and human behavior. These specializations are related to the particularities of the field through a core curriculum requiring an understanding of the history of cities and a general awareness of the components of an urban system as well as how these interact. In recent years many urban studies programs, in recognition of community needs and changes in the student pool, have enhanced their offerings in areas related to economic development and urbanization in developing countries.

Employment following training in this field can be both scholarly and applied. Until recently, the majority of Ph.D. graduates were finding jobs in teaching and research. As their numbers

Urban Studies (continued)

increase, the tendency is for many of them to serve as policy advisers or research technicians in major urban, regional, or state agencies. On the master's level, graduates are finding jobs as middle-level technicians in public and private research and consulting agencies, in social service agencies, and in planning organizations. Current development in the field indicates a growing emphasis on methodological training and competence in research techniques. Success in the field also requires a developed ability to synthesize and relate to complex systems. As cities continue to grow and resources available to them diminish, the need will arise for urban studies graduates who are trained in the understanding of the decision-making process, the assessment and development of priorities, and the development of alternative solutions.

Nohad A. Toulan, Dean
School of Urban and Public Affairs
Portland State University

Psychology

Psychology The sprawling field of psychology is so diverse that specialists in one subarea may have difficulty communicating effectively about their work with specialists in another subarea. The kinds of questions with which different psychologists deal are exceedingly varied, and methods for trying to answer them include formal experiment, systematic measurement, and controlled observation. Yet psychologists may be divided roughly into two large, partly overlapping, groups: academic or research psychologists, who teach and do scholarly research on principles of human and animal behavior, and professional or practicing psychologists, who apply what is known about behavior to the alleviation of suffering and to the enhancement of human welfare. In spite of this division, all psychologists share two significant orientations: an interest in behavior or conduct (whether of humans or animals or both and whether of an individual, a group, or people or organisms in general) and an evidential approach (that is, a concern with data, facts, and observations rather than only speculation in the absence of solid empirical evidence).

Academic or research psychology is devoted to a wide spectrum of issues that range from natural science to social science and the gray areas in between, as illustrated by such subfields as behavioral neuroscience, behavioral genetics, perception, cognition, information processing, learning, developmental psychology, psychopathology, psycholinguistics, personality, and social psychology. Fields of professional or applied psychology also cover a broad range, from human engineering (designing machinery so that humans can interact with it effectively) and other aspects of industrial and organizational psychology through consumer psychology, opinion measurement, educational psychology, and school psychology to counseling (on occupational, academic, and personal problems) and clinical psychology (including diagnosis and assessment as well as interventions, such as individual and group psychotherapy for behavioral and emotional disorders whose severity can range from mild to extreme).

Currently there appears to be an inverse relationship between how difficult it is to become accepted as a graduate student in a particular specialty in psychology and the employment opportunities for individuals trained in that specialty. In terms of the number of vacancies in graduate programs and the number of applications for those vacancies, it is, on a purely statistical basis, far harder to get accepted into a nationally accredited graduate program in clinical psychology than into a medical school, but the employment opportunities for those with a doctorate in clinical psychology continue to be promising. In most other fields in psychology, the competition, while still significant, is less severe for getting into graduate school, but the employment outlook is much less rosy, as the academic marketplace generally continues to be bleak. Yet it appears likely that there will continue to be a demand, though only a fairly modest one, for bright, well-motivated, and well-trained Ph.D.'s in all fields of psychology.

Michael Wertheimer
Department of Psychology
University of Colorado at Boulder

Clinical Psychology Clinical psychology is a form of applied psychology that emphasizes the understanding, assessment, diagnosis, and treatment of individuals in psychological distress. Like all other subdivisions of applied psychological knowledge, it has for

Clinical Psychology (continued)

its foundation the scientific methods of experimental and statistical analysis inherited from its laboratory forebears. It differs from other areas of applied psychology primarily in that the focus of attention is "personalogical," considering psychological and personality variables as they converge in individual persons. At the same time, understanding of the impact of the larger systems in which an individual operates, such as the family, the school, and other social institutions, is essential to the understanding of an individual's problems.

The most widely accepted model for training in clinical psychology today is that of the scientist-professional, who usually has earned a Ph.D. from a university psychology department and completed an internship in a clinical setting. This type of psychologist is expected to be broadly grounded in the fields of human development, psychopathology, and research. Usually the competencies necessary for clinical intervention are acquired during the internship or following the formal training. More recently, professional training programs in clinical psychology have been developed, some leading to the Doctor of Psychology degree (Psy.D.). Usually in these programs greater emphasis is placed on practitioner skills, with required areas of instruction paralleled by relevant clinical experience.

Most clinical psychologists develop competence in both diagnostics and intervention. In the first area, specific techniques range from individual interviews, psychological testing, neuropsychological evaluation, and adjunctive diagnostic procedures to concepts of systems analysis and program management. In the second area, techniques range from individual psychotherapy, group therapy, and family therapy to community consultation and education. More recently, there has been a good bit of attention focused on prevention intervention techniques. Opportunities for employment are currently quite good, particularly for individuals who wish to work in clinical settings, such as community mental health centers, state hospitals, correctional systems, and outpatient facilities. With the advent of licensing for psychologists in most states, the ability to develop a private practice in clinical psychology has grown significantly.

Jules C. Abrams
Director of the Division of Psychology
Hahnemann University

Counseling Psychology The primary goal of the field of counseling psychology is to maximize growth in three major life areas: family, work, and education. A secondary goal is early intervention to prevent major psychological stress in these areas. To meet these goals the counseling psychologist employs therapeutic and educational modalities to facilitate the individual's ability to contend effectively with a variety of life-span concerns.

Since counseling psychologists serve a wide range of clients and developmental concerns, their therapeutic training is in individual, group, marriage, and family counseling as well as in skills in the areas of careers, vocational and educational counseling and assessment, rehabilitation, and research.

Counseling psychologists also function as consultants in developing strategies for modifying institutions with which they are involved. They recognize that personal concerns are often a product of these systems impinging directly on the individual.

Employment opportunities for counseling psychologists are excellent. Graduates find employment in universities, community mental health centers, VA and medical hospitals, business and industry, private practice, schools, and a variety of service-based centers.

Richard J. Malnati, Chairperson and Professor of
Counseling Psychology
and
David J. Reynolds, Professor of Counseling Psychology
Temple University

Developmental Psychology Developmental psychology focuses on the transitions that people experience during their lifetime. These include changes in perceiving, learning, thinking, feeling, and relating to others. Most of the field covers the development of these processes during childhood, though a growing amount of attention is being devoted to development during adulthood and old age as well. One reason that so much of the emphasis is given to children's development is that there is such an impressive magnitude of changes occurring during that period. Some capabilities, such as perception, undergo their greatest changes during infancy. Others, such as language, show especially dramatic changes in the preschool period. Yet others, such as problem solving and reasoning, show large changes in early childhood and continue to do so during later childhood and adolescence.

Developmental Psychology (continued)

Most developmental psychologists study a particular aspect of development and a particular age group. The focus might be on the development of the visual system in infancy, on the development of mathematical knowledge in the early school years, or on the development of social interaction skills in adolescence. Some developmental psychologists also adopt a particular theoretical approach to their work. For example, among psychologists who study children's conceptual understanding, some are heavily influenced by Piaget's theory, others follow a learning theory, and yet others adopt information-processing approaches. Most graduate programs expose students to all of these viewpoints, though most also emphasize one or another. Two important considerations in choosing a graduate program are the number and quality of faculty members interested in the content area that the student finds most interesting and the compatibility of the theoretical ideas that are most heavily represented with the student's preferences.

Developmental psychologists study both applied and theoretical problems. This diversity is reflected in the different settings in which they are employed. A large number work in universities; most of these people focus on theoretical issues. Another large number work in government programs that deliver services to children, in toy companies, as heads of day-care and head-start centers, and in other applied settings. Still others merge their interests in children and in clinical work and become child clinical psychologists. With this large variety of occupational opportunities, it is not surprising that the job market in developmental psychology has been favorable for many years. Both university departments and other employers have been hiring large numbers of new graduates.

Robert S. Siegler
Department of Psychology
Carnegie-Mellon University

Experimental Psychology Psychologists study behavior and the factors that influence it. Experimental psychologists use experimental methods, with independent and dependent variables, to carry out their analysis.

Behavior comprises everything an individual does, whether that individual is a person or an animal. Behavior usually occurs as a continuous, smooth, well-integrated series of activities that are goal directed. Nonetheless, for analysis these behaviors are often divided into various groups, such as sensation and perception (seeing, hearing, etc.), motivation (eating, drinking, etc.), cognition (memory, problem solving, etc.), and motor action (reflexes, skilled athletics, etc.). The preceding list is illustrative and not exhaustive. If you can describe and measure a behavior, experimental psychology can study it.

Experimental psychology also investigates the variables that affect behavior. Many types of variables are considered, and these may occur at different levels of analysis. Biological variables include the influence of the brain, drugs, and the pressures of the environment in which an individual lives. Cognitive variables include the way in which information is remembered, the influence of language on thinking, and the ways in which expectations can influence the perception and memory of an event. Behavioral variables include the number of times that an individual has been successful in making a particular response, the number of hours of sleep deprivation, and the amount of food eaten. Again, these examples are illustrative and not exhaustive.

The experimental method is one in which the experimenter manipulates an independent variable and observes its effects on a dependent variable. The independent variable is called that because it is not under the control of the individual being tested. Rather, it is manipulated by the experimenter. The dependent variable *is* under the control of the individual being tested; it is the response of that individual. By analyzing the changes in dependent variables as a result of manipulation of independent variables, experimental psychologists describe the processes that are involved.

Attempts to divide disciplines into discrete categories encounter problems with boundary conditions. The same is true for the division of psychology into components. The illustrations used here provide some examples of ways in which psychologists commonly classify their activities. However, any classification scheme is subject to modification. The term "experimental" is often used in conjunction with another adjective to describe psychology, such as experimental social psychology or experimental developmental psychology. In general, a department within a university is a department of psychology, rather than a particular type of psychology. Nonetheless, departments specialize in the types of information they teach. Consequently, an understanding of the relative emphasis of a department should help students decide which department and which university is most appropriate.

Training in experimental psychology can be applied in any setting in which understanding the behavior of other individuals is

Experimental Psychology (continued)

helpful. The principles of experimental psychology are useful in such applied settings as social work, behavioral medicine, interactions of people and machines, and management. Students who wish to pursue graduate work in psychology will find that emphasis in experimental psychology provides excellent background.

David S. Olton, Chairman
Department of Psychology
Johns Hopkins University

Industrial and Organizational Psychology Industrial and organizational (I/O) psychology is both a field of scientific inquiry within the discipline of psychology and an area of action research and application of psychological knowledge to solving problems of human behavior and interaction in organizational settings. Organizational psychology is a relatively new field of professional interest and specialization, having emerged in the last few decades in part out of the more narrow fields of industrial and personnel psychology. Contemporary organizational psychology is concerned with the behavior and social-psychological situation of people in organizations, the relationship between the individual and his or her work group and organization, the structure and functioning of human organizations, and organization-environment relations.

Traditionally, industrial psychology focused mainly on personnel selection, training, and placement; on personnel testing and performance evaluation; and on problems of employee productivity, absenteeism, and turnover. In addition, it has been concerned with the assessment of employee aptitudes, interests, motivation, and attitudes; with labor relations; and with problems of supervision, management, and leadership in industrial and manufacturing organizations. Eventually, however, interest in the study of these phenomena was extended to all types of organizations, both profit and nonprofit in both the public and private sectors, including business firms, hospitals, schools, labor unions, government agencies, insurance companies, military organizations, and professional associations. Equally important, research interests have been broadened to encompass the study of all aspects of organizational behavior at the individual, group, and total organization (system) levels.

Currently, the research interests of organizational and industrial psychology include problems of human relations and human resources; job satisfaction; employee motivation, incentives, and rewards; the meaning of work; member participation in decision making and adjustment to the requirements of organization and technology; problems of coordination and control; related problems of job design, organization design, and organization development; individual and group performance; the social environment of work and quality of work life; adaptation to the external environment; and other subjects. In the study of these complex and difficult problems, organizational psychology has increasingly drawn upon knowledge not only from other fields of psychology (e.g., social psychology, motivation, learning, and personality) but also from other disciplines, especially sociology, administrative science, economics, and political science. As a consequence, it has cultivated, and to some extent relied on, a broad interdisciplinary orientation and a wide range of research methodologies. Its purpose has been to promote the generation and use of dependable knowledge, irrespective of its disciplinary source, that can help us explain human behavior and interaction in organizations at the individual, group, and total organization levels. In fact, today some of the problems mentioned above are being studied not only by I/O psychologists but also by other social and behavioral scientists who are interested in understanding the behavior of individuals in social settings or the effectiveness of human groups and organizations.

Training in I/O psychology requires graduate work. Graduate studies are generally offered either in departments of psychology or at schools of management and business. Professional specialization in this field typically requires study at the doctoral level. Doctoral programs offering specialization in I/O psychology typically train students for research and teaching careers (including teaching at schools of business) or for professional practice in nonacademic organizations. Some psychology departments offer mostly applied programs in traditional industrial or personnel psychology, while some offer more basic research- and theory-oriented programs in organizational psychology. Doctoral programs in organizational behavior at schools of management and business typically have an applied orientation, emphasize action research and the study of profit-making organizations, and prepare their students mainly for professional practice careers in such areas as personnel, human resources, management consulting, and organization development. Current demand for admission to doctoral programs in I/O psychology is both strong and growing, and the number of qualified

Industrial and Organizational Psychology (continued)

applicants well exceeds the number of students accepted at major universities.

Employment opportunities in nonacademic positions for I/O psychologists with doctoral training exceed the available supply and have been expanding at a rather rapid rate in recent years. Opportunities for academic positions in schools of management and business, where the establishment of graduate programs in organizational behavior has been proliferating, also have been excellent. Openings in psychology departments, on the other hand, have been much less numerous though still considerable. Staff growth and financial compensation have favored the business schools over psychology departments. Overall, the demand for organizational psychologists is likely to continue to increase in the foreseeable future.

Basil S. Georgopoulos, Professor and Chairman
Doctoral Program in Organizational Psychology
University of Michigan

School Psychology School psychology is a rapidly growing, dynamic area of applied psychology. As the title implies, school psychologists are well trained in the application of psychological and educational principles and technology, with their primary foundation in psychology. It is one of the four areas of applied professional psychology, which also include clinical, counseling, and industrial/ organizational psychology.

School psychologists offer a comprehensive range of psychological services, including consultation regarding mental health, behavioral, and educational problems; psychological assessment; primary and secondary prevention; individual, group, and family counseling and intervention; in-service training and organization development; program planning and evaluation; and applied research. While much of their practice is with handicapped students, school psychologists serve all members of the educational community. They work with children from birth through age 21, with their families, and with educational personnel and organizations. Training programs in school psychology vary in the emphasis they place on the development of skills in these various job functions, and prospective students are advised to ascertain the philosophical and theoretical orientation of programs to which they apply. While most programs are practitioner-oriented, some doctoral programs have an academic emphasis.

School psychology programs are housed within various administrative units, including departments of psychology and educational psychology. Training at the specialist degree level (which involves 60 semester hours of course work with a one-year internship) is generally recognized as appropriate for entry into the profession, although the doctoral degree is becoming increasingly popular. A strong undergraduate background in psychology (including child/adolescent, developmental, and abnormal psychology; learning; personality; and statistics) is usually preferred for admission.

Two national organizations represent school psychology: the National Association of School Psychologists (NASP) and Division 16 (School Psychology) of the American Psychological Association (APA). Currently, both organizations accredit training programs. NASP does so through the National Council for Accreditation of Teacher Education (NCATE) at both the specialist and doctoral levels, while APA accredits programs solely at the doctoral level. Although NASP and APA differ on issues such as training and credentialing, a continuing dialogue is taking place to resolve these differences.

School psychologists have had one of the lowest rates of unemployment in psychology in recent years. Although most are employed in educational settings, an increasing number (especially at the doctoral level) work in hospitals, community mental health centers, university-based training programs, and private practice. The employment outlook continues to be very positive in most of the country.

Joseph E. Zins, Associate Professor
School Psychology Program
University of Cincinnati

Social Psychology   Social psychology is the study of how people are affected by others and by their social environment. As such, social psychology encompasses a diverse array of basic and applied research and applications involving direct work with individuals and

Social Psychology (continued)

groups. Research in social psychology ranges from basic studies of attitude formation and decision-making processes to applied studies of problems such as the effects of racial integration on schoolchildren and the recovery of surgical patients who have received different types of information about their condition. Social psychologists also work with schools and other organizations to improve individual and group effectiveness, to evaluate programs, and to redesign physical and social environments. The underlying orientation of social psychologists is to understand relationships among individuals and their social environment.

Graduate study in social psychology is offered by departments of psychology and, in some cases, by sociology departments. Often, graduate training in social psychology is linked to training in personality theory and research. Training programs focus on theory of individual and group behavior and on research methodology, and they include study of a number of problem areas, such as intergroup relations and conflict resolution. The Ph.D. is the usual degree sought by social psychologists, although it is increasingly possible to receive a terminal master's degree. M.A. programs are often developed around subspecialties, such as organizational behavior or evaluation research. Ph.D. programs train students for careers in university teaching and for basic and applied research. Currently, graduate programs in social psychology differ in their emphasis on basic or applied research and the degree to which training is focused on preparation for academic and nonacademic careers. Programs also vary in the substantive interests of faculty (i.e., orientation to basic research and interests in specific substantive problems) and the variety of research experiences and internships available.

Social psychology developed at a rapid rate during the 1960s and 1970s as the need grew for teachers and researchers interested in individual-society relations and social change issues. This growth has leveled off but may increase in the future as academic positions again become available. In addition, an increasing number of jobs for social psychologists in applied settings are becoming available. Social psychologists are being hired to work for private industry in training, evaluation, and market research; in addition, government and organizations receiving government research funds employ social psychologists to conduct applied research. There also appears to be an increasing market for social psychologists as faculty members in schools of business and management, in medical and public health schools, and in schools of education. The broad training received by social psychologists provides considerable flexibility as employment possibilities for researchers, teachers, and practitioners evolve.

Leonard Saxe, Associate Professor
Department of Psychology
Boston University

Social Work

The broad purposes of social work are to help people cope with stress stemming from interpersonal or social problems while simultaneously enhancing society's responsiveness to those in need. It is a profession with a dual focus: on people (individuals, families, and groups) and on the environments with which they interact (social networks, organizations, and communities). Social work interventions take into account the developmental problems, life crises, and pathologies of persons along with the ways in which social situations have an impact on them. Social workers look to transactional events as sources of data on which to base their helping: the person affecting his or her environment and the environment affecting the person.

Depending on their interests, social workers may engage in clinical practice, in the development of programs and policies in service agencies, in the administration of social programs, or in social research. Graduate schools of social work require 900 hours of supervised internship and ordinarily offer students an emphasis in one of the four areas above, although some graduate schools offer a mix of these areas. Whether as clinicians, program planners, administrators, or researchers, social workers are expected to employ a rigorous methodology—collecting data on the individual or group and on the impinging environment, assessing problems, planning and enacting interventions, and evaluating outcomes. In addition to the profession's own rich tradition, social work knowledge and skill draw on psychology, sociology, political science, public health, computer science, economics, and medicine.

Students are also ordinarily called on to develop expertise in at least one social problem area or particular field of social work practice: health, mental health, drug and alcohol abuse, developmental disabilities, child welfare, corrections, family services, industrial social work, or services to the aged.

Social workers are employed in a vast array of settings, for example, mental health clinics, hospitals, psychiatric settings,

Social Work (continued)

research and development offices of government, social service units in public welfare, settlement houses, nursing homes, courts, residential treatment institutions, industry, labor unions, and even private offices. During a period of generally declining employment in 1982, the number of social work positions increased nationwide and the Department of Labor projects a further expansion of 24 percent during the remainder of the decade. Employment opportunities vary among fields of practice, with the number of positions in industry, unions, health settings, and services to the aged predicted to rise at a faster pace than in other areas. Indeed, gerontological social work has been projected by the Department of Labor to be the second of ten major growth industries by 1990.

George Brager, Professor
School of Social Work
Columbia University

Sociology, Anthropology, and Archaeology

Anthropology By definition, anthropology is the study of the human species. Conventionally, the study of anthropology has also subsumed the study of nonhuman primates and certain elements of prehistory that merge with the topical concerns of historians. When the breadth of interests these activities represent is contemplated, it can be seen that anthropology spans the life sciences, the social sciences, and the humanities. In a very real sense, its multidisciplinary roots make anthropology the quintessential liberal arts discipline. This place at the center of the liberal arts curriculum has made the study of anthropology attractive to students who have not yet arrived at a final decision concerning career goals and wish to learn as much about themselves and their culture and other cultures as possible while selecting a professional career. Historically, anthropology has also had a strong attraction for students returning to graduate study from business or professional careers. A number of leading professional anthropologists are the product of such career changes.

Anthropology is generally divided into four major subfields. These are archaeology, social/cultural anthropology, physical anthropology, and linguistics. The subfields are, in turn, subdivided into a number of major areas of interest. For instance, one archaeologist may be concerned with archival work oriented toward improved understanding of prehistory, while another archaeologist may be engaged in the excavation of the site of an American Indian village. What is shared by them is an interest in the cultural history of a human population as investigated by quite different methods. Increased awareness of the importance and urgency of preserving the material evidence of earlier cultures has stimulated public concern for the conservation of these materials for future generations. Academic interest in museum studies and cultural resource management has paralleled increased public concern, with the result that the training of archaeologists now often incorporates programs designed to satisfy this growing need. This is perhaps the fastest-growing area of academic anthropology and one that promises to provide employment opportunities in the future.

Social/cultural anthropologists study the interactions of humans as shaped by their cultures. One segment of this area of anthropological study is concerned with the nature of culture itself and with comparisons of the distinguishing features of different cultures both past and present. The role of the environment in determining the characteristics of a culture and ultimately the behavior of its members is a thread of continuity that can be found in most studies of social/cultural anthropology.

Physical anthropology subsumes topics as diverse as the study of nonhuman primate anatomy and behavior, human variation and its genetic determinants, hominid and prehominid paleontology, and human adaptability, growth, development, and aging. While many of these topics require a firm grasp of principles imbedded in the biological sciences, they share an emphasis on concern with the understanding of humans, their origins, and their relationships to other organisms that defines anthropology.

Linguistics, the study of human language, is studied by anthropologists who seek understanding of the interaction of language and culture. The role of spoken and written communication in transmitting knowledge and values across time and space is unique to our species and has had an important influence on the way in which individuals within a culture perceive themselves and their relationships with others and with the culture at large. Through the medium of ethnolinguistics and comparative linguistics, anthropologists strengthen the understanding of the factors that control and define human behavior.

It must be pointed out that each of the areas described can be pursued from the perspective of a "pure" or applied science. Applied

Anthropology (continued)

anthropology often combines the interests of two or more subfields, as occurs in the collaborative efforts designated medical anthropology, developmental anthropology, and human ecology. Since contemporary anthropology is both heterogeneous and dynamic, new combinations of interest continue to emerge, allowing the student to apply his or her talents to addressing questions arising from a broad spectrum of human experience. Finally, the synergistic nature of the four anthropological subdisciplines should be underscored. Anthropology is a holistic discipline, and to understand the origin, development, and current diversity of humankind often requires simultaneous and integrated input from all four areas of anthropological inquiry.

William A. Stini, Head
Department of Anthropology
University of Arizona

Archaeology   Archaeology is concerned with the recovery and interpretation of the material record of our past. Most of this record is not readily available and has to be extricated from fragmentary, ruined, and accumulated deposits. The tasks of archaeologists include excavation, surveying, recording, classification, and interpretation; their aims are an understanding of human activities, development, and interaction with the environment from the primitive to the highest levels. The archaeologist is a prehistorian, historian, economic and art historian, and anthropologist; to obtain the greatest possible proportion of the information embedded in the material residue of the past, the archaeologist calls upon, and must understand, the work of scientific and technical specialists (physical anthropologists, zooarchaeologists, and paleobotanists; geomorphologists and palynologists; and metallurgists, ceramologists, and practitioners of all new sciences concerned with the dating of physical evidence from the past). Archaeologists must know their history and languages when their research is set in a historical period, and they must make the best use of modern analytical and statistical techniques.

Archaeology is taught in anthropology departments (theory, methodology, American archaeology, and Old World prehistory), in classics departments (classical and preclassical Mediterranean archaeology), in history of art departments (Greek and Roman, Egyptian, Mesopotamian, Indian, Chinese, Japanese, and pre-

Columbian art and architecture), in departments of Near Eastern studies (archaeology of Western Asia and Egypt), and increasingly in departments of archaeology (with a general perspective or a concentration in specific periods and areas).

Prospective graduate students should select the program most suitable to their interests and prepare for it in college. The archaeologist who specializes in complex, literate societies needs a preparation in ancient history, ancient and modern languages, and history of art. The prehistorian and world archaeologist needs anthropology, sciences, geography, geology, and computer technology, as well as modern languages. Field training is essential; many graduate programs offer courses and practicums in excavation. The graduate programs are diverse and lead to careers in the academic world, in museums, in federal or state organizations (cultural resource management), in historic preservation, in contract and salvage archaeology, and in editorial work and publishing.

Machteld J. Mellink, Professor
Department of Classical and Near Eastern Archaeology
Bryn Mawr College

Sociology   Sociology is an academic discipline devoted to the study of human social life. Social life appears in many forms, from the interaction of two individuals to the behavior of nations and empires, and sociologists study it in all those variations. They attempt to understand how small groups and large institutions behave—what their regular patterns of action are and what the reasons are for those patterns and for deviations from those patterns.

The specific topics currently studied by many sociologists include the ways that individuals' social class positions (jobs and income) influence their life-styles, beliefs, personal relationships, and political activities; what factors are leading to the decline in birthrates in Western societies; the ways that men and women systematically deal with one another; the evolution of American metropolitan areas into new spatial and economic forms; and how different organization structures affect their efficiency and their members' loyalty. These are but a few illustrations of the hundreds of topics that sociologists study.

These issues are studied in a variety of ways: by directly observing behavior of groups, such as working in a factory in order to describe its operations; by conducting surveys, such as interviewing people about their religious beliefs; by doing historical research, such as studying the diaries of nineteenth-century people

Sociology (continued)

to see how attitudes toward family life changed; and by other techniques as well. In all cases, sociologists try to discover how and why patterns and changes occur, explaining them in terms of social factors (rather than psychological ones or historical accidents).

Practicing sociologists are employed typically in universities and colleges, although an increasing number are playing important roles in government and private industry, working there to help research and understand the social factors that both must deal with.

Claude S. Fischer, Professor
Chair, Department of Sociology
University of California, Berkeley

Women's Studies

The field of women's studies is an interdisciplinary one that focuses on the social creation and maintenance of gender: the ways in which human behavior, social roles, and feelings have been divided into appropriate male and female categories and the ways in which men and women are trained and constrained to act these out. Women's studies grew out of critical work in every discipline, as scholars first sought to add knowledge about women and, later, to reexamine the explanations of male/female difference that built on assumptions of natural, biological differences, as well as of necessary gender specialization. Anthropologists pointed out that while men and women did different work in every society, the particular work assigned to men and women varied from place to place and from one historical period to another. Economists questioned why occupational segregation existed: the segregation of women and men in the labor force and the difference in pay for men's and women's jobs. Faculty members in English literature departments recovered women writers whose work had not been included in the teaching canon; they argued both that men's imaginative experience of the world was not the same as women's and that men's criticism had been formed in appreciation of male authors and not of the women whose world they did not comprehend. Historians and sociologists pointed out the varieties of family organization and women's and men's relative positions in families, reminding us that the family is an organic and changing social entity. Political theorists and philosophers treated women's position the same as men's in evaluating the equity of any particular theory, and they also reformulated definitions of personhood and power as women's experience was incorporated into political theory. Many scholars are now developing research and theory through intensive examination of women's lives and experiences; other scholars emphasize research and theory to understand men's lives and male patterns of exclusion and dominance of women. Scholars from both perspectives work in most disciplines and programs.

As a discipline profoundly influenced by political movements on women's behalf, the field of women's studies also makes the assumption that the social differentiation of men and women allowed men greater privilege and power in all societies. The goals of the discipline, therefore, are both to understand the means by which male authority is maintained and to construct plans for social change to create more equitable societies. As a consequence, many women's studies programs require internships.

Women's studies programs usually have three distinct sets of courses: those, usually in the humanities, that focus on women's experience and comprehension of the world; those, usually in the social sciences, that examine the social institutions that channel men's and women's behavior into different activities; and those that study the influence of government policy and law on women's and men's relative positions.

As an interdisciplinary field that examines all of human culture, society, and politics, women's studies can be pursued through the combination of a number of disciplines and with a number of career goals. The most common programs in the United States are specialties in women's history within degree programs in history; specialties in counseling within counseling, social work, or graduate psychology programs; and women's literature specialties within graduate English and comparative literature departments. Women's studies programs per se offer a variety of disciplinary graduate courses on women, as well as core, integrating courses. It is possible to complete enough disciplinary course work to graduate with a Ph.D. in a traditional discipline. Other graduates work in women's organizations devoted to particular social problems such as spouse abuse, employment training, or child-care advocacy. Many graduates work in women's organizations, in advocacy groups, and in policymaking institutions.

Phyllis Palmer, Academic Director
Women's Studies Program and Policy Center
George Washington University

Interdisciplinary Humanities and Social Sciences

Humanities Traditionally the field of humanities includes all divisions of language and literature (both ancient and modern), philosophy, religion, art, music, and occasionally history. The question of whether history belongs in the humanities or the social sciences is itself a clue to what the field as a whole represents. Insofar as history studies what people have thought, written, or spoken about themselves, or about being human, it would fall within the general parameters of the humanities; insofar as it emphasizes quantitative techniques or a particular culture's development, it would seem to be a social science. The place of history is further complicated by the fact that study within all divisions of the humanities has itself been, and largely continues to be, historical—the history of movements and ideas, of artistic styles and forms, of iconographic and linguistic periods, of the developing work of a single figure.

Over the last few decades, however, other approaches have begun to compete with historical studies across the humanities. Newer theories of language and narrative as the structural systems determining all thought and expression have opened alternative research areas known generally as structuralism and poststructuralism, semiotics, hermeneutics, and so forth. Newer theories of how and why certain kinds of narratives are produced within specific eras or cultures have stimulated interest in such areas as Marxism and post-Marxism, feminism, and New Historicism. Not only have such approaches weakened the once-firm boundaries segregating the individual disciplines within the humanities, but they have also called into serious question the distinction between the humanities and the social sciences. Today the study of a particular text—literary, artistic, musical, or philosophical—frequently involves the methods and the interests of psychoanalysis, sociology, anthropology, and even political science, as well as more traditional humanities interests. A second consequence of the newer approaches is the fairly widespread shift from questions of *what* a given text, painting, or philosophical/religious system means to ones of *how* such objects mean anything at all. To this extent it could be argued that the center of humanities study is moving away from history as such and more toward the linguistic, political, and philosophical analysis of all sign systems.

Graduate programs in the humanities are designed primarily to train budding academics. In the 1970s, when academic jobs across the country were extremely scarce, graduate enrollments in humanities programs seriously declined. In the 1980s, however, enrollments are steadily increasing, as are employment prospects in the nation's colleges and universities. With these increases as well as the new areas of interdisciplinary research currently being developed, the next decade promises to be a very exciting one for all humanities programs.

A. Leigh DeNeef
Department of English
Duke University

Social Sciences   Social science programs are designed to provide interdisciplinary education for students whose needs cannot be met in traditional disciplinary departments. Social science training involves faculty from a variety of disciplines and often includes experience with ongoing research. There are three general types of studies undertaken by social science students: research on the boundaries of the social science disciplines, exploration of methodological problems, and intensive study of substantive areas.

Research on the disciplinary boundaries requires extensive work in at least two social science disciplines (e.g., history and anthropology). Students who wish to study new research questions in which there is not yet a formal curriculum can develop individualized programs.

Students interested in the methods of the social sciences need access to faculty in philosophy and mathematics as well as to methodological specialists. The rapid growth of the social sciences has resulted in different methodological assumptions, research techniques, and standard statistical conventions. Social science programs often support such studies by involving faculty from the sciences and humanities.

The growing field of policy research and the emphasis on accountability in public programs have offered a wide range of research opportunities. Social science students may select a substantive area (e.g., the health-care delivery system or the metropolis) and explore this area from the perspective of sociology, political science, geography, and economics in order to acquire a comprehensive and sophisticated understanding of the complex problems presented.

The several schools that offer programs in social science vary in their emphases on these options, the disciplines involved, and the substantive areas that are emphasized. Students applying to such

Social Sciences (continued)

programs should provide as much information as possible about their own interests, expectations, and research plans.

John Agnew
Director, Social Science Program
Maxwell School of Citizenship and Public Affairs
Syracuse University

Biological, Agricultural, and Health Sciences

Biological Sciences

Biology and Biomedical Sciences

Biology Biology, "the science of life," is a comprehensive term covering all aspects of the structure, function, development, and behavior of living organisms. Its boundaries with physical, earth and marine, and behavioral sciences are not easily defined. Considerations of the origin of life also link biology to cosmology and planetary astronomy; methodological analogies to computer science and mathematics; and the applications of biology to medicine, biological engineering, and agriculture.

The organization of biological studies varies greatly from institution to institution in a way that can be most confusing to the student not familiar with these bureaucratic niceties. At some institutions, a single department embraces most or all of the subdisciplines. Others may divide biology by taxonomic categories, e.g., zoology, botany, bacteriology, and protozoology. Still others (especially medical schools) distinguish functional subdisciplines, such as biochemistry, biophysics, anatomy, physiology, microbiology, genetics, pharmacology, pathology, immunology, and neurobiology. Elsewhere biology is organized into molecular biology, developmental biology, structural biology, and organismic and systemic biology. Increasingly, molecular genetics is providing a common thread to a degree that work in physiology may be almost indistinguishable from that in structural biology.

Some schools aid students seeking guidance through these thickets by providing a university-wide center for receiving and responding to applications for graduate study. Others leave this task to each department separately, and the student may find that he or she has missed a precious opportunity by not seeking full information on the range of opportunities available throughout the institution.

This organizational turmoil is testimony to the exciting pace of contemporary biological research and its application to every facet of human affairs.

Graduate students in biology are expected to have a good basic grounding in physics, chemistry, and mathematics, as well as curricular experience in various biological subjects depending on the

Biology (continued)

discipline. Ph.D.'s have wide-ranging job opportunities at universities, in government, and in industry, the excitement in biotechnology being only the most recent manifestation. Some students may find a broad-ranging department of biology most suited to their interests and level of training; others with a firm idea of the specialized interest will thrive in a small department that matches this precisely. Above all the student must be informed about the complexity of these various programs in order to make an appropriate choice.

Joshua Lederberg, President
Rockefeller University

Biomedical Sciences   The biomedical sciences may be considered to include all of the scientific disciplines that are represented by the academic programs and research conducted in a medical setting. The more medically oriented disciplines include anatomy, physiology, pharmacology and toxicology, pathology, reproductive biology and endocrinology, neurobiology, immunology, medical physics and nuclear medicine, and microbiology and virology. Other, more basic biomedical science disciplines include biochemistry, molecular biology, cell biology, biophysics, and biomathematics.

However, an inventory of the biomedical science disciplines does not provide a realistic view of this field, for research in any of these disciplines is rarely conducted in isolation, free from the influence of any other. The interdisciplinary nature of most biomedical research has made its assignment to disciplinary categories very difficult, if not meaningless in some cases. For example, studies in an animal model on the expression of genes that are responsible for tumor induction may involve technical and conceptual fundamentals from physiology, genetics, biochemistry, molecular biology, virology, and cell biology. While varying emphasis may be placed on different disciplines at various stages of the investigation, at any one stage the involvement of more than one discipline is readily identifiable.

In recognition of the interdisciplinary interactions that characterize biomedical research and the fundamentals that each discipline must contribute to permit successful investigations, the area of biomedical science has evolved an identity as a field that transcends the disciplines it subsumes. This evolution has consequences on the formulation of graduate education in biomedical science, in that students must be instructed in the fundamentals of several disciplines, with special concentration on the disciplines to be emphasized in their thesis research. Thus, breadth of study, which provides a core of biomedical science knowledge, and depth of study in one or more disciplines are characteristic features of graduate programs in biomedical science, regardless of whether the programs are developed within traditional disciplinary departments or by interdepartmental, interdisciplinary faculties of biomedical science.

Dr. Roger R. Hewitt, Associate Dean
Graduate School of Biomedical Sciences
University of Texas Health Science Center at Houston

Anatomy

Anatomy today is a discipline concerned not only with structure, but also with the function and development of the cells, tissues, and organs constituting the animal body. Because the anatomy department is usually at the medical school, it also has an important role to play in bridging the gap between basic and clinical sciences. Microscopic anatomy consists of studies on the structure of cells and tissues, using the light and electron microscopes. Research advances in this area have been dramatic in the past two decades. Because the practical resolution of the ordinary transmission electron microscope is better than 1 nm, molecules can be visualized and the gap between chemistry and morphology bridged. Thus, it is possible today to correlate the ultrastructure of cell organelles like mitochondria with molecular composition and function. Anatomists whose studies correlate the ultrastructure and biochemistry of cells and subcellular organelles are called cell biologists. This is a very important research area today. Cell biologists who study morphogenesis are called developmental biologists. Neuroanatomists study the structure and function of the nervous system, reproductive biologists the reproductive system, and so on. In some cases the emphasis may be on correlation of physiology with structure or on the combination

Anatomy (continued)

of experimental approaches with morphological and biochemical analytical procedures. Gross anatomy deals with structure that can be observed at the gross level, that is, with the naked eye and by dissection. Research at this level today is mainly carried out by anthropologists, some of whom are located in anatomy departments.

The largest instruments in use in anatomy departments today are the various electron microscopes. The ordinary transmission electron microscope sends a broad beam of electrons through the specimen, whereas the transmission scanning electron microscope sends a tiny roving beam across the thin specimen; deflected as well as transmitted electrons can be gathered and X-ray and energy analysis as well as visual analysis carried out. The scanning electron microscope per se produces a visual image of the reflected rather than the transmitted beam and thus can be used to scan the surface of nontransparent (thick) objects. Specialized light microscopes include the polarizing microscope, the phase contrast microscope, the phase interference (Nomarski) microscope, and the fluorescence microscope. The latter is in wide use today for visualizing fluorescent-labeled antibodies in tissues, an approach called immunohistochemistry. Radioimmune assay, immunoelectro-phoresis, optical and X-ray diffraction, freeze-etch, cell fractionation, enzyme histochemistry, organ and tissue culture, and autoradiography are some of the other techniques in widespread use in anatomy departments. One of the recent developments that is gaining use in anatomy departments is molecular biology combined with in situ hybridization for localization of mRNA in developing tissues.

Career opportunities in anatomy departments continue to be excellent because of the consistent demand for well-taught courses for first-year medical students in the areas of gross anatomy, cell biology and microscopic anatomy (histology), developmental biology (embryology), and neuroanatomy. An understanding of the structure and substructure of the human body and its development is fundamental to the pursuit of a career in medicine. These are the traditional teaching areas of the anatomy department. Anatomists, however, also teach graduate courses that emphasize research in the areas described above. Most departments offer a Ph.D. in anatomy and also participate in interdisciplinary graduate student training programs and in M.D./Ph.D. programs. Some members of anatomy faculties hold the M.D. or Ph.D. degree, but most hold the Ph.D. alone. Most anatomy graduate students seek careers in anatomy departments, but the Ph.D. degree qualifies the innovative investigator for a career in a research institution, hospital, or undergraduate biology department.

Elizabeth D. Hay, M.D., Professor and Chairperson
Department of Anatomy and Cellular Biology
Harvard Medical School

Biochemistry

Biochemistry is a study that utilizes chemistry and other physical sciences to understand all life processes and the products of such processes. The study of biochemistry, therefore, is broad in its disciplinary application and is broad in the subjects and materials on which the scientist works. The biochemist thus interacts closely with geneticists to use chemistry to understand the mechanism of genetic transmission and the mechanism of expression of genetic information. The biochemist also interacts with molecular biologists to understand how nuclear material is expressed in functional cellular components. When the cellular components are studied in the context of the entire organism, there is interaction with such biologists as physiologists and pharmacologists. Finally, principles and methods of chemistry and other physical sciences are used to investigate the products that result from biological systems, such as the food supply, energy transduction, waste disposal, and toxicants. Biochemists, because of their acquaintance with chemical tools, have been largely responsible for many recent developments in the treatment of disease and the understanding of disease processes.

Dr. Hector F. DeLuca
Steenbock Research Professor
Department of Biochemistry
University of Wisconsin–Madison

Biophysics

The interdisciplinary field of biophysics involves the application of physical techniques and the analytical methods of physics to the solution of biological problems. Biophysics has defied a precise and universal definition because of its diversity and because its

Biophysics (continued)

component areas of research receive different relative emphasis in different institutions. Biophysics departments and interdepartmental committee programs often specialize in a particular subfield of biophysical investigation, such as macromolecular structure, membrane transport, or neural function.

Although it would seem that the acknowledged field of biophysics is relatively young, its continual impact in the life sciences has been substantial: many of the important discoveries in biology have been made by biophysicists. Early biophysicists included Leonardo da Vinci, who analyzed flight mechanisms of birds; Galvani, who studied bioelectric phenomena in frog muscle; Helmholtz, with his early analysis of vision; and even Roentgen, who discovered X rays. The subfields of biophysics and areas in which biophysicists have made important contributions to the life sciences include molecular biophysics, with emphasis upon the structures and interactions of biological macromolecules; genetic fine structure; photobiology, including photosynthesis; radiation biology; bioenergetics; membrane structure and transport phenomena; contractile mechanisms and muscle function; the structure and ultrastructure of the cell; nerve function and sensory biophysics; mathematical modeling of biological processes; nonequilibrium thermodynamics; and bioelectric phenomena. However, it is not the particular biological system or technology that is important so much as the background and scientific attitude of the investigator. The biophysicist, like other life scientists, devotes his attention to solving biological problems, but his training is such that he can speak the language of the physicist and the physical chemist. He thus fulfills an important role in communicating across the boundaries of the traditional disciplines. The arbitrary distinctions between the fields of physics, chemistry, and biology are blurred in the realm of biophysics, and the relationships between biophysics, biochemistry, and molecular biology or physiology are interwoven.

Specialization in biophysical science generally occurs at the graduate and/or postdoctoral level. Biophysics students usually begin their careers with a solid grounding in undergraduate mathematics, physics, and physical chemistry. Their focus on research problems in biology develops at a later time. It is more difficult, although not impossible, to attempt the reverse.

Many trained biophysicists choose academic careers in departments of biological sciences in universities. However, research institutes and the chemical and drug companies also offer positions for researchers with the unique cross-disciplinary training of the biophysicist. As with other fields in the life sciences, the credentials for employment depend as much or more on the actual evidence of creative research productivity as on the particular designation of the graduate degree. Some specialized areas for employment exist in biophysics. Within radiation biology there are jobs for people trained in health physics, which involves the assessment of radiation hazards. Another specialized area is medical instrumentation and bioengineering. However, biophysics is much more than the use of sophisticated instrumentation. It may involve the creative development and application of instrumentation to solve problems. A promising new area of medical biophysics is acoustic imaging, in which sound waves are used to probe biological structure.

Dr. Robert D. Simoni
Professor and Chairman, Department of Biological Sciences
Director, Biophysics Program
Stanford University

Biotechnology

Biotechnology involves the application of biological principles to produce useful products or understanding of biological processes that may subsequently lead to the production of useful products.

Particular areas of research where an education in biotechnology is useful include genetic engineering, protein engineering, applied microbiology, biochemical engineering, mammalian cell technology, applied enzymology, biomaterials, and drug delivery systems. The understanding of these areas either individually or in concert is important to biotechnology.

The biological sciences, chemistry, and chemical engineering are of great importance in the study of biotechnology. An integrated approach to the study of these disciplines is essential for a scientist if he or she is to have a broad understanding of biotechnology and biotechnological processes.

Biotechnology is a profession that can result in revolutionary changes in the types of products available and in enabling new processes to exist. It is now possible to make many novel pharmaceuticals and specialty chemicals, to re-engineer cells to acquire new functions and properties. Biotechnology will have an impact on many areas of science and technology. Areas it has already impacted include health care, personal care, veterinary applications, chemical and food industries, and many others.

Biotechnology (continued)

The challenges of the biotechnologist are great, and the development of strong interdisciplinary skills becomes critical in trying to solve such diverse problems as are necessary in developing new products. In particular, it becomes critical in biotechnology to be able to re-engineer organisms using gene-cloning techniques, to determine how best to grow those organisms, to separate the products or enzymes that organism produces, and to stablize and deliver those products in an appropriate manner. As an educational discipline, biotechnology is just beginning in many universities. The design of appropriate programs and courses will be critical to the future of this important field.

Robert S. Langer
Professor of Biochemical Engineering
Department of Applied Biological Sciences
Massachusetts Institute of Technology

Botany and Plant Sciences

Botany and Plant Sciences Botany, a major branch of the biological sciences dealing with the plant kingdom, is concerned with classification, environmental adaptation, evolution, functional processes, plant diseases and their controls, and the role of plants in society. Botany is also a basic science related to applied plant sciences such as agronomy, horticulture, and forestry.

Botany offers numerous graduate programs of study because of the diverse areas of specialization. In many cases there is an overlapping of these areas, as in physiology, genetics, systematics, ecology, anatomy, morphology, paleobotany, and plant pathology. In addition there are distinctive areas of study, such as mycology, phycology, bryology, and lichenology, dealing with specialized organisms. Plant (crop) science graduate studies deal with basic and applied research of specific crop disciplines.

Modern biology has changed the scope of the traditional botanical fields. Investigations have led to important advances in cell and molecular biology. The future in these areas is exciting and should contribute greatly to plant biology. The various levels of modern biology, although unique, are often interrelated.

Because of the scope of the sciences, job opportunities for students with advanced degrees are quite diverse. A high percentage of graduates in botany and plant sciences are employed to teach and to conduct research and extension activities at universities and colleges. Others are employed by government agencies or private industry in research and administrative positions. In addition, M.S. and Ph.D. graduates find positions in federal, state, and local governments; at agricultural experiment stations; in extension services; in environmental and natural resource agencies; and in public health services. Universities, museums, botanical gardens, private consulting groups, herbaria, and nature organizations employ plant scientists in technical, administrative, and research positions. M.S. graduates often teach biology at the high school and junior college levels.

Dr. Edward J. Klos, Chairman
Department of Botany and Plant Pathology
Michigan State University

Plant Pathology   Plant pathology is a science, based on a broad group of disciplines, in which the goals are to determine the causes of disease in plants, to understand how and why the various causal agents affect plants, and to determine how diseases can be controlled. Because the environment interacts with both the causal agent and the host plant, this relationship is often referred to as the "disease triangle," indicating the interdependence of host, pathogen, and environment.

The causal agents of plant diseases include fungi, bacteria, "fastidious" bacteria, rickettsia-like organisms, mycoplasma-like organisms, spiroplasmas, parasitic higher plants, viruses, viroids, nematodes, protozoa, and many nonbiological factors. Among the latter are air pollutants; an excess, lack, or imbalance of nutrients; and certain deleterious environmental factors.

Academic backgrounds of plant pathologists may vary but will usually include a basic knowledge of chemistry, physics, mathematics, botany, plant physiology, genetics, mycology, virology, bacteriology, biochemistry, and soil science. Agricultural backgrounds in horticulture, agronomy, and forestry are also valuable. In some specialized fields of plant pathology students may need to seek advanced expertise in one or more of the fields mentioned. For instance, the part of plant pathology that seeks to understand how a causal agent affects the plant often requires a high

Plant Pathology (continued)

level of knowledge in plant physiology, biochemistry, and molecular biology. The part that seeks to understand epidemiology requires an advanced understanding of mathematics, statistics, and computer technology. Molecular biology and genetic engineering have contributed to fundamental concepts on the effects of pathogens on hosts and are accordingly being emphasized currently.

The ultimate goal of plant pathology is to control diseases. However, the rationale for improving the efficiency of control methodology is through more basic research on the nature of the causal agents and how these agents induce disease. There is therefore a broad spectrum of research approaches ranging from the practical to the basic. The interaction of all these approaches is necessary for a thorough understanding of plant diseases and how to control them.

At the M.S. or M.A. level, positions are available as research technicians in university, governmental, and commercial laboratories; farm advisers in agricultural extension; developers and salespersons for commercially produced pesticides; and agricultural consultants in regulatory and diagnostic agencies.

Positions are available at the Ph.D. level in universities in research and teaching and/or extension; in some state colleges and universities in teaching; in the U.S. Department of Agriculture in research; in commercial companies that develop fungicides, nematicides, and bactericides; in plant-breeding companies; in companies that consult and advise agriculturists on control of diseases; in state departments of agriculture and other agencies that diagnose diseases and regulate pesticide application; and in companies involved with the genetic engineering of plants. The field of integrated pest management includes plant pathologists with expertise in team research, extension, and related disciplines.

Dr. Donald C. Erwin
Professor of Plant Pathology
University of California, Riverside

Cell and Molecular Biology

Cell Biology   Cell biology is the study of how animal and plant cells work. It is an interdisciplinary, problem-oriented field, applying cell culture, biochemical, biophysical, microscopic, genetic, and immunological techniques to answer questions about cellular structure and function. In the best laboratories a graduate student can expect to use several of these different approaches to investigate a single question. Some of the exciting problems now under investigation in cell biology are the structure, function, and biosynthesis of membranes, endocytosis and secretion, cell motility, cell-to-cell communication, biogenesis and function of organelles, packaging of DNA in chromosomes, regulation of the cell cycle, and nuclear-cytoplasmic transport. Cell biologists are attempting to determine the mechanisms of these cellular functions at the molecular level.

The study of cell biology encompasses and unites the fields of biochemistry, molecular biology, physiology, and structural biology. An important trend in the field is the elucidation of normal cellular functions through studies on the pathogenesis of human diseases. Graduates with interdisciplinary training in cell biology can qualify for positions in cell biology as well as many traditional academic departments, including biology, biochemistry, anatomy, zoology, and botany. In addition, there appear to be expanding opportunities for cell biologists in the biotechnology industry.

> *Thomas D. Pollard, M.D., Professor and Director*
> *Department of Cell Biology and Anatomy*
> *Graduate Program in Biochemistry, Cellular and*
> *Molecular Biology*
> *Johns Hopkins Medical School*

Molecular Biology Molecular biology developed originally in response to the need for the systematic study of the molecular and structural basis for the storage, modification, transmission, and expression of genetic information. With time, however, this approach to structure and function as it pertained to DNA and chromatin was extended to the macromolecular systems, which provide the basis for structure and function in cell organelles other than the nucleus. Today's molecular biology curriculum finds students examining the relation of molecular domain organization in membranes to signal transduction and immune reactions, or the relation of the molecular organization of mitochondria and

Molecular Biology (continued)

chloroplasts to energy transduction and thermodynamics, or the macromolecular organization of hormone receptors in relation to gene expression. Thus, molecular biology has increasingly taken unto itself the general study of the relationship between macromolecular organization and cellular function.

Alongside this broadening of the boundaries of the discipline there has been an almost explosive growth of the core in the form of DNA research and technology, including sequencing, gene structure, recombinant DNA, and gene mapping and cataloging, so that today, the prospects of unraveling the fine structure of genes, of the permutations of gene sequence organization within chromosomes, and of the relations of the permutations to gene expression (transcription) are very bright. New developments in DNA recombination and cloning also presage rapid growth in our knowledge of gene programming and regulation. Areas such as receptor structure and function, studied from the level of gene expression to that of membrane synthesis, have gained in prominence, while the modulation of gene expression by variations in transcription and/or processing of gene sequences is now a recognized field of study.

The application of this new knowledge to the synthesis of artificial genes, to the production of defined genotypes, and to the correction of genetic deficiencies, errors, and pathologies can be expected to occur in the near future. In effect, the science of molecular biology, less than three decades old, has already produced an offspring, the infant technology of genetic engineering, and is rapidly penetrating the domain of the pharmaceutical industry in the search for agents that can predictably modulate gene expression.

The explosive growth of the field has produced a companion development, namely the high-tech biology industry based on genetic engineering, which bids fair to be the true growth industry dominating the pharmaceutical and medical fields. The industry is based on the greatly reduced time of transfer of basic research to the production of gene products. Mastery of the underlying theory and technology will give the graduate access to jobs at all levels, from manager to high-level technologist.

Dr. Robert J. Rutman
Professor of Biochemistry
University of Pennsylvania

Ecology, Environmental Biology, and Evolutionary Biology

Ecology Ecology, in its broadest sense, deals with the study of mechanisms controlling the structure and functional processes of ecological systems. This includes those mechanisms governing the abundance, persistence, and evolution of species populations, the spatial and temporal organization of species assemblages, and the interactions among the component species. Ecology especially involves research on larger landscape-scale ecosystems, such as lakes, rivers, estuarine systems, and forests, and the modifying impact of man on these systems. Ecologists, along with economists, political scientists, sociologists, and environmental engineers, frequently join forces in examining the interconnections between the diverse life-supporting natural ecosystems and technically driven agricultural and cultural and social systems.

Professional ecologists are trained through a wide variety of graduate programs, depending on the student's career plans. Training in ecology and evolutionary biology is usually available through traditional botany, zoology, and biology departments or through specialized departments of ecology and evolutionary biology. Training in ecology and the environmental sciences can be found in environmental biology departments or programs in departments and schools of environmental studies and environmental sciences. Training involving the integration of "biological" ecology and the environmental and social sciences can also be found in broad interdepartmental degree programs that make use of expertise in these disciplines. All such ecological-environmental training requires an undergraduate background in biology and the natural sciences as well as training in economics, geography, and human cultural and social systems. Most graduate students in ecological programs must also develop their quantitative skills, including computer programming, statistics, and special areas of mathematics.

Professional ecologists with the Ph.D. degree find traditional employment in universities and colleges, although these opportunities have diminished over the past few years. Federal and state environmental laboratories and government field research and management programs are a source of employment for both master's- and doctoral-level ecologists. Larger private industries have also developed environmental programs, which, together with a large number of environmental consulting agencies, provide a

Ecology (continued)

diverse source of employment opportunities for professional ecologists.

Dr. Alan E. Stiven, Chairman
Curriculum in Ecology
University of North Carolina at Chapel Hill

Environmental Biology   Environmental biology encompasses a wide array of disciplinary studies related to ecological requirements, attributes, adaptations, and survival of species, communities, and ecosystems. In the modern world, societal problems concerning pollution, human population, natural resource management, and energy require a trained cadre of professional environmental biologists for their effective solution.

Many programs in environmental biology build on traditional education in botany, zoology, entomology, and fish and wildlife biology. Related to these are somewhat newer and more synthetic disciplines that carry labels like ecology, limnology and oceanography, ecotoxicology, population genetics, and environmental science. Regardless of the name, all programs generally permit two approaches. One, delineated by environmental, geographical, or functional units, attempts to understand the biotic components of these systems. The other approach begins with individuals, populations, or species and focuses on characterization of the environmental complex that governs their growth, behavior, and reproduction. In all of these activities, the overriding concern is the continuance of sufficient environmental quality to sustain human populations at an acceptable standard in relation to the ultimate carrying capacity of the biosphere.

Different graduate schools provide different programs, depending on their locations, faculty, past history and tradition, and the general scientific and economic climate prevailing in the state, region, or nation. For most professional positions, a Ph.D. in some aspect of environmental biology is required. During periods of national economic decline, jobs in environmental fields are often in short supply. Conditions are subject to state and local situations, however, and the impacts of federal and state legislation, regulatory requirements, and rates of land-use change.

Most programs require advanced training in mathematics, statistics, and computers in addition to advanced biology. Often, exposure to formal course work in soils, geology, meteorology, chemistry, and hydrology is encouraged or required. Most programs require the successful solution of a problem through a thesis or dissertation based on original research, although nonthesis options for the master's degree are becoming increasingly available. Students should explore a variety of programs to ensure compatibility with their backgrounds, aims, and objectives.

While much rhetoric has characterized the last decade, it is still true that continuing ecosystem function is fundamental to the survival of the human race. Scientists trained in environmental biology will continue to play a key role in education, resource management, and decision making as these relate to the preservation and enhancement of environmental quality and the maintenance of the priceless biological heritage of the earth.

Dr. Robert L. Burgess, Chairman
Faculty of Environmental and Forest Biology
State University of New York
College of Environmental Science and Forestry

Evolutionary Biology   Evolutionary biology deals with the genetic determination of traits and comparative structure of the genome, patterns of genealogical relationship of organisms and phenotypic traits, and the processes that generate those relationships. Evolutionary biologists seek to understand the mechanisms that regulate the pattern and rate of evolutionary divergence within and among species. This includes the study of mechanisms of heredity, population processes that regulate the presence and abundance of genes, factors that regulate the appearance and extinction of species, and methods for determining the relationships among taxonomic groups. A knowledge of traditional comparative biology, transmission genetics, theoretical and empirical population genetics, molecular genetics, biostatistics, methods of classification, paleontology, and developmental biology all contribute to a successful foundation for the understanding and solution of evolutionary problems. On the larger scale, training in paleontology and geology are required to understand the factors behind the major features of the history of life. Because of the broad nature of evolutionary biology, students tend to specialize in one area, though an appreciation of the broader context is essential for intellectual development.

Evolutionary Biology (continued)

Evolutionary biologists are trained in a variety of graduate programs, but they find themselves most often in departments of zoology, botany, or biology or a number of departments specializing in ecology and evolutionary biology. Training in evolutionary biology requires an undergraduate background in biology, with a possible focus in biochemistry, genetics, and systematics, but a background in mathematics or statistics is also quite useful. At the graduate level, development of quantitative skills is quite important.

Evolutionary biologists usually seek employment in universities and colleges, though positions in a wide variety of private and government research laboratories are also common. Opportunities in industry are in general fairly restricted, although the statistical and mathematical skills that are often acquired by evolutionary biologists are very useful in some medical, epidemiological, and environmental applications.

Jeffrey S. Levinton
Department of Ecology and Evolution
State University of New York at Stony Brook

Entomology

Man has long been fascinated by insects and their activities. It is the competition, however, between man and insects for food and fiber resources of the world that gives rise to the historical importance of entomology. Graduate students in entomology delve into the basic areas of insect systematics, morphology, physiology, behavior, biology, ecology, population dynamics, genetics and the applied areas of biological control, chemical control, insect pathology, medical and veterinary entomology, apiculture, insecticide toxicology, host plant resistance to insects, and, more recently, integrated pest management. The basic and applied aspects are synergistic in that effective and environmentally acceptable insect pest management systems must rest on sound fundamental knowledge of the pest(s) involved. Thus, today's basic research often turns into applied research in a few years and may eventually develop into a population management tactic.

Most land-grant institutions offer M.S. and Ph.D. degrees in fundamental areas as well as the more applied aspects of plant and animal protection. Graduate training in entomology is also available in biology or zoology departments in many other universities and institutions. Since job opportunities are better for students with training in plant and animal protection than for those with training in only the more basic areas of entomology (for example, systematics, morphology, and physiology), most students are training in universities with full-fledged entomology departments.

Because of the need for trained personnel in the plant and animal protection areas, several universities are now offering degree programs (Master of Agriculture, etc.) that substitute an internship and additional courses for the usual thesis requirements.

Jerry B. Graves, Professor
Department of Entomology
Louisiana State University

Genetics and Developmental Biology

Developmental Biology Developmental biology is a broad, multidisciplinary branch of biological science concerned with the establishment, maintenance, and senescence of biological systems at all levels of organization and in all organisms—animal, plant, and microbial. It includes the major subdivisions of reproductive biology, embryology, tissue maintenance and repair, regeneration, and aging. The field of genetics, or at least certain aspects of genetics, is also included by many scholars as a subdivision of developmental biology because development is directly related to regulation of the genome and gene expression. Regardless of how it is classified, no high-quality program in developmental biology can exist without a strong component of genetics. Developmental biology shares many common interests with certain fields of medicine, such as pathology, oncology, hematology, obstetrics-gynecology, and pediatrics, because many of the same general mechanisms that operate during normal development appear to operate to produce pathologic or abnormal conditions, e.g., cancer and birth defects, to name just two. For this reason, programs in these fields sometimes include training in special aspects of developmental biology.

Because of its multidisciplinary nature, developmental biology has many areas of subspecialization, including developmental biochemistry, developmental genetics, developmental physiology, developmental morphology, developmental cell and molecular biology, and developmental neurobiology. Current work in all of these areas seeks to discover and describe the basic mechanisms of

Developmental Biology (continued)

development and to apply current knowledge to prevent or correct developmental anomalies, to increase or improve the food supply, and to furnish new products for industrial exploitation, especially in the biomedical, pharmaceutical, and food industries.

Although there has been a lessening of demand for developmental biologists in academic institutions during the past several years, employment opportunities for university and college faculty are reasonably strong. Opportunities have increased in private and government basic research laboratories as well as in industrial applied research laboratories. There appears to be an increasing demand for professional developmental biologists in biomedical and food-production facilities.

Due to the breadth and diversity of the field, no graduate program can offer comprehensive coverage of all aspects of developmental biology. Each program is highly individualistic and reflects the skills and interests of its faculty. Thus the requirements and goals of each program vary somewhat. The student should take these factors into consideration when choosing a graduate program in developmental biology.

J. Douglas Caston
Professor of Developmental Genetics and Anatomy
Case Western Reserve University

Genetics   Genetics is the study of the inheritance of characteristics from organism to organism and the mechanisms of gene function that specify these characteristics. A wide spectrum of specializations is included in this definition. At one end of the spectrum, molecular geneticists study how mutations—alterations in the nucleotide sequence in the DNA—alter the gene expression and hence physical characteristics; at the other end, population geneticists study how genes are conserved or lost in large groups of organisms and how new species arise. The range of organisms so studied is striking—bacteriophages, animal and plant viruses, bacteria, invertebrates from protozoa to fruit flies, and vertebrates from fish to human beings—although the basic concepts are quite generalized.

Current areas of activity in genetic research include the study of specific genes, using cloning techniques to determine the products and their control; the ways in which genes are put together into chromosomal arrays and the mechanisms by which chromosomes are distributed between daughter cells; inherited metabolic diseases of human beings and animals; damage to genetic material caused by environmental hazards; and the production of new, useful forms of life by genetic engineering.

Opportunities for careers in genetics are at a high point, largely because of an expanding interest in the commercial applications of gene cloning methods. In general, Ph.D.'s in genetics have tended to work in university facilities, in commercial biotechnology facilities, or in government laboratories. Well-trained students with M.S. degrees are finding positions in such areas as environmental mutagen screening programs and as technical support personnel in private and public laboratories.

Dr. Stanley A. Zahler, Professor
Dr. Peter J. Bruns, Professor
Section of Genetics and Development
Cornell University, Ithaca

Microbiological Sciences and Immunology

Bacteriology   In a strict sense, bacteriology refers only to the study of bacteria, although nearly every modern department of bacteriology also studies viruses and more complicated organisms, including eukaryotes. Thus, the term "bacteriology" is often synonymous in practice with the more general term "microbiology."

The many different types of studies that may be undertaken in a department of bacteriology range from the highly applied (e.g., industrial microbiology, bacterial ecology or epidemiology, and the microbiology of dairy products) to sophisticated studies of the molecular genetics and biochemistry of various prokaryotes or eukaryotes. The disciplines of recombinant DNA research and molecular immunology found their origins in bacteriology and are used heavily by many students of bacterial structure and function. The techniques of bacterial genetics are basic to the expanding use of recombinant DNA in universities and industry. Thus bacteriology, now a relatively old discipline, is still in a healthy state of growth.

There is considerable interest in many departments of bacteriology in use of the full array of techniques of molecular biology and immunology to study pathogenic bacteria (bacteria that cause disease in humans, animals, or plants) or ecologically crucial microorganisms such as those involved in nitrogen fixation or marine biological processes. Many fundamental problems are profitably studied in bacteria, including recombination, protein secretion,

Bacteriology (continued)

DNA-protein interactions, phase variation and genomic rearrangements, and mechanisms of transposition. We live in a world that is massively populated by bacteria, only a few of which are well understood. New uses for bacteria, as well as problems caused by bacteria, are being discovered at a rapid pace.

P. Frederick Sparling, M.D., Chairman
Department of Microbiology and Immunology
University of North Carolina at Chapel Hill

Immunology   Immunology is the study of the response to foreign (nonself) substances, whether or not their origins are extrinsic, such as viruses or bacteria, or intrinsic, such as red-cell or basement-membrane antigens or acetylcholine receptors. Immunology includes a broad sweep of activities that range from basic biochemical studies (such as definition of the structure of antibody molecules and the regulation of antibody production) to clinically related investigations, such as the study of autoimmune diseases caused by antibody to receptors or analysis of the acquired immunodeficiency syndrome. In recent years there has been much emphasis on how the immune response is genetically regulated and on the complex interactions between various types of lymphocytes—processes that may result in a protective immune response or an undesired response such as rejection of a transplanted heart or kidney. The recent structural definition of antigen receptors on T cells, the biochemical analysis of the major histocompatibility complex, and the recognition of gene rearrangements related to immune function of lymphocytes are examples of current research advances that have extensive implications in biology and medicine. Discovery of the complex array of mediators that enhance immune responses of lymphocytes as well as the appearance of regulatory (anti-idiotype) antibodies during an immune response has provided new insights into the complicated workings of the immune system. Some of this information has found direct clinical application.

Techniques of molecular genetics have been applied by immunologists, resulting in the identification of defective gene control in the synthesis of the various structural regions of the antibody molecule. In turn, this information has provided biochemists with a better understanding of the regulation and control of protein synthesis. As a result of the genetic mapping leading to a greater understanding of factors controlling synthesis of the antibody molecule, it has been possible to understand the basis for diversity of antibody molecules found in certain individuals.

As with any scientific area, the field of immunology is gradually evolving into highly specialized areas of study such as immunoglobulin structure, cellular immunology, inflammatory mediators, immunogenetics, immunoregulation, and immuno-pathology. Immunologists find professional placement in industry, research institutes, and universities. University positions are especially concentrated in medical schools; even here, immunologists may find their homes in basic science departments (microbiology, biochemistry, etc.) as well as in clinical departments (pediatrics, internal medicine, surgery, pathology, etc.).

Like many other long-standing scientific disciplines, immunology has now achieved a degree of maturation, evidenced by its diversity, the large number of immunologists in the Western world, the rapid application of basic knowledge in immunology to clinical disorders, and the high standing accorded immunology by the scientific community, one indication of which is the many scientific honors awarded to immunologists, including Nobel prizes. It is probably fair to say that the rapid growth of immunology over the past three decades is a reflection of its vigor and its acceptance by the world scientific community as an important scientific discipline.

Peter A. Ward, M.D., Professor and Chairman
Department of Pathology
University of Michigan Medical School

Medical Microbiology Microbiology and bacteriology are fundamentally related fields of study, as one can determine from the definitions presented in this section. In the strictest sense, microbiology is a somewhat broader term than bacteriology, encompassing the study of not only bacteria but also mycoplasmas, rickettsiae, chlamydiae, viruses, protozoa, and fungi. Medical microbiology also encompasses the study of these microorganisms, but with an emphasis on relevance and application to medicine. Individual programs of study may vary, depending on the area(s) of medical microbiology emphasized by a given department. However, course work generally includes offerings in basic microbiological principles (e.g., microbial physiology and metabolism, molecular genetics) as well as course offerings with a diagnostic or clinical emphasis. Such courses would include medical bacteriology,

Medical Microbiology (continued)

virology, immunology, parasitology, mycology, antimicrobial agents and chemotherapy, and pathogenic microbiology and/or infectious diseases. In addition to basic course work, some medical microbiology programs may provide formal interaction between students and clinicians—students might, for example, participate in infectious disease rounds.

Career opportunities for those with M.S. or Ph.D. degrees in medical microbiology range from employment in a clinical or industrial setting to teaching and/or research, depending on such individual factors as level of graduate education and emphasis of program of study. At present, the future for careers in medical microbiology, as in other health-related professions, appears bright for the student well educated in this field.

Richard V. Goering, Ph.D., Associate Professor
Department of Medical Microbiology
School of Medicine
Creighton University

Microbiology Modern microbiology is an extremely broad, multidisciplinary field. It arose from two separate branches of biology: the observation of microscopic life and the study of infectious disease. When the role of microbes in human and animal disease became apparent, the two branches merged. Today microbiologists study all sorts of organisms, from those that parasitize animals or plants to those whose metabolic activities are indispensable for life in our biosphere. Immunologists, who study in addition the host responses to parasitism, are usually included among microbiologists. Thus, the organisms whose study comprises the field of microbiology range from viruses with sufficient genetic material for only two or three genes to tapeworms, which can grow to several feet in length. The processes that microbiologists investigate range from gene expression at the molecular level and the biochemistry of cell surfaces to the composition of cell populations in the spleen and the role of various organisms in the biodegradation of organic compounds in the soil. Microbiologists use the techniques of genetics, chemistry, biochemistry, physiology, ecology, and pathology. They are united by their interest in the biology of the cells they study. The ability to manipulate the biology of microbial cells has been one of the most important foundations of biotechnology, much of which is applied microbiology.

Preparation for graduate work in microbiology should emphasize a strong background in the physical sciences, particularly mathematics and chemistry, together with broad training in biology. It is impossible not to specialize as a graduate student; even general microbiology is a subdiscipline within the field. Thus, breadth in biology should be acquired as early as possible. In choosing a graduate program a student should bear in mind that a department may be strong in one area and not in another; thus care should be taken to choose a program whose strengths match the student's interests.

The employment opportunities for microbiologists are varied, ranging across the fields of academia, health care, industry, and government. An M.S. degree prepares students for technical work in hospitals and in laboratories of all kinds and (with appropriate certification) for secondary school teaching. Often it is also a useful, although not essential, first step toward a Ph.D.

The recent surge of interest in biotechnology has greatly increased the number of opportunities available to those holding a Ph.D. in microbiology. Although molecular biology has been most widely publicized, numerous opportunities are available in industry and academia for immunologists, microbial physiologists and ecologists, general microbiologists, and virologists, as well as geneticists and molecular biologists. Governmental opportunities are also available, at both state and federal levels. It seems clear that, for the foreseeable future, microbiology and the techniques developed in the discipline will continue to be extremely important in solving both basic problems and practical problems in biology.

Dr. Paul T. Magee, Professor and Chairman
Department of Microbiology and Public Health
Michigan State University

Parasitology   Broadly defined, parasitology is a branch of ecology dealing with organisms that obtain their sustenance on or within another organism. In general practice, the study of parasitology, the interests of its scientific societies, and the published articles in journals of parasitology indicate that it is a branch of zoology, i.e., animal parasitology. Thus, parasitologists have focused their investigations on host-parasite relationships of protozoa, helminths,

Parasitology (continued)

and arthropods. In the context of parasitology, arthropods have been studied as animals that may live on or within another organism, and also in their very important role of transferring protozoa and helminths from one host to another, usually serving as a habitat en route. Other invertebrates, notably mollusca, also serve as intermediate hosts in the life cycles of parasites.

Parasitology is concerned with the recognition, identification, classification, and morphology, including ultrastructure, of parasites; however, the foundation of the science is the study of the life cycle of the parasite. Life cycles may be simple or complex. Parasitologists have brought to bear on these phenomena the modern disciplines of biochemistry, immunology, physiology, genetics, entomology, and ecology. Parasitology is a science that also has made important contributions to medicine. Because many parasites induce disease within their hosts, a medical parasitology has evolved that embraces two related disciplines: pathology and epidemiology.

The broad spectrum of parasitology offers individuals a diversity of opportunities for scientific inquiry. Trained parasitologists (usually those holding doctoral degrees) find employment opportunities in a wide variety of institutional positions, including undergraduate and graduate teaching and research in universities and basic and applied research in both industrial and government health- and agriculture-oriented organizations. Many of the parasites of man are particularly prevalent in the tropical developing countries of the world because environmental conditions and sanitary facilities in these areas tend to promote the life cycles of human and animal parasites. Thus, the tropical zones offer unusual opportunities for trained parasitologists to assist in Third World solutions to many parasite-associated public health problems. Recently, many collateral disciplines have developed an intense interest in parasites as models for the study of problems in immunology, biochemistry, physiology, etc. During the past five years the fields of molecular biology and microbial genetics have become important adjuncts to the study of parasites. As detailed knowledge of the genetic apparatuses and regulatory mechanisms in parasites has accumulated, the use of biotechnology in the development of vaccines against parasites has become an important aspect of the discipline. An increasing demand in developing countries and in pharmaceutical centers, worldwide, for individuals trained in molecular genetics of parasites has emerged. Excellent opportunities exist for basic and applied research in this area by individuals holding doctoral degrees in parasitology. Upon receipt of their degrees, individuals trained in modern parasitology can find a broad base of postdoctoral positions in these various disciplines.

Dr. Lionel G. Warren
Professor and Coordinator of Graduate Studies
Parasitology Section
Department of Microbiology, Immunology and Parasitology
Louisiana State University Medical Center

Virology   Viruses are very small, simple biologic entities that infect cells. There are viruses of bacteria, plants, insects, and mammals. In short, no cellular organism appears to be exempt from virus infection. In simple terms, viruses require living cells for their multiplication. They bring into the infected cells one or more chromosomes carrying a few to perhaps as many as a hundred genes. As a consequence of the expression of these genes, the cells die or can acquire different properties. In eukaryotic organisms, viral infections can cause disease or even death through cell destruction, and in some instances cancer may result from modification of some intrinsic properties of cells.

Current interest in viruses stems from several considerations. Foremost, viruses are the cause of significant human, animal, and plant disease. Because their genomes are small, viruses are particularly useful for studies of gene organization and expression. Viruses are excellent probes for the study of cellular functions inasmuch as they use many of the cellular pathways and organelles for the synthesis of their own gene products. In recent years, the ability of viruses to transform cells from normal to malignant cancerous cells has led to the development of model systems for the study of the mechanisms and causes of cancer and to the discovery of genes that mediate the process of malignant transformation. Viruses and viral genes are increasingly being used as carriers or vectors of genetic information not only of prokaryotic cells (bacteria) but also of eukaryotic (animal) cells.

Virology is a broad field, encompassing studies on the structure and multiplication of viruses and their effects on cells. Its tools include those of molecular biology, genetics, immunology, and epidemiology. Training in virology has been and continues to be an excellent base on which to build research and teaching careers in many fields of cell and developmental biology, molecular biology, genetic engineering, oncology, etc. Opportunities for graduates

Virology (continued)

abound and will probably continue to be plentiful in the future in universities, research institutes, and industry—especially in the field of genetic engineering.

Dr. Bernard Roizman
Joseph Regenstein Distinguished Service Professor of Virology
Chairman, Department of Molecular Genetics and Cell Biology
University of Chicago

Neurobiology and Biopsychology

Biopsychology Biopsychology spans a wide range of disciplines, extending from neurochemistry up through the biology of social behavior. Its central aim is to understand the biological factors governing psychological and behavioral processes. Researchers have many perspectives on what it means to "understand" behavior. For some, this means specification of the mechanisms responsible for the observed process, defined at the chemical, hormonal, physiological, and anatomical levels. What brain systems are active during perception, learning, thinking, or behavior? What neuroanatomical pathways are involved? Which neurotransmitters are associated with these pathways? What patterns of electrophysiological activity, regional cerebral blood flow, or regional cerebral metabolism are observed? How do hormones affect and modulate neural activity? Other researchers concentrate their attention on trying to understand the historical antecedents of behavior. How and why did a particular behavior evolve? What are the genetic mechanisms controlling the development of neural and behavioral function? How do experiential factors affect the nervous system and hormonal function? To what extent are variations in neurobehavioral function among members of a species due to variations in genes, to variations in environmental experiences, or to nonadditive interactions between the two?

Depending on a student's particular interest, the study of biopsychology may be pursued in departments of psychology, biology, biochemistry, molecular biology, genetics, or, at some universities, in specialized programs in the neurosciences or biopsychology. A good undergraduate background in the natural sciences (general and organic chemistry; general biology, genetics, and developmental biology; one year of physics; and mathematics through calculus) and courses in the behavioral sciences are usually strongly recommended and are sometimes prerequisites for admission to graduate programs. Graduate study typically entails advanced courses in the physiological bases of behavior and general neuroscience courses in neuroanatomy, neurophysiology, neurochemistry, and, depending on the student's interest, neuropharmacology or psychopharmacology. Many departments or programs require a minor research project, equivalent to a master's thesis, in addition to the Ph.D. dissertation, with the student becoming involved in laboratory research during the first year of graduate study.

Job opportunities vary widely for different areas of biopsychology. Neuropsychologists who study the brain mechanisms of psychological function in people are employed in clinics and hospitals, where they assess behavioral function in brain-damaged patients, and as teachers and researchers in psychology departments. Pharmaceutical companies offer excellent research settings for neuropharmacologists or psychopharmacologists with interests in the development of new drugs for the treatment of behavioral disabilities. Government or private research laboratories employ many investigators in the neurosciences, in some cases for specific goal-oriented research, in others for basic research in an area chosen by the scientist. Most biopsychologists hold faculty positions in universities, where their time is spent in undergraduate and graduate teaching and in research.

Students who plan to pursue a graduate career in biopsychology need to know the particular subdiscipline in which their interests lie, since programs vary widely in the training offered. No single program or department is likely to encompass all the different areas within the broad field of biopsychology. Involvement in undergraduate research is an excellent method for students to identify their particular interests.

Jerre Levy, Ph.D.
Professor, Committee on Biopsychology
University of Chicago

Neurobiology Neurobiology is the study of nervous systems and how they function. It is broad in subject matter and interdisciplinary in its approach. It includes studies of nervous systems ranging in complexity from primitive nerve nets through those with more

Neurobiology (continued)

complex organization, up to and including man. It encompasses study of the development (neuroembryology), structure (neuroanatomy), chemistry (neurochemistry), and function (neurophysiology) of nervous systems and the behavior they produce (behavioral neurobiology and neuropsychology). Aspects of the closely related areas of neuroimmunology, neuroendocrinology, neuropharmacology, psychopharmacology, and experimental neuropathology form an integral part of many neurobiology programs. Given the breadth of the field and the variety of approaches used, programs vary greatly in their orientation, content, and core material. Individual programs should be assessed in accordance with the interests and career plans of the student.

Programs in neurobiology appear to have grown up in two general ways. Some of the earliest programs were developed de novo by bringing together individuals from several different subdisciplines. Other programs have arisen by expansion from a previously existing group in one of the traditional disciplines, such as biology, anatomy, physiology, psychology, or pharmacology. Thus there are programs that deal almost exclusively with simple invertebrate nervous systems; programs oriented primarily in anatomical, neurochemical, behavioral, or physiologic directions; and even programs devoted largely to the study of higher cortical functions. In general, programs that have grown out of a traditional discipline tend to maintain strength in that discipline while broadening out through the acquisition of faculty with other backgrounds. Programs that have grown up de novo are likely to be less focused as to research discipline and tend to be more problem oriented. They usually attempt to bring a variety of disciplinary approaches to bear on a particular neurobiological problem or group of problems. For example, a group interested in the visual system might include anatomists looking at synaptic organization, physiologists doing single-cell recording from nerve cells, immunocytochemists looking at the distribution of neurotransmitter-related enzymes, behavioral neurobiologists training animals in visually restricted environments, and neurochemists studying the characteristics of neurotransmitters and receptors in the visual pathway.

Career opportunities vary widely depending on the type of training one has undertaken and one's subspecialization within the field. They include positions in government laboratories, regulatory agencies, and university and medical school departments as well as positions in the pharmaceutical, pesticide, and chemical industries for those trained in neuropharmacology or neurotoxicology. Some of the more psychologically oriented programs even include training appropriate for clinical psychology positions in hospitals and clinics.

Students should base selection of a program on their area of interest and career goals as well as on their aptitude for scholarship and research. No single department offers all areas of training or all available research techniques. Experience in a neurobiology laboratory as an undergraduate is useful in developing the student's interests and in providing information that will allow selection of an appropriate program.

Robert M. Herndon, M.D.
Professor and Director
Center for Brain Research
University of Rochester

Pathology

Pathology is the discipline in medical sciences that is concerned with the study of disease and disease mechanisms. Because pathology includes features of both clinical and basic medical sciences, its province includes study of human disease and human disease mechanisms. Pathology represents one of the most multidisciplinary areas in modern medical research today. All of the conceptual and technical aspects of other disciplines may have to be understood in order to unravel mechanisms of a particular disease. In any given department of pathology, there may be an emphasis on subspecialty pathology or there may be individuals who approach the diseases of many different organ systems from a common disciplinary approach. Examples of the former include those specializing in renal pathology, cardiovascular pathology, neuropathology, pulmonary pathology, bone pathology, liver and gastrointestinal pathology, surgical pathology, and general autopsy pathology. Investigators interested in cell injury, biochemical pathology, and immunopathology frequently work with many different organ systems. Although morphological studies, from gross to light microscopic and ultrastructural, remain an important part of pathology today, morphology is no more or less important than the application of techniques and principles from physiology, biochemistry, molecular biology, and immunology. Both within a given department and among pathology departments nationally, heterogeneity in emphasis

Pathology (continued)

exists because of the broad areas of potential interest in the study of disease mechanisms.

Most departments that offer graduate programs are similar in that their primary goal is to train master's and Ph.D. candidates as independent investigators. Most diagnostic pathology, which is the clinical branch of pathology, is practiced by licensed physicians or veterinarians. Most graduate programs require basic grounding in the principles and understanding of human pathology; research concepts and training, rather than the in-depth diagnostic skills that would be necessary for residents in pathology, are then emphasized.

The full range of instrumentation and technical skills that would exist in any of the other basic science departments of anatomy, biochemistry, physiology, pharmacology, microbiology, or immunology may exist in any given department of pathology. Such varied instrumentation as transmission and scanning electron microscopes may coexist with amino acid analyzers and the most modern approaches toward recombinant DNA technology.

Career opportunities for pathology graduates remain excellent in academic, government, and industrial positions. The majority of positions available to pathology graduates involve research, since teaching positions in pathology in medical and veterinary schools are most often filled by M.D. and D.V.M. graduates who have been trained to teach clinical as well as research skills. Because of an expanding need for research-oriented pathologists—for example, in areas of toxicologic pathology in industry and government—opportunities remain excellent. Pathology graduates have broad career opportunities open to them. By supplementing Ph.D. work with postdoctoral research training, a pathology graduate may be accepted into any of the other basic science departments in a medical, veterinary, or dental school or into general university basic science departments.

Darell D. Bigner, M.D., Ph.D.
Professor of Pathology
Duke University

Pharmacology and Toxicology

Pharmacology Pharmacology is the study of the actions of chemical substances on living systems or on material derived from living systems. Historically, pharmacology evolved from pharmacognosy, therapeutics, and its inseparable companion, toxicology. Little more than a century ago the rational approach to the study of drugs was inaugurated with the classical experiments of Claude Bernard on the actions of curare at the neuromuscular junction. During the next several decades, drugs became major tools in the armamentarium of the physiologist, and much insight was gained into normal physiological processes by the use of agents that modify these events in one or more ways. In like manner, more recently, drugs and other chemical agents have proven invaluable to biochemists and molecular biologists in their investigations of molecular mechanisms in biology.

Simultaneously, pharmacologists have advanced from investigating the actions of drugs on whole animals to performing innumerable studies on isolated organs and tissues and conducting investigations of the actions of drugs at the cellular, subcellular, and molecular levels. The level of sophistication in chemical pharmacology is increasing rapidly, and direct studies of drug-receptor interactions can now be performed in many systems. In a few instances it is now possible to define the chemical features a drug must possess in order to produce specific pharmacological effects. Paul Ehrlich's prediction that "magic bullets" for the treatment of disease would someday be synthesized, based on our knowledge of chemical structure and biological activity, is in the early stages of becoming a commonplace occurrence. In the not-too-distant future, rational drug design may supplant empirical chemical structural modification and pharmacological profile screening.

Within the past two decades, the science of pharmacology has expanded further. In addition to adapting the tools and scientific advances of physiology, biochemistry, cellular and molecular biology, and physical and theoretical chemistry to elucidate the mechanisms of drug action, pharmacologists have initiated many studies on the effects of drugs on behavior and have contributed much to the modern techniques and knowledge of the experimental and clinical psychologist. The tremendous burgeoning of new and useful therapeutic agents in the treatment of cardiovascular, infectious, neurological, psychiatric, and other diseases and in the treatment of cancer has created new demands for pharmacologists who are trained in clinical medicine and therapeutics and who are capable of developing and implementing meaningful drug evaluation studies in the clinic. The increasing appreciation that drugs, industrial chemicals, and other environmental pollutants are responsible for a considerable amount of morbidity and mortality, as a consequence of their liability to produce acute and chronic

Pharmacology (continued)

toxicities and teratologic and carcinogenic effects, has created a considerable demand for basic and clinical toxicologists. Drug use and drug abuse have become so widespread that major problems of both economic and sociological significance have been created in our society. In the reasoned approach to the solution of these socioeconomic problems, the advice and counsel of trained pharmacologists will be sought.

The increasing horizons of the broadly trained pharmacologist are creating increasing demands for his or her unique talents in medical, pharmacy, and graduate schools; in undergraduate education; in the chemical and pharmaceutical industry; in research institutes; in clinical centers; and in the regulatory and policymaking agencies of government. Assuming that the public and private sectors continue their commitment to biomedical research, it is anticipated that these demands will increase in the future, providing more opportunities for graduates of pharmacology and toxicology training programs in the decades ahead.

Dr. Norman Weiner, Chairman
Department of Pharmacology
University of Colorado Health Sciences Center

Toxicology Toxicology offers the student who is fascinated by matters biological an opportunity to marry concern with the environment to laboratory work in the natural sciences. Toxicologists study the adverse effects of chemicals on living organisms and try to determine just how these effects occur. Graduate training in toxicology should guide the student toward making significant research contributions that bear upon questions of high relevance to society's problems. Any substance that is suspected of causing the organism to be less fit, whatever the mechanism of action, will be studied by the toxicologist. Some of these, such as mercury, asbestos and lead, occur naturally. Others, such as the many pesticides, herbicides, and preservatives, are the products of modern industry.

In their laboratory studies of the adverse effects of chemicals, toxicologists use techniques developed in such fields as biochemistry, molecular biology, pharmacology, physiology, immunology, and even psychology. Their major emphasis is usually on determining how the chemical exerts its biological effects; in this emphasis upon mechanisms, toxicologists resemble other biological scientists. However, some toxicologists spend time assessing the likelihood of effects in the population at large, given particular experimental results determined with lower animals. In this type of activity, they may interact with biostatisticians and epidemiologists. Because of their broad interests, toxicologists are frequently in demand by such organizations as the Environmental Protection Agency, where they may deal with regulatory questions.

Because no one person can hope to master every aspect of toxicology, a number of relatively distinct areas have appeared. The largest deals with the physiological and biochemical mechanisms involved in determining how toxic substances act. Other areas of current interest include reproductive, developmental, genetic, marine, clinical, forensic, inhalation, and neurobehavioral toxicology, with each school choosing to specialize in a small group of these.

Most applicants to toxicology programs have stressed the study of biology or chemistry (or both) as undergraduates. But it is quite possible for the engineer or psychology major to take graduate training in toxicology, given at least some background in biology and chemistry and a willingness to make up any deficiencies once in graduate school.

Each doctoral program in toxicology has a distinct flavor, imparted by its context. More programs are to be found in medical schools than anywhere else, but toxicology programs are offered in schools of pharmacy, veterinary medicine, and public health as well. In medical schools, more are in departments of pharmacology than elsewhere, but they are also located in other preclinical departments or in divisions that span several departments. If it is at all possible, the prospective student should visit the schools under serious consideration in order to assess their strengths and weaknesses.

Victor G. Laties, Ph.D.
Professor of Toxicology and Director
of the Toxicology Training Program
School of Medicine and Dentistry
University of Rochester

Physiology

Physiology concerns the mechanisms of animal function, from the level of the cell to that of the whole organism. Physiological research

Physiology (continued)

overlaps the study of biochemistry at one end and psychology at the other, and in between there exist a wide variety of challenging problems at many levels.

The following examples of problems, taken from the area of neurophysiology, exemplify the spectrum of interest. At the molecular level, one can ask how a neurotransmitter molecule binds to its membrane receptor in a way that leads to an alteration in the postsynaptic membrane's ion permeability. At the cellular level, one can ask how a limited number of neurons interact to control very simple behaviors. At the organ level, one might ask how the nutrients available to brain cells are affected by the blood and food concentrations of these substances. At the whole-animal level, one might ask how the nervous system receives and manipulates sensory information so that it correctly regulates the heart during exercise. Questions at all four levels are being asked about how animals move; how they respire; how nutrients, metabolites, and gases are circulated and regulated; how nutrients are obtained from food and used by cells; and how animal nervous systems control behavior.

Physiology departments often contain endocrinologists, anatomists, membrane biophysicists, and biochemists as well as physiologists, all interested in determining the mechanisms by which animals function. Some areas of physiology are relatively well developed (for example, the ionic basis of action potentials), while other areas are essentially unexplored (for instance, the neuronal basis of higher mental functions). Research in physiology often has indirect (or even direct) application to clinical medicine.

Many departments of physiology are associated with both the graduate school and the medical school of their university. Careers for the postdoctoral physiologist are found mainly in teaching and basic research in the academic community. In recent years, job opportunities for Ph.D.'s have been restricted, but there have consistently been positions available for those who have demonstrated a gift for original research. Medical school faculties have continued to grow.

Dr. Lawrence B. Cohen, Professor
Department of Physiology
School of Medicine
Yale University

Radiation Biology

Radiation biology as a field is very inclusive. It can be defined as studies of the actions of radiation, mostly ionizing, on molecules, cells, and whole biological organisms. These studies can range, however, from particle physics and basic interactions with biological tissue to cancer causation and treatment.

All living systems are perturbed by radiation; these perturbations are often very subtle but very important. They range from mutation to DNA strand breaks, to chromosomal aberrations, to inhibition of cell division, to cell death. Cells, in turn, have developed elaborate repair systems that respond to radiation damage; the final expression of a radiation insult is the product of the initial damage and the response of repair systems to this damage. Interpretation of the induction of the initial lesions leans more on genetic and molecular experiments. Work with whole organisms may include physiological studies as well.

In the past, radiation biological studies have helped to open up whole new areas to research in genetics, molecular and cell biology, and physiology—and they continue to do so.

Dr. Robert K. Mortimer, Professor and Chairman
Department of Biophysics and Medical Physics
University of California, Berkeley

Zoology

Marine Biology   The following definition of marine biology and the related but distinct discipline of biological oceanography is adapted largely from Publication 1492, a report of the Committee on Oceanography, Division of Earth Sciences, National Academy of Sciences.

Marine biology is concerned primarily with understanding biological principles and processes having broad applications to living things; the ocean environment is largely incidental. Various marine organisms are chosen for study for different reasons. They may be convenient objects for the particular line of research, or they may exhibit extraordinary manifestations of processes observed elsewhere, or the marine process may be an expression that differs from terrestrial or freshwater processes in such a way as to reveal

Marine Biology (continued)

broad generalizations. A good background in biological sciences, biochemistry, and physics is very important for students of marine biology.

Biological oceanography, on the other hand, is concerned primarily with marine organisms as part of the total oceanic system and with the ocean as a habitat for life. It seeks to understand the interactions of organisms with their environment and with each other. It seeks to understand how oceanic environments affect the distribution, behavior, evolution, and life processes of the organisms and how the organisms modify the environment. It is particularly concerned with the flow of energy and matter through the marine realm. Students in biological oceanography need a knowledge of basic biology and biochemistry. In addition, knowledge of various aspects of physical, chemical, and geological oceanography is very important in understanding the properties of the medium in which the organisms live.

Basil G. Nafpaktitis
Professor of Biological Sciences
University of Southern California

Zoology   Zoology focuses on interests in animal biology, covering a spectrum from traditional natural history and field biology to the mammalian biology underlying medical research. In spite of its traditional place as a subdivision of biology, zoology has, through its animal orientation, fostered some of the most relevant and exciting research being conducted today: in immunology and immunogenetics, in hormonal action, in genetic regulation in development, and in animal behavior and social structure. Many of these are concerns shared by functionally oriented departments or fields, but zoology is the focal point of all. The student of zoology usually receives broad training in the physiology, development, and evolution of animals on a comparative basis and normally is able to meet the challenge of moving from one interest to another within animal studies.

Training in zoology may lead to academic employment, where breadth may be an advantage, or to jobs in research laboratories of government agencies or private industry, e.g., drug manufacturers. Earning the Ph.D. degree is the usual means of attaining these objectives. Students competing for admission to medical or veterinary programs often find training in zoology to be a logical basic-science alternative and discover that study toward the master's degree is a realistic interim goal. Laboratory skills in cellular and physiological zoology may provide tools for various kinds of paramedical employment.

Several areas of applied biology have an animal focus; depending on the academic institution, zoology may be organizationally combined with these, may provide a background for their graduate programs, or may have interdisciplinary ties with them. Noteworthy among these applied areas are entomology, wildlife studies, and some programs in marine biology.

Dr. Peter E. Thompson, Professor
Department of Zoology
University of Georgia

Agricultural and Natural Resource Sciences

Agricultural Sciences

Agricultural Sciences The agricultural sciences include those disciplines that, traditionally, have provided man with food, fiber, and shelter. The animal and plant sciences are concerned with the production of food and fiber, and forestry and wildlife-related disciplines are concerned with materials for shelter and resources for recreation.

Some of the new areas of study and research build on a broad background in the basic sciences and include management of soil, water, and air; the quality of renewable resources (forests and waters); biomass for energy production; energy conservation and management; modeling of the growth and yield of plants; integrated pest management; agricultural climatology; agricultural mechanization; and land-use planning for food and fiber production and wildlife resources. Emerging technological advances in such areas as computer modeling, genetic engineering, and tissue culture are examples of the high-tech nature of today's agricultural sciences. Increased attention is being given to the use and regulation of foods and processed products, agricultural drugs, and pesticides and other chemicals. Other special areas not related to food and fiber, such as turfgrass, ornamental horticulture, floriculture, tobacco, recreation, and horses and other pets, are also included in the agricultural sciences.

Agricultural Sciences (continued)

Because agriculture is of prime importance to this nation's economy, standard of living, and international trade; to world peace and understanding; and to the protection and preservation of the environment and our natural resources, good career opportunities in the field of agricultural sciences are assured.

Dr. James R. Nichols, Dean
College of Agriculture and Life Sciences
Virginia Polytechnic Institute and State University

Agronomy and Soil Sciences   The disciplines of agronomy, crop science, and soil science are closely related, and the term agronomy is sometimes used to denote all three disciplines. In the narrowest sense, agronomy treats the interrelationships of crops and soils. Crop science emphasizes the breeding, ecology, genetics, and physiology of plants, which may include field crops, pastures, turfgrass, or vegetable crops. Soil science involves the chemistry, classification, conservation, fertility, genesis, microbiology, mineralogy, and physical properties of soils. Most often, soil properties are related to plant growth, engineering uses, waste disposal, land reclamation, or other environmental considerations. In the disciplines of agronomy, crop science, and soil science, plants, plant products, soils, water, and climate—all essential parts of the environment—are treated in relation to their characteristics, changes, conservation, development, and use.

The biological sciences, chemistry, geology, mathematics, and physics are of great importance in the study of agronomy and soil science. These sciences are used in the study of plants as photosynthetic organisms essential to man's existence and of soils as natural dynamic biochemical systems. They also support the development of ecologically sound practices of crop culture and soil management. Use of genetic engineering in plant breeding and in manipulation of soil organisms presents challenges and opportunities in the agronomic aspects of agricultural biotechnology.

Agronomy is the profession that feeds the world. Challenges are great in such areas as crop management for different environmental situations; crop breeding for higher yield, drought and salt tolerance, pest resistance, better quality, and photosynthetic efficiency; crops as an energy source; and soil science for basic properties of soils, fertility relationships, soil-water-air relationships, microbiological activity, and trends in soil development. Career opportunities are available in breeding, management, science, industry, environmental protection, or acquisition and dissemination of knowledge through research, teaching, or extension.

Dr. M. H. Milford, Professor
Department of Soil and Crop Sciences
Texas A&M University

Animal Sciences   Animal sciences are concerned with the breeding, husbandry (production), marketing, and reproduction of domesticated animals (livestock and poultry) and wildlife for clothing, food, power, and recreation. Areas of study in animal science are behavior, biochemistry, biotechnology, breeding and genetics, growth and development, husbandry and management (production), nutrition, physiology, and reproduction. Studies on the composition and quality of animal products, e.g., eggs, meat, milk, and wool, are carried out in animal science and related departments.

There are a variety of career opportunities for graduates at all degree levels in government and university extension work, production of animals and animal products, college and university teaching, and government, industry, and university research. Positions available in agricultural industries also include those of breeder, consultant, and nutritionist.

Dr. R. T. Berg, Dean
Faculty of Agriculture and Forestry
University of Alberta

Food Science and Technology   Food science and technology encompass both fundamental and applied science. Research in food science is concerned with the development of fundamental information concerning the chemical, physical, and biological properties and interactions of foods and food components. This information is necessary for the development of optimum processes and conditions for the maintenance of the nutritional value, safety, and quality of foods. Food technology involves the integrated application of several basic disciplines (chemistry, animal and plant biology, biochemistry, nutrition, physiology, microbiology,

237

Food Science and Technology (continued)

fermentation, engineering, economics, sociology, and psychology) to the processing, packaging, and merchandising of foods.

Dr. Richard A. Ledford, Chairman
Department of Food Science
Cornell University

Horticulture   Horticulture, by strict definition, is garden culture. It is more properly defined as the intensive, and, more recently, extensive cultivation of garden plants including fruits (pomology), vegetables (olericulture), flower crops (floriculture), and landscape and nursery crops (ornamental or landscape horticulture). Unlike the field of agronomy, which deals with a relatively few extensively grown species, horticulture deals with hundreds of species with a very wide range of environmental and cultural requirements. A student generally specializes in a crop or crops within one of these groups; more important, the student designs a program to emphasize crop physiology, crop culture and management, or plant breeding and genetics. The crop physiologist stresses training and experience in identification and solution of fundamental problems in the basic life processes of horticultural plants, including photosynthesis, respiration, flowering and fruiting, growth regulation, and nutrient relations. The specialist in crop culture and management, like the crop physiologist, is well grounded in plant physiology but is more likely to be concerned with applied cropping problems such as mineral nutrition, postharvest storage, seed production, weed control, technological applications from seeding through harvest, irrigation, temperature relations, and many others. The student of plant breeding and genetics designs a program based upon a strong background in genetics, molecular biology, and cytogenetics and supporting work in plant pathology, plant physiology, and statistics. There is a trend in horticultural graduate programs to stress interaction among the commodity groupings and discipline areas.

The major areas of research being stressed by horticulturists offer numerous opportunities for the graduate student. The maintenance, manipulation, and utilization of genetic diversity, including the use of recombinant DNA technology, molecular biology, and tissue culture; cultivar development; and classical plant breeding are the primary goals of plant breeders. The management of biological stress (resistance, tolerance, avoidance of biotic stresses, and integrated pest management) and of environmental stress (cold, drought, heat, and chemicals) is important to all the discipline areas. The proper utilization and preservation of horticultural land, integrated crop or farm management, energy efficiency, and weather-crop interactions are timely areas for research and practical application for the graduate in horticulture. The requirements for consumer acceptance, including the considerations of taste, flavor, texture, safety, and nutritional composition, together with those for reduction in losses due to spoilage, present many challenges to the horticulturist. Development of systems for management of small family-owned farms poses special challenges to the horticulturist with an interest in socioeconomic problems. For the horticulturist interested in the technology of the finished crop there are challenges in the management of crop residues and in food processing, packaging, and utilization. The above represent the ten areas designated for priority attention by the American Society for Horticultural Science in 1982.

The rewards and challenges possible in the field of horticultural science are diverse and include making contributions to feeding the world's population, preserving the environment, improving the aesthetics of the environment, supporting an important part of the economy, and adding to man's knowledge in the plant sciences. The job opportunities are likewise diverse and include the positions of plant breeder, farm manager, greenhouse manager, research scientist, research technician or technologist, extension agent or specialist, technical representative, university professor, international development specialist, research director, and technical product sales representative. Many persons with graduate degrees in horticulture achieve positions of leadership beyond the scope described herein.

In selecting a program for graduate study in horticulture, the student should attempt to at least partially narrow the field of interest prior to making contacts.

John F. Kelly, Professor and Chairperson
Department of Horticulture
Michigan State University

Natural Resource Sciences

Environmental Sciences   Environmental sciences curricula stress interdisciplinary education and research for effective resource use, resource conservation, and environmental protection. During the last three decades, a global consciousness has emerged in regard to the well-being of the environment. The finite boundaries and resources of "spaceship" Earth have been illustrated spectacularly by photographs taken on the Moon. A burgeoning human population coupled with increasing demands for food, fiber, and fuel has resulted in large-scale disturbance of the environment. Polluted air and water, land areas made derelict by mining, energy-intensive agricultural practices, the use of pesticides, large-scale industrial growth with its attendant waste products, unprecedented numbers of automobiles, networks of roadways, and expanding urbanization set the stage for the birth of environmental awareness in its positive and activist roles.

Landmark legislation (e.g., the National Environmental Policy Act of 1969, the Clean Air Amendments of 1970, the Federal Water Pollution Control Amendments of 1972, the Endangered Species Act of 1973, and the Surface Mining Control and Reclamation Act of 1977) has been enacted to guard against irrevocable decisions and irreversible damage to biological resources. However, the fulfillment of each legislative mandate poses new questions never before asked and demands new information never before collected. Solutions to these contemporary problems transcend disciplinary boundaries.

Future environmental scientists must combine a strong grounding in traditional disciplines with a keen awareness of a number of ancillary fields. Their effectiveness will be felt most in bringing about a transfer of technology from experimental to real-world situations. Such breadth precludes a rigid curriculum. A comprehensive curriculum for graduate study in environmental sciences must incorporate, within the framework of issues of environmental policy, planning, and regulation, several appropriate concentrations. These often include training in energy resources and their utilization and conservation, land use, water resources, urban environments, waste management, and environmental communication.

Each of these concentrations should be founded in both modern scientific methods and techniques and a quest for innovation within a given economic-social-political framework. Students are strongly advised to pursue at least one area of special concentration. Environmental scientists may be employed in educational and research institutions; in industry; in local, state, and federal government; and in private consulting firms.

Mohan K. Wali, Professor
State University of New York
College of Environmental Science and Forestry

Fish, Game, and Wildlife Management   Fish and wildlife management is the art of treating land and water in the regulation of wild plants and animals to maintain or increase their value to man and to help ensure a healthy environment. The management of game, the harvested species, is a subfield of wildlife management. Built on a broad background in biological sciences, with emphasis on ecology, chemistry, mathematics, social sciences, and communications, programs in fisheries and wildlife management prepare students to manage these resources by offering a broad overview of human beings' place in the ecosystem and of the impact of their actions on other living components. In-depth studies develop understanding of these effects on the ecosystem and the ability to formulate and implement techniques by which they can be modified.

Students with baccalaureate and graduate degrees have a variety of employment opportunities. Most enter public employment with local, state, and federal natural resource agencies. Jobs with government agencies include positions in law enforcement, management, research, and public relations/communications. Other graduates are privately employed by firms involved in environmental assessment, fish and wildlife propagation, and similar enterprises. Individuals who complete graduate degrees are also employed as educators and research scientists. Competition for employment in the fields of fisheries and wildlife management is very keen, with work experience often being of equal importance to the degree received.

Thomas M. Stockdale, Professor
Fisheries and Wildlife Management
School of Natural Resources
Ohio State University

Forestry   Forestry encompasses a wide array of information needs and activities. These range from growing trees to manufacturing products derived from trees. The field is also concerned with forest-

Forestry (continued)

related resources and services, such as water, wildlife, and recreational facilities. The diverse nature of forests requires a diversity of backgrounds among the professionals who must manage the soils, wildlife, water, wood, forage, and landscape. In the case of wood alone, special knowledge of growing, harvesting, processing, utilization, and marketing is needed. A special strength of the forestry profession has been its ability to integrate knowledge and techniques drawn from a variety of disciplines.

To accommodate the diverse requirements of the profession, graduate study in forest resources generally takes one of two formats: professional specialization in one or more areas covered during undergraduate training or in-depth study of one or more academic disciplines from the natural, physical, or engineering sciences in the context of forestry. In correspondence with this dichotomy, two types of degrees are awarded: professional degrees—the Master of Forestry and the Doctor of Forestry—and degrees with a greater disciplinary focus—the Master of Science and the Doctor of Philosophy. A wide array of disciplines may be included, depending on the emphasis of the program. A program in forest hydrology, for example, would have strong ties to geological sciences and engineering, while a program in forest economics would be based on general economics. Programs in wood chemistry or wood physics would draw on the resources of chemistry, chemical engineering, physics, and mechanical engineering programs. Forest ecology, silviculture, and tree physiology programs would draw heavily on basic ecology, study of soils, and plant physiology but would have a research emphasis on forests. Forest logging engineering or forest harvesting programs would apply engineering principles to the cutting and extraction of the wood crop.

To generalize, graduate studies in forestry and forest sciences encompass a broad array of disciplines. The programs are not self-contained but depend on the contributions of other scientific or professional programs at the institution at which they are offered.

Forestry is a dynamic field with many new and expanding specialties. The application of computer technology to all areas of forestry is one example of the new skills needed in forestry. Marketing of forest products, especially internationally, is also a field receiving heavy emphasis at many institutions.

Students completing graduate programs in forest resources have generally found employment possibilities reasonably good. As in all fields, there are year-to-year fluctuations related to general economic conditions. Employment opportunities have tended to be very good in the area of pulp and paper in both the private sector and educational and research institutions. Wood science and technology is generally short of adequately trained people, while general environmental fields are oversupplied. Excellent opportunities for minority students exist throughout all of forestry.

Dr. Gerard F. Schreuder
Professor of Forest Statistics and Economics
Chairman, Forest Products and Engineering
College of Forest Resources
University of Washington

Natural Resources   The term natural resources generally describes an association of several fields of science or graduate study. It is not, and should not be, defined as a field of study unto itself. Academic departments or schools using the term in their titles frequently encompass all or several of the following disciplines: forestry, wood sciences, wildlife science, fisheries and aquatic ecology, hydrology, atmospheric science, outdoor recreation, and resource economics. Rarely is soil science or geoscience included, these areas having been long established as separate disciplines. Occasionally, environmental law and engineering are included in or at least associated with natural resource programs.

Thorough preparation in math, chemistry, and physics is essential in all areas of natural resources. Fundamental training in biology is necessary in some areas. Economics and social and political science courses are frequently desirable or even essential.

Students with strong aptitude in science and an interest in natural history or the physical environment should find one of the subject disciplines of natural resources appealing and rewarding. Most of the disciplines entail extensive public contact or public involvement. Thus, the ability and willingness to work with people is essential in most areas. There are few opportunities for the recluse in natural resources science or management careers.

Job opportunities vary with the area and the economic and political climate. In the fields of forestry and wood science, private industry is the principal employer, although significant public service positions exist. The public sector offers the greatest number of positions in wildlife science, fisheries, and recreation.

Mason C. Carter, Dean
College of Agriculture
Louisiana State University

Range Science Rangelands are a diverse land type that occupies a major portion of the world's land surface and over 50 percent of the United States. Though typically construed as arid and unproductive regions, rangelands include a vast variety of environments and vegetative arrays. Any landscape that is composed of herbaceous and/or shrub species, contains one or more inherent physical limitations to its productivity (such as aridity, low soil fertility, or potentially high rates of erosion), and has a history of herbivory can be correctly included as rangeland.

As a discipline that encompasses such widely dissimilar land types, range science represents a broad scope of scientific and management endeavors. From basic studies in plant physiology to applied studies in management requirements of livestock grazing systems, range science as a research discipline defies easy categorization.

This is equally true of the various curricula and programs emphasized at universities, most notably the land-grant colleges, that offer graduate training in range science. Additionally, range science programs are housed within a variety of schools or colleges, including agriculture, forestry, and natural resources, as well as occasionally sharing departmental resources with the fields of animal science, agronomy, botany, forestry, wildlife, and land reclamation. In selecting a program, a prospective graduate student should thoroughly assess a program's orientation, the specialty areas of its faculty, the particular research facilities available, and the type of rangelands most probably encountered within that university's geographical location. From this overall assessment, potential graduate students will be better able to match a range program to their needs and career goals.

Successful candidates for an advanced degree in range science can find employment in many settings, including foreign assignments. The current focus on rangelands as a resource for meeting energy needs, recreational demands, and wildlife habitat concerns as well as a purveyor of food and fiber products has generated a host of employment opportunities. These include agricultural businesses, land resource consultant firms, land reclamation operations, and chances for self-employment. Typically, federal land resource management agencies have provided the bulk of suitable jobs; however, in many areas of the nation, this responsibility has shifted to the state, and opportunities with state departments associated with land resource management and agricultural extension are now increasing. Research with state agricultural experiment stations and federal research service centers also provides employment avenues for Ph.D. and occasionally M.S. graduates.

Range science can best be described as a conglomeration of subject areas. These areas include, but are not limited to, soil science, plant ecology, livestock management, arid-land hydrology, and wildlife management. The opportunities for the enterprising graduate student for both studies and career placement in any aspect of this economic, social, and politically important land resource discipline are impressive and extensive.

Dr. Kris Havstad, Associate Professor
Department of Animal and Range Sciences
Montana State University

Health-Care Professions

Allied Health Professions

Dental Hygiene   A dental hygienist is a licensed professional and a member of the health-care team who functions as an oral health educator, patient advocate, and practitioner promoting preventive dental care. The health services that may be rendered by a dental hygienist are regulated by state statutes and therefore vary widely from state to state.

A dental hygienist conducts patient assessments, including the health and dental history, blood pressure measurements, and intraoral and extraoral examinations; provides instruction in dental disease prevention and control; exposes dental radiographs; scales, root planes, and polishes the teeth; applies topical fluoride and pit and fissure sealants for dental caries control; takes dental impressions; and fabricates dental models and protective mouth guards. Supplementary procedures encompass a variety of expanded responsibilities.

In addition to these functions, a person with the Master of Science degree in dental hygiene may engage in dental hygiene education and administration, management, consulting, and research. Through training in specialized skills, master's graduates are prepared to assume leadership roles in improving dental hygiene care and in advancing knowledge and practice of dental hygiene.

Research in dental hygiene has focused on the organization, delivery, and evaluation of dental hygiene services; the effectiveness

Dental Hygiene (continued)

of instruction in professional and continuing education; the effectiveness of dental disease control on the oral health status of special-needs populations; the acquisition of clinical skills in dental hygiene; and oral health behaviors and oral health status. The influence of curricula on the competence and performance of dental hygiene students is of particular concern, along with mandatory continuing education requirements for dental hygiene relicensure, role delineation of the dental hygienist, and interdisciplinary approaches to dental hygiene education and practice.

Dental hygiene is a challenging and demanding profession continually evolving with new perspectives and options for study and employment.

Dental hygienists, depending on their educational background, are employed in general and specialty dental practice, elementary and secondary schools, higher education and administration, community and public health settings, dental product sales, hospitals, and research. Dental hygienists can also find employment abroad.

Michele Darby, M.S., RDH, Chairman
Department of Dental Hygiene and Dental Assisting
Old Dominion University

Medical Physics   Graduate work in medical physics in the United States is concerned primarily with the applications of physics to radiological sciences. These usually include applications of physics to the treatment of cancer with radiation therapy and radioactivity; applications of physics in nuclear medicine, with an emphasis on imaging; applications of physics in diagnostic radiology—especially in computerized tomography and imaging techniques; applications of ultrasound for diagnostic imaging; and new applications of physics, such as nuclear magnetic resonance.

Many graduate programs in medical physics are affiliated with the department of radiology of a medical school, and some of these are referred to as radiological sciences programs. They are often offered in conjunction with a graduate program in the field of radiation biology.

Some graduate programs in medical physics include the option of specialization in radiation protection (health physics). Other programs may cover areas that include medical instrumentation and are sometimes referred to as biomedical engineering.

Master of Science degree programs prepare physicists to work in hospitals or industrial facilities, while Ph.D. programs lead primarily to research and teaching in medical schools.

John R. Cameron, Emeritus Professor
and F. H. Attix, Professor and Chairman
Department of Medical Physics
University of Wisconsin Medical School

Medical Technology Medical technology (clinical laboratory science) provides a vital component of patient care by assisting in identification of the course of disease, contributing to management of the disease process, and aiding in health maintenance. A wide variety of physical, chemical, and microscopic analyses of body fluids and tissues are performed by the various professionals who constitute the laboratory team.

Included in the education of the professionals are four clinical science disciplines: clinical chemistry, clinical microbiology, clinical immunology, and clinical hematology. The integration of knowledge in areas of these disciplines is not only critical to high-quality laboratory services and patient care, but also provides a broad base of scientific knowledge and skills that enable the medical technologist to fill a variety of positions or to pursue additional graduate study.

Medical technologists with graduate degrees have a variety of employment opportunities. They may work in clinical laboratories in hospitals; in research laboratories in medical schools, institutes, or industry; in public health and government facilities; as faculty members in educational programs in hospitals, community colleges, industry, and four-year colleges and universities; or as site evaluators of laboratory standards.

National certifying examinations are given at the baccalaureate level for medical technologists, and specialty examinations are given at the master's and doctoral levels in the four clinical science areas previously noted. Some states set minimum personnel standards for clinical laboratories that include a master's degree as a qualification for a new supervisor. A limited number of states have personnel licensing. Federal personnel requirements, described in Medicare regulations, include those for master's-level personnel.

Many master's programs in medical technology require the applicant to be certified at the baccalaureate level or to have experience in the clinical laboratory. At the master's level the student specializes in one of the four clinical discipline areas or selects an

Medical Technology (continued)

option in education or administration. The last two options require course work in the clinical discipline areas, focused toward a career in clinical laboratory science education or an administrative role in the clinical laboratory. Students in a Ph.D. program select a clinical specialty, while students in an Ed.D. or D.A. program specialize in education. There are ongoing discussions regarding the feasibility of developing doctoral programs in medical technology.

The medical laboratory industry is burgeoning, having increased the output of procedures performed by about 15 percent per year over the last fifteen years. The advances in science and technology that have made this possible require highly educated researchers and laboratory practitioners with supervisory and teaching capabilities.

Nellie May Bering
Professor of Medical Technology
College of Allied Health Professions
Temple University

Occupational Therapy   Occupational therapy is a health profession based on the art and science of using occupation (work, play and leisure, and self-care activities) to help individuals maintain or improve the state of their health. These purposeful activities and their interpersonal and environmental context are used with sick or at-risk individuals to promote their adaptation and ability to carry out essential functions and roles.

Two types of master's degree programs are available: professional and postprofessional. Professional master's-level programs are for those with an undergraduate degree in a field other than occupational therapy. Generally two years long, they include both didactic and fieldwork courses, are designed to develop competency as an occupational therapist, and lead to eligibility to take a national professional credentialing examination. A good undergraduate background in biological sciences, psychology, and sociology is strongly recommended; most programs have specific prerequisites in these areas. Postprofessional master's degree programs are for those who are already occupational therapists. They vary considerably in content, degree of focus, and emphasis on research. Some are generic, relating to the science of occupation and its general use to promote health. Others are specialized, focusing on an area of practice such as pediatric occupational therapy or a role such as teaching or management. At some institutions postprofessional study is offered as part of an allied health master's degree program. Some universities have combined the two types of master's degrees—students start at different points but graduate with the same competencies.

A few universities offer doctoral study in occupational therapy or programs offered in conjunction with other departments. Current research relates to the nature of occupation, its effect on various parameters of human function, development of clinical and research measurement instruments, and educational and administrative problems of the field.

Graduates with a professional master's degree in occupational therapy find jobs in a variety of clinical settings. Employment in outpatient, community, and home health facilities; in schools; and in private practice is becoming more common. Occupational therapists with postprofessional and doctoral degrees often obtain faculty positions or assume administrative or clinician-researcher roles.

Patti A. Maurer, Ph.D., OTR, FAOTA
Professor of Occupational Therapy
Medical College of Virginia
Virginia Commonwealth University

Physical Therapy   Physical therapy is a health profession that is concerned primarily with human movement and movement dysfunction. Because problems in any biological system may contribute to problems of movement, the physical therapist may treat widely diversified disabilities resulting from industrial injuries, burns, stroke, fractures, postural strain, heart and respiratory disease, and birth defects, to name only the more prevalent causes of disability. The practice of physical therapy includes the performance and interpretation of tests to assess the nature of movement dysfunction, potential or actual, and the development and administration of treatment programs employing physical agents, activities, and devices for the prevention or remediation of movement dysfunction.

Pathokinesiology, the study of movement dysfunction at all levels of physiological organization, and therapeutic kinesiology, the use of movement to prevent or remediate movement dysfunction, are the principal scientific bases for the practice of physical therapy.

Physical Therapy (continued)

At the graduate (postentry) level, education in physical therapy tends to specialize in one of several major areas: musculoskeletal (orthopedic), neurological, or cardiovascular. In the past, some graduate programs have emphasized education and administration, but specialization in clinical areas is a growing trend. Other areas of specialization in physical therapy are possible; these tend to be specialized applications of orthopedic, neurological, and cardiopulmonary principles and include geriatrics, pediatrics, hand rehabilitation, cancer rehabilitation, community health, and sports physical therapy, among others.

There are now at least four doctoral programs in physical therapy that combine basic and clinical sciences to produce teacher-researchers in the field. Research is greatly needed to establish the scientific bases of empirical techniques developed by clinicians to meet immediate patient problems. As professional entry-level education moves to the postbaccalaureate-degree level, there will be an increased demand for teacher-researchers trained at the doctoral level. Master clinicians trained at the postentry graduate level are, and will continue to be, in great demand for clinical, clinical education, and academic positions. According to the U.S. Department of Labor, physical therapists will be in high demand at least through 1990.

Otto D. Payton, Ph.D., PT
Chairman, Department of Physical Therapy
Medical College of Virginia
Virginia Commonwealth University

Speech-Language Pathology and Audiology Speech-language pathology and audiology are two related professional disciplines that fit under the generic academic discipline called communication disorders. The latter term refers to handicaps that some members of society face in the production, reception, and/or comprehension of speech and language.

Speech-language pathologists, who are clinically certified at the master's degree level, are concerned with the evaluation and treatment of various types of communication impairments. Included among these are disorders of phonology (the speech sounds of the language), voice quality, fluency of speech (stuttering), and language (the ability to understand and express oneself verbally or nonverbally). These impairments may result from organic causes (e.g., cleft palate, brain injury, and hearing loss) or may be related to learning, environment, or unknown factors.

Audiologists, who are also clinically certified at the master's degree level, are concerned primarily with measuring hearing acuity, providing medically related information pertaining to hearing loss, and planning for and providing appropriate amplification and remedial assistance to those with hearing losses. Recent technological advances have resulted in more sophisticated evaluation procedures than were once thought possible, with the result that educational programs for audiologists will likely have significant modifications within the decade.

Professionals in the areas of speech-language pathology and audiology share a base of knowledge concerning normal speech and hearing processes and development. While clinicians trained at the master's degree level are primarily engaged in the assessment and treatment of people with communication handicaps, those trained at the doctoral level (usually a Ph.D., sometimes an Ed.D. or Sc.D.) often have their primary commitment to teaching and research. Researchers and teachers at the doctoral level whose main interests are in normal communication processes are often labeled speech and hearing scientists. Some of these individuals also have an interest in disordered communication and thus are closely connected to the field.

Speech-language pathologists and audiologists are employed by hospitals, clinics, public school systems, and state and federal institutions, and an increasing number are engaged in private practice. According to a report from the U.S. Department of Labor, the job outlook for these professions will be above average throughout the 1980s. There is currently a critical shortage of such professionals in rural areas of the United States.

Dr. Nicholas W. Bankson, Professor and Chairman
Department of Communication Disorders
Boston University

Chiropractic

Chiropractic   Chiropractic is a branch of the healing arts that is concerned with processes of human health and disease. Doctors of chiropractic are physicians who consider man as an integrated being

Chiropractic (continued)

but give special attention to spinal mechanics; subluxations of the spine; and musculoskeletal, neurological, vascular, nutritional, and environmental relationships.

The Council on Chiropractic Education has adopted the following definition: "Chiropractic science concerns itself with the relationship between structure, primarily the spine, and function, primarily coordinated by the nervous system, of the human body as that relationship may affect the restoration and preservation of health."

All states, the District of Columbia, and Puerto Rico have statutes recognizing and regulating the practice of chiropractic as an independent health service. The practice of chiropractic is officially regulated in nine of the provinces of Canada and in Switzerland, West Germany, New Zealand, Australia, and Bolivia and is acknowledged and accepted in the Scandinavian countries, France, Italy, the British Isles, South Africa, Rhodesia, Japan, Venezuela, Peru, and the Virgin Islands.

Dr. Beatrice B. Hagen
President, Logan College of Chiropractic
President, Council on Chiropractic Education

Straight Chiropractic   At its annual meeting in December 1984, the Federation of Straight Chiropractic Organizations adopted the following definition of straight chiropractic: "Straight Chiropractic is a vitalistic philosophy of life and health based upon the recognition that living things have an innate striving to maintain health; and the art and science of correcting vertebral subluxation(s) in accordance with that philosophy."

Subluxations are slight articular disrelationships within the vertebral column that disturb nerve function. The practice objective of straight chiropractic is to contribute to health by correcting subluxations.

It should be noted that two schools of thought exist within the chiropractic profession. Straight chiropractic is distinguished by its commitment to the analysis and correction of vertebral subluxation—it does not adopt the medical objective of treating disease.

T. A. Gelardi, D.C., President
Sherman College of Straight Chiropractic

Dentistry and Oral Sciences

Dentistry Dentistry is a health profession dedicated to the prevention and treatment of oral diseases. During a four-year training period, the dental student acquires the required knowledge and skills to carry out this mission using a variety of diagnostic and treatment procedures all founded on a comprehensive biological basis. Thus, the early years of education include such courses as human anatomy, biochemistry, microbiology, pathology, physiology, and pharmacology. Following this thorough grounding in the scientific basis for clinical treatment, the student enters upon a two- to three-year period of training in the various clinical subdisciplines of dentistry, such as restorative dentistry, prosthodontics, periodontics, orthodontics, endodontics, oral surgery, pediatric dentistry, oral diagnosis, oral medicine, oral radiology, dental materials, and community dentistry.

Upon successfully completing this curriculum, the student earns the degree of Doctor of Dental Medicine or Doctor of Dental Surgery. These degrees are equivalent in all aspects of training and professional recognition. Many graduates seek postgraduate training in one of the eight dental specialties approved by the American Dental Association. The majority of graduates enter the private practice of dentistry; others combine practice with research and/or teaching. Changing patterns of dental disease and systems of oral health–care delivery have resulted in a variety of practice settings for the graduate.

In recent years, the enrollment of dental students has decreased, and as a result the supply and demand for dentists are expected to move closer to a balance. More people now have dental insurance to cover dental expenses. Aging of the general population is occurring. Fewer of these adults are losing their teeth due, in part, to a decrease in childhood caries resulting from good care and successful preventive efforts. Therefore, more adults are retaining their teeth and are expected to require more dental services. These

Dentistry (continued)

factors make the outlook for dentistry as a profession brighter. From all standpoints, dentistry is a most satisfying and rewarding calling for the student devoted to improving the health and well-being of people of all ages.

Ralph S. Kaslick, D.D.S., Dean
Fairleigh S. Dickinson, Jr., College of Dental Medicine
Fairleigh Dickinson University

Oral and Dental Sciences   Advanced education in oral and dental sciences includes a multitude of programs. Individuals with a professional degree in dentistry may enter postgraduate training in one of the eight recognized dental specialties: dental public health, endodontics, oral and maxillofacial surgery, oral pathology, orthodontics, pedodontics, periodontics, and prosthodontics.

Postgraduate programs may be based within a dental college, a dental center devoted to advanced education, a teaching hospital, or a combination of these facilities. All programs providing accepted training are accredited by the American Dental Association and offer a Certificate of Specialization upon successful completion of the program.

Programs are designed to prepare individuals to practice in the specialty area and be eligible to complete examinations for diplomate status or state board registration in their chosen specialty. In many states, diplomate status or the successful completion of a state specialty board examination is required for dentists to declare themselves a specialist.

Some advanced training facilities offer a program leading to the award of a Certificate of Specialization in combination with a graduate degree (M.S. or Ph.D.). M.S. programs include a significant research component and are designed for individuals interested in preparing for a full-time or part-time career in clinically oriented dental education or research. Doctoral programs are usually offered in the area of oral biology or oral sciences and are structured with an emphasis in one of the pure sciences: biochemistry, microbiology, immunology, anatomy, physiology, biomechanics, or pharmacology. Research activities apply the science to a dentally related problem. Graduates of doctoral programs seek educational and research positions with dental colleges or research positions in industry following completion of their training.

Current research in dental science areas is diverse. Microbiologic and immunologic endeavors are answering questions regarding the etiologic factors responsible for the two most common forms of dental disease: dental caries and periodontal diseases. Such information is making it possible to integrate pharmacological principles into therapy modalities. Biomechanical research is addressing problems of developing better materials to aid in the restoration or replacement of teeth damaged or lost because of dental diseases. Public health research is investigating the pandemic nature of dental diseases and evaluating the effect of public care measures on their progression.

Kenneth L. Kalkwarf, D.D.S., M.S.
Director, Graduate and Postgraduate Studies
College of Dentistry
University of Nebraska Medical Center

Medicine

Allopathic Medicine   Allopathic medicine is a label describing the predominant mode of education practiced by most schools of medicine in the United States today. Individuals educated in allopathic medical schools acquire the fundamental skills and abilities needed to provide high-quality health care to individuals of all ages and sexes. The process of education has two major stages: medical school education, where one obtains the M.D. degree, and graduate medical education, where one develops the skills and abilities to be a specialist or subspecialist.

Each year about 34,000 students apply to 125 medical schools in the United States for about 16,000 openings. Admissions are made on the basis of college grades, performance on the Medical College Admission Test (MCAT), recommendations concerning the character of the applicant, and the applicant's extracurricular activities. In the last twenty years there has been a significant increase in the number of women both applying to and being accepted into medical schools. Today nearly 40 percent of the applicants and enrollees are women. In the last five years the number of applicants has leveled off, and over the past two years there has been a slight annual decrease in the number of applicants.

Most medical schools have a 4-year curriculum, but in some cases it has been condensed to 3 or 3½ years. The curriculum is

Allopathic Medicine (continued)

traditionally divided into basic science and clinical science components, each lasting approximately 2 years. The basic science component consists of courses such as human anatomy, human physiology, biochemistry, pathology, microbiology, pharmacology, and human behavior. During the first 2 years, many medical schools also teach students how to perform a physical examination and diagnose illness. Instruction is carried out through lectures, self-paced learning programs (some of which involve computer-based instruction), laboratory experience such as dissection of a cadaver, microbiologic evaluations of specimens from sick patients, and actual encounters with real and simulated patients. Students are also taught to use computers to access large databases to answer specific scientific and clinical questions.

The second half of medical education consists of instruction in the clinical sciences, such as pediatrics, surgery, psychiatry, internal medicine, radiology, neurology, anesthesiology, obstetrics, gynecology, and family practice. During the clinical years students spend one- to two-month blocks of time (clerkships) learning about most of the major specialties. The student works in teams with faculty mentors, residents in each discipline, nurses, and other health-care personnel. As a member of the team the student receives practical instruction in caring for patients in a variety of settings, including the physician's office, hospital outpatient departments, emergency rooms, and hospital inpatient departments (general wards/intensive care units). Allopathic medical students interview patients, perform physical examinations, perform certain diagnostic studies, write reports on the patient's condition, and at times participate in providing a variety of treatment modalities. All of these actions are performed under the close scrutiny of licensed physicians in settings that have been accredited by national organizations. During this two-year period, students receive a general professional education and are prepared to enter the next phase of medical education. There is for each of the various disciplines of allopathic medicine a set of skills and abilities that must be mastered to be a competent practitioner of that discipline. Because the scope of these skills and abilities is so vast, no graduate of an allopathic school in the United States is prepared to immediately participate in the independent practice of medicine.

Almost all U.S. medical school graduates seek further training in one of the twenty-three medical specialties approved by the American Board of Medical Specialties: allergy and immunology, anesthesiology, colon and rectal surgery, dermatology, emergency medicine, family practice, internal medicine, neurological surgery, nuclear medicine, obstetrics and gynecology, ophthalmology, orthopedic surgery, otolaryngology, pathology, pediatrics, physical medicine and rehabilitation, plastic surgery, preventive medicine, psychiatry and neurology, radiology, surgery, thoracic surgery, and urology. The training lasts from three to seven years, depending on the specialty. During this time the student learns the specific skills and abilities that are needed for assuming responsibility for patients in the independent practice of medicine. With each passing year the resident physician assumes more responsibility for progressively more complex cases. At this stage nearly all learning occurs in the context of caring for patients. This experience includes care of both hospitalized patients and patients seeking care at a physician's office or clinic. At the conclusion of this stage of educational process, the physician is prepared for the independent practice of medicine without supervision.

Following the conclusion of the graduate years, physicians enter a variety of settings. Most go into the office practice of medicine, usually with groups of other physicians and rarely as a solo practitioner. Others go into academic medicine, where they provide patient care, educate medical students and residents, and conduct research. Some physicians involve themselves in other professional fields, such as business, engineering, and education.

Fredric D. Burg, M.D.
Associate Dean for Academic Programs
School of Medicine
University of Pennsylvania
Professor of Pediatrics
Children's Hospital of Philadelphia

Osteopathic Medicine   Osteopathic medicine began in the 1870s as a reform movement that sought to make American health care more effective and more scientific. Today, it is the fastest-growing health-care field, with nearly 25,000 practitioners and fifteen colleges—triple the number in 1969. While the overwhelming majority of doctors of osteopathy (D.O.'s) engage in the practice of medicine, others are primarily teachers, researchers, or health-care-policy leaders. In the latter arena, D.O.'s serve on state and national medical advisory commissions, as presidents of state medical boards, and as high-ranking medical corps officers in the military. A D.O. is currently director of one of the National Institutes of Health.

Osteopathic Medicine (continued)

Admission to osteopathic medical schools is very selective. On the average, only 1 out of every 13 students who apply is accepted. Osteopathic medical students are, with rare exception, required to earn a bachelor's degree prior to admittance, and many have master's and doctoral degrees in other disciplines. Specific courses in such fields as biology, chemistry, physics, and the behavioral sciences are required for admission. In most osteopathic medical schools the first two years are devoted primarily to the basic sciences, which include anatomy, pharmacology, physiology, microbiology, immunology, medical biochemistry, pathology, hematology, neurology, and psychiatry. The second two years are more heavily clinical in orientation, and the student spends much of his or her time in hospitals, clinics, and doctors' offices to learn the science and art of patient care. Osteopathic medical students are taught the use of all accepted methods of diagnosis and treatment, including drugs, surgery, radiation, and manipulation. Clinical instruction emphasizes looking at the whole patient and how various body systems interrelate, rather than focusing on the particular disease or illness causing the most immediate problem. Close attention is also paid to the ways in which the musculoskeletal and nervous systems influence the functioning of the rest of the body.

This "total body" approach is part of a distinct philosophy of health care that is taught to osteopathic students. Disease is seen as a disruption of the body's normal state of health, and treatment is viewed as a way of enhancing the body's natural defense mechanisms. This philosophy, which was propounded in the writings of early osteopathic educators, has gained wide acceptance in most medical circles in recent years.

Before entering practice, a D.O. must complete four years of osteopathic medical school and a yearlong internship in an osteopathic or military hospital. After the internship, most D.O.'s continue their medical studies in a specialty residency of one to five years. About 60 to 70 percent of D.O.'s go into family medicine or one of the other primary care fields—pediatrics, obstetrics and gynecology, internal medicine, or emergency medicine.

In today's medical world, most D.O.'s and M.D.'s have a high regard for the professional education and clinical skills of their associates from the other profession. It is common for a D.O. family physician to refer a patient to an M.D. specialist or for an M.D. family doctor to refer to a D.O. specialist. The best example of cooperation is probably the armed services, where D.O.'s and M.D.'s work side by side, the health care of the men and women in uniform being their primary concern.

Dr. Frank W. Myers, Dean
College of Osteopathic Medicine
Ohio University

Naturopathic Medicine

The term naturopathic medicine was first used in the late nineteenth century to describe the growing coalition of physicians and healers who believed that treating the person and promoting health were more important than simply alleviating the symptoms of disease. While the profession is not much more than a hundred years old, the practice of naturopathic medicine has been alive as long as people have used food, plants, water, thought, air, light—the forces of nature—to heal themselves. Hippocrates said, "Let your food be your medicine, and your medicine be your food," and "Do no harm." Naturopathic physicians still subscribe to these principles.

Today, naturopathic physicians provide primary health care that blends centuries-old knowledge of natural nontoxic therapies with current advances in the understanding of health and human systems. The scope of practice includes all aspects of family care, from natural childbirth through geriatrics.

The philosophical approach of naturopathic medicine includes prevention of disease, encouragement of the body's inherent healing abilities, natural treatment of the whole person, personal responsibility for one's health, and education of patients in health-promoting life-styles.

The U.S. Department of Labor defines the naturopathic physician as one who "diagnoses, treats, and cares for patients, using a system of practice that bases its treatment of all physiological functions and abnormal conditions on natural laws governing the body, utilizes physiological, psychological and mechanical methods, such as air, water, heat, earth, phytotherapy (treatment by use of plants), electrotherapy, physiotherapy, minor or orificial surgery, mechanotherapy, naturopathic corrections and manipulation, and all natural methods or modalities, together with natural medicines, natural processed foods, and herbs, and natural remedies. Excludes major surgery, therapeutic use of x-ray and radium, and use of drugs, except those assimilable substances containing elements or

Naturopathic Medicine (continued)

compounds which are compounds of bodily tissues and are physiologically compatible to body processes for maintenance of life.

"Most naturopathic doctors are in private practice. There are a growing number of clinics and interdisciplinary practices. Naturopaths are also involved in education and research."

Peggy Smith, N.D.
Dean of Admissions
John Bastyr College

Nursing

Nursing Nursing is a health science that encompasses a range of academic options. Through graduate education in nursing, students may prepare for a variety of roles in the health-care-delivery system. Degrees available include the M.N., M.S.N., M.S., M.A., and, at the doctoral level, the N.D., D.N.S., D.N.Sc., Ed.D., and Ph.D. Specialization at the graduate level may be according to clinical area, e.g., nurse anesthesia, community health nursing, gerontological nursing, medical-surgical nursing, psychiatric mental health nursing, and nurse midwifery; according to age group, e.g., child-health nursing and nursing of the adult; or according to functional area, e.g., teaching and administration. Programs that prepare generalists are also available. Graduate preparation is widely becoming accepted as a basic requirement for advanced certification.

Nursing as a professional discipline is concerned with human responses to actual and potential health problems. Current research in nursing is focused on nursing practice, including human responses to acute and chronic health problems, health promotion and health maintenance, and nursing interventions; nursing-care delivery; nursing education; the profession of nursing, including professional socialization and behavior, ethics, and clinical judgment; and international nursing.

Doctoral education in nursing may be undertaken in any of four types of programs: the N.D. (Doctor of Nursing), the professional doctorate; the D.N.S. or D.N.Sc. (Doctor of Nursing Science), the advanced clinical doctorate or the clinical research doctorate; the Ph.D. (Doctor of Philosophy in nursing), the research doctorate; and the Ed.D. (Doctor of Education), the education doctorate. Doctoral education prepares the graduate for a variety of positions, depending primarily on the type of program. These include positions as faculty members in schools of nursing, nurse executives in academic and health-care-service settings, and workers in research, consultation, and expert clinical practice. Currently, there exists some difference of opinion in the field regarding the distinctions between D.N.S. or D.N.Sc. and Ph.D. programs. In some cases the choice of the academic degree is based primarily on university guidelines.

Joyce J. Fitzpatrick, Ph.D., FAAN
Professor and Dean
Frances Payne Bolton School of Nursing
Case Western Reserve University

Child-Care Nursing   Child-care nursing is a specialty field offered at the master's level in many graduate nursing programs and in a few doctoral programs in nursing. The specialty offerings appear under a variety of titles, including pediatric nursing, nursing of children, family-child nursing, parent-child nursing, maternal-child nursing, or child-health nursing. The programs usually offer generalist preparation, with optional or required functional-role preparation in clinical specialization, teaching, or administration. Doctoral programs with a nursing major are too few to comment on trends. Doctoral programs in child-care nursing emphasize in-depth study of children vis-à-vis theories from related disciplines, independent study, and original research of a problem in the field. Many nurses pursue a doctorate in a related field such as family or child development or education and opt for a minor in nursing.

Master's programs vary in length from one to two years of study and lead to the M.N., M.S.N., or M.S. degree. Building upon theories of family and child development, the course of study places emphasis upon promoting positive parent-child interaction and optimum growth and development of the children in the family. Clinical experiences focus on maintaining wellness and promoting a positive response of the child and family to illness throughout childhood. Some programs selectively emphasize one age group (e.g., the newborn or adolescents) or category of health deviations (e.g., pulmonary dysfunctions, handicaps). Usually the master's program requires independent investigation of a problem either as a case study, project, or thesis. Clinical experiences occur in a variety of settings such as acute- or chronic-care institutions, community health agencies, and, more recently, ambulatory-care facilities.

Child-Care Nursing (continued)

Research in child-care nursing focuses primarily on clinical studies of responses to illness, children's understanding of their health/illness situation, and strategies to support children in stressful situations, such as impending surgery. Another focus of research deals with family/parent/sibling as the supportive milieu for a child, their reactions to the child's health/illness situation, and approaches to anticipatory guidance. Because the subject population consists of minors, much research in child-care nursing is descriptive in nature, although increasing numbers of studies are exploring the effects of nursing interventions.

Graduates of master's programs in child-care nursing find positions in a broad range of settings, from clinical to academic institutions. The graduate may elect to work in acute-care hospitals, long-term institutions, or primary-care settings as clinical nurse specialists, nurse clinicians, parent-family educators, or nurse practitioners. Another opportunity for employment is in educational institutions as a teacher of child-care nursing. This position requires additional preparation in educational theory and practice. Understanding of management principles and institutional policymaking is useful in all of these roles.

Doctoral work usually prepares the graduate for faculty positions in schools of nursing and concomitant work in administration, research, and consultation.

Virginia Hagemann, RN, Ph.D.
Professor, Graduate Nursing Program
University of Missouri–Columbia

Gerontological Nursing Gerontological nursing—nursing care of the older adult—is a specialty available at the master's and doctoral levels. Specialization may be offered as a major or as a minor (for example, specialization in community health nursing with an emphasis on gerontological nursing). Programs that specialize in gerontological nursing are usually of a generalist nature—that is, they examine the various health-care needs of the older adult in a variety of health-care settings—and prepare the nurse for clinical specialization or advanced practice. Programs that offer gerontological nursing as a minor are designed to be focused on the setting, e.g., community, home health care, and acute care.

Two options for specialization are the gerontological clinical specialist and the gerontological nurse practitioner. The clinical nurse specialist in gerontological nursing is expected to be able to function as a clinician, educator, researcher, and consultant. The geriatric nurse practitioner is expected to be able to provide primary care and is prepared to manage the nursing and medical aspects of selected acute and chronic health problems. Some states require licensure or certification in addition to the basic RN licensure.

A variety of curricula may be found, and most include a study of various aspects of aging: biological, psychological, social, cultural, legislative, and environmental. Clinical course work in gerontological nursing is based on ANA standards of gerontological nursing practice. Programs at the doctoral level are likely to offer interdisciplinary programs and/or opportunities.

Current research in areas of gerontological nursing can be grouped into four categories—research on clinical or practice problems, research on education and service programs, research related to sites, and research on policy pertaining to gerontological nursing. Much of gerontological nursing research is exploratory in design; however, increasingly experimental and quasi-experimental designs, and multidisciplinary approaches, are being used. Examples of these interdisciplinary research and training programs are the Teaching Nursing Homes, funded by the National Institute on Aging and the Robert Wood Johnson Foundation.

Nurses with master's degrees in nursing and specialization in gerontological nursing find employment opportunities in many settings. The gerontological clinical specialist is finding placement in long-term-care facilities, home health and community health agencies, and acute-care hospitals. Positions as clinical nurse specialist, nurse clinician, or clinical nurse coordinator are becoming more common, particularly in large long-term facilities and HMOs. Many opportunities are available for management positions, including administration in skilled nursing facilities. It is wise for nurses to include course work in management or leadership in their programs. A nursing home administrator's license may be obtained with adequate educational preparation. Nurses with primary-care skills may obtain positions as nurse practitioners, usually in outpatient clinics, nursing homes, and/or collaborative practice with a physician. Graduates of doctoral programs usually obtain faculty positions, although they may also assume administrative, consultative, or research roles.

In selecting a program, prospective graduate students should examine the philosophy and goals of the program, the size and

Gerontological Nursing (continued)

qualifications of its faculty, the availability of additional (non-nursing) gerontological resources on campus, clinical opportunities, and the breadth and depth of the program.

Glen C. Doyle, RN, Ed.D.
Associate Clinical Professor
School of Nursing
University of California, San Francisco

Maternity Nursing Maternal-newborn nursing is the study and nursing care of the mother and her newborn child during the childbearing and early childrearing experience. Theory and nursing practice related to the well woman's health and to the family and the community as they are affected by the childbearing/early childrearing experience are also included.

Career opportunities for nurses with a master's degree exist in the nursing care of the childbearing/early childrearing family in acute-care, community, or public health settings. Nurses choosing to work in acute-care or community settings usually pursue the clinical specialist role, which prepares them to provide expert nursing care to a select group of patients. Nurses interested in a community or public health setting may prepare to be nurse midwives or nurse practitioners in the obstetrical-gynecological area. In addition to the clinical specialist or nurse practitioner role, teaching at the junior college and undergraduate-level college or university and nursing service administrative positions are other career choices. Research skills are integral to master's degree preparation in maternal-newborn nursing.

There are many leadership positions available for nurses with a doctoral degree. These career opportunities can be in academia, clinical practice, administration, consultation, government, private business, and research.

Rene M. Reeb, RN, CNM, Ph.D., Associate Professor
Maternal-Newborn Nursing Graduate Program
University of Mississippi Medical Center

Medical-Surgical Nursing Medical-surgical nursing is the diagnosis and treatment of adult patients with actual or potential health problems in medical and surgical areas. The science of medical-surgical nursing is based on selected theories and principles from the physical and behavioral sciences as well as medical and nursing theories.

Medical-surgical nursing encompasses all aspects of the nursing care of patients who are treated by medical and surgical methods. It is an area of clinical nursing specialization that is available at both master's and doctoral levels.

The graduate of a master's-level program in medical-surgical nursing is prepared for advanced practice as a clinical nurse specialist in general medical-surgical nursing or in such nursing subspecialties as cardiovascular, respiratory, renal, oncology, neurological, gerontological, critical-care, recovery room, perioperating room, trauma, or neurosurgical nursing. Master's-level preparation is also useful to a head nurse, a supervisor, a clinical teacher, or an administrator of a medical and/or surgical nursing division or department.

Doctoral study in medical-surgical nursing provides preparation for research, teaching, or administration in medical-surgical nursing or one of its subspecialties in an academic setting as well as a health-care institution. Graduates usually conduct and/or direct research related to the nursing care of patients with medical-surgical problems, and the knowledge generated from their research contributes to nursing education and practice.

Mi Ja Kim, RN, Ph.D., FAAN
Professor, Associate Dean for Research, and
Director, Office of Graduate Studies
College of Nursing
University of Illinois at Chicago

Nurse Anesthesia   Nurse anesthesia is a profession with great appeal to the registered professional nurse interested in expanded responsibility, challenge, self-fulfillment, and satisfaction. The anesthetist's role is practically as old as the nursing profession itself. As an essential member of the surgical team, the nurse anesthetist's primary function involves providing for the patient a state of insensibility to pain during surgical, diagnostic, and therapeutic procedures and the management of patients so affected. Although anesthesia is usually administered in the operating room, the nurse anesthetist may also perform vital services for obstetrical departments, intensive care units, emergency rooms, psychiatric departments, inhalation therapy departments, and dental offices. The patient-nurse relationship is probably more important in this

Nurse Anesthesia (continued)

field than in any other type of nursing. The nurse anesthetist must apply the finest theoretical principles, technical skills, and psychology of bedside nursing to each patient.

Educational, medical, and scientific achievements are advancing at an overwhelming rate. It is the goal of the nurse anesthesia profession to stay abreast of these developments. Within the past few years, nurse anesthetists have become increasingly active in contributing to these achievements and advancements. Anesthetists are continuing to pursue scientific research in clinical, educational, and administrative areas to further the science of anesthesia. The American Association of Nurse Anesthetists (the professional organization for the nurse anesthetist) keeps its members informed of advances in the science of nurse anesthesiology through its publications and continuing education programs leading to biennial recertification. Although a variety of curricula, program lengths (minimum twenty-four months), and degrees are offered, all nationally accredited programs in nurse anesthesia must meet the high educational standards and directives as set by the Council on Accreditation of Nurse Anesthesia Educational Programs/Schools, the official accrediting body for all nurse anesthesia programs. In the near future, all programs in nurse anesthesia not already structured at the graduate degree level will be required to comply.

Today's nurse anesthetist works in a variety of settings. In spring 1986, 47 percent were employed by hospitals, 38 percent were employed in anesthesiologist group practice, and 12 percent contracted their services on a fee-for-service basis. Nurse anesthetists administer more than half of the estimated 20 million anesthetics administered each year. Salaries for the nurse anesthetist are equal to and usually exceed those of top nursing positions. Nurse anesthetists legally practice in all fifty states, the armed services, and many foreign countries. The need for nurse anesthetists is continually growing. New hospitals are being built while older ones are being expanded to provide for the growing number of patients and expanding applications of modern surgery. Issues concerning cost containment and quality care in the health-care-delivery system are more prevalent than ever before. These changes and others in health-care services add emphasis to the ever-growing need for additional nurse anesthesia personnel. Nurse anesthesia is unquestionably one of today's most demanding careers, offering security and a rewarding future to those who enter this special kind of nursing as a certified registered nurse anesthetist (CRNA).

Herbert T. Watson, CRNA, M.Ed.
Professor and Chairman
Department of Nurse Anesthesia
Medical College of Virginia
Virginia Commonwealth University

Nurse Midwifery The American College of Nurse Midwives (ACNM) adopted the following definition of nurse midwifery in 1978: "Nurse-midwifery practice is the independent management of the care of essentially normal newborns and women, antepartally, intrapartally, postpartally, and/or gynecologically, occurring within a health-care system which provides for medical consultation, collaborative management, or referral and is in accord with the 'Functions, Standards and Qualifications for Nurse-Midwifery Practice' as defined by the A.C.N.M."

Nurse midwives are educated in the two disciplines of nursing and midwifery. They bring a broad knowledge of the behavioral and biological sciences into focus in delivering primary care to women during their reproductive years. Nurse midwives believe that women and their families deserve individualized care and that people have the right and even the obligation to participate in decisions made about their health care. Nurse midwifery practice includes a strong emphasis on client education. Work toward enhancement of the client's resources to improve or maintain health is central to the work of the nurse midwife/client team.

Outside the office setting, nurse midwives have been active supporters of improvement in the delivery of services to women and infants. Nurse midwives are active at all levels of government, working to influence policy aimed at reducing maternal and infant mortality and morbidity. ACNM has issued a statement in support of universal access to prenatal and infant care. The value of nurse midwives in improving maternal and child health has been recognized by the National Academy of Sciences' Institute of Medicine Committee, who recently called for "more reliance on nurse midwives . . . to increase access to prenatal care for hard-to-reach, often high-risk groups."

Nurse midwives practice in a variety of settings. Many nurse midwives are employed by hospitals, health maintenance

Nurse Midwifery (continued)

organizations, and other institutions that deliver health care. Other nurse midwives are in private practice. Nurse midwives attend births in hospitals, in birth centers, and at home according to their individual philosophy of practice and state and local legal requirements. Wherever nurse midwives practice, formal arrangements for physician consultation must be set up.

Employment and practice opportunities for nurse midwives have been growing dramatically in recent years in many, but not all, states. There are now 2,600 nurse midwives in the United States and increased opportunities for consumers to elect nurse midwifery care. Passage of legislation permitting nurse midwifery practice and mandating third-party reimbursement for nurse midwifery services has added to practice opportunities.

Nurse midwifery education is standardized through the Accreditation Division of the American College of Nurse Midwives. All nurse midwifery programs, whether leading to a graduate degree or a certificate, must include in the curriculum the necessary content to prepare the graduate to perform the core competencies of nurse midwifery practice identified by ACNM. Education in nurse midwifery has a strong clinical focus. Clinical teaching is tutorial in nature; the usual faculty-to-student ratio in the clinical areas is 1:1 or 1:2. Many educational programs employ mastery learning curricula, which are designed to take advantage of the students' previous learning and foster mature self-directed learning. Programs that do not use mastery learning are able to offer students more continuity of care experience if their curricula provide the flexibility necessary to follow clients through the phases of childbearing. Graduate-degree programs add to the basic core competency curriculum content intended to strengthen nurse midwifery practice and prepare graduates for leadership positions. Various programs emphasize research, public health, administration, education, or general higher education content directed at enhancing advanced professional practice. Those seeking graduate nurse midwifery education should evaluate the various programs in light of their personal professional goals.

Patricia Aikins Murphy, CNM, M.S., Instructor
Graduate Nurse-Midwifery Major
School of Nursing
Columbia University

Nurse Practitioner Studies Nurse practitioners are nurse specialists who autonomously provide comprehensive health-care services that are focused on patient education and counseling to promote health and prevent disease and include obtaining health histories, performing physical examinations, utilizing diagnostic/laboratory tests, and diagnosing and managing health needs and problems. This includes acts of medical diagnosis and medical management, consulting with physicians if and when necessary. The scope of services provided by nurse practitioners thus includes both nursing care and what has heretofore been defined as medical care.

Educational programs to prepare nurse practitioners, initiated in about 1960 at the continuing education level, have become an integral part of master's programs in nursing. The term nurse practitioner refers to a nursing role, not a field of study. The field of study in which most nurse practitioners are prepared is primary care, the day-to-day preventive and curative health care required by most people to meet most of their health needs throughout life.

Most of the educational programs currently established prepare family or adult primary-care nurse practitioners; however, there are programs that prepare nurse practitioners to care for other populations, such as children and the elderly, as well as programs that provide preparation in other fields of study, such as care of cancer patients.

In addition to the core study typically required of all students in master's nursing programs, curricula preparing nurse practitioners as primary-care specialists emphasize didactic and clinical experiences related to providing nursing services that are aimed at health promotion and disease prevention and focused on the diagnostic process and management of common acute and chronic illnesses such as hypertension, diabetes, and minor infections. Programs do vary nationally in the degree to which they emphasize medical diagnosis and management, but the focus on health promotion and disease prevention services is a commonality.

Research in primary-care nursing, usually descriptive in nature because of the newness of the specialty, is focused on the promotion of health and alternative strategies for managing health problems. Primary-care nursing is increasingly becoming available as a research option in doctoral nursing programs, and this will greatly enhance the amount and quality of primary-care nursing research. Most master's-prepared nurse practitioners seek employment as clinicians, i.e., positions in which they are predominantly involved in providing direct patient-care services but can also engage in other nurse

Nurse Practitioner Studies (continued)

specialist activities such as consultation, research, education, and administration. Employment opportunities for nurse practitioners are many and varied, limited only by any legal constraints imposed by the state in which the nurse practitioner is working. Most nurse practitioners are employed in ambulatory-care settings, such as outpatient clinics, HMOs, family health centers, or private doctors' offices or are engaged in private practice. Other common sites employing nurse practitioners are student health services, occupational health sites, and geriatric long-term-care centers.

In selecting a nurse practitioner program, applicants should first assure themselves that the philosophy and objectives of the program and its faculty are compatible with their professional goals. In addition, it is critical that applicants to a nurse practitioner program determine the eligibility of graduates of that program for legal certification, if any, in the state in which they anticipate practicing upon graduation.

Shirley A. Negley, CRNP, RN,C, M.N.Ed.
Associate Professor and Program Director
Family Nurse Practitioner Program
School of Nursing
University of Pittsburgh

Nursing Administration   Nursing administration is a specialty that is available at the master's and doctoral levels. Specialization may be offered as a major or as a minor (for example, major in psychiatric nursing with an emphasis on administration in the psychiatric nursing setting). The purpose of nursing administration programs is to prepare professional practicing nurses to administer nursing services at a variety of levels, in the acute-care and community settings. Some programs specifically state that the preparation is for the nurse executive level, while others are less specific on the organizational level of placement for their graduates. Programs with nursing administration as a minor are more setting-specific and generally prepare the nurse for a middle-management role.

A variety of curricula may be found, but most emphasize an interdisciplinary approach with other administration majors such as business, public, and health administration. The foundation for this interdisciplinary approach is that nursing administration draws on the theories of administration, organization, leadership, and systems to direct nursing practice. Often students take courses offered in business, health, or public administration departments or taught by faculty from those departments. A few programs offer a joint Master of Nursing and Master of Business Administration or Master of Health Administration degree. Additionally, all programs have a core of nursing courses related to nursing theory, roles, and research. The major in nursing administration also usually includes courses in financial management, information systems, policy and law, economics, and marketing; these courses are not included for the minor in nursing administration. All programs include a practicum with a practicing nurse administrator, which may be spread throughout the entire curriculum or may be a terminal experience.

Nurses with a master's degree in nursing administration find positions as director/vice president of nursing, clinical supervisor/director, or head nurse. These nurses are also particularly well prepared for positions as director of in-service, quality assurance, or infection control programs. Graduates of doctoral programs may obtain faculty or nurse executive positions.

In selecting a program, prospective graduate students should examine the philosophy and the goals of the program, the qualifications and research interests of the faculty, the nature of the interdisciplinary offerings, the availability of clinical resources for practicum experiences, and the flexibility of the program to meet the career goals of the specific nurse.

Judith W. Alexander, RN, Ph.D.
Assistant Professor
College of Nursing
University of South Carolina

Nursing Education   One of the purposes of graduate education in nursing is to prepare nurse educators, leaders in nursing with the ability to transmit nursing knowledge, values, and skills. Master's preparation for this role includes concentrated study and practice in a clinical area, in the functional area of teaching, and in research methodologies. Doctoral preparation tends to emphasize leadership, administrative, and investigative functions.

Preparation for a role in academic nursing requires advanced nursing practice in a particular clinical area. Complex nursing-care

Nursing Education (continued)

problems involving individual patients as well as families and community groups are studied. Such problems provide an opportunity to study the theory and practice of nursing, to develop and test nursing theories, and to think through alternative ways of providing health care. Advanced clinical study may be pursued in parent/child, family, medical/surgical, adult, psychiatric/mental health, community health, or gerontological nursing or in a subspecialty area, such as cardiovascular, oncology, neonatal intensive care, or community mental health nursing.

Preparation for the teaching role includes study of the history and philosophy of higher education, curriculum development and evaluation, learning theories, and teaching methodologies. Practice teaching under the supervision of an experienced teacher can provide the opportunity to plan, implement, and evaluate learning experiences and teaching methods in actual classroom and clinical settings. Doctoral preparation is recommended for those interested in administrative or leadership roles.

For many years, research in nursing tended to be centered on nursing, its practitioners, and its various roles and functions. Today, clinical investigation of nursing-care problems for developing and testing nursing diagnoses and nursing theory, for more effective nursing practice, and for developing alternative delivery systems is being encouraged. Nurses with the master's degree are prepared in beginning research skills, such as analyzing practice problems in nursing, evaluating clinical nursing practice, and applying research findings to clinical nursing practice. It is expected that nurses with master's-level preparation will be contributors to or collaborators in research. Nurses interested in developing nursing theory or in providing the leadership to advance nursing practice should consider doctoral preparation.

Graduate nursing programs vary in location, philosophical understanding of the nursing role, curricular emphasis on the scholarly role versus the teaching role, and clinical opportunities for advanced practice. Choosing a graduate nursing program that differs in significant aspects from one's undergraduate education can broaden and strengthen one's nursing as well as one's academic background. For those interested in a career in academic nursing, graduate education in a program with a strong research emphasis is recommended. Research and other scholarly activities are expected of nursing faculty and are major criteria in the promotion and tenure process.

A master's degree in nursing with functional preparation in teaching is required for a faculty position in nationally accredited nursing programs. Nurses with this level of education may also obtain jobs as staff educators or administrators in nursing staff development departments or as patient educators in clinical settings. Doctoral preparation is required for a teaching position in a graduate program or for an administrative position in the academic setting.

Helen E. King, RN, Ph.D., Dean
School of Nursing
Loma Linda University

Oncology Nursing   The term cancer represents a variety of disease processes, some of which are curable and many of which are chronic. Oncology nursing encompasses the delivery of specialized nursing care to cancer patients and their families over the course of the disease.

Specialization in oncology nursing is made available at the master's level of education. Some master's programs offer courses in the physiology and pathology of cancer, as well as nursing courses designed to prepare the graduate to address psychosocial concerns of the patient and the family while practicing within a highly technological environment. This type of master's program prepares oncology clinical nurse specialists, which is a nursing role recognized for its excellence of nursing-care assessment, planning, and delivery. The oncology clinical nurse specialist often serves as a clinical preceptor to students, frequently undertakes classroom teaching, and generally functions as a practitioner within an interdisciplinary health-care team.

Graduate education in oncology nursing may also serve to prepare the registered nurse for a career in research or administration. Cancer research is an ongoing biomedical endeavor, and oncology nurses continue to contribute significantly to many such research efforts. Nursing administrators with advanced oncology education manage the care of large groups of cancer patients and their families within both hospitals and home-care settings, through all phases of the disease.

Oncology nurses are making important contributions in areas of health care that affect large segments of the population. New opportunities for master's-prepared oncology nurses are emerging

Oncology Nursing (continued)

as the value of this type of nursing care is increasingly recognized and rewarded.

Jo Ann Wegmann, RN, Ph.D.
Associate Director of Nursing, Foster McGaw Hospital, and
Associate Professor, School of Nursing
Loyola University of Chicago Medical Center

Psychiatric Nursing Psychiatric nursing is a specialized area of nursing practice requiring preparation at the master's level or beyond. It includes an emphasis on both mental health and mental illness. Students may elect from a number of options within the field, such as child psychiatric nursing, adult psychiatric nursing, geriatric psychiatric nursing, rural mental health, forensic psychiatric nursing, family mental health and treatment, and psychiatric liaison nursing. Graduate curricula in psychiatric nursing may also offer preparation for teaching and administrative roles. Most master's programs prepare their students for the role of clinical specialist in psychiatric nursing; however, some prepare students for a more generalist practice in psychiatric nursing. Doctoral programs prepare researchers, consultants, and administrators; they may or may not offer much clinical practice in psychiatric nursing.

Students who plan to pursue a career in psychiatric nursing should examine carefully the philosophy, objectives, and course offerings of the programs they are considering. Attention should also be paid to the type and nature of the clinical placements that are utilized in the program as well as the faculty responsible for clinical supervision and teaching. The curriculum should also provide for the development of research skills and the integration of research findings into psychiatric nursing practice. A graduate program in psychiatric nursing builds on knowledge and skills obtained at the baccalaureate level. Master's degree programs should enable the graduate to go on for doctoral study.

A wide range of positions are open to nurses completing a master's degree in psychiatric nursing. Those prepared as clinical specialists often take positions in hospitals, either as members of the nursing staff of psychiatric inpatient units or outpatient psychiatric clinics or as liaison nurses consulting with personnel about patients in nonpsychiatric units. Many take positions in community mental health centers, providing direct care to clients as well as mental health education and consultation services in the community. Some go into private practice either on their own or with a group of mental health professionals. Those prepared as teachers assume faculty positions in schools of nursing or in hospital in-service education programs. Psychiatric nurses prepared at the master's level in administration usually fill middle-management positions in hospitals, such as head nurse or supervisor, depending upon their experience in the field and requirements for the position. Those working in community facilities often take positions as directors of service programs. Graduates of doctoral programs usually assume faculty or administrative positions and combine these with research or consultation.

Future predictions of the need for psychiatric nursing services in the United States indicate that there will be a serious shortage of practitioners in this specialty. Many opportunities for exciting and rewarding careers are available in this specialty now and will continue to be so for many years to come.

Patricia Ryan Wahl, RN, Ph.D., Associate Professor and Chair
Graduate Department of Psychiatric–Mental Health Nursing
University of Cincinnati

Public Health Nursing　"The Definition and Role of Public Health Nursing in the Delivery of Health Care," published by the Public Health Nursing Section of the American Public Health Association, states: "The specialty of public health nursing is professional nursing directed toward a total community or population group. Consideration is given to environmental, social, and personal health factors affecting health status. Its practice includes identification of subgroups or aggregates within the community or population who are at risk of illness or poor recovery and targeting its resources toward those groups and families and individuals who comprise them. Emphasis is on planning for a community as a whole rather than on individual health care. Its purpose, to improve the health of the commmunity through nursing intervention, is achieved by working with and through community leaders, health-related groups, groups at risk, families and individuals and by becoming involved in relevant social action. Participation of the public is an essential ingredient in the process."

Public health nursing specialists holding master's or doctoral degrees have received advanced training in nursing theory and practice and in the sciences of public health, including epidemiology, biostatistics, and environmental sciences. Knowledge of public

Public Health Nursing (continued)

health philosophy, organization, and management are included in their preparation. Readings in the social and behavioral sciences also provide a framework for understanding the formulation and implementation of health policy and the application of techniques of prevention and health promotion. Public health nursing specialists are expected to provide leadership in public health nursing practice, teaching, administration, consultation, and research. The essential knowledge needed for practice is the synthesis of public health science and professional nursing theories.

The content and approach of some community health nursing programs are the same as those of public health nursing programs. Other graduate programs in community health nursing, however, also prepare primary-health-care providers, such as community health nurse practitioners, family nurse practitioners, and other types of nurse practitioners. Other examples of subspecialization in public and community health nursing include school health, occupational health, and community mental health.

Nurses interested in public and community health graduate education should carefully assess the congruence of their career goals and the programs they are considering. The requirements of specific types of employment or specialty certification as well as other factors need to be investigated before an appropriate program can be selected.

Iris R. Shannon, RN, M.A., FAAN
Associate Professor
College of Nursing
Rush University

Rehabilitation Nursing   The field of rehabilitation is concerned with maximizing human potential among the disabled. Rehabilitators prepare and assist the disabled to participate in society at the highest level of functioning possible within the limits of a disability. Rehabilitation nursing seeks to intervene when an individual's ability to interact dynamically with the environment is adversely affected by the presence of a disabling condition.

In rehabilitation, the nurse is an indispensable member of an interdisciplinary health team. The nurse's knowledge of the theory and process of rehabilitation and rehabilitation nursing provides the basis for the nursing contribution to the team approach. The nurse acts as a team coordinator and uses the nursing process for planning rehabilitation programs for disabled individuals and their families.

Rehabilitation nursing interventions take the form of direct client/family contacts as well as interdisciplinary and community involvement to eliminate or minimize factors that adversely affect the rehabilitation process. In rehabilitation nursing, the caring relationship is conceptualized as an action-oriented process in which the client implements the program of rehabilitation while the nurse facilitates such implementation.

Master's degree education in rehabilitation nursing should prepare the student for professional practice as a teacher, administrator, expert clinician, or researcher. In selecting a suitable graduate program, prospective students should consider the following: The program must incorporate the scientific principles and rehabilitation theory that nurses need to assist clients and their families in making a positive adaptive response to the presence of a disability. Emphasis should be placed on planning and implementing rehabilitation programs for severely disabled individuals and their families. The framework of the program should be such that it is ideally suited to educate students not only in one clinical subspecialty but also in the broader dimensions of rehabilitation. The philosophy of the rehabilitation nursing specialty must be consistent with that of the school of nursing in which it resides; both philosophies should address the issue of maximizing human potential.

Pamela G. Watson, Sc.D., Associate Professor and Chair
Department of Rehabilitation,
Medical-Surgical, and Gerontologic Nursing
School of Nursing
Boston University

Nutrition

A student contemplating graduate work in nutrition should, in general, acquire a strong background in the basic sciences of chemistry, biochemistry, and biology. The student should also determine the area of nutrition that is of primary interest and plan the undergraduate curriculum accordingly. Areas of specialization in graduate work include nutritional biochemistry, human nutrition, clinical nutrition, international nutrition, community nutrition, nutrition education, and foods. Students intending to concentrate in

Nutrition (continued)

nutritional biochemistry should undertake courses in math and physics in addition to work in chemistry, biochemistry, and biology. Students planning a concentration in international nutrition should demonstrate a commitment to international work through, for example, service as a Peace Corps volunteer or any relevant experience of a responsible nature in a developing country. Students interested in community nutrition should include areas such as communications, sociology, and psychology in their curriculum, in addition to the basic sciences. A typical premed curriculum offers good preparation for graduate work in clinical nutrition. There is a common misconception that an undergraduate program in any major provides adequate preparation for graduate work in nutrition. This is definitely not the case. The more selective programs require a solid science background and will not admit applicants with deficiencies.

Many programs require applicants to submit satisfactory scores on the Graduate Record Examinations. Some may require scores on both the General Test and a Subject Test. Since a Subject Test is not given in nutrition, students with adequate preparation in chemistry or biology usually take the Subject Test in one of these fields.

Success in graduate work in nutrition depends to a considerable extent upon the student's aptitude for research. Most master's and doctoral programs require a satisfactory research thesis, planned and executed in consultation with a faculty adviser. Graduate programs in nutrition usually also require students to select one or two minor subjects appropriate to their area of concentration. Practical experience is a requirement in many programs in nutrition. Students interested in clinical nutrition need to acquire hospital experience, or a suitable alternative, to satisfy the requirements of the American Dietetic Association for certification as a registered dietitian (RD). Students in international nutrition are often expected to carry out their research in a developing country. Those in community nutrition carry out research projects that entail contact with people. Because graduate work is highly individualized, the M.S. or Ph.D. varies. In most programs a minimum of one year of residence for the M.S. is required, three years for the Ph.D. Actual duration of graduate study is typically two to three years for the M.S. and five years for the Ph.D.

Graduate stipends from fellowships, research assistantships, and teaching assistantships are becoming increasingly difficult to obtain, especially for foreign applicants. Foreign applicants should make every effort to obtain support from their own governments, the

United Nations University, or from private sources. U.S. citizens with superior academic credentials can sometimes obtain support from the National Science Foundation or other granting institutions.

At present the job market for graduates with the M.S. or Ph.D. in nutrition is good. Ph.D. graduates in nutrition are in demand for positions on university faculties, in national or international government, and in the pharmaceutical or food industries. For many positions in community nutrition and nutrition education, employers look for job candidates holding the M.S. degree. For positions in clinical nutrition, the M.S. degree together with the RD is the most common preparation, although the Ph.D. provides access to positions of greatest responsibility.

B. A. Lewis, Ph.D., Professor
Graduate Faculty Representative, Nutrition
Cornell University

Optometry and Vision Sciences

Optometry Doctors of Optometry (O.D.) determine the presence of vision problems, eye diseases, and other abnormalities. They gather information on the visual system during optometric examinations, diagnose any conditions discovered, and prescribe optometric treatment, such as corrective lenses, contact lenses, or vision therapy. They also detect ailments, such as glaucoma, cataract, diabetes, or hypertension, that require referral to other health-care practitioners.

Optometrists receive a four-year graduate education, which includes training in the visual sciences, the basic health sciences, psychology, and public health matters emphasizing preventive care and early detection of diseases. Training includes the use of pharmaceuticals for both diagnostic and therapeutic uses. Clinical activity and patient exposure usually begin during the first year and continue with clinical rotations both on and off campus during the remaining three years.

Students prepare for a career in optometry at one of the eighteen schools of optometry in the United States, Canada, and Puerto Rico. Applicants must satisfy specific prerequisites, take the Optometry Admission Test, and, as a rule, visit the college for a personal interview. Most students enter with a baccalaureate or advanced degree, although some schools may grant admission after

Optometry (continued)

only two years of college. Upon graduation, students must meet state licensure requirements before entering full optometric practice. These requirements often include passing of the National Board Examinations as well as state exams.

Optometrists find employment in private or associated practices, industry, the military, hospitals and health maintenance organizations, or teaching and research. One-year clinical residencies are available at a number of the colleges and at Veterans Administration facilities. Some also offer a doctorate in physiological optics, intended to prepare graduate O.D.'s for teaching or research. One college offers an accelerated program in which students with a doctorate in the sciences may earn the O.D. degree in two calendar years.

One of the latest changes affecting the profession of optometry allows optometrists to use therapeutic pharmaceuticals. Eleven states now permit such use. Further developments in this area, plus the advent of health service delivery in commercial settings, may lead to some changes in the profession of optometry and optometric practices.

Sylvio Dupuis, O.D.
President, New England College of Optometry

Vision Sciences The subject matter of the vision (or visual) sciences ranges from the physical principles involved in the absorption of light quanta by receptor pigments to the psychology of perception; accordingly, vision is one of the most interdisciplinary areas of study in all of science. Whether one is interested in biochemistry, anatomy, physiology, neural information transfer, or the psychology of perception, it will often be found that the most advanced work in the area is being completed by investigators who are identified as vision scientists. For example, a typical department of vision sciences might include biochemists investigating receptor proteins, anatomists working on questions about the development of retinal neural mechanisms, investigators using electro-physiological techniques to study the processing of neural information within the visual pathways, psychophysicists who use behavioral techniques to study the spatial, temporal, or color-resolving capacities of human vision, theorists who use engineering-based information transmission models to study the limitations of visual perception, and clinically oriented investigators whose research concerns health-related problems of vision.

Traditionally, vision scientists have worked within the administrative units of their discipline, such as anatomy, physiology, or psychology; however, because of rapid advances in the field of vision, there have been some relatively recent reorganizations that served to assemble these scientists within a single unit. Often, these units are associated with ophthalmological or optometric institutions, some of which have used the term physiological optics to refer to postprofessional graduate work in vision. (The term has its historical roots in the title of Helmholtz's monumental treatise on vision.)

Because of the interdisciplinary nature of the field, vision science programs often have very flexible requirements for graduate degrees, and it is sometimes useful for prospective students to investigate the possibility of strong affiliations with more than one department within a university. They may also consider pursuing a combined degree, such as the O.D./Ph.D., which is offered by several schools of optometry and provides solid clinical and research training.

Career opportunities in the vision sciences have tended to remain strong in comparison to those in many academic disciplines, not only because of teaching and research needs within the fields of optometry and ophthalmology, but also because of the enormous variety of applied problems that involve human image processing in the military and private sectors.

Dr. S. Lee Guth, Chairman
Graduate Program in Visual Sciences and Physiological Optics
Indiana University

Pharmacy and Pharmaceutical Sciences

Pharmaceutical Sciences Graduate study in the pharmaceutical sciences offers an opportunity to apply chemical, physical, and biological principles to the design of drugs and the characterization of their biodisposition. The pharmaceutical sciences encompass a number of disciplines, including medicinal chemistry, pharmaceutical chemistry, physical pharmacy, pharmaceutics, biopharmaceutics, and pharmacology. Although the plethora of

Pharmaceutical Sciences (continued)

names is confusing, these disciplines are interrelated, as outlined below.

Students in medicinal chemistry, pharmaceutical chemistry, or pharmacognosy are trained in the disciplines of chemistry so that they may carry out chemical investigations on compounds of biological interest. In medicinal chemistry or pharmaceutical chemistry research may involve studies relating to drug design and synthesis, reaction mechanisms, bioorganic chemistry, structure-activity relationships, the mechanism of action of drugs (including drug-receptor binding), isolation of active compounds from natural sources, drug metabolism, biochemical toxicology, the relationship between physicochemical properties and biological function, and the techniques of computer-assisted drug design, including computer graphics. At some schools, programs in pharmacognosy are devoted to the isolation of active compounds from natural sources and the elucidation of their biosynthesis.

Men and women interested in pharmaceutics undertake studies in pharmacokinetics (the absorption, distribution, metabolism, and excretion of drugs in man and animals), pharmacodynamics, drug-drug interactions, transport mechanisms, biopharmaceutics (dosage form and physiologic factors influencing drug availability and absorption), physical pharmacy (physicochemical factors influencing the design of pharmaceutical systems), the development of new drug delivery systems, and drug metabolism. Programs offering pharmacology as a major generally include study of the mechanism of action of drugs, pharmacokinetics, pharmacodynamics, and drug metabolism.

A bachelor's degree in pharmacy, chemistry, or biochemistry usually provides an adequate background for graduate work in the pharmaceutical sciences. The curriculum, normally tailored to the needs of each student, includes training in chemistry, pharmacology, and biochemistry. Specialized instrumentation used by many students in the pharmaceutical sciences includes mass spectrometry, especially newer techniques for the analysis of compounds of higher molecular weight. Nuclear magnetic resonance spectrometry, including two-dimensional NMR, is of special importance to students in medicinal chemistry, as are computer graphic techniques. Students in the pharmaceutical sciences should learn to use biomedical data management systems, such as the PROPHET Computer Resource of the National Institutes of Health, for data management, graphics, statistical analyses, and molecular and mathematical modeling.

Men and women who complete an up-to-date graduate program in the pharmaceutical sciences are well prepared for a variety of interesting positions in academia, government, and industry. Typical data from a large department show that 40 percent of the graduates pursue academic careers, 30 percent undertake research and fulfill administrative functions in industry, and 20 percent hold research and administrative positions in government research institutes. Especially well qualified men and women may hold high administrative positions in more than one area—government, industry, and academia—at various times in their careers. Transfer from one of these areas to another is not uncommon at lower as well as at higher levels.

Regardless of the names given to areas in the pharmaceutical sciences, the emphases and depth of these programs may vary widely from school to school. It is important for the prospective student to examine the offerings of each institution carefully to ensure that the proposed program is consistent with his or her interests.

Dr. George L. Kenyon
Professor of Chemistry and Biochemistry
Chairman, Department of Pharmaceutical Chemistry
University of California, San Francisco

Pharmacy Pharmacy has long enjoyed a respected position, beginning with the early history of medicine. The clinical aspects of pharmacy, involving the therapeutic application of drug knowledge, have led to the utilization of the pharmacist in a variety of positions unheard of just a few years ago. Doctor of Pharmacy programs prepare highly skilled individuals sophisticated in the application of drug therapy and the knowledge needed to improve patient care through individualization of drug regimens and drug consultation and monitoring. To accomplish this, programs provide the student with a solid academic foundation on which extensive, well-structured clinical experiences are based.

Students acquire a comprehensive background in pathophysiology, therapeutics, pharmacokinetics, and toxicology. They then undertake an extensive program of clinical experience in medical, surgical, and subspecialty areas in hospitals and other health-care sites. Students learn to assess patient problems, design and initiate therapeutic plans, solve drug therapy problems, monitor and assess therapeutic and adverse effects of drugs, and manage patients' drug therapy. Skills in communication, utilization of drug literature, and research methods, together with a sense of personal responsibility to patients for their drug therapy, are developed in the clinical program.

The expertise of clinical pharmacists is being employed more extensively in clinical research on drugs. The pharmacokinetic properties of individual agents, the use of experimental agents in humans, and the application of existing drugs for new therapeutic purposes are all areas of research available to the clinical pharmacist. Pharmacists most often work in interdisciplinary collaborative research teams with other health-care professionals.

Most Doctor of Pharmacy graduates assume positions in pharmacy practice or pharmacy education. An increasing number of current graduates are accepting positions as specialty practitioners in such areas as pediatrics, oncology, and infectious disease, developing pharmacokinetic services, engaging in clinical research, serving as primary-care practitioners, developing practices in community settings, or exploring the diversity of opportunities in the pharmaceutical industry. A Doctor of Pharmacy degree prepares pharmacists to meet the changing pharmacy practice needs of society.

George E. Downs, Pharm.D.
Professor of Clinical Pharmacy
Director of Pharmacy Practice
Philadelphia College of Pharmacy and Science

Podiatric Medicine

Podiatric medicine is that specialty of medicine that seeks to diagnose, treat, and prevent diseases and disorders of the human foot. Podiatric medicine has developed in response to the need for specialized care in this area of medical practice. Podiatric services range from routine podiatric care to reconstructive surgery for congenital deformities; within the growing podiatric medical specialty are subspecialties ranging from podo-pediatrics to podo-geriatrics. The podiatrist's scope of practice may include a combination of routine care, podiatric surgery, sports medicine, and treatment of chronic disorders of the elderly.

Within the podiatric profession are various academies and colleges affiliated with the American Podiatric Medical Association, including (but not limited to) the American College of Foot Orthopaedists, the American College of Podiatric Dermatologists, and the American College of Foot Surgeons. There are at present two recognized Certifying Boards: the American Board of Podiatric Surgery and the American Board of Podiatric Orthopaedics.

By helping to keep people ambulatory, active, and healthy, podiatrists make a major contribution to the society in which they live.

Thomas V. Melillo, D.P.M., President
Ohio College of Podiatric Medicine

Public and Community Health

Public and Community Health   Public health is a field that includes several disciplines. The fields that are generally regarded as forming the foundation for academic programs in public health are biostatistics, epidemiology, health promotion and health education, environmental health, and health administration or health policy and management. Many schools of public health, depending on their respective traditions and institutional resources, also have programs in health nutrition, tropical medicine and public health, occupational medicine, maternal and child health, population dynamics, and international health.

The field of public health attracts both researchers and practitioners, as well as those who choose to integrate research with public health practice. These two foci of interest are manifested in the various degree programs offered by schools of public health; many institutions intend that their M.S. and Ph.D. programs will be especially attractive to those wishing to enhance their research skills, while those who already have research training or who are experienced practitioners will be more likely to choose M.P.H. or Dr.P.H. programs.

Public health is a field in which intercourse across numerous disciplines is absolutely essential. It is difficult, if not impossible, to think of a contemporary public health problem that is the exclusive province of a single public health discipline. Assessing the risk for exposure to a given toxic hazard, for example, is a frequently presented public health problem that requires collaborative activities of researchers across many disciplines.

Public and Community Health (continued)

As with many other fields, employment opportunities depend in part upon the area within public health in which the student specializes, as well as the prior educational and professional experience the student has. Although municipal, state, and federal public health agencies and health-care programs have long been employers of graduates of schools of public health, in recent years both manufacturing and service companies in the for-profit sector have been sources of considerable employment. Positions available in such firms range from epidemiologists in pharmaceutical companies to toxicologists with computer manufacturers to administrators of health maintenance organizations.

Students selecting an academic program should consider the institutional resources available to them. It is helpful to assess not only the number of faculty members and their qualifications, but also the extent to which students may work with established investigators on their research and service projects. It is also important to determine if the programs offered are accredited by the Council on Education for Public Health.

Andrew Sorensen, Director
Division of Public Health
University of Massachusetts at Amherst

Environmental and Occupational Health   The field of environmental health sciences is the study of interactions between humans and their environment and the characteristic conditions that affect human health. The status of human health represents the end result of complex interactions between the biological system—man (the internal environment)—and the total surroundings (the external environment).

Environmental health is the branch of public health that concentrates on the factors, which may be substances, forces, forms of life, and/or general conditions, in our surroundings that may have impact upon human health with the overall goal of preventing such factors from adversely affecting human health status. The purview of environmental health includes both the natural surroundings (the general environment) and the workplace (the occupational environment).

Occupational health is the specialty within the environmental health sciences that addresses factors that may affect human health status in the workplace. The following types of activities are within the scope of occupational health: assessing the source(s) and degree of exposure to potential hazards, defining the expected/potential results of such biological interactions on employees, protecting employees from known workplace hazards, educating and training managers and the employees they supervise in areas related to worker health and safety, and maintaining operational health and safety programs in order to provide a safe and healthful workplace environment.

The World Health Organization's definition of environmental health also included the effects of the quality of life within the domain of this specialty. This approach may include a concern with ecological and aesthetic values as well as health in a more strict sense. The quality of life is related directly to the quality of our environment. Our world is a very finite ecosystem with limited quantities of natural resources (land, water, air, food, etc.) that do have direct impact upon human life and health status. Concepts such as pure water, pure food, clean air, and clean neighborhoods reflect newer areas of concern within the field and an understanding of environmental health as meaning more than the absence of disease.

There are many areas in the world today where the level of environmental quality needed to ensure the bare survival of inhabitants has not yet been attained. Malnutrition, lack of sanitary conditions, and vector-borne diseases such as malaria and schistosomiasis are extensive health problems in many countries. In the United States we still have health problems involving food-borne illnesses such as infectious hepatitis, food poisoning such as salmonellosis, botulism, and staphylococcal poisoning and outbreaks of vector-borne diseases including encephalitis and Rocky Mountain spotted fever. The use of potentially toxic materials originating from man-made and natural sources has added to health hazards associated with the general environment and the workplace environment, as exemplified by instances of lead poisoning in children, lung cancer and asbestosis from exposure to asbestos, lung cancer in industrial workers exposed to vinyl chloride, chronic effects from aflatoxins in grains, and effects on reproduction caused by medicinals such as diethylstilbestrol (DES).

Problem solving in the multidisciplinary areas of the environmental health sciences involves principles and methods not only of the physical and life sciences, mathematics, engineering, and other areas of public health and medicine but also of the social sciences in order to deal with the complex interactions of humans,

Environmental and Occupational Health (continued)

their activities, and the many perturbations caused by varying life-styles, the environment, and possibly acceptable "trade-offs."

Dr. Edward O. Oswald, Chairman
Department of Environmental Health Sciences
School of Public Health
University of South Carolina

Epidemiology Epidemiology is defined as a branch of science that deals with the causes of diseases of human beings as inferred from studies of human beings. Early in this century, epidemiologists dealt primarily with infectious diseases such as yellow fever, malaria, and tuberculosis. In the modern era, methods of controlling these ancient scourges must still be kept in place; however, most epidemiologic research and service is now directed against the contemporary plagues: heart disease, cancer, and mental illness among others.

Educational opportunities in epidemiology and in public health, the broader field of which it is a part, remain quite limited at the undergraduate level. Opportunities for graduate study, on the other hand, are abundant. Many universities offer courses or degree programs in this area through a medical school, a school of allied health sciences, or a school of public health.

At the master's level, the program most often selected leads to the Master of Public Health (M.P.H.) degree. This is a broadly based program in public health in which about 30 percent of study is concerned with epidemiology. The alternative master's program leads to the Master of Science in Public Health (M.S.P.H.) degree and is more focused on epidemiology and, usually, biostatistics; these areas together occupy about 75 percent of the curriculum. One to two years are usually required to complete either type of program. Doctoral programs lead to the Doctor of Public Health (Dr.P.H.) or the Doctor of Philosophy (Ph.D.) degree and usually take two to four years to complete. These programs are given over to the study of epidemiology, biostatistics, and computer sciences. Virtually all degree programs in epidemiology, master's or doctoral, include courses in human physiology and pathophysiology for students without such training.

Epidemiology is a very exciting, dynamic field that is now growing rapidly and is becoming well recognized by the lay public as well as by legislators, regulators, and policymakers as the science that provides the basis for modern public health policy. Employment opportunities in epidemiology have always exceeded the supply of trained personnel, and this will remain so for the foreseeable future. Graduates work in universities; federal, state, and local government agencies; hospitals; and large corporations. Activities include research into the causes of disease and control efforts to detect and reduce early indices of disease, such as high blood pressure or early signs of cancer.

Students considering a career in epidemiology might wish to contact the head of the department of epidemiology at a school of public health for information and advice.

Philip Cole, M.D., Dr.P.H., Professor and Chairman
Department of Epidemiology
School of Public Health
University of Alabama at Birmingham

Health Physics/Radiological Health   Health physics/radiological health spans a wide range of disciplines, including radiation chemistry, radiation biology, nuclear engineering, environmental health, public health, and medical physics. Health physicists are professionals dedicated to the protection of man and his environment from the harmful effects of radiation while recognizing that there are benefits to be derived from the use of radiation in many areas of daily life. Their concerns include ionizing radiation (such as X rays and gamma rays) as well as nonionizing radiation (such as microwaves and ultraviolet). For the above reasons a health physicist should have a broad background in chemistry, biology, and physics, with a strong grounding in mathematics.

A student interested in the field should recognize that, with only a few exceptions, concentrated study begins at the graduate level. A strong undergraduate course of study in the above-mentioned areas is the appropriate preparation for graduate study if an undergraduate health physics/radiological health curriculum is not available.

At the graduate level, the student has an opportunity to select a health physics/radiological health program based on a primary interest. For example, some programs are found in schools of engineering, whereas others are in a school of public health or environmental health. Programs are also offered through divisions of biology (or radiobiology) and/or associated with medical

Health Physics/Radiological Health (continued)

programs. While all programs are based on a fundamental understanding of ionizing and nonionizing radiation, individual programs concentrate in a specific subdiscipline of health physics. Several universities, however, offer less-restricted programs that allow a student to mix several areas of interest with a core curriculum common to all areas of health physics/radiological health.

Graduate programs in the field have widely varying requirements for the master's degree. Most require a thesis or a major research project. However, programs are available in which the student has the option of substituting course work for the thesis. The length of programs is also quite variable. Some are arranged to be completed in approximately 1 year (including the summer session), while others may involve a commitment of up to 2½ years. Study leading to the Ph.D. degree is also available at some universities.

Job opportunities for health physicists vary widely. Many graduates are placed in electric utilities that operate nuclear-electric generating facilities. Most research facilities, including universities, national laboratories, and research hospitals, employ health physicists. Industrial opportunities are too numerous to mention, but essentially any company utilizing radiation to control a process or using radioactive material in a process will employ one or more health physicists. Government service also offers career opportunities. Positions are available in regulatory agencies as well as in research facilities operated by these agencies.

Dr. John W. Poston, Professor
Department of Nuclear Engineering
Texas A&M University

Veterinary Medicine and Sciences

Veterinary Medicine   Veterinary medicine is a broad professional discipline that applies the biomedical sciences to the health and welfare of animals and deals with the public health aspects of interaction between animals and humans.

The study of veterinary medicine involves a minimum of two years of preprofessional education in animal and biologic science in a university followed by a four-year professional degree curriculum. Admission to the four-year program is highly competitive and will require experience with animals as well as excellent preprofessional academic performance. Preprofessional education may be obtained at almost any accredited university, while education for the professional degree is available at only twenty-seven locations in the United States. The professional academic program leads to a Doctor of Veterinary Medicine (D.V.M.) degree.

Completion of the D.V.M. degree allows the graduate to sit for state licensing examinations and permits entry into the private practice of veterinary medicine. The graduate also has many opportunities in industry, government regulatory activity, and continued academic programs leading to M.S. or Ph.D. degrees in the biological sciences and/or board certification in the various clinical specialties.

Students holding B.S. or B.A. degrees and wishing to enter graduate degree programs in colleges of veterinary medicine may generally do so only in the basic science areas. Graduate programs in clinical science will usually require the applicant to have completed the D.V.M. professional degree program.

In general, veterinarians wishing academic or research careers will complete an M.S./Ph.D. program after the D.V.M. degree. Veterinarians wishing to specialize in clinically related veterinary activities will complete a minimum of an M.S. degree and several years of specialized training leading to certification by a veterinary medical specialty board.

Recently completed studies indicate that the demand for veterinarians in clinical practice will grow very slowly in the near future while the demand for veterinarians with advanced degrees and specialty training will continue to expand.

Billy E. Hooper, D.V.M., Ph.D.
Executive Director
Association of American Veterinary Medical Colleges

Veterinary Sciences Postgraduate training in veterinary medical sciences encompasses a broad range of disciplines. Students can pursue advanced training and research leading to graduate degrees in anatomical sciences, biochemistry, bioengineering, immunology, microbiology, nuclear medicine, nutrition, parasitology, pathology, pharmacology, and physiology as well as the more clinically oriented areas of anesthesiology, internal medicine, radiology, surgery, and theriogenology.

Depending on career goals, individuals who pursue advanced training in veterinary sciences may proceed in one of two general

Veterinary Sciences (continued)

directions. The first path leads through graduate courses and research in the basic sciences and culminates in the Ph.D. degree. An individual with this background is most likely to pursue a career in an academic or research setting.

The second type of program emphasizes increased individual expertise in diagnostic skills or in a specific clinical skill, such as surgery. These programs, which are classified as residency programs, usually include completion of the M.S. or the Ph.D. degree. Prior completion of the D.V.M. degree or the equivalent is usually required for entrance into these applied programs. After completing these training programs, individuals may take certification examinations to become board certified in such areas as surgery, internal medicine, toxicology, and theriogenology.

Students who complete degrees in veterinary sciences have a wide variety of career options available to them. They can meet the need for teachers or researchers in a variety of academic, governmental, or industrial situations. Research on biomedical problems of importance to both human and animal populations is an important component of programs in veterinary medicine. In recent years, increased emphasis on research support for disease problems in food animals has resulted in significant growth of opportunities in this important area. Also, the increasing application of genetic technology to problems of disease prevention and animal productivity has greatly expanded the options for new trainees. Jobs can be found in the academic sector, government, industry, and, for persons trained to be private practitioners, in specialty referral clinics. The broad comparative training of a veterinary scientist is excellent preparation for research on biomedical, environmental, public health, and food-animal problems of a most diverse nature.

Dr. William C. Wagner, Professor and Head
Department of Veterinary Biosciences
College of Veterinary Medicine
University of Illinois at Urbana-Champaign

Physical Sciences and Mathematics

Astronomy and Astrophysics

Astronomy Astronomy is concerned with the study of the properties of all bodies external to the earth that can be examined by means of instruments located within the solar system and with the understanding of these properties in terms of physical processes that have their foundation in experimental physics. Current instrumentation allows the study of light emitted by external bodies over a considerable range in wavelength: less than 3,300 (ultraviolet, X-ray, and gamma-ray telescopes in space), 6,000–12,000 and 1.2–200 microns (infrared mountaintop telescopes), 3,000–6,000 (optical telescopes at all elevations on Earth and in space), and 1 millimeter to 20 meters (radio telescopes at all elevations). Objects of study range from galaxies, consisting of billions of stars and interstellar gas in bound systems, to stars and interstellar molecules within our own galaxy and in the local group of galaxies. Galaxies vary in type from quasars, which are thought to be bound systems possibly deriving their immense power from massive black holes that are swallowing stars, to ordinary galaxies such as our own, which contain light stars as old as the universe itself. Much of the matter in the universe, including most of the matter in galaxies, is thought to be in the form of "dark" matter, whose presence is known only by its gravitational effect on luminous objects. Stars vary in type from very young, bright stars that ultimately become supernovae to very condensed objects—such as white dwarfs, neutron stars, and black holes—which are thought to represent the final dying stages of stars that have exhausted their original store of nuclear fuel.

Careers for the Ph.D. astronomer may be found in the academic community (teaching and basic research), industry (instrument design and computer programming), and the space program (applied and basic research). In recent years, job opportunities for Ph.D.'s have been somewhat restricted, but there have consistently been positions available for those who have demonstrated a gift for innovative research. It is to be hoped that capable students with a real interest in and talent for astronomical research will not be dissuaded by past and future vagaries in the job

Physical Sciences and Mathematics

Astronomy (continued)

market from entering a most fascinating and intellectually rewarding field.

Icko Iben Jr.
Departments of Astronomy and of Physics
University of Illinois at Urbana-Champaign

Astrophysics   Astrophysics is the study of astronomical phenomena in terms of the underlying physical processes. The investigation of these phenomena involves virtually every subfield of physics—for example, nuclear physics (stellar evolution, supernovae, element formation in the early universe), atomic and molecular physics (stellar atmospheres, molecular clouds and the interstellar medium), plasma physics (stellar interiors, supernovae, radio galaxies), condensed-matter physics (neutron stars), relativity and gravitation (neutron stars–pulsars, black holes, large-scale structure of the universe, big bang theory), and elementary particle and field theory (the early universe and the nature of dark matter).

Much of the excitement in astrophysics has been generated by several important "unsolved problems." These include the missing mass in galaxies and clusters, the solar neutrino problem, the isotropy of the cosmic background, the formation of galaxies, the energy sources in quasars and active galaxies, and the ultimate fate of the universe. Experimental evidence relevant to these and other problems comes primarily from astronomical observations with X-ray, optical, infrared, and radio telescopes, although neutrino and gravitational wave telescopes have been constructed, and laboratory experiments in nuclear and atomic physics are sometimes motivated by astrophysical problems.

Since astrophysics is a subfield of physics, graduate preparation is essentially the same as for physics in general. Many physics departments, especially those that are combined with astronomy departments, have strong programs in astrophysics. Permanent positions for Ph.D. astrophysicists at academic institutions are in short supply, as is the case for most other areas of physics. However, because of their background in physics,

294

astrophysicists find that job prospects in industrial and governmental research facilities are quite good.

Professor Stephen P. Boughn
Department of Physics
Princeton University

Chemistry

Chemistry is the science of matter. It is primarily an experimental science with active research areas, including chemical synthesis and analysis, chemical dynamics and quantum chemistry, chemical instrumentation, structural chemistry, and solid-state and polymer chemistry. Research in chemistry provides the basis for developments in other important areas, such as microelectronics, oceanography, and atmospheric science.

Chemistry is the principal link between biological and physical science. The development of chemical methodology and phenomenological understanding during the last half century has served as the foundation on which modern, molecularly oriented biological sciences are built. While traditional classifications such as analytical, biological, inorganic, organic, and physical chemistry are still widely used, the subject has expanded to overlap with physics, geology, biology, biochemistry, physiology, bacteriology and microbiology, metallurgy, materials science, medicinal chemistry and pharmacology, computer science, environmental science, biotechnology, and other emerging areas.

Career opportunities for chemists who have received doctoral, master's, and bachelor's degrees abound. National employment remains above 99 percent, and chemical, petrochemical, and pharmacological corporations continue to lead the nation's economy. Societal needs, especially in health, environmental, and energy concerns, are making ever-increasing demands on the supply of well-trained chemists. Chemists are managerial as well as scientific leaders in industry, government, and academia. Chemistry is likely to remain one of the largest professions in the nation throughout the twentieth and into the twenty-first century.

Thomas L. Isenhour
Dean of Science
Utah State University

Earth and Planetary Sciences

Earth Sciences   The earth sciences today connote a very diverse area of study, including the various pursuits of traditional geology (mineralogy, petrology, geomorphology, glacial geology, volcanology, sedimentation, stratigraphy, tectonics, etc.) as well as geochemistry, geophysics, glaciology, hydrology, oceanography (chemical, geological, and physical), and paleontology. These disciplines cover the study of the solid, liquid, and gaseous parts of the earth and other planets of the solar system, including studies of their magnetic and gravitational fields. Virtually all of the earth sciences are interdisciplinary in that they are the application of chemistry, biology, mathematics, and physics to their special area of study.

All of the disciplines of the earth sciences have an orientation toward the study of processes. These studies vary widely from erosion, sedimentation, and volcanism on earth, other planets, and their satellites to organic evolution and to the processes that move the earth's crustal plates, produce ocean tides and currents, and modify the weather (long and short term). Most of the disciplines have a historical aspect leading to the history and evolution of the earth, its continents, mountains, oceans, etc., as well as the other planets and their major features.

Much research in the earth sciences has been directed to exploration for nonrenewable essential minerals and fossil fuels (oil, gas, and coal), as well as to alternative energy sources. Most recently, because there has been a great concern for decreasing supplies of clean surface and underground water as well as for pollution of this necessary resource, demand for specialists in hydrology and hydrogeology has been very high.

Herbert Tischler, Chairman
Department of Earth Sciences
University of New Hampshire

Geochemistry   Geochemistry, broadly construed, is the application of the principles of chemistry to earth and planetary sciences. We may broadly distinguish two main categories, organic and inorganic, although many terrestrial subjects clearly involve both types.

Geochemistry has enjoyed a remarkable flowering in the past thirty years, chiefly because of the increased capabilities brought about by advances in instrumentation and technology. We are now able to sustain static pressures in the laboratory exceeding half a million bars, attain plasma temperatures of several thousand degrees C, and detect atomic and isotopic abundances in favorable circumstances to less than a part per billion.

Individual fields have grown up around analytical capabilities, such as mass spectrometry; gas chromatography; X-ray diffraction and fluorescence; instrumental and radiochemical neutron activation; atomic absorption; Mössbauer, optical, and infrared spectroscopy; and electron and ion microanalysis, among others. Materials investigated include living systems; fossil flora and fauna; petroleum; natural gas; coal; igneous, sedimentary, and metamorphic rocks; volcanic emanations; hydrothermal and connate fluids; ore deposits; lunar rocks; and meteorites. Particular disciplines involve the study of major and trace-element distribution, radioactive and stable isotope fractionations, experimental phase equilibria, and thermochemical computation and modeling.

Employment opportunities, as might be anticipated, are as diverse as the subject covered by the term geochemistry. Geochemists are utilized in the mineral resource industries (working on fissionable and fossil fuels and ore deposits), earth and space sciences, environmental sciences (including hydrology), and several branches of chemical science and technology.

W. G. Ernst
Professor of Geology and Geophysics
Department of Earth and Space Sciences
University of California, Los Angeles

Geodetic Sciences   The task of geodetic science is to determine the size and shape of the Earth and carry out measurements and computations necessary for accurate mapping of the Earth's surface. With man's conquest of space this task extends itself to celestial bodies other than the Earth.

Geodetic science techniques find many applications in engineering, architecture, geology, agriculture, archaeology, and geography, to mention but a few.

The study of geodetic science can be built only on a solid foundation, which includes mathematics, physics, astronomy, and geophysics. Thus, while the undergraduate student may qualify for the baccalaureate degree in geodetic science, this field is necessarily one that is pursued more intensively by the graduate student.

Geodetic Sciences (continued)

The field of geodetic science usually includes geodesy, photogrammetry, and cartography.

Some consider geodesy to be the oldest earth science. It has the general goals of precisely determining positions on the Earth's surface, determining the Earth's size and shape, determining the Earth's gravity field, and measuring and representing geodynamic phenomena.

Photogrammetry obtains reliable information about physical objects and the environment by recording, measuring, and interpreting photographic images and patterns of electromagnetic radiant energy and other phenomena. A conventional application of photogrammetry has been the compilation of topographic maps and surveys based on measurements and information obtained from aerial and space photographs with optical analog instruments and/ or analytic computations.

Cartography describes an environment by graphical and/or digital means. The irreversible trend in cartography today is toward computer-assisted methods of mapping and data manipulation. The cartographer's goal is to organize the data of an environment into an efficient land (or geographic) information system. For example, a graphical or analog land (or geographic) information system would be a topographic or thematic map. A digital (or geographic) information system would exist in a computer and would be accessible via appropriate terminals.

Geodetic science forms the basis of studies in the mapping sciences. Until a few years ago, the only maps available were those printed on material such as paper. Today the mapping sciences stand on the threshold of an exciting and ever-expanding future. The computer now allows the mapping scientist to produce maps on computer graphics terminals. Some maps can reside in a computer, in complete numerical (or digital) form, from which a user can extract needed information. The computer and its peripherals, such as digitizers, plotters, file management systems, and graphics terminals, are used today in all stages of map production.

Ivan I. Mueller, Professor
Department of Geodetic Science and Surveying
Ohio State University

Geology   Geology is the study of the Earth, especially the solid part of the Earth and its interactions with the fluids and gases within and above it. The concerns of geology, now frequently called geological sciences or included in earth and planetary sciences, have traditionally been with the rocks and structures of the crust of the Earth as exposed at the surface or studied in bore holes or mines up to a few kilometers beneath the surface. In the last generations the subject has come to include the geochemistry and geophysics of the Earth and its relation to the other planets as integral parts of the geological sciences. Modern geologists not only study their rocks directly in the field but study them by remote sensing from satellites and by using geophysical and geochemical exploration techniques. They carry the rocks to the laboratory and there analyze them physically and chemically. Experiments on rock synthesis, deformation, and destruction constitute an important part of the field.

There are two major aspects to the study of geology: how the Earth operates as a dynamic system today and its historical evolution as a planet. The first aspect concerns the current forces shaping the surface and interior of the Earth, from mountains to the floors of the oceans, from the sedimentary processes by which the products of erosion are deposited as sedimentary layers to the dynamics of volcanism and earthquakes, and all of the other processes that continue to move and modify the structure and form of the Earth. The second aspect, usually lumped under the subject historical geology, includes the study of the Earth through its 4½-billion-year history. From historical geological studies we are able to learn the dynamics of very slow processes. In almost all of the subfields of geology—stratigraphy, paleontology, sedimentology, mineralogy and petrology, structural geology, and geomorphology—there are new and exciting developments, many of them linked to the major new theory that has swept the geological sciences in the past fifteen years—plate tectonics. Geophysics and geochemistry have been broadly joined to geology, particularly in the study of the development of the ocean basins, the origin of mountain belts, and the evolution of continental landmasses.

Researches in geology have extreme practical value: the energy and mineral resources of the Earth are largely contained in its crustal layers. The geologists, in particular those engaged in the hunt for fossil fuels (oil and gas, coal, shale oil, and tar sands) and those hunting for the mineral resources that we use for much of our industry (ores of various metals, nonmetallic mineral resources such as phosphate, and others), are in great demand by the energy and mineral resource industry. There is a great deal of research going on into both fundamental and applied aspects of the origin of various economically important deposits. Mining has been extended to the

Geology (continued)

seafloor, and so, as with many other areas of geology, the study of the oceans has become an important division of the subject: marine geology, geophysics, and geochemistry are integral parts of the field.

Because of the great breadth of the geological sciences and their relation to all of the other sciences, the advanced student needs to know not only a great deal about the Earth but also physics, chemistry, and mathematics in order to be able to carry on the newer researches in the field. With a good background in related sciences and in geological sciences, geologists are having enormous successes in understanding the ways in which the Earth is formed and in which its economically useful products may be recovered.

Raymond Siever
Professor of Geology
Department of Geological Sciences
Harvard University

Geophysics   Geophysics means physics of the Earth. Because the Earth is a vast and complicated object, geophysics is a broad subject and includes, for example, meteorology (the science of the weather) and oceanography (the science of the oceans, their currents, waves, and tides). Solid-earth geophysics is concerned with the problems of the internal constitution of the Earth and its evolution. What causes mountains to form, volcanoes to erupt? What are earthquakes? What accounts for the heat that seeps out of the Earth, or for its magnetic field? What causes continents to move, or the seafloor to be constantly renewed as it spreads from places where new crust is formed to places where it sinks back down into the depths? These are some of the questions that geophysics tries to answer in studies of the structure and internal composition of the Earth; seismology (the science of earthquakes and of the propagation through the Earth of the elastic waves they generate); studies of the gravitational, electrical, and magnetic fields of the Earth; studies of heat sources, heat transfer, and temperature distribution within the Earth; and laboratory studies of the physical and chemical properties of minerals under the conditions of high pressure and temperature that are present within the Earth.

Geophysics is clearly an interdisciplinary field. On the one hand, it is very closely related to geology, the study of rocks and the record of the Earth's history that can be read from them. On the other hand, it is closely related to physics as it attempts to explain geological observations in terms of experimentally verifiable physical laws. It is also related to chemistry and to the branch of that science (geochemistry) that deals with the distribution of chemical elements and chemical compounds (minerals) that form the Earth. Mathematics is an indispensable tool of geophysics, as it is of physics.

Geophysics also has some highly practical applications, closely related to engineering. Much of the search for economically valuable deposits of metals and petroleum, for example, is conducted by geophysical means, such as by detecting the effects these bodies have on gravity or on the electrical or magnetic fields on the Earth's surface. Geophysicists are called upon to study the mechanical properties of rocks on which the foundations of dams or other large structures may be laid; they evaluate earthquake hazards and design instruments for the exploration of the moon and other planets. They find employment in academic institutions in teaching and research, in government and industrial research laboratories, and in companies involved in exploration for petroleum and mineral deposits. They work in the laboratory and in the field and spend much time exploring the more distant corners of the Earth, from the rift valleys of equatorial Africa or the volcanoes of the Pacific to the glaciers of Antarctica. Geophysics, perhaps more than any other science, is essentially an international effort, inasmuch as all geophysicists, regardless of nationality, are concerned with one and the same Earth.

Lane R. Johnson, Professor
Department of Geology and Geophysics
University of California, Berkeley

Planetary Sciences Planetary sciences refer to the study of the nature, origin, and history of the solar system, applying the principles of all the other branches of the physical sciences, especially those that play important roles in the geosciences and astronomy. Our understanding of the solar system is benefiting greatly from the wealth of data returned from space probes, which have now visited all but the most distant planets and have opened up whole new "planetary systems" (the satellite and ring systems of Jupiter, Saturn, and Uranus) for detailed study. Space-probe data are combined with observations from the ground and from Earth orbit, laboratory measurements, and theoretical analyses in an attempt to understand the scientific issues posed by our nearby cosmic environment.

Planetary Sciences (continued)

Planetary sciences also involve studies of the chemistry, mineralogy, and history of extraterrestrial materials (meteorites and lunar samples) and an analysis of extraterrestrial processes that have modified Earth history (impacts by meteorites or comets, tidal influences, changes in the Earth's orbit caused by other planets, solar variability, and other possible causes of climatic variation).

Much of planetary sciences is interdisciplinary and defies categorization into subdisciplines. However, specializations within the field are often one of four areas that define regions of a body: the external region of plasmas and fields, the atmosphere, the surface (if there is one), and the interior. Scientists concerned with the external region study the behavior of charged plasmas in space and how they interact with the planetary magnetic field and the outermost regions of the planet. Their tools include radio astronomy and the direct measurement of magnetic fields and plasmas by spacecraft. Atmospheric scientists include dynamicists and chemists; they wish to understand the thermal structure, composition, energy balance, spatial and temporal variability, global circulation, winds, atmospheric waves, clouds, and interactions of the atmosphere with the regions above and below. Their database includes IR and UV spectra, imaging at visible wavelengths, and (in the cases of Mars and Venus) direct sampling of the atmosphere. Planetary geologists interpret the surfaces of solid bodies using techniques developed in terrestrial geomorphology as well as other techniques developed within planetary sciences, such as interpretation of the number density and morphology of impact craters. Their data include high-resolution imaging and infrared mapping by spacecraft. Scientists who work on the properties of planetary interiors must synthesize the information from other areas together with gravity field, heat flow data, and laboratory and theoretical information on the properties of materials at high pressures. In each subdiscipline, "planet" can also mean "satellite," because there are many satellites in the solar system with histories and structures as complex as a conventionally defined planet. Asteroids and comets also have a sufficiently rich phenomenology to demand specialized attention. All of these areas of interest require a comparative approach in which similarities and differences between planets not only provide the basis for a cosmic synthesis but also help us to understand the Earth better.

Exciting possibilities exist in planetary science for people who are talented in physics, mathematics, and chemistry. In addition to ongoing and planned planetary missions (Voyager, Galileo, Venus

Radar Mapper, Mars Observer, comet rendezvous, and Titan probe/ Saturn orbiter), new data continue to be gathered from ground-based and Earth-orbit observations. People with training in planetary science are also well suited to a variety of geoscience or astronomy careers. The long-term stability of funding for planetary science and NASA missions is uncertain, but there is the profound hope that planetary exploration is much too important a human endeavor to be permanently affected by these uncertainties.

David J. Stevenson
Professor of Planetary Science
Division of Geological and Planetary Sciences
California Institute of Technology

Marine Sciences/Oceanography

Oceanography, viewed broadly, is the study of the processes, both physical and biological, occurring in the sea. The field is traditionally divided into four disciplines: physical oceanography, marine chemistry, marine geology, and marine biology or biological oceanography. The boundary lines between the fields are overlapping, and much of oceanography is truly interdisciplinary in nature.

Physical oceanography deals with mechanisms of energy transfer through the sea and across its boundaries and with physical interactions within the seas. Included are air-sea interactions and climatology, the general circulation of the oceans, fluctuations of currents, properties of waves, the thermodynamic description of the sea as a nonequilibrium system, and the optical and acoustic properties of the sea.

Marine chemistry deals with chemical processes operating within the marine environment and with the interactions of the components of seawater with the atmosphere, with sediments, and with organisms. Research in marine chemistry relates strongly to all of the disciplines of oceanography and includes biochemistry as well as inorganic and organic chemistry.

Marine geology is concerned with the origin, nature, and history of ocean basins and their shores and sediments and with the geological processes that affect them. Studies include tectonics and volcanism, geomorphology of the ocean crust and margins,

Marine Sciences/Oceanography (continued)

sedimentation, stratigraphy and paleontology, petrology, geochemistry, and geophysics.

Biological oceanography is concerned with the interactions of populations of marine organisms with one another and with the environment. Studies range from population dynamics of single species and investigations of the structure of communities and ecosystems to primary productivity and the physiological and biochemical adaptations of organisms.

A newly emerging area is applied ocean sciences, which is concerned with the application of engineering techniques to the solution of basic and applied research problems in the sea. Its goal is to produce oceanographers who are knowledgeable of modern engineering and engineers who know about the sea.

Oceanography is a synthetic graduate subject. Students who wish to pursue graduate study in one of the fields of oceanography should acquire a strong background in one or more of the basic sciences, mathematics, or engineering.

Graduates with degrees in one of the disciplines of oceanography have found jobs in a variety of areas—universities, federal and state government laboratories and agencies, and private industry.

Richard Rosenblatt, Professor
Graduate Department
Scripps Institution of Oceanography

Mathematical Sciences

Applied Mathematics The American tradition of mathematical education neglected the study of applied mathematics as a full-fledged academic discipline until the time of the Second World War, when the exigencies of wartime research drew attention to a shortage of American-trained applied mathematicians. The first U.S. universities to introduce systematic programs in this field were New York University under Richard Courant and Brown University under William Prager, who were, through their backgrounds, able to draw on the long-standing European tradition of teaching pure and applied mathematics in an integrated manner.

The training of applied mathematicians has two fairly distinct aspects: they have to provide themselves with a broad arsenal of mathematical methods and techniques that will be essential to them in their professional life, and they have to study one or more application areas in order to learn firsthand how mathematics is used in actual, real-life problems—whether these be problems in a physical, biological, or social science; in engineering; or in industry and government. In their study of mathematics they will naturally gravitate toward the more applicable subdisciplines, and in applications, toward those currently posing mathematical challenge and promise. The latter have changed over the years. "Classical" applied mathematics principally addressed itself to the mathematical problems posed by the mechanics of particles, of rigid and deformable bodies, and of fluids and also by electromagnetic theory.

Although there are still many outstanding and challenging problems in these "classical" fields—for instance, those concerning unorthodox materials—the purview of applied mathematics has been considerably broadened since, perhaps, the middle 1950s. This is partly due to advances in mathematics itself, many stimulated by applications, but largely to the fact that we can now profitably attack more complex and less idealized problems than before; the tool of computer simulation has been added to our armory. Large-scale scientific computation has in fact become an important subfield of applied mathematics, yielding challenging analytical and algorithmic problems. In addition, the recent prominence given to large-scale scientific computing and the emergence of supercomputers—both vector machines and massively parallel processors—is providing new challenges to applied mathematicians: these computers will require different mathematical methods for their efficient utilization from those implemented on orthodox architectures and numerical algorithms of a different sort for the solution of large-scale problems in meteorology, oil exploration, economic forecasting, aircraft and spacecraft design, nuclear technology, etc. In addition to the physical sciences, the biological and social sciences now provide a host of stimulating applications for mathematical analysis. With this has come a widening of job opportunities for graduates. No longer do they largely enter the academic profession. Industry, commerce, and government have come to appreciate the analytical and computational skills of Ph.D. graduates trained in the better applied mathematics departments.

Walter Freiberger, Professor and Chairman
Graduate Program Committee
Division of Applied Mathematics
Brown University

Biometrics The field of biometrics is concerned with the application of quantitative methodology to biological or, more generally, scientific problems concerning natural phenomena. In scope, biometrics can refer to such diverse fields as medicine, meteorology, genetics, agriculture, sociology, chemistry, epidemiology, physics, and demography. One specialty is medical information sciences, relating to medical information processing by computers.

Biometrics is a natural field of further study for the student with strength in both mathematics and biology and the desire to utilize his or her background in both areas and in a professional field where employment opportunities remain good.

In complexity, the practice of biometrics can range from the simple calculation of an average to the derivation of original quantitative theory or the development of sophisticated computer software. A student's background should generally include matrix algebra and analysis (calculus and differential equations), chemistry, general biology, genetics, physiology, and exposure to computers.

Richard H. Jones, Professor
Department of Preventive Medicine and Biometrics
University of Colorado School of Medicine

Biostatistics Biostatistics is an integral part of biomedical and health research. Statistical models of observed phenomena and randomization in the design of experiments form the basis for inductive reasoning. Generalizations from such studies involve statistics in planning, analysis, and interpretation. The specialized statistical approaches for variables and investigations that are biomedical, epidemiologic, and health-service related constitute the field of biostatistics. Biostatistics has developed as a separate field of statistics not just because it is an intrinsic part of life science but because of society's concern over the quality of the environment, the development of new medical treatments, the provision of health services, the prevention of disease, and the assurance of the efficacy and safety of drug regimens.

Graduate study in biostatistics at the master's level prepares students for careers in the application of statistical methods to the design and analysis of biomedical and clinical research studies and the planning and evaluation of epidemiologic investigations and health services programs. In addition, doctoral study provides the opportunity for research on biostatistical methodology and greater responsibility and leadership in collaborative research. The demand for biostatistics graduates at both the master's and doctoral levels is very high, and it is anticipated that the demand will continue to grow.

The understanding and development of biostatistical methodology requires a background in mathematics, at least through calculus and linear algebra. Thus the primary preparation for graduate study in biostatistics is in mathematics. Course work in statistics and a cognate area related to health, but not necessarily biology itself, is needed at the undergraduate level mainly to stimulate interest in the application of mathematics and statistics to the health sciences and to provide the motivation for graduate study and a career in biostatistics.

Richard G. Cornell, Professor
Department of Biostatistics
University of Michigan

Mathematics   Mathematics is the broadest of all scientific fields, ranging over an enormous and ever-growing variety of subjects, styles, and applications. Yet a common structure subtly links the various branches, and the unity of mathematics is triumphantly demonstrated over and over again by discoveries of the unsuspected relevance of results and methods of one field to another one, seemingly far removed. No mathematician understands more than a fraction of the body of mathematics, except on a superficial level; no single department, even among the largest ones, can adequately teach all of it.

The origins of mathematics lie in concrete problems outside of mathematics; yet most mathematics develops as an autonomous subject, and its branches are usually taught as such. This line of development has been crowned with many recent successes, in topology (classification of 4 manifolds), in number theory (rational solution of algebraic equations), in algebra (classification of finite simple groups), in differential geometry, in several complex variables, etc. There is also a strong recent trend back to external sources. The study of dynamical systems is flourishing, spurred by recent startling discoveries (new classes of completely integrable systems and their stability, solitons, universal features of chaotic behavior). Fluid dynamics has undergone a similar recrudescence (strange attractors and other aspects of turbulence, propagation of shock waves). Mathematics has made new contacts with physics, in particular in statistical mechanics, quantum field theories, and

Mathematics (continued)

plasma dynamics; relatively new applied branches are beginning to emerge, such as mathematical physiology, biology, and ecology; and attempts are being made to mathematicize some of the social sciences. Much, though not all, of this resurgence of interest in applied topics has been stimulated by the availability of powerful computer systems, which has made numerical modeling possible for purposes of design and to discover new phenomena. Computing is becoming an increasingly powerful tool in pure mathematics as well; furthermore, the problem of utilizing computers efficiently and the study of the structure of computer programs are emerging as separate disciplines on the border between mathematics, logic, and computer science.

In view of this diversity, no two departments of mathematics are alike. Prospective graduate students should try to match their interests with those of the department where they plan to study; they should make sure that they are evaluating departments on the basis of up-to-date information.

There are today good positions available for teaching and research in departments of mathematics. There are also good opportunities for employment to do research in industrial or national laboratories; previous acquaintance with the spirit and some of the substance of applied mathematics is good preparation for such positions, where mathematicians often work in collaboration with physicists, engineers, or even biologists.

Mathematics is a highly technical subject; advanced graduate training is partly an apprenticeship, and the Ph.D. dissertation is partly a demonstration of the candidate's proficiency in using the tools of the trade. However, the motive for doing mathematics is not to overcome technical difficulties but rather to gain understanding.

Peter D. Lax
Professor of Mathematics
Courant Institute of Mathematical Sciences
New York University

Statistics Statistics deals with the collection, description, and analysis of data. The field is broad with respect to the theory-applications spectrum and also in terms of the diversity of fields of applications. Statistics is widely applied in the social, biological, chemical, and management sciences. Research topics in statistics reflect the breadth of the field in both of the above dimensions.

Graduate work typically requires a strong undergraduate math background; some computer background is helpful and is becoming increasingly important.

Employment opportunities for statisticians at the M.S. and Ph.D. levels are excellent and promise to be so for the foreseeable future. Opportunities exist in universities, federal and state government agencies, and industry. Notable examples include federal health agencies such as NIH and FDA; the National Bureau of Standards; the biopharmaceutical, chemical, automotive, and communications industries; and private consulting firms.

William E. Strawderman, Professor
Department of Statistics
Rutgers University

Meteorology and Atmospheric Sciences

The field of meteorology or atmospheric science is a relative newcomer as an academic discipline. Most graduate programs in meteorology/atmospheric science were established during the 1950s and 1960s. During that time period, the discipline experienced rapid growth, which has continued into the present era.

Many advances in meteorology/atmospheric science can be attributed to breakthroughs in related areas of mathematics, physics, engineering, and technology. Supercomputers, weather radars, meteorological satellites, and the latest in other remote-sensing technologies have been applied not only to scientific inquiry but also in hour-to-hour and minute-to-minute operational weather forecasting. Some meteorological research is devoted to the observation, numerical simulation, and prediction of weather systems such as hurricanes and typhoons, cyclones, severe storms, and heavy snow events. Other meteorologists/atmospheric scientists perform research in such diverse areas as atmospheric dynamics, atmospheric chemistry, climate modeling and climate change, turbulence, precipitation physics, and solar-terrestrial interactions. Historically, meteorologists have been at the forefront in the use of all sizes of computers and peripheral devices for data handling, modeling, and the graphical display of results. Supercomputers and the latest supercomputing techniques are an integral part of the science of meteorology.

Meteorological research and graduate education span a continuum from highly theoretical to more applied projects and

Meteorology and Atmospheric Sciences (continued)

courses. Graduate students are recruited and usually receive financial support to tackle these tough scientific problems under the guidance of a faculty member with a research grant. Graduate student research projects might focus on the derivation of a new mathematical theory to describe the behavior of hurricanes, the application of a remote-sensing technique to severe storm and tornado detection, the complex mechanisms that produce acid precipitation, or the effects of climate variability on wheat production.

Graduate students in meteorology or atmospheric science come from a variety of undergraduate backgrounds. Some have B.S. degrees in meteorology or atmospheric science. Others come with undergraduate majors in mathematics, physics, chemistry, computer science, or one of the engineering disciplines. A thorough grounding in differential equations and physics is the most important requirement for admission to a graduate program in meteorology/ atmospheric science.

Graduate degree recipients in meteorology/atmospheric science have traditionally sought employment within the federal government or the academic community. However, a growing number have found employment within the private sector. A recent study showed that 30 percent of the master's degree and 17 percent of the Ph.D. recipients in meteorology are now entering promising career paths in private companies.

James F. Kimpel, Director
School of Meteorology
University of Oklahoma

Physics

Acoustics   Acoustics is the science of sound. It contains a large number of subfields, many of which are interdisciplinary. Some of the subfields are architectural, musical, noise control, physical, physiological, psychological, speech communication, ultrasonic, and underwater acoustics. Several of these branches of acoustics are concerned with how we produce and perceive sound and how we use it to communicate information and emotions. Others use sound to learn more about our environment, sensing the properties of crystals, parts of the human body, or objects in the ocean. A graduate degree in acoustics can lead to employment as a research scientist in an industrial, government, or university setting. The appropriate preparation for graduate study in acoustics depends on the branch(es) of acoustics one desires to study and on how one desires to contribute to that field. A solid undergraduate physics program is recommended, with special attention to classical mechanics, the wave equation and its application to problems involving boundary conditions, and Fourier and Laplace transforms. Electrical engineering courses are helpful for work in signal processing, and experience with computers is useful. Some knowledge of mechanical engineering is particularly suitable for design of transducers and control of noise and vibration.

Gary L. Gibian
Assistant Professor of Physics and Audio Technology
American University

Applied Physics Applied physics is not a well-defined branch of physics, such as solid-state or nuclear physics; rather, it is an umbrella designation for a group of fields, akin to physics, with a fascinating diversity. In fact, most fields of human intellectual activity have received contributions from physics in one form or another, and frequently a separate branch of applied physics arose out of the need of a certain field. Biophysics, geophysics, electrophysics, medical physics, and others are well known, yet there are also contributions of physics to archaeology and history, to the fine arts, and to forensic sciences. Best known, of course, are those applied physics areas that are related to engineering disciplines, e.g., electronics, semiconductor devices, microwaves, computer technology, nuclear fission, aerospace, and optics and lasers.

New areas of applied physics appear as our knowledge of physics advances. Sometimes these new fields emerge slowly, sometimes quickly. We are told that Wilhelm Roentgen's discovery of X rays was followed, within days, by the first radiological examination of a bone fracture in a local hospital, marking the appearance of a new field of applied physics, now called radiology. On the other hand, almost half a century passed between Lord Rutherford's basic discovery of α scattering by nuclei and the application of this technique to the study of surfaces and of thin films.

What is the best preparation for a career in applied physics? A thorough familiarity with basic physics is almost always necessary. Usually this knowledge is acquired by taking graduate courses in

Applied Physics (continued)

quantum mechanics, classical mechanics, electricity and magnetism, thermodynamics, and mathematical methods of physics. Some specialized courses should also be taken; their selection is indicated by the applied physics branch selected by the student. These courses may or may not be in physics. For example, a student interested in semiconductor devices may wish to take solid-state physics and electrical engineering courses. A flair for experimental work, for data analysis, and for data reporting (technical writing) would be an asset. Skill courses such as FORTRAN programming may have been taken as part of the undergraduate curriculum.

Students considering applied physics as a career should be cautioned: If you wish to succeed in applied physics, you must be able to work professionally with nonphysicists. You, as a physicist, are interested in the basic laws of nature; their interests may be quite different. You must learn to understand and to respect their motives. If you can do this, and if your academic preparation is adequate, then you will find that a career in applied physics is both stimulating and rewarding.

Gunter H. R. Kegel, Professor
Department of Physics and Applied Physics
College of Pure and Applied Science
University of Lowell

Mathematical Physics Mathematical physics is a specialty that encompasses activities ranging from the construction of apparatus to abstract theorizing. For example, the design of a machine to study plasma fusion employs many mathematical physicists in the study of the electromagnetic fields in a particular geometry, how the plasma interacts because of the fields and conductor geometry, and how practical an eventual configuration design is for applications. On a more abstract level, mathematical physicists study models of physical theories that are analytically tractable. Into these models more and more "reality" is injected to improve the description of the model. The aim here is to demonstrate the mathematical soundness or existence of a particular model.

Between these two extremes and mixed with them, there is an area of theorizing that is closely connected with mathematical forms of expression. General relativity—a highly abstruse field of study— proceeds from very few physical assumptions to very far reaching conclusions through analysis of the mathematical properties of the theory. The existence of black holes is a subject stimulated by the study of the singular solutions to the Einstein field equations. More recently, the study of nonlinear waves has received a great impetus from a few simple but startling discoveries. Computer analyses led to analytical studies of nonlinear field theories. These analytical studies, in turn, stimulated a significant amount of thinking about the physical systems that the theories described. The result of this thinking is that the generality of certain physical theories, especially quantum field theory, is recognizably much greater than had been anticipated. This is one of the best examples of a situation in physics where a theory and the language in which it is expressed are developed simultaneously.

Many areas of mathematical physics have become traditional. One of the more important of these, because of its connections with quantum theory, is group theory. Contemporary studies of this important area focus on nonlinear representations of groups, especially Lie groups, and their related algebras. This subject is applied broadly in the physical sciences and is the topic of regular international conferences.

Philip B. Burt, Professor
Department of Physics and Astronomy
Clemson University

Optical Sciences   Optics, the study of light, is both an important branch of physics and an exciting field in engineering. In optics, basic scientific discoveries are being made each year, and each year optical physicists and engineering scientists are making useful new applications combining lasers, electronics, and computers. This renaissance in optics started with the application of communications theory, an engineering science, to optics and continued with the invention of the hologram and the laser. Today optical scientists and engineers are working on electronic printing and imaging, phase conjugation, laser radar, laser fusion, laser lithography, laser optical disks, and new optoelectronic materials.

Optics is a science that greatly enriches other areas of science and technology. Optical techniques are used in physics, chemistry, and biology laboratories for measuring lengths, illuminating samples, forming images, and detecting emitted radiation. Optical data acquisition is a key aspect of many space programs and ranges from the detection of environmental pollutants to the discovery of the characteristics of the Martian landscape. Lasers are now used in

Optical Sciences (continued)

everyday life, in such applications as laying drainpipe, providing automatic scanners for supermarket checkout systems, and automating industrial process control. As the telephone industry switches from conventional copper cable to fiber optics, it will require the services of many more engineering scientists trained in optics. Advanced optical technology now includes lasers, fast electrooptic and acoustooptic modulators, low-loss fibers, wideband detectors, integrated circuits, and holographic recording.

Optics is a field with far-ranging appeal. Whether students aspire to become theoreticians, experimentalists, engineering scientists, or design engineers, the field of optics is broad enough to provide a challenging career and a rewarding profession. For example, students with a bachelor's degree in physics, mathematics, or any discipline of engineering can obtain an M.S. in optics with one year of graduate education and be well prepared to enter the field at a highly professional level. Students whose career goal is to conduct basic research in the optical sciences are well advised to continue their studies through the Ph.D. Whether or not the graduating Ph.D. wishes to be known professionally as an optical physicist or an optical engineer is largely a matter of choice depending on which area of specialization he or she elects. In the optical sciences it is important for the graduate student to have rigorous core courses in the principles of optics, including electromagnetic theory, quantum mechanics, and mathematics. The industrial community expects a Ph.D. recipient to be highly competent in each of three specialized areas: optical systems and instrumentation—conception and design of telescopes, lens groupings for imaging, information processing, or energy transfer; fields and waves, including coherency—propagation and statistical optics; and quantum optics—interaction of light and matter, and device physics (lasers, detectors, and active elements).

Nicholas George, Professor
Institute of Optics
University of Rochester

Physics The goal of physics is to discover the fundamental laws of nature. "What man knows about inanimate nature is physics—or, rather, the most lasting and universal things that he knows make up physics" (*Physics in Perspective,* National Academy of Sciences, 1972).

Physics is an experimental science. Experiments range in scale from those performed using very large accelerators at national laboratories to those carried out in small laboratories on college campuses. There is also a large effort in theoretical physics aimed at understanding past experiments and predicting the results of future experiments.

Physics naturally divides itself into subfields: astrophysics and relativity, plasma and fluid physics, acoustics, optics, condensed-matter (solid-state) physics, atomic and molecular physics, nuclear physics, and elementary particle physics. Although this division is useful, it is not unusual for a single experiment to overlap several subfields, e.g., optical techniques used to study atomic transitions in a plasma.

The goal of graduate study in physics is to prepare for a research career in an academic institution, an industrial research laboratory, or a government research center. Employment prospects are, in general, quite good, though there is a shortage of permanent positions at academic institutions. Students who have completed graduate work in physics are in great demand by industrial employers. This strong demand is due in part to the physicist's ability to bring his or her research training to bear on a very broad spectrum of problems. The national need to solve technical problems, such as the current energy problem, promises a bright future for employment in this field.

Thomas A. Griffy
Professor of Physics
University of Texas at Austin

Plasma Physics   Plasma is the state of matter at temperatures so high that an appreciable fraction of the molecules and atoms are dissociated into ions and electrons. Stellar and interstellar matter is mostly in the plasma state, as is matter in the magnetosphere, the ionosphere, flames, chemical and nuclear explosions, and electrical discharges. In addition, a number of current high-technology areas involve matter in the plasma state, including gas lasers, free-electron lasers, certain microwave amplifiers, and plasma deposition and etching operations. Also, very significantly, the working fuel in a controlled thermonuclear reactor would be in the plasma state, and it has been largely the study and development of this "fusion reactor"

Plasma Physics (continued)

concept for large-scale electric power generation that has led to our extensive current knowledge of plasmas. Fusion power would utilize, in a socially and ecologically safe way, the almost limitless nuclear energy that is potentially extractable from the world's abundant resources of the light elements, particularly hydrogen and lithium. The kindling temperature for the very slow nuclear burning envisioned for a fusion reactor is around 100,000,000° C, many times hotter than the center of the sun, a fact that explains why the reacting fuel is necessarily in the plasma state.

In terms of gross properties, plasma differs from ordinary (unionized) gas by its very high electrical and thermal conductivity and by the emission of electromagnetic radiation such as microwaves, light, bremsstrahlung, and even X rays. At high temperatures, interparticle collisions, which dominate ordinary gas behavior, become very infrequent, and mean free paths many times longer than the apparatus dimensions are commonly achieved in laboratory experiments. Plasmas may therefore exhibit fascinating "memory" effects and can respond in dramatic ways to electric and magnetic fields.

Plasma physics is not a specialized discipline but broadly spans modern experimental and theoretical physics and technology. On the academic front, the study and the teaching of plasma physics invoke the blending of knowledge from electricity and magnetism, atomic physics, statistical mechanics and kinetic theory, computer science, and applied mathematics. Graduate curricula in plasma physics typically include the canonical graduate physics courses in quantum mechanics, electromagnetic theory, and statistical mechanics, together with advanced work in magnetohydrodynamics, plasma waves and instabilities, irreversible processes, and nonlinear interactions. Research laboratories with sophisticated apparatus, diagnostics, and data-handling facilities are associated with almost every institution offering graduate plasma programs and offer students invaluable training in current experimental research using state-of-the-art techniques.

Because of the manifold possibilities for interaction among its different aspects, plasma physics provides extraordinarily diverse, fertile, and still largely unexplored ground for fundamental theoretical and experimental research. Plasma physics is itself a large field and in many of its aspects is still a young field with challenging applications in astrophysics, space physics, electronics, materials sciences, and fusion research—where success in our understanding will have enormous impact on reaching a satisfactory long-range solution of the world's energy problems.

Thomas H. Stix, Associate Chairman
Department of Astrophysical Sciences
Princeton University

Engineering and Applied Sciences

Engineering

Engineering is the profession in which a knowledge of mathematics and natural sciences gained by study, experience, and practice is applied with judgment and social consciousness to develop ways to economically utilize the materials and forces of nature with a concern for the environment and for the benefit of mankind. Engineering deals with all aspects of the physical world. Engineers must also have a fundamental knowledge of the sciences, primarily physics and chemistry, mathematics, logic, sociology, earth sciences, and the humanities. Vitally important to an engineer is a spirit of teamwork and a keen sense of social and other impacts of the product of his or her labors on humanity, the community, and the world around us. A knowledge of cultures, language, communicative skills, and social sciences is essential to engineers. All of these provide the necessary base that interacts with the physical reality of engineering design through the creative engineering process.

The engineer must be prepared to solve the technological problems of society, which requires the ability to devise a system, component, or process to meet desired needs. This is what design is all about—a decision-making process in which the total knowledge of the engineer is applied to convert resources to meet a stated objective.

Engineering can be an end in itself as a profession. However, an engineering education offers its graduates possibilities to use knowledge gained as an engineer as a background for other professions. Engineers are particularly adept at moving into such nonengineering professions as law, medicine, management, sales, and administration, all of which require additional specialized education. National surveys show that over 60 percent of U.S. middle- and upper-management personnel have one or more degrees in engineering. Engineering education in today's world of technology may be defined as the most liberal education available at the baccalaureate level.

Practicing engineers can be found in over ninety different specialties, from macrocomputers, lasers, fiber optics, space structures, and oceanography to bridges, highways, genetics, biology, medicine, and nuclear reactors. The definition of an engineering specialty is up to each individual practitioner, based on his or her education. Many engineering specialties combine complementary disciplines such as bioengineering, patent law, and medical engineering.

Graduate study in engineering is becoming increasingly important for those pursuing an engineering career. Graduate programs offer the opportunity to gain in-depth knowledge in a given discipline. This usually provides the student with theoretical knowledge of the state of the art at a level that allows him or her to perform as an engineer in a specialized area. The level and depth of new knowledge is such that the compressed education of the baccalaureate only opens the door to more extensive educational needs for a high level of proficiency. Most graduate programs provide an opportunity for research work. The experience is valuable not only to those seeking positions in that area, but also to those wishing to enter education. A Ph.D. or its equivalent is almost mandatory for anyone wishing to enter engineering education and academic or other research activities. Because of the accelerated rate of new advances in engineering, a graduate education is most desirable for all engineers and is usually recognized by employers, who pay a premium for employees with a graduate education.

There are many fields within the engineering discipline. Each field also contains several subfields. Not all colleges of engineering will offer all fields or all subfields. The student must be careful in investigating what is available at various institutions through college catalogs, professional journals, and course offerings and by talking to his or her own undergraduate faculty.

Following is a list of the basic fields of engineering together with the more popular subfields. A complete list would contain over 100 entries. (The word engineering has been deleted as a qualifier from each notation; however, it is implied.)

Aeronautical—aerodynamics, aeronautics, astronautics, airframes, structures, propulsion

Agricultural—energy and power, farm machinery, food processing

Ceramic—ceramics, glass, refractories

Chemical—polymers, process control, unit operations, transport phenomena

Civil—structures, soils, materials, sanitary, transportation

Electrical—power, electronics, communications, computers, systems, fields and waves, energy

Industrial—operations research, production planning, quality

Engineering (continued)

Mechanical—air-conditioning, heating, ventilation, refrigeration, controls, fluid power, manufacturing processes

Metallurgical—extraction, forming, welding, mineral processes

Nuclear—reactions, instrumentation, radiation, fuels

A number of new programs that focus on the relationship between "living" organisms and engineering have been developed; these fall under the generic title of bioengineering. The main thrust of these new programs is, in some cases, apparent from their name—biomechanical engineering, biochemical engineering, and biomedical engineering, for example.

The computer has caused a major change in today's technological world, and new programs related to computers are being developed almost on a daily basis. Within engineering, programs in computer engineering, data-processing engineering, etc., are being offered either as complete programs or as major components of others.

Manufacturing engineering is also becoming a prominent field. As of this writing, not many programs are being offered in this area, but several subspecialties, sometimes offered within the scope of other major disciplines, are becoming well known. Special mention should be made of computer-aided design, computer-aided manufacturing, and robotics.

Another disciplinary area that cuts across traditional fields is management engineering. Many programs in this area are currently found in industrial engineering departments, which also offer operations research, a special subfield in industrial engineering that is slowly becoming its own independent area—or is highly mathematical in its orientation and involves much mathematical modeling.

David R. Reyes-Guerra, PE
Executive Director
Accreditation Board for Engineering and Technology

Agricultural Engineering

Graduate study in agricultural engineering encompasses the search for solutions to engineering problems in agriculture. This search may demand the development of new knowledge of the physical and biological systems that make up the food production, handling, and processing system, as well as a synthesis of solutions using current knowledge in the biological, physical, and engineering sciences. Engineering knowledge often enhances the development of a deeper and more precise understanding of the biological systems. Recently there has been widespread development of the use of microprocessor and microcomputer technology for the monitoring and control of the biological and physical systems used in the production, processing, and utilization of foods and feeds. In addition, artificial intelligence and expert systems are being explored as means for solving engineering problems of agricultural and food production systems. Some examples of the use of this emerging technology are computer-controlled environmental control systems for product storage, ventilation of greenhouses, and animal environments. Coupled with the use of microprocessor technology is the emerging use of robots in agriculture. Robots are being developed for sheep shearing, fruit and vegetable picking, and other repetitive tasks of agricultural production and food processing.

The ultimate goal of agricultural engineering research is to create technological advances in food, feed, and fiber production by discovering new knowledge as well as utilizing technological advances of other scientific and engineering disciplines. A recent development has been the utilization of advances in biotechnology to better enhance food and fiber production as well as to research the engineering scale-up of new products' (enzymes, plant propagation) production.

Specific studies in the field include the application of mechanical power to production and harvesting of field crops along with the development of related equipment. Food, feed, and fiber production and quality control are furthered by studies of the soil, water, and air environments around plants. Animal growth and the production of animal products are considered in the studies of animal environment and related animal physiology. Proper management of soil and water resources results in improved food production and waste disposal. Many graduate students in this field examine problems in the processing of food, feed, and fiber to maintain and enhance product quality and acceptability. Some students study forest engineering, aquacultural engineering, or international agricultural development.

Graduates of advanced degree programs in agricultural engineering are in strong demand by private industry, government, and educational institutions. Continual improvements in machinery,

Agricultural Engineering (continued)

equipment, buildings, and other facilities require many research and development engineers. Demands for solutions to and control of environmental pollution and waste management have increased the number of agricultural engineers employed by regulatory agencies and consulting firms. The current demand for doctoral degree recipients by academic institutions exceeds the supply; usually, there are several available for each Ph.D. recipient in agricultural engineering.

Gerald E. Rehkugler
Professor and Chairman, Department of Agricultural Engineering
Cornell University

Biomedical Engineering

Biomedical engineering can be broadly defined as the application of engineering concepts, methods, and techniques to biology and medicine. Because of the breadth of the field, several subspecialties have been emerging.

Bioengineering is concerned with the quantitative analysis, both theoretical and experimental, of the structural and functional properties of the components of biological systems (cells, tissues, and organs) as well as their organization into integrated organisms. Career opportunities are concentrated primarily in academia and biomedical research.

Medical engineering, or biomedical technology, deals with the design, development, application, and evaluation of instrumentation, computers, materials, diagnostic and therapeutic devices, artificial organs and prostheses, and medical information systems for use in medical research and practice. Within this category, rehabilitation engineering addresses specifically the needs of the rapidly increasing population of physically handicapped individuals. A wide variety of career opportunities exist in universities, government agencies, and various industries.

Clinical engineering uses engineering concepts and technology to improve health-care delivery in hospitals and clinics. Career opportunities include positions in private and public health-care delivery systems as well as in industry and federal agencies.

Health-care systems engineering deals with problems in the analysis of health-care concepts and health-care systems, such as socioeconomic and psychosocial determinants of health. It is also concerned with the design and implementation of more efficient and less costly modes of health-care delivery. Career opportunities include positions in health planning agencies, private industry, and state, federal, and international health organizations.

Biochemical engineering, agrobioengineering, and genetic engineering are now emerging as new subspecialties in the rapidly developing field of biotechnology. These fields of study deal with the analysis of cellular and subcellular structures and processes in a variety of organisms, as well as with the application of engineering methods to production processes and their control in agriculture, environmental protection, and industry. Employment opportunities exist in government and private research institutions as well as in industry.

E. O. Attinger, Forsyth Professor and
Chairman, Division of Biomedical Engineering
University of Virginia

Chemical Engineering

Chemical engineering is the discipline in which chemistry, physics, and mathematics are combined with basic engineering principles to solve environmental, biomedical, societal, or technological problems arising in the application of chemistry.

Perhaps the broadest of the engineering fields, chemical engineering includes such subdisciplines as process synthesis, optimization and control, energy technology, environmental technology, electrochemical processes, bioengineering, materials engineering, kinetics and catalysis, chemical reactor engineering, thermodynamics, separation techniques, heat transfer, mass transport, fluid mechanics, corrosion, rheology, and particle technology. These form the scientific and engineering basis for a broad spectrum of new technological and industrial developments and also provide the tools for addressing a wide range of pressing societal problems. Some current areas of concern where chemical engineering expertise is critical include energy resource development and conservation, the more efficient production of food, new nonpetroleum feedstocks for our chemical industry, environmental quality assessment and control, materials shortages (recycling/reprocessing) and alternative materials, development and

Chemical Engineering (continued)

efficient production of semiconductor materials for electronics, and new developments in biotechnology.

Because of the shortage of Ph.D.'s in chemical engineering, very attractive professional opportunities (and high starting salaries) await the graduate. Demand is high both from industry and from academic institutions. Although essentially every major industry employs chemical engineers, Ph.D.'s find industrial employment principally in the oil, chemical, pharmaceutical, metals, pulp and paper, food, and electronics industries. In addition, the government employs chemical engineers with advanced degrees in such areas as air and water quality control.

All signs point to a quickening evolution of technology in general, and of chemical engineering in particular. Graduate study is an essential educational prerequisite for those who want to be at the forefront of these developments.

W. Harmon Ray, Steenbock Professor
Department of Chemical Engineering
University of Wisconsin–Madison

Civil and Environmental Engineering

Architectural Engineering Architectural engineering is concerned with the engineering and construction of buildings. It encompasses structural engineering, environmental systems, construction processes, and construction management. For those who enter this field, an understanding of basic principles of architecture is also important, so that they may ensure that the form and function of buildings are optimal.

Graduate study in architectural engineering is founded upon a strong undergraduate base. Calculus, physics, mechanics, materials, computer programming, and chemistry are important basic courses for the architectural engineer. Advanced undergraduate courses in structures include structural analysis, design of steel, concrete, masonry, wood structures, soil mechanics, and advanced structural analysis. Materials and methods of construction, engineering economy, contracts, specifications, and cost estimating are important courses in materials and construction. For environmental systems, important subjects are fluid mechanics, thermodynamics, mechanical equipment of buildings, air-conditioning and heating, acoustics, and plumbing and electrical systems. Several courses in architectural design are also included in the undergraduate curriculum. Graduate study includes advanced courses in one or more of the primary technical areas: structural engineering, environmental systems, and construction management.

Graduates of advanced degree programs in architectural engineering are in strong demand by the building industry, government agencies, and educational institutions. Structural engineering consulting firms, which work with architectural firms, employ many graduates. These firms are typically small, but the opportunities are good. Many students find employment with construction and construction management firms. The complexity of building systems necessitates the involvement of architectural engineers in their construction. The emphasis on energy conservation has created a strong demand for architectural engineers to design environmental systems for buildings. And many other industries such as the oil companies seek architectural engineering graduates.

Joseph F. Malina Jr.
C. W. Cook Professor of Environmental Engineering
Chairman, Department of Civil Engineering
University of Texas at Austin

Civil Engineering Civil engineering is the planning, design, construction, and economics of the systems and physical facilities related to public and private works.

The professional civil engineer of future years must be well grounded in the sciences, educated in social and humanistic studies, and cognizant of economic factors and have competent knowledge of the principles that underlie the broad practice of the profession.

Civil engineering includes the following major areas of professional specialization.

Construction engineering deals with the management and engineering required to plan and execute construction projects and to control their cost and timely completion. It is concerned with the fundamental principles that underlie planning, organizing, financing, managing, and operating construction enterprises and estimating the probable performance of construction organizations under specific conditions.

Civil Engineering (continued)

Photogrammetry and surveying embody the sciences concerned with precise measurement of the earth's surface to obtain reliable data for engineering design and location.

Geotechnical engineering encompasses the fields of soil mechanics, foundation engineering, geological engineering, rock mechanics, and highway materials engineering.

Hydraulic and coastal engineering deals with the control of water in all its physical aspects. Hydrological phenomena are considered from a scientific and engineering viewpoint. The conception and design of systems and structures for water-power development, flood control and irrigation projects, river and harbor development, coastal and ocean engineering, and hydraulic aspects of water pollution control are among the major technical aspects of hydraulic engineering.

Water resources engineering encompasses a broad approach to the problems and systems involved in surface and groundwater resources development and in water quality management for a multiplicity of beneficial uses.

Sanitary and environmental engineering involves the engineering control of the environment. Primary emphasis is given to the scientific and engineering development, design, and operation of water resource quality management systems involving agricultural, industrial, and municipal water supply treatment; wastewater treatment; and disposal and reclamation (recycling). Also included are gaseous- (air pollution) and solid-waste analysis, as well as process and control system design and management.

Structural engineering is concerned with the analysis and design of all types of structures. Engineers have to assess the loadings the structure will be called on to resist during its life and assess its safety, its endurance, and the possible effects of vibration, shock, or temperature change. They must know the properties of the materials in the structure and be able to select materials with suitable characteristics for maximum economy and safety as well as for aesthetic appeal.

Transportation engineering is concerned with the planning, design, construction, and operation of transportation systems and facilities, such as highways, railroads, urban transit, and air transportation and the associated terminals. Transportation engineers are oriented toward the total system. In order to perform their professional duties adequately, they must have a well-developed knowledge of administration, economics, land-use planning, environmental impacts, and methods of performance evaluation of transport systems.

James K. Mitchell
Department of Civil Engineering
University of California, Berkeley

Environmental Engineering The American Academy of Environmental Engineers has defined environmental engineering as "the professional application of scientific principles and technical practices to the protection and improvement of the health and well-being of humans and their surroundings. It involves the management and optimum use of air, water and land resources, and the provision of facilities and the control of conditions for living, working and recreation that will contribute positively to human health, comfort and well-being." Within the range of activities included in that definition, water pollution control, air pollution control, hazardous-waste management, and water supply engineering are major current environmental engineering activities.

No academic program in environmental engineering is known to comprehensively embrace all facets of the field as broadly defined by the academy. The diverse activities of environmental engineers are unified, however, because all require a fundamental understanding of the chemical, physical, and biological factors controlling the quality of natural and engineered environments. Graduate-level training in environmental engineering is founded on basic knowledge of the chemical, physical, and biological phenomena that control environmental quality. These foundations are acquired at the undergraduate level and strengthened by basic and applied graduate course work.

Many graduate educational programs in environmental engineering teach the engineering application of chemical, physical, and biological concepts primarily in the context of the water environment. Some environmental engineering programs offer specialization in air pollution, and some emphasize land pollution or hazardous-waste management. Other programs embrace land and air quality control as they relate primarily to water quality control (for example, by considering the land application of wastewaters, agricultural utilization of wastewater sludges, combustion of wastewater sludges, or stripping of volatile organic compounds from groundwaters).

Environmental Engineering (continued)

The work of environmental engineers differs from that of environmental scientists in that the end product is a technique or facility for environmental quality control. Like environmental scientists, environmental engineers study and develop analyses of environmental problems; however, the end product of the environmental engineer's work is the design (and, sometimes, construction) of an environmental quality control technique. For example, an environmental engineer's end product might be the design of an industrial-wastewater treatment facility; a scheme for obtaining, treating, and distributing potable water for a municipality; or a plan for cleaning up a hazardous-waste site. These design activities require basic engineering training.

Because environmental engineering involves the application of complex and diverse chemical, biological, and physical concepts, graduate-level training (at least to the master's degree level) is common. Graduates find employment in private consulting engineering practice, at all levels of government, and in industries with pollution control problems or products. Past failure to responsibly manage wastes, protect environmental quality, and maintain public infrastructure have created a backlog of challenging opportunities for the environmental engineers of the future.

Richard I. Dick
Joseph P. Ripley Professor of Engineering
School of Civil and Environmental Engineering
Cornell University

Fire Protection Engineering   Fire protection engineering (FPE) is a specialty field aimed at using the tools of science and technology to solve fire safety problems. The field intersects in many ways with electrical, mechanical, civil, industrial, and chemical engineering; architecture; the behavioral sciences; management; and economics.

Good job opportunities have been holding strong over the years. The 3,400-member Society of Fire Protection Engineers (Boston) reports that major employers of FPEs include business and industrial firms, consulting engineering firms, and the insurance industry. Men and women specializing in fire protection engineering are also found in federal and state government agencies, the military, local fire departments, building code agencies, trade associations, research organizations, hardware systems companies, and academia.

From Boeing to Burger King, the variety of employers and interesting work environments is extensive.

Fire protection engineering curricula generally include subjects such as theories of fire ignition, growth, and spread; explosions; design and evaluation of fire detection, alarm, and suppression systems; industrial processes and risk evaluation; fire safety decision analysis; building fire safety design; codes and standards; insurance and risk management; and public fire protection. Normally admission to graduate study requires a baccalaureate degree in engineering or the physical sciences.

Over the past decade, sponsored research has emphasized combustion and fire phenomena (understanding the thermodynamics, chemistry, and fluid mechanics of unwanted fires and resulting smoke/toxic gases) along with investigation of fire suppression systems and devices. Mission-related research covers a broad spectrum and includes ignition and burning properties of materials, methods for evaluating furnishings, marine shipboard fire protection, implications for space vehicles, fire protection of nuclear power facilities, explosion detection and suppression, mathematical modeling of fires, engineering methods for predicting fire performance of structural steel building frames, and computer applications.

It is generally agreed that fire protection engineering is making the transition from what was once more of an art to a mature engineering discipline. This is evidenced by the more quantitative tone of papers given at symposia and professional meetings and the emergence of graduate programs of study. In 1981, the National Council of Engineering Examiners began making professional engineer registration examinations available nationally in the FPE specialty. Overall indications are that fire protection engineering will be a growth field, with still some room for pioneering.

David A. Lucht, Director
Center for Firesafety Studies
Worcester Polytechnic Institute

Geotechnical Engineering Geotechnical engineering is a discipline within civil engineering that deals with the adaptation of earth material for engineering purposes. Earth material in this context is defined as naturally occurring soil and rock and man-made waste by-products. This material may be used in many ways: as a

Geotechnical Engineering (continued)

supporting medium for a surface structure, host of an underground facility, primary building material for surface structures such as dams, and containment medium for either natural resources such as groundwater or by-products of civilization. In all of these uses, the geotechnical engineer must consider the earth material as an engineering material and evaluate its behavior under a multitude of environmental loading conditions. These loadings may include gravity, wind, earthquakes, storm waves offshore, ice loads in the Arctic, extreme pressures on the deep-sea floor, or even vacuum conditions on the moon.

New challenges that require new technologies to solve the associated problems are being posed constantly to the geotechnical engineer. Among the recent challenges have been the design of oil production facilities in the North Sea, construction of the Alaska pipeline, mining of tar sands in Alberta and oil shale in Colorado, development of a national nuclear-waste repository, and even the engineering of spacecraft footings to make safe landings on the moon. This scope of activities provides a wide range of excellent opportunities for careers in teaching, research, industry, government, and private consulting or construction practice.

Preparation for a career in geotechnical engineering requires a broad base of training in the basic and engineering sciences. The mechanics of solids and fluids, materials science, and computer skills are particularly important in this regard. Geological principles play a major role, and biological principles are becoming important. Design and construction knowledge is necessary, and written and oral communicative skills are vital. A B.S. in civil engineering provides the broad-based fundamental training, but an advanced degree is normally required to develop specialized knowledge in the discipline. In a large majority of geotechnical engineering organizations, the M.S. is considered to be the entry degree, and the Ph.D. is becoming increasingly common.

Geotechnical engineering is a challenging and demanding profession. It requires a sound knowledge of principles, an understanding of complex material behavior, the capability to get a project constructed even under adverse field conditions, and the willingness to tackle a difficult challenge.

Fred H. Kulhawy, Professor
School of Civil and Environmental Engineering
Cornell University

Structural Engineering Structural engineering is concerned with the application of structural theory, theoretical and applied mechanics, and optimization to the design, analysis, and evaluation of building structures, bridges, and shell structures. The science of structural engineering includes the understanding of the physical properties of engineering materials, the development of methods of analysis, the study of the relative merits of various types of structures and methods of fabrication, and the evaluation of their safety, reliability, and performance.

Graduate study in structural engineering may emphasize structural design in either steel or concrete, classical analysis, numerical computer analysis of structures, solid mechanics, probabilistic methods, or some combination of the above. The types of structures involved in a typical structural engineering program include bridges, buildings, offshore platforms, containment vessels, reactor vessels, and dams. Research in structural engineering can include such topics as computer graphics, computer analysis and design, stress analysis, structural dynamics, structural fatigue, structural mechanics, structural models and experimental methods, structural safety and reliability, and structural stability.

Graduates of advanced degree programs in structural engineering are in great demand by consulting firms, private industry, government and national laboratories, and educational institutions. Recent demands for improvements of the nation's infrastructure, which includes, among other public facilities, the highway system and over 550,000 bridges, have increased the number of structural engineers employed by highway departments and consulting firms. The current demand for recipients of doctoral degrees by academic as well as private and government research institutions far exceeds the supply, especially in the areas of experimental works, large-scale computer applications, computer-aided design and engineering, interactive graphics, and knowledge-based expert systems.

W. F. Chen, Professor
Head of Structural Engineering
School of Civil Engineering
Purdue University

Transportation and Highway Engineering Transportation and highway engineering is that portion of civil engineering dealing with the planning, design, and operation of facilities and systems used for

Transportation and Highway Engineering (continued)

the movement of persons and goods. As an engineering discipline, transportation and highway engineering involves the application of physical and mathematical sciences to the solution of societal problems relating to transportation.

Although some transportation engineers are involved in activities relating to only one mode of transportation, such as a designer of highways, others are involved in making fundamental decisions leading to a choice of mode. For example, a problem of transporting metallic ore from a mine to a port might require consideration of a highway, a railroad, a belt conveyor, or an aerial tramway. Urban transit problems similarly may involve a choice between the alternatives of rail and bus. The subject matter addressed by transportation and highway engineers also includes airports and inland waterway facilities and systems.

Specific activities suggesting the scope of transportation and highway engineering include highway planning, traffic engineering, railroad maintenance engineering, and the design of airports. Research in these and many other areas of transportation engineering is guided by the Transportation Research Board, National Research Council, National Academy of Sciences.

Since most transportation facilities are planned, constructed, and operated by public entities, many transportation and highway engineers are employed by government agencies. Others are employed by engineering consulting firms that provide the specialized planning and design services required by public entities. In many of these activities, transportation and highway engineers serve as members of an interdisciplinary team that works closely with citizen groups and members of the general public. Railroad and pipeline companies represent the other principal demand for transportation engineers.

R. L. Carstens
Professor of Civil Engineering
Iowa State University

Water Resources   Water resources is an applied multidisciplinary field concerned with the development and utilization of local, regional, and national surface water and groundwater. The multidisciplinary aspects of the field are manifested by its components derived from natural sciences (hydrology, physics, meteorology, biology, mathematics, and statistics) and from the social sciences (economics, public administration, political science, and law).

The central issue in water resources arises from the discrepancy between water supply characteristics—location, time distribution, quality, and institutional framework—and desired availability. Water must be transported to centers of demand, it has to be stored (on the surface or in aquifers) so as to regulate its flow, its quality has to be maintained or improved, and the laws and regulations governing its development and utilization may need updating and/or revision.

Basic to the field of water resources is the science of hydrology. Hydrological phenomena are represented in the analysis of water resources systems by mathematical models that emphasize either the physical aspects of the precipitation-streamflow phenomena or their stochastic characteristics.

Water resources systems are synthesized so as to respond to a broad range of magnitudes of hydrologic events, from droughts to floods. Extremes of this range can have serious economic and social consequences that need to be mitigated, at least. The problems to be solved are increasingly complex, in particular the competition between different user categories for finite (and increasingly scarce) regional water resources. The three main issues facing us today are (a) management of water quality, (b) operation of complex surface and groundwater systems, and (c) the institutional-legal aspects of water resources. Consequently, the field of water resources is continuously developing analytical capabilities for the better understanding of natural (hydrological) and socioeconomic phenomena, as well as creating approaches to synthesizing alternative systems that would resolve these problems.

Nathan Buras, Professor
Head, Department of Hydrology and Water Resources
University of Arizona

Computer and Information Sciences

Computer Science Computer science is a well-established discipline concerned with the study of the phenomena related to computers. More specifically, it emphasizes the creation, analysis, and implementation of algorithms at all levels in the computer

Computer Science (continued)

hierarchy—from circuits at the binary representation level to the more macroscopic description of algorithms by programming languages. The research methodology is similar to that of other sciences: experimentation and observation of complex systems and algorithms leads to the formulation and revision of descriptive theories. Computer engineering is a related field that overlaps the subject areas of computer science. There is no well-defined boundary between these disciplines, but computer engineering certainly includes the lower-level, hardware aspects of computers and those areas in which implementation and cost effectiveness are dominant concerns.

Sometimes departmental titles such as Computer and Information Sciences are used. However, the use of the term information science runs the risk of confusion with other subject areas using the same designation. For example, this title is sometimes used to label library science, the study of communication media, or certain aspects of signal processing in electrical engineering.

As in other disciplines, there are many subfields in computer science, and some of them are briefly delineated here. Again, the boundaries are difficult to define. Indeed, many computer scientists feel strongly that the principal contributions by the discipline are the result of the broadly applicable, specialty-bridging aspects of the field.

Numerical computation is a field that predates electronic digital computers, but the emphases and possibilities have changed dramatically, particularly in the era of highly parallel supercomputers. The creation of efficient algorithms to numerically solve the equations describing physical systems is the dominant interest. The effects of discretization and approximation in algorithms are analyzed with many of the conventional tools of mathematical analysis, but the emphasis is on algorithms as opposed to the existence and properties of static systems.

The theory of computation is increasingly important in the development of computer science. Complexity theory, which measures the computational difficulty of algorithms in terms of problem size, is an important part of this specialty. But other areas involving language theory and the semantics of programming languages are also active areas of study.

As mentioned, computer technology and its implications for the design of computers are included in both computer science and computer engineering. Topics such as the design of integrated circuits require some knowledge of physical electronics, but the related design process is very algorithm oriented and is often included under the computer science heading. The higher-level study of computer design, usually called computer architecture, is an active area because of the increasing interest in specialized, parallel systems.

Artificial intelligence deals with the creation of algorithms and systems that exhibit intelligent behavior. This broad definition includes activities such as heuristic and adaptive programming. The development of expert systems, which use heuristics to solve problems in specialized knowledge domains, is a rapidly developing subarea. The underlying problem of understanding and modeling cognitive processes continues to provide the fundamental direction.

The creation and development of programming languages continues to play a central role. In an era of increasing specialization, languages dedicated to particular problem areas, and their implementation on various computers, are ever more important. Also languages designed to permit formal verification of algorithms are of great interest. This subject area subsumes the topics related to compilers and compiling algorithms.

The programs that control computer systems are called operating systems. The study and implementation of such programs involves issues of scheduling, hardware/software interfaces, memory management, and communications. Simulation and analytic modeling of systems are important related topics.

Database systems are very often at the center of large computer applications. The study and design of databases includes the various structural alternatives, the formulation and processing of queries, and the design and efficiency issues related to the use of hierarchical storage systems. The technological possibilities for distributed databases have raised additional problems of synchronization, consistency, and reliability, and these are active areas of research.

As the name suggests, software engineering is concerned with the methodology of designing and implementing large, complex programs. The topics include techniques for the generation of structured programs; systems for maintenance of consistent, updated program modules; and the automation of programmer intercommunication. The resultant programs for the engineering of large programs are themselves complex and interact with other system components, such as the operating systems.

These brief descriptions of areas within computer science are, at best, examples, but even these few suggest the near indivisibility of the discipline. Databases and operating systems are implemented

Computer Science (continued)

with various languages via software engineering. When theory shows that necessary algorithms are not effectively computable, there must be recourse to the heuristic techniques of artificial intelligence. Perhaps the most independent area is numerical computation, but here, too, complexity theory is applicable and the interaction with technology and computer architecture is increasing as systems for specialized numerical computation become feasible.

Bruce W. Arden, Professor and Dean
College of Engineering and Applied Science
University of Rochester

Information Science   The importance of data and information to modern technological society has resulted in the establishment of a new scientific field of information studies. Information science brings together several of the physical and social disciplines—mathematics, computer science, communications, linguistics, philosophy, psychology, and sociology—in preparing information professionals at several levels to deal with the nature of information itself and the character of the information transfer process.

This new interdisciplinary field is concerned with signals, data, information, and knowledge, plus the successive transformations that eventually result in information transfer to the human mind and in its effective utilization. The scholar in this field will study the cycle of generation of information, recording in various media (e.g., print, film, and magnetic), analysis and organization, selective dissemination, and use. Fundamental principles and laws of data-handling systems and networks are developed in the science and technology aspects of information science; the transformations that result in data becoming information and knowledge are developed in the behavioral aspects; and the interface between information systems and people is a particular focus of study and research.

All indices point to the presence of a kind of Malthusian law for the growth of knowledge, building at a faster rate than society's ability to assimilate it. The challenge to information scientists is to develop effective systems for the storage and dissemination of knowledge, using appropriate technologies, and to evaluate these systems in terms of their ability to serve and to be operated by the wide variety of individuals pursuing the solution of problems in a society of increasing complexity.

The tools of the information scientist include computers, communication systems, and telecommunication networks. The interdisciplinary skills needed include (1) foundations (behavioral, philosophical, and sociological), dealing with the needs of information users, how users function in information-rich environments, the theories and models of problem formation and solution, and human communications; (2) basic science, to develop the intellectual tools for dealing with information as a human experience through study of philosophy, mathematics, statistics, cybernetics, artificial intelligence, pattern recognition, automata, modeling and simulation, coding theory, and operations research; (3) technology and systems, concerned with the means through which people deal with data and information transfer—including technology; man-machine communications; analysis, design, implementation, management, and evaluation of information systems and networks; and analysis of the impact of information systems; and (4) computers and programming, to permit the effective and efficient use of computers, through study of computer architecture, operating systems, programming systems, file structures, and database management systems.

Research in this field addresses problems of information system design and evaluation, vocabulary control, graphic display, cognition, relevance, simulation modeling, database management, and information transfer.

Applications of information science and employment opportunities for information science graduates are found throughout society in banking, law, administration of justice, health records, industry, libraries, communications, agriculture, education, and government agencies.

Information resources management represents one of the most rapidly expanding areas in both the public and the private sector. Economists estimate that employment in agriculture, manufacturing, and service occupations has now been surpassed in the United States by employment in occupations based entirely on the production, utilization, and transfer of data and information, with the information sector of the economy accounting for 53 percent of total national compensation. Accordingly, increasing numbers of information professionals are needed to provide leadership in this information-based society; professionals include information scientists (Ph.D.); information managers, systems specialists, and

Information Science (continued)

counselors (M.S.I.S.); and information technologists (B.S.I.S.). They are in short supply now, and the demand for their services is expected to remain high. Critical shortages are currently being experienced in the telecommunications industry.

Allen Kent, Distinguished Service Professor
Interdisciplinary Department of Information Science
School of Library and Information Science
University of Pittsburgh

Software Engineering Software engineering is concerned with developing and modifying the software components of systems that incorporate digital computers. Computing systems are composed of hardware, software, and people. While software engineers are primarily concerned with software issues, the fundamental goal of a software engineer is to ensure that the total system satisfies the users' needs in a cost-effective manner. Because the functional or performance characteristics of computing systems can be changed by reprogramming, modification of existing systems is a major concern of software engineers.

Software engineering is a young and emerging discipline based on computer science, computing technology, management, and engineering economics. A pragmatic approach to problem solving is the hallmark of a software engineer. Software engineers combine theoretical and practical considerations of technology, cost, and social impact in order to produce systems that are both effective and efficient.

A strong graduate curriculum in software engineering requires an undergraduate background in computer science topics such as assembly language, computer architecture, block-structured programming languages, data structures, and discrete mathematics. In addition, graduate programs in software engineering often require practical work experience of the entering student. Master's programs in software engineering typically include courses in computer systems, software development methodology, management, and projects that emphasize teamwork.

Courses in the computer systems area cover topics such as operating systems, database systems, compilers, and computer networks. Courses in software development methodology cover tools and techniques for analysis, design, implementation, documentation, validation, and modification of software systems. Management courses cover the roles of computing systems and data processing within organizations, as well as techniques for planning and controlling software projects and leading project teams.

Employment opportunities for software engineers are excellent and seem likely to improve in the future. Software engineers are in demand in every segment of society affected by computing technology. Typical employers include companies that build and sell computers, software companies, research and development laboratories, aerospace contractors, banks, insurance companies, and manufacturing organizations.

Richard E. Fairley
Chairman of the Faculty
School of Information Technology
Wang Institute of Graduate Studies

Electrical and Power Engineering

Computer Engineering   In recent years a new area in engineering has emerged, called computer engineering. This broad-based field of study has incorporated the fields of electrical engineering and computer science. Thus, a computer engineering program becomes a balance among hardware, software, and applications of computers and related digital systems.

In a computer engineering program, knowledge of a wide range of computer languages becomes necessary. This includes exposure to assembly language programming and micro-programming as well as high-level modern languages. In addition, exposure to data structures, operating systems, and system software, such as editors, compilers, and debuggers, becomes an integral part of this field of study. Thus, the skills needed for software design and utilization, as well as the structure and manipulation of data, are developed in a computer engineering program.

With respect to hardware considerations, a computer engineering curriculum again is broad based. Studies range from logic design concepts, which emphasize the realization and interconnection of basic digital building blocks and digital design techniques, through digital system design, which emphasizes the architectural aspects, data flow, and control-signal flow of entire digital systems. In addition, the integration of software and hardware

Computer Engineering (continued)

concepts becomes eminent in the areas of interfacing and communication aspects of digital devices and systems.

The diversification of computer engineering is most noticeable when considering the several areas of specialization, of which a few will be mentioned. Computer-aided design involves the use of computers in the design of other systems. Computer graphics is concerned with the highly effective means of handling information in graphic form. Fault-tolerant computing is concerned with the design of highly reliable digital systems, an important area as the usage and complexity of digital systems have grown while their sizes have decreased as a result of very large scale integration. In an effort to provide for high performance, studies of advanced architectures and parallel processing become important. Theoretical studies of digital systems for the purpose of establishing formal analysis and design procedures are a part of the automata theory area. Application areas of computers include artificial intelligence, which involves, for example, expert systems and robotic systems. Finally, other important areas of computer engineering involve the utilization of very large scale integration technology for the design of digital systems and computer communications networks.

Donald D. Givone, Professor
Department of Electrical and Computer Engineering
State University of New York at Buffalo

Electrical Engineering   Electrical engineering is a broad field that continues to expand and diversify as it exploits new scientific discoveries and technological advances to better serve the needs of industry, commerce, and the individual. The Institute of Electrical and Electronics Engineers (IEEE), with more than 250,000 members, is the world's largest professional organization. The diversity of electrical engineering is mirrored by the IEEE's thirty-one professional groups, which are devoted to specialties that range from acoustics through antennas, communications, computers, control systems, industrial electronics, microwaves, and power to vehicular technology.

The field of electrical engineering can be roughly divided into two realms, one more closely related to physics and devices and the other to systems that schedule, coordinate, and operate the devices.

In the communications area, a good example is the transatlantic telephone cable. Its electronic repeater amplifiers are devices that must operate reliably for many years on the floor of the ocean while being operated by a system that allows two conversations to share a single line by inserting the second conversation when there is a pause in the first. Similarly, the antenna and receiver circuits in a satellite communications system perform more effectively when the system coordinates users so as to reduce the probability that two will block each other by transmitting at the same time.

Electrophysics areas of current interest include materials, such as semiconductors and plasmas; devices, such as laser diodes, optical fibers, and integrated-circuit chips with etched components of ever-decreasing dimensions; and wave propagation phenomena, such as electromagnetic, optical, acoustic, and magnetostatic.

Some research and development areas in electrical systems are telecommunications (television, cellular mobile radio, fiber optics, radar, and sonar, in addition to the systems mentioned above), image processing (digitization of pictures; storing, transmitting, and reconstructing images; correcting images for noise and distortion; and automatic recognition of objects, e.g., tumors in X-ray pictures or in CAT scan records), automatic control (flight control of aircraft and space vehicles, automatic manufacturing systems, precision robots, and variable-speed AC motors), and computer architecture (parallel processing for higher computational speed and greater data-handling capability, and fault-tolerant structures for greater reliability and safety).

It is important to recognize that in addition to a thorough understanding of fundamental principles and current knowledge of electrical technology, the essential tools needed by an electrical engineer include effective communication skills. A good educational program should include preparation of proposals, reports, and theses to develop skills in organizing and presenting complex technical concepts and plans, both orally and in writing. Ability to use electronic computers for analysis, computer-aided design, and text processing must also be cultivated.

The recent growth in the need for electrical engineers seems likely to continue, in view of the high-technology trend in our society. Graduate study and continuing education will be of increasing value for engineers who wish to keep up with advances and to maintain their professional options. Industry and government have recognized these needs, as evidenced by the emphasis on renovating university laboratories, novel plans for continuing education,

Electrical Engineering (continued)

satellite broadcasting of courses, and fellowship programs to train doctoral students who plan to pursue academic careers.

Leonard Shaw, Head
Department of Electrical Engineering and Computer Science
Polytechnic University

Power Engineering The field of electrical engineering has widened over the years so that it now has a number of individual disciplines that at first sight seem almost unrelated. A closer scrutiny shows that there are still many common elements among these disciplines, such as electromagnetic theory and circuit theory. Inevitably, with increasing understanding in science and the burgeoning growth of technology, individuals have found it necessary to specialize in one discipline or another. One of these specialties is electric power engineering. It is one of the oldest and one of the most fundamental.

Programs in electric power engineering seek to educate and train engineers for that part of the industry that is concerned with the generation, delivery, and utilization of electrical energy. It addresses the business of the utility industry—how electric power systems are planned, designed, and operated to produce economical and secure service for society—but it is also concerned with the design and construction of the vast array of power equipment, such as generators, transformers, power circuit breakers, and transmission lines, that constitutes the system. Finally, in the area of utilization, it deals with the many ways in which electrical energy is put to use in industry. This embraces such disparate items as arc and induction furnaces, drive systems for steel mills, and power applications in land and sea transportation.

Modern technology from other fields has had a marked impact on electric power. Computers are everywhere used for data processing and analysis. Microelectronics have found their place in sophisticated control systems. Microwaves, satellites, and fiber optics are being used for rapid communication. Moreover, there has always been a strong connection with mechanical engineering since so much in power equipment design depends upon mechanical and thermal considerations. Similarly, in the generation area there is a tie with nuclear engineering. In this environment there are therefore opportunities for people in a very wide range of interests.

In many electrical engineering departments the "power option," which represents their offering in the electric power field, is quite limited. Interested students would therefore be well advised to examine carefully the depth and breadth of the program offered and the size and reputation of the faculty. Since graduate study is almost essential for a sound preparation for a professional career in electric power, a well-established graduate program is an important consideration.

Allan Greenwood
Philip Sporn Professor
Chairman, Department of Electric Power Engineering
Rensselaer Polytechnic Institute

Engineering Design

Design is the most essential and fundamental engineering activity. It results from an expression of need for a component, product, or system and entails several steps in producing a solution to fill that need. These steps typically include a precise definition of design requirements, determination and analysis of alternative possible solutions, and the selection, after several iterations, of a solution that will best satisfy the constraints of technical feasibility, economics, time, and human factors. In a broader sense, the solution must also take into account legal and government requirements; environmental, social, and ethical considerations; aesthetics; and various other factors.

Today's successful engineering designer must be well schooled in mathematics and engineering sciences and be conversant with computers. Success is dependent upon an ability to apply these skills to actual problems in a creative way. The design effort is almost always a team effort, with several engineers, technicians, draftsmen, and individuals from nontechnical areas being involved. Thus, an aptitude for working well with people and, eventually, for planning and directing the work of others is also necessary. Finally, it is absolutely essential that every engineering designer be able to communicate effectively in speech, in writing, and through drawings, especially in computer-aided systems.

The ever-increasing level of sophistication in technology presents great challenges for the designer and necessitates keeping abreast of the changes and advances being made. A career in engineering design offers immediate and expanding responsibility to those who are willing and able to accept it. Engineers working in the area of design can find rewarding opportunities in industry, government, and private practice.

Harrison Streeter
Department of General Engineering
University of Illinois at Urbana-Champaign

Engineering Physics

Engineering physics, or applied physics, is concerned with the application of new concepts developed in the basic sciences, particularly physics, to engineering problems and, at the same time, with the application of devices and techniques developed in engineering disciplines to important problems in physics. This transfer of technology between the basic sciences and the engineering sciences is often inhibited by our history of educating researchers within narrow academic disciplines. Engineering physics is a broad field that aims at overcoming the enormous differences in emphasis and course work in the teaching of students in physics and engineering. Engineering physics students pursue a broad curriculum that includes courses in both areas as preparation for graduate research.

Research in engineering physics is best defined by examples: studies of surfaces and materials using lasers, electron and ion beams, and neutrons; development of solid-state devices; laser and electron-beam studies of fluids, gases, and plasmas; precision measurements of fundamental constants; accelerator design; computational physics; and space and planetary physics. Research in engineering physics is closely associated with that in electrical engineering, aerospace and mechanical engineering, nuclear engineering, and materials science. Although the particular research emphasis varies somewhat from program to program, the goals stated earlier are typical of all programs.

Students obtaining degrees in engineering physics have excellent employment opportunities. Traditionally most students have obtained positions in universities, government research laboratories, and the laboratories of high-technology-oriented industries. Because of the recent increased interest of both engineering schools and physics departments in the applied sciences, there has been a corresponding increase in the number of academic positions available for those with Ph.D.'s in engineering physics or applied physics. The number of other employment opportunities has also continued to increase along with the gradual increase in the number of engineering physics programs. Because of their flexible academic and research backgrounds, graduating students have been relatively unaffected by the cyclical changes in the job market affecting most engineering and science fields. Finally and more important, it has been well established in all research fields and industries that Ph.D. holders with broad training are able to adjust their interests as old problems are solved and new directions are emphasized. Engineering physics is therefore appropriate training for work in applied science in the future.

T. G. Williamson
Chairman, Department of Nuclear Engineering
and Engineering Physics
University of Virginia

Food Engineering

Food engineering is a broad field that is concerned with the application of engineering principles and concepts to the handling, manufacturing, processing, and distribution of foods. This relatively new branch of engineering encompasses the knowledge required to design processes and systems for an efficient food chain extending from the producer to the consumer.

The U.S. food industry is the largest industry in the country with regard to total employment, value added, and total value of shipments. Estimates indicate that over 17,000 people working in the food industry identify themselves as engineers.

The handling of foods from production to consumption includes many variables, and engineers often have to resort to adapting mathematical procedures developed for nonbiological materials. Research in food engineering includes improving our understanding, on a quantitative basis, of changes occurring in foods as a result of the various conversion processes. The large number of food items available in today's supermarket is possible partly

Food Engineering (continued)

because of the application of basic concepts of physics, chemistry, microbiology, and engineering to foods.

The food engineering educational programs at many institutions in the United States are offered jointly by departments of agricultural engineering, chemical engineering, and food science and technology. The curriculum emphasizes engineering course work with additional exposure to microbiology, chemistry, biochemistry, nutrition, and food science. In addition, the students take course work in unit operations important to the food industry. Topics such as rheology, liquid- and solid-food handling, size-reduction processes, separation processes including sedimentation and centrifugation, membrane processes, and mixing and blending systems encompass the mechanical unit operations. Thermal operations such as heat transfer in heat exchangers, food freezing, evaporation, dehydration, and preservation are taught with a particular reference to the unique requirements of foods during processing.

Food engineering educational and research programs offer a challenge to improve traditional methods of food handling and innovate systems for the future that will ensure a healthful and plentiful food supply for consumers. The need for food engineering is likely to stay at a high level in the future, in view of the changing needs of our society. Future trends indicate increasing emphasis on prepared foods as more spouses enter the job market. The additional disposable income allows greater emphasis on quality of foods. This shift will require continued improvements and innovations in engineering systems for food processing and manufacturing. Educational programs in food engineering are expected to expand to meet the increasing needs of the food industry.

R. Paul Singh
Professor of Food Engineering
University of California, Davis

Geological, Mineral/Mining, and Petroleum Engineering

Geological Engineering Geological engineering, broadly defined, is the application of geology to engineering works such as highway and dam construction, building foundation investigations, mining, petroleum production, and other works of man. A graduate degree in geological engineering can be obtained at fourteen schools in the United States. Typically, students who have a B.S. degree in geology may be accepted into these departments with the provision that they make up deficiencies as may pertain to engineering subjects.

Many engineering geologists go to work for geotechnical or groundwater hydrology firms or mining and petroleum companies. Many graduates acquire a professional engineering certificate. When seeking employment, graduates with geological engineering degrees generally have an advantage over graduates with geology degrees in that, because of their familiarity with engineering, they are better able to quantitatively assess situations and offer specific solutions to problems. For this reason, geological engineering graduates typically find better job opportunities than geology graduates.

Perry H. Rahn, Professor
Department of Geology and Geological Engineering
South Dakota School of Mines and Technology

Mineral/Mining Engineering Essential to modern civilization, mining engineering provides the basic mineral raw materials needed to sustain our economy and society. Yet it also has the responsibility to develop new technologies to conserve and recycle natural resources, to solve problems of energy supply, and to create safe and productive mining conditions. These topics of worldwide concern place mining engineers in a critical role, as their professional decisions affect our standard of living. Knowledge of recent advances in environmental technology, health and safety, and high-tech computer technology is vital to meet the continuing challenges of the minerals industry. As preparation for a career in this field, the mining engineering curriculum uses the basic and engineering sciences to develop and define the specific activities of a mining engineer— mineral exploration, evaluation, development, extraction, beneficiation, and conservation; protection of the environment; and mineral economics.

Employment opportunities in mining and mineral engineering exist in virtually every state in the United States, as well as throughout the world. Mining operations can be found in nearly every state, and it will be increasingly prudent for the United States to develop and rely on its own mineral resources as its dependence on the minerals industries of other nations could be jeopardized by

Mineral/Mining Engineering (continued)

conditions resulting from international instability. In addition, the growing demand for alternative energy resources signals a growth in the coal industry, which will strengthen career opportunities.

Current research in mineral and mining engineering includes production of the geological environment and the ground control/ operational systems interface necessary to optimize production and safety at minimum cost. Other major areas include exploration, rock characterization, ground control/systems interface, systems simulation, innovative systems, production planning and control, environmental considerations, and systems/ore body integration.

A major subgroup of mineral and mining engineering is the field of mineral processing, which is the technology of transforming ores into salable products. Research into mineral processing includes slurry flow and rheology, particle sizing and characterization, surface chemistry, computer simulation, and process control. Similar to mineral processing and gaining increasing importance by the need to bolster the domestic fuel supply is coal preparation, which is concerned with the removal of impurities such as ash and sulfur from coal so it can burn cleanly and efficiently and become an environmentally accepted replacement for petroleum and natural gas.

J. Richard Lucas, Head
Department of Mining and Minerals Engineering
Virginia Polytechnic Institute and State University

Petroleum Engineering Petroleum engineering can be broadly defined as the application of engineering concepts, methods, and techniques to explore and drill for, produce, and extract petroleum from underground reservoirs. A specialized branch of mineral engineering, petroleum engineering encompasses broad applications of mechanical engineering, chemistry, mathematics, and geology. These applications include drilling engineering, which involves mechanics of solids and fluids as well as mechanical design of well equipment; production engineering, which is concerned with surface equipment, subsurface pumping methods, and automated production techniques; and reservoir engineering, which includes pressure testing of wells and is concerned with the flow of fluids through rocks and methods to extract maximum recovery of petroleum by various techniques, often simulated by mathematical models.

Integral elements of a petroleum engineering education include rock mechanics, well logging, reservoir simulation by computer modeling, and the geological relationships of reservoir rocks to fluid flow through porous media. Areas in the forefront of research include enhanced recovery of petroleum in existing fields by newly developed methods, including chemical flooding, thermal flooding, and miscible displacement techniques. Allied areas of research include geothermal energy, which applies petroleum engineering principles to extraction of heat energy from the earth, in situ leaching of uranium ore from rocks, and solution mining of salt domes for strategic storage of petroleum.

Today, the demand for petroleum engineers with graduate degrees remains high. M.S. degree graduates command salaries of about $38,000, and Ph.D.'s begin at about $10,000 a year higher. Only a limited number of universities offer advanced degree programs of extensive size in petroleum engineering; these include the University of Texas at Austin, University of Southern California, and Stanford University. The University of Texas and Stanford have turned out some 75 percent of all Ph.D.'s working in this field.

Myron H. Dorfman
Chairman, Department of Petroleum Engineering
University of Texas at Austin

Industrial/Management Engineering, Operations Research, and Systems Engineering

Industrial/Management Engineering The professional industrial and management engineer creates efficient and effective systems that provide products and services for human consumption. The integration of people, materials, capital, equipment, and energy into productive systems is the main concern of the profession. The process involves the analysis, evaluation, synthesis, design, and management of systems that range from a single component to very large and complex assemblages of resources of all types. A multidisciplinary approach to systems design is used. Industrial and management engineers draw upon specialized knowledge in the mathematical, physical, and social sciences as well as upon the

Industrial/Management Engineering (continued)

principles and methods of engineering analysis and design to specify, predict, and evaluate the results to be obtained from systems.

Industrial and management engineers will be leading the nation's "reindustrialization" efforts. Sometimes called "productivity engineers," these professionals are pioneering in such fields as robotics, computer-integrated manufacturing, decision support systems, energy management, quality circles, and participative management.

The industrial and management engineer may follow a career in almost any type of enterprise: manufacturing companies; service organizations, such as insurance companies, banks, and hospitals; or government agencies, at the city, state, and federal levels. The industrial and management engineer's position in an organization is usually that of a management adviser—a technical resource person in contact with every phase of the organization. Because of the breadth of his or her background, the industrial and management engineer is especially well qualified to rise to positions of leadership and authority within an organization.

An increasing number of students with B.S. degrees in other branches of engineering are pursuing M.S. degrees in industrial and management engineering. This is an especially attractive alternative for students who wish to prepare for careers in the management of technical organizations.

Joe H. Mize, Regents Professor
School of Industrial Engineering and Management
Oklahoma State University

Operations Research Operations research (OR) deals with the analytical study of operational systems, where the latter are defined as systems that are subject to human decision. This is a vast collection that includes, among others, production, transportation, warehousing, agriculture, communications, education, forestry, defense, trade, economic, and government systems. OR is mainly concerned with the study of the structure of such systems and with observing their behavior to first gain basic understanding of their nature and of the factors that influence their performance and, secondly, modify their performance, with an eye toward improving such performance. Such improvement is achieved through the optimal allocation of resources or the optimal utilization of existing resources. The approach of OR is in harmony with the classical view of the scientific approach, which embodies observation, modeling and establishing hypotheses to explain the phenomena under study, the validation of both models and hypotheses, and the use of these theories and models to describe the performance of the system under modified conditions.

Operations research is strongly based in the mathematical, physical, and engineering sciences, with the computer and its technology playing an increasingly important role in the implementation of its findings. Its methodology borrows from and contributes to the fields of mathematical programming, discrete mathematics, stochastic processes, control and optimal control, and economics and econometrics, among others. An OR study may concern itself with a small system, such as an individual assembly line or a truck route, or with a large system, such as a multimodal evacuation system in case of emergency.

Typically, OR is a graduate program of instruction, with introductory treatment given at the undergraduate level in departments of mathematics, statistics, industrial engineering, and business. Its graduates are in high demand at both the master's and doctoral levels in industry, consulting, research centers, universities, and government.

Salah E. Elmaghraby, University Professor
Director, Operations Research Program
North Carolina State University at Raleigh

Safety Engineering   Safety engineering is a specialized discipline of professional practice that applies mathematics and the physical laws of nature to the identification, elimination, or modification of activities, conditions, and events that possess the potential for causing harm or damage to people, property, or the environment in both public and private systems. The identification of such activities, conditions, and events may be carried out by analytical means or by the development of standards and codes of practice against which comparisons may be made. The potential for harm or damage is resolved into components of severity and of probability or frequency of occurrence. These components are evaluated actuarially, analytically, or through the application of professional judgment. The need for modification of activities, conditions, and events is evident when it is recognized that the harm or damage that may result exceeds a level deemed acceptable.

Within safety engineering, the practice of specialized subdisciplines is common. These treat particular areas of activities,

Safety Engineering (continued)

including product safety, occupational safety and health, mining safety, and construction safety. The subdiscipline specialty of system safety engineering has wide application in aerospace, consumer products, defense-related industries, and manufacturing operations. It characteristically involves a systematic application of analytical techniques, evaluation methodology, and management skills, and it emphasizes preventive aspects with considerable attention directed to engineering design and procedural analysis. With system failure minimization as a major objective, system safety engineering is involved in all aspects of the planning, design, development, fabrication, test, installation, maintenance, and operation of man-machine-environmental systems.

The foundation subjects for university programs in safety engineering focus on mathematical disciplines, engineering sciences, engineering control mechanisms, analysis, and design. Blended within the curriculum will be instruction in codes and standards, economics, energy analysis, ergonomics, management sciences, materials, processes, and risk assessment techniques. Many engineers from other disciplines enter graduate programs in safety engineering, where they find a rich field for research and the opportunity to apply their engineering knowledge and skills.

Safety engineers find rewarding career opportunities in aerospace, construction, defense industries, government service, manufacturing, and service industries. The casualty insurance industry is probably the largest single employer of safety engineers. Some of the most rewarding opportunities for safety engineers exist in the subdisciplines of system safety engineering and product safety engineering, in which failure analysis, energy analysis, and risk assessment techniques predominate.

Ralph J. Vernon, Professor
Industrial Hygiene and Safety Engineering Program
Department of Industrial Engineering
Texas A&M University

Systems Engineering   Engineering is the application of science and technology in supplying human needs. Systems engineering is distinguished primarily in terms of the complexity of the system to be designed. Engineering takes such forms as the design of a valve for a process controller or the design and development of a satellite communication system. The first of these two engineering tasks is relatively straightforward in terms of problem definition, if not in terms of technological difficulty. The second task involves considerable interaction among physical, social, economic, and political factors. Initially, the objectives in system design may be unclear, or even conflicting. Yet the motivation behind the task may be strong, e.g., the inadequacy of the present long-distance communication system. The specific objectives are often formulated as the project develops. Thus, systems engineering is a term that describes activities near one extreme of the continuum of engineering work. It involves the design of relatively large-scale, relatively complex systems.

The development of large-scale electrical systems—the telephone network and the power distribution network—was an early driving force in the cultivation of a systems approach in engineering. The techniques originally developed in these fields are now being applied to many complex problems of society, such as integrated manufacturing and public transportation. Systems engineers are crucial to the development, design, and management of high-technology systems such as modern telecommunications systems and military weapon systems. These complex systems typically include important human, computer, control, and information-handling components.

The development of computers has been an important factor in the development of systems engineering as a discipline. It has made possible the realistic modeling and simulated operation of large-scale systems. Furthermore, most systems include computers as information-processing components.

Most engineering disciplines are distinguished by some subfield of the sciences, such as electricity, mechanics, and chemistry. Systems engineering, on the other hand, cuts across all of the sciences. The basic foundation of systems engineering is in mathematics and in an understanding of the interactions among the variables of the system. The terminal characteristics of system components and the manner in which the components are interconnected are of more significance in system design than is the manner of operation of individual components.

The foundation subjects for university programs in systems engineering focus on mathematical disciplines, including probabilistic methods, system modeling and simulation, system control, and optimization theory. Economic and legal implications and man-machine interactions are usually treated as well.

Most of the engineering work in communications, control, decision making, and resource allocation depends upon the mathematical tools of systems engineering. Therefore, these disciplines are often coupled with university programs in systems engineering.

Since the initiation in 1953 of a graduate program in systems engineering, such programs have become increasingly attractive to students seeking leadership roles in the planning, development, and management of sophisticated systems. Government and the private sector have become increasingly aware of the need for and value of systems engineers.

C. Nelson Dorny, Professor
Chairman, Department of Systems Engineering
Moore School of Electrical Engineering
University of Pennsylvania

Materials Sciences and Engineering

Ceramic Sciences and Engineering Ceramics are inorganic, nonmetallic materials generally processed at elevated temperatures. Along with metals and polymers, they are the primary materials used in manufacturing. The industry that produces ceramic products is a major force in the U.S. economy, with sales of over $50-billion. These products include glass, cements, electronic materials from ferrites to insulators, refractories, whitewares, consumer products, abrasives, structural products, and nuclear products, to name just a few. Recent developments in fiber optics have generated substantial expansion in this field. Other areas growing rapidly include new applications of ceramics in electronics, carbides and nitrides, and bioceramics. Bioceramics are used as replacement parts in humans and in medical technology. Carbides and nitrides are used in structural applications in engines, space vehicles, etc. The coming decade could well see revolutionary changes in the use of ceramic materials. The transportation engines of the 1990s may be made entirely from ceramic materials. The result will be engine efficiencies as high as 40 percent greater.

Ceramic engineers/scientists are educated to understand the behavior of these materials and their applications. They are concerned with the design of ceramic materials having a specific set of properties for a given application, the design of processes for production of ceramics, and the incorporation or application of ceramic materials in the design of other machines, systems, or products.

At the graduate level of study, the ceramic engineer/scientist is trained to participate in all phases of research and development. Some prefer fundamental areas of investigation; others attack problems preventing the introduction of a material into a new application. Regardless of whether the program emphasizes basic or applied research, the engineer must use both analysis and synthesis to create new ceramic products or processes.

The opportunities in the field are quite substantial. The American Ceramic Society estimates that the ceramic industry will need about 1,500 new ceramic engineers every year at the B.S., M.S., and Ph.D. levels. However, at present only 500 are graduated annually.

W. Richard Ott, Dean
New York State College of Ceramics
Alfred University

Materials Engineering   Materials engineering is concerned with solving engineering problems through the specialized use of materials. It involves topics as diverse as the design and development of new materials for special purposes, the characterization of the mechanical response of materials under service conditions, and the creation of material systems that optimize the use of materials for a given engineering task. The field differs from materials science more in philosophy than in substance, but the distinction is clear: materials engineering is concerned with engineering, i.e., with application of knowledge to the technical problems of society.

Materials engineering has experienced an exciting period of growth in the last five to ten years. First, the development of microcircuitry revolutionized the electronics industry and brought about what may be the most significant single development in engineering history—the modern digital computer. Then, the age of space brought demands not only for new materials but for new design philosophies for the use of materials. The new materials such as plastics and composites have found their way into nearly every home. The new design philosophies have created whole new disciplines, such as fracture mechanics, fatigue studies, and material design.

This field is just beginning its most exciting phase. High-technology requirements in fields such as robotics, transportation,

355

Materials Engineering (continued)

energy, and defense provide a broad and diverse horizon of opportunities for research and development in materials engineering. New fields such as high-temperature composites offer a special opportunity for interdisciplinary study combining information and technology from chemistry, physics, and mechanics.

Demand for people in this area far exceeds supply. The most vigorous market is in the high-technology industries, including transportation and energy systems, as well as in aerospace groups. Numerous research and development laboratories also employ materials engineers.

K. L. Reifsnider
Chairman, Materials Engineering Group
College of Engineering
Virginia Polytechnic Institute and State University

Materials Sciences   Materials science is concerned with the relation between the structure and properties of materials, the factors controlling the internal structure of solids, and the processes for altering the structure and properties of solids. It brings together in a unified discipline the developments in physical metallurgy, ceramics, polymers, and the physics and chemistry of solids.

The following are typical of the kinds of questions asked and answered in materials science. What determines the structure of a material and how does this structure affect its mechanical and electronic properties? What are the basic energy constraints that determine how materials can be made and what they do? What controls the stability of materials, and how rapidly can changes be made to occur? How can we describe and creatively change those factors that control mechanical and electronic properties?

Materials are playing an increasingly important role in modern society. At many points in the energy program, for example, the limiting factor is the type of material available. We need alloys for reactors, materials that are strong enough at high temperatures to be used in advanced engines, new types of materials to serve as electric batteries in storage systems, new low-loss transmission-line materials, innovative methods to prepare materials in ways and forms not known previously, and materials systems for the conversion of solar energy into useful thermal and electrical energy. These examples from the energy field could be multiplied many times over as the needs of many rapidly growing areas are considered. The graduate degree recipient in materials science has a singularly wide range of knowledge that extends from materials synthesis, to materials characterization, to the measurement of properties, to the interpretation and theoretical understanding of these properties, to device design and optimization.

R. H. Bube, Professor
Chairman, Department of Materials Science and Engineering
Stanford University

Metallurgical Engineering Metallurgical engineering is the discipline and the profession in which the principles of basic science, engineering science, and engineering design are used to understand and utilize metals. By contrast, materials engineering uses these same principles with respect to a broader class of materials, including metals, ceramics, polymers, and hybrids, such as semiconductors. Materials science, on the other hand, entails the same breadth as materials engineering but is devoid of strong considerations of engineering design and practicality.

There are currently about eighty-five departments or programs in the United States that are variously titled and have a significant component of metallurgical engineering in their curricula. While most provide some opportunity for graduate study, only a small number have programs of significant scope and international acclaim. Financial support for such programs, including tuition and living stipends for students, is supplied predominantly through federal research grants (e.g., through the National Science Foundation, the DOD agencies, DOE, and NASA) and to a lesser extent through industrially sponsored research or fellowships.

Basic subject matter in most curricula draws heavily on chemical thermodynamics (e.g., thermochemical reactions and phase diagrams), transport properties and phenomena (e.g., diffusion and heat flow), and materials structure (e.g., crystal structure and defect structure). Other course offerings usually include phase transformations and strengthening mechanisms in solids, deformation and fracture behavior of materials, the theory of alloy phases, solidification processing, analysis of metallurgical operations, and the physical chemistry of metallurgical reactions and solutions. Studies are both theoretical and experimental, the former often involving the use of applied mathematics and computer-aided modeling and the latter often involving the use of modern analytical

Metallurgical Engineering (continued)

techniques such as electron microscopy, Auger spectroscopy, and automated techniques for diffraction and mechanical testing.

Typical areas of research include chemical and extractive metallurgy, which deals with the winning of metals from their ores and subsequent refining; physical metallurgy, which deals with the physical properties of metals, such as their microstructure and their electrical and magnetic properties; and mechanical metallurgy, which deals with the interrelationship of such factors as strength, ductility, and susceptibility to fracture, including microstructural and design considerations.

Students who pursue graduate studies in this field generally have undergraduate backgrounds in the field itself or in allied areas, such as mechanical engineering, chemical engineering, chemistry, physics, and mathematics.

I. M. Bernstein, Professor
Head, Department of Metallurgical Engineering
and Materials Science
Carnegie-Mellon University

Metallurgy   Metallurgy is the study of the structure of metals and alloys as related to properties important in their technological utilization. It bridges the basic sciences of the physics and chemistry of materials and the design disciplines such as civil engineering, mechanical engineering, and electrical engineering. Traditionally, it has encompassed the extraction of metals from their ores and continues with principles of alloying into combinations that have utility, beauty, and efficiency of use combined with low cost. Extractive metallurgy traditionally has used grinding, flotation, and chemical methods of extraction of metals from complex ores. As mineral ores become ever leaner, more sensitive chemical and biological methods are being used for extraction. The sensitivity of chemical extraction may be noted by the current practice of refining gold, whereby ores of gold content as low as 1 gram of gold per ton of rock are economically feasible.

Once ores have been refined to the pure metal, then the task of combining them physically or chemically into useful combinations—alloys—is also the province of the metallurgist. Optical microscopy, long the accepted technique of examining the grain structure and precipitate arrangement, is accompanied by sensitive physical and chemical methods of analysis such as electron microscopy, Auger systems, mass spectrometry, electron spectroscopy, and other electron-optical methods. Nuclear magnetic resonance is a prominent technique of analysis.

Application of alloys to products is ruled now by economy and performance. As technological applications place ever-increasing demands on performance and reliability, the metallurgist must design alloys with ever more severe demands on performance, at the same time keeping production costs low. Manufacturing products from carefully controlled powders and forming to near-net shape is being utilized increasingly.

Most metals and alloys are crystalline, but a class of materials termed glassy metals or amorphous materials is becoming increasingly important. Rapid enough quenching from the molten state can provide an amorphous solid with unusual properties. Applications in specialized areas such as magnetic pickups and high-performance transformers is an important application of amorphous solids. Improvements in permanent magnet alloys have come rapidly—one can now buy permanent magnets with five times the strength of the standard alnico magnets of just a few years ago.

Applications of metallurgy to electronic components are enormously important. As integrated circuit components become more densely packed and as demands for reduced response time of circuits increase, the fashioning of interconnecting lead wires between electronic components becomes increasingly more difficult. Metal-ceramic interfaces place greater demands on the design engineer.

The profession of metallurgy is an exciting field. The interplay between technological design of products and the underlying basic sciences of solid-state physics and chemistry is fascinating and demanding. Learning how to utilize the unique characteristics of a particular alloy to solve a pressing problem of technology is a satisfying experience.

Charles Wert
Professor of Metallurgy
University of Illinois at Urbana-Champaign

Polymer Science/Plastics Engineering   Polymer science and engineering deals with the synthesis, characterization, properties, processing, and use of macromolecules. These include synthetic polymers of practical interest as materials as well as natural

Polymer Science/Plastics Engineering (continued)

biopolymers, often of interest because of their biological role. Polymers may be studied and used in solution or in their solid state. Solid polymers include plastics, rubbers, and fibers. The production and consumption of polymers is rapidly increasing and is rivaling that of more conventional materials in the construction of automobiles, aircraft, containers, building materials, and fabrics. A reason is the possibility of energy-efficient production of lightweight products having high strength and other special properties.

Important advances in the understanding of the physics, chemistry, and engineering of these materials has made possible the design and construction of articles with tailored properties. This presents a challenge to the synthetic chemist to devise ways of synthesizing large molecules having well-controlled specific structures, to the physicist and physical chemist in devising means for characterizing these structures and predicting their relationship to their properties, and to the engineer in dealing with the design of structures from these often complex materials, which may be anisotropic, viscoelastic, and nonlinear.

While the principal activity in the field has been concerned with "commodity polymers" such as polystyrene, polyvinyl chloride (vinyl), polyethylene, and polyethylene terephthalate (polyester), which are relatively low value added materials whose cost is largely based upon that of the starting materials, often petrochemicals, economics and use patterns are resulting in a change. The production of the commodity polymers is increasingly being carried out in the petroleum-producing nations, and the activity in the United States, Western Europe, and Japan is shifting toward more high value added materials. These include high-strength fibers (Kevlar) made using liquid crystal technology, membranes used for artificial kidneys and controlled drug release, multilayered materials for food containers, and polymers with special electrical properties for use in xerography, microelectronic fabrication, and electrooptical application. The development of these materials requires a high level of interdisciplinary research, often accomplished through collaboration of people in chemistry, chemical engineering, materials science, and polymer departments.

Richard S. Stein, Director
Polymer Research Institute
University of Massachusetts at Amherst

Textile Sciences and Engineering Textile sciences are concerned with the performance properties of fibers, molecular structure relating to these properties, and the interaction of fibers in structures. Manufacturing processes, machinery, process dynamics, and management also enter into the scope of the textile sciences. The textile sciences deal with the physics and engineering requirements for the production, control, and evaluation of fibers, yarns, and fabrics. Since the usual course of fabric manufacture inherently implies a preparation, coloration, and finishing sequence, the textile sciences also deal with the properties and physical aspects of mechanical and chemical fabric treatments.

Graduate degree recipients find employment in the textile manufacturing, fiber, and machinery industries; research and development laboratories; government agencies; and universities. Starting salaries have been commensurate with other basic science and applied engineering disciplines.

E. A. Vaughn
Director, School of Textiles
Clemson University

Mechanical Engineering, Mechanics, and Aerospace/Aeronautical Engineering

Aerospace/Aeronautical Engineering Aerospace engineering is the branch of engineering that deals with all aspects of aircraft and spacecraft. This succinct description, although correct, is superficial because it does not address a method of approach that has characterized this field since its inception. Because weight, power, a sometimes hostile environment, and other important constraints had to be dealt with, even in building the earliest aircraft, it was necessary to consider trade-offs, to optimize—in short, to use what has become known formally as a systems approach. It is their grounding in this approach to vehicle design that has made aerospace engineers unique and valuable in other fields of endeavor.

Even in its infancy, aerospace engineering involved the melding of several disciplines, the most notable then being aerodynamics, structural mechanics, and propulsion. As aircraft and now spacecraft performance have been pushed to ever greater limits, the vehicles have become much more complex, and the corresponding need for aerospace engineers to be familiar with many more disciplines has given them a richness of background found in few other fields. In many cases, the extraordinary demands imposed by special vehicle applications have led to significant advances in these various disciplines.

Most departments of aerospace engineering provide a core program of training in aerodynamics, propulsion, structures, flight dynamics and control, and design, in addition to the usual first two years of general engineering subjects. Special interests may then be pursued in elective courses. Qualified students are encouraged to pursue graduate work leading to a master's degree, with the option of specializing in one or two areas of work. The usual Ph.D. program is highly specialized and provides training for those interested in doing original research work.

Graduates of a degree program in aerospace engineering can look forward to a career in what is broadly referred to as the aerospace industry. This covers a wide gamut of possibilities ranging from manufacturers of private aircraft to companies that make the largest jet transports and from manufacturers of small satellites to builders of the space shuttle. Positions are also available at government research laboratories, and growing numbers of aerospace engineering graduates are being offered employment in industries other than aerospace.

Thomas C. Adamson Jr.
Professor and Chairman
Department of Aerospace Engineering
University of Michigan

Mechanical Engineering   Mechanical engineering is the application of the principles of mechanics, thermodynamics, and material properties to the solution of human problems. The field of mechanical engineering is very broad. Over the course of history, a number of its areas have developed into disciplines recognized in their own right, e.g., aeronautical, chemical, and nuclear engineering. The activities of members of the profession range from research in basic science and applied mathematics to management.

Among the basic areas recognized by the American Society of Mechanical Engineers are applied mechanics, computer engineering dynamic systems and control, bioengineering, fluids engineering, heat transfer, lubrication, materials, noise control and acoustics, and ocean engineering. There are also a number of general engineering areas common to many industries, such as mechanical design, materials handling, plant engineering and maintenance, nondestructive testing, production engineering, air pollution control, and safety and management. Large numbers of mechanical engineers are employed by the automotive, aerospace, coal, petroleum, pressure vessel and piping, food and chemical processing, rail transportation, and textile industries. The many industries concerned with energy conversion are primary employers of mechanical engineers: diesel and gas engine manufacturing, turbines, and electric power generation.

R. D. Finch, Professor
Department of Mechanical Engineering
University of Houston

Mechanics Mechanics, which is an engineering science base for nearly all branches of contemporary engineering, has a lineage stemming from Archimedes, Leonardo da Vinci, and Newton. It should be noted, however, that the engineering community has nurtured the growth of mechanics to its current vitality and importance over the last half century.

Mechanics is the study of forces on matter or systems and involves, by contemporary definition, the identification and description of such systems by cause-and-effect associations.

A partial list of subjects of study would include such diverse areas as analytical dynamics and celestial mechanics; mechanics of deformable media, or rheological mechanics of solids, fluids, metals, polymers, rocks, and soils; mechanics of failure processes such as brittle fracture, ductile fracture, fatigue, and creep; experimental mechanics; computational mechanics; biomechanics; electromagnetism in deformable media and interpenetrating continuum mechanics in general; surface mechanics; and interbody mechanics in general.

Mechanics (continued)

Today, mechanics is probably the most important ingredient in computer-aided design. Moreover, it is relevant to computer-aided manufacturing and microcomputer systems.

Frederick F. Ling
William Howard Hart Professor
Chairman, Department of Mechanical and
Aeronautical Engineering and Mechanics
Rensselaer Polytechnic Institute

Nuclear Engineering

Nuclear engineering is concerned with the safe and reliable production, control, and utilization of energy derived from nuclear sources and systems by the process of nuclear fission or fusion. It includes the design and development of nuclear reactors, radioisotopes for medical applications, and other applications of radiation, such as in the processing of materials, the construction of electronic circuitry, and nondestructive evaluations. Nuclear engineering is closely associated with mechanical, chemical, materials, and electrical engineering technologies. The goals of producing nuclear energy are to be attained by the nuclear engineer through means that are safe, reliable, economical, and without deleterious effects on human health and the environment.

A strong graduate nuclear engineering curriculum provides a basic background in mathematics, physics, basic engineering, and chemistry as a foundation for advanced courses in nuclear reactor physics and engineering, engineering sciences, mathematics, atomic and nuclear physics, and associated computer and laboratory experience so as to allow a graduate degree recipient to be prepared in the analysis, synthesis, design, and utilization of radiation techniques and nuclear power systems. Because of the merging boundaries of other fields, research in nuclear engineering can include topics that border on the mechanical and structural properties of reactor components (e.g., fuel fabrication and pressure vessels), fluid and heat transfer properties of the working fluid, reliability analysis and safety, economics of fuel loading and cycles, processing and radioactive wastes, and radiation surveillance and monitoring. Nuclear engineers are actively involved in fusion engineering and will be even more heavily involved in fusion technology as soon as it becomes clear that economical power can be derived from nuclear fusion.

In spite of a slowdown in the ordering of new nuclear power plants in the last few years, the job market is strong and is projected to remain strong.

R. T. Lahey Jr., Chairman
Department of Nuclear Engineering and Science
Rensselaer Polytechnic Institute

Ocean Engineering

Ocean engineering exists as a discipline for much the same reason as aerospace engineering—because engineering in a specific environment is dominated by considerations imposed by that environment. Waves, wind, current, corrosion, and high pressure combine to control the design of engineering systems in the ocean. And, since ocean systems generally play essential functions in the activities of society, they must be designed integrally with those larger systems.

The earliest ocean engineering systems were ships, and the design, construction, and use of ships is still an important part of ocean engineering. A modern ship is a complicated structure, which must be able to withstand the loads imposed by waves, its own motions, thermal stresses, the weight of its cargo, and sometimes ice. It must have adequate power to drive itself and support its internal systems, and its power has to be converted into a propulsive force. It must serve a purpose—for example, carrying heavy cargoes in world commerce or providing national defense.

The most rapidly growing aspect of ocean engineering today is concerned with the exploitation of ocean resources, most notably exploration for and production of oil and gas. Some geologists maintain that over 50 percent of the undiscovered oil and gas in the world is located underwater, and so this part of ocean engineering can be expected to grow steadily. The development and use of ocean drilling systems requires knowledge and experience similar to that needed in ship design and operations; for example, waves, currents, and wind create major environmental loads that must be accommodated. But there is no decades-old reservoir of knowledge on which to base even the simplest engineering decisions. A single platform may cost as much as a billion dollars. So the design of

365

Ocean Engineering (continued)

drilling platforms is undertaken only after extended research has been conducted.

Working in the ocean also requires the capability for observing and measuring phenomena that occur there. Ocean acoustics is a science of rather recent origin. Its purpose is precisely to allow engineers, scientists, and operators to gather knowledge about the ocean environment.

Two frontiers of special interest to ocean engineers are Arctic and deep-submergence operations: (1) Although the Arctic Ocean was of interest even hundreds of years ago, because of Europe's preoccupation with finding the Northwest Passage, it is newly important for two reasons: (a) it is the site of large discoveries of fossil fuels (in areas controlled by friendly and stable nations), and (b) it is the major US/USSR frontier, an area of increasing military importance. But its environment is, at the same time, among the most hostile and the most fragile in the world. Engineering in the Arctic requires entirely new concepts and, frequently, new scientific foundations. (2) The deep-ocean environment has become economically important because of the possibility of finding energy sources there, as well as major sources of scarce and expensive minerals other than fossil fuels. The deep ocean presents challenges and rewards similar to those of exploring space; for example, the recent discovery of seabed vents led to the further discovery of life systems that are fundamentally different from any previously known.

Graduate study in ocean engineering can include any of these areas and the fields that provide their scientific foundations. In addition, ocean engineers recognize the necessity to integrate their field into activities of society, and so studies are vigorously pursued on the interrelationships between ocean engineering and economics, law, political science, operations research, and management.

T. Francis Ogilvie, Head
Department of Ocean Engineering
Massachusetts Institute of Technology

Solar Engineering

The solar engineer is involved in converting scientific theory into useful applications. The applications include climate control in buildings, the generation of power, and the production of foods and fuels. Solar engineering applications in buildings include building design, building use and operation, building control systems, energy conservation, and active and passive solar heating and cooling systems, including daylighting and strategies for daylighting design.

Solar engineering also relates to solar industrial process heat systems, wind energy systems, photovoltaics, biomass, and ocean thermal energy conversion systems. Solar industrial process heat systems include applications in manufacturing, food processing, and service industries. Wind energy systems include wind machine configurations, energy storage, and large- and small-scale power generation. Photovoltaic applications include power generation for data acquisition and transmission at remote sites, irrigation, crop drying, manufacturing, and domestic needs in some locations.

Biomass applications include direct combustion, gasification, pyrolysis, and aerobic digestion and fermentation for use in the production of steam, electricity, electric power and gas, heat, and gasohol. Ocean thermal energy conversion applications relate primarily to power production.

The solar engineer should have a good background in the fundamental processes involved in the specific areas of interest. A student interested in thermal processes should obtain a strong background in the thermal sciences. Rather than specialize in solar engineering, prospective solar engineers should study one of the basic engineering disciplines, such as mechanical or chemical engineering, in order to obtain a good background in the fundamentals. They may then elect to take specific courses relating to solar engineering in order to obtain the specific information. This approach will greatly enhance their prospects for employment.

C. Byron Winn, Professor and Head
Department of Mechanical Engineering
Colorado State University

Technology Management and Policy

Energy Management and Policy   Energy management and policy is defined as the process of organizing, planning, controlling, and activating energy activities in order to coordinate those elements of the sociotechnical system that contribute to the judicious and effective use of energy. The energy manager/policymaker is the

Energy Management and Policy (continued)

catalyst who (a) determines objectives and policy, (b) explores alternatives in achieving goals, (c) identifies potential problems, (d) evaluates resources, (e) selects an avenue of action, and (f) then puts into motion and controls the resources needed to accomplish objectives. The scope of energy management and policymaking encompasses utilization and supply of energy, conservation, optimal choice of fuels, and contingency planning for energy curtailment. The total objective function for energy management and policymaking is thus exceedingly complex. In addition, any policies or projects must be evaluated in terms of their cost-effectiveness relative to other investment opportunities.

Much of energy management and policy is based on the study of a variety of long-established disciplines—e.g., economics, administration, physics, thermodynamics, industrial engineering, power engineering, and petroleum engineering—and in fact it is commonly studied as a side subject in some graduate courses in these disciplines. However, there are certain topics germane only to energy management and policy, such as (but not limited to) energy auditing, energy analysis, automatic control systems, energy economics, and HVAC. As a result, and particularly since the 1973 energy shortages and resultant price increases, a growing number of universities and colleges are offering either entire degrees or specializations in energy management and policy. These programs appear to be following two general thrusts: (a) educating and training personnel to work in industrial, commercial, and residential facilities and related consulting areas, and (b) schooling individuals in the national or regional energy policy, planning, and budgeting arena. While research opportunities abound in both program thrusts, the latter appears to be on the wane while the former is becoming increasingly important.

Similarly, job opportunities appear to lie more in the facilities and related areas. For example, a small but steadily growing number of industrial energy management career opportunities continue to open up each year, and upper management is now viewing the energy function as one of the pathways to top managerial levels. As another example, some engineering firms are experiencing shortages of trained personnel in all areas of energy conservation consulting—these same firms currently enjoy a several months' backlog of jobs. As a final example, it is probably in academia that the shortage of qualified individuals is most acutely felt. Anyone expecting to enter this field should be cautioned, however, that energy marketplace dynamics will continue to have short-term impacts on job prospects.

Furthermore, while solar energy appears to be the glamour topic among many of today's graduate students (and the schools are doing little to discourage this), there are virtually no job prospects in the solar field outside of a few select research centers and universities.

Barry G. Silverman, Professor
Energy/Environmental Management Concentration Coordinator
Engineering Administration Department
George Washington University

Engineering Management Engineering management may be broadly defined as management of those activities for which knowledge of engineering or applied science is important to success. Engineering managers are distinguished from other managers in that they possess both an ability to apply engineering principles and a skill in organizing and directing people and projects. They are especially qualified for two types of management jobs: management of the technical functions (design, production line, and staff) in almost any enterprise or management of broader functions (marketing or general management) in high-technology enterprises. Further, management is the *normal* career progression of engineers: about two thirds of engineers can expect to spend about two thirds of their careers managing.

Graduate degree programs to train engineers in management skills have grown explosively in recent years, from six in 1960 to sixteen in 1970 to seventy-odd by 1982. Engineering Management is the most frequent degree title, but many degrees carry other titles, such as Engineering Administration, Management Engineering, Industrial Management/Administration, or Management Science or are (engineering) management options within an industrial or systems engineering program.

Most, but not all, engineering management graduate programs require a bachelor's degree in engineering or science for admission. Most M.S. degree programs require 30 to 36 semester hours of work; they do not require the "remedial" undergraduate business courses that stretch M.B.A. programs to 46–60 semester hours for engineers. Engineering management programs may be full-time or part-time; most schools offer both, and the majority of M.S. students are part-

Engineering Management (continued)

time. Doctoral programs are available in perhaps fifteen universities; these typically require two years of work beyond the M.S. degree.

Daniel L. Babcock, Professor
Department of Engineering Management
University of Missouri–Rolla
Executive Director
American Society for Engineering Management

Technology and Public Policy   Interactions between technology and society are nothing new. Such interactions have gone on since the beginning of civilization, in all cultures. The twentieth century has seen a number of important changes in the nature of these interactions—changes in people's expectations, changes in the scale of possible impacts, and changes in the degree of interconnection between our technical and social systems. Graduate programs in this area are concerned with the study of these interactions, and, in particular, with the development of direct and indirect techniques for their management and control.

In most engineering fields, the graduate programs that are represented display many similarities in institutional structure, research problems and paradigms, and types of degrees granted. This is not true in technology and public policy, and the student who is intent on making reasonable choices among programs in this field should make a careful effort to identify and understand the nature of their differences.

The programs are different for at least two important reasons. First, they are interdisciplinary programs that have grown up in widely different institutional settings and thus reflect the unique imprint of their local academic environments. Building successful interdisciplinary efforts in U.S. universities is an exceedingly difficult job that requires substantial compromise and accommodation from many parties. That the solutions worked out at the various institutions offering such programs are different from each other should come as no surprise. Second, the programs are different because they have different educational philosophies, and they identify different kinds of problems and methodologies as being interesting and important.

Since the judgments required are highly subjective, it would be inappropriate to attempt to compare or classify the programs.

Rather, identified below are five of the key variables that should be used in such a classification effort. Potential graduate students may consider them in developing their own comparisons.

1. *The role of technology in the problems studied.* Problems in technology and public policy can almost be laid out along a continuum that ranges from those where the technology sets the general context and boundary conditions but the policy questions can be dealt with essentially independently of the technical or scientific details to those where the technical and policy questions are intimately interconnected and cannot be decoupled. Different programs choose to operate over different regions of this continuum.

2. *The nature and power of the analytical tools used.* Some programs take a highly quantitative analytical approach. Others are far more qualitative. Some have a substantial commitment to specific techniques or methodologies. Others take a rather more freewheeling "whatever works on the problem at hand" attitude.

3. *The level of formal science and engineering background.* Some programs require an undergraduate-level background in science or engineering, and, of these, a few require substantial additional graduate-level training in science and engineering. Some programs require relatively little formal background in science and engineering. Clearly, there is some correlation between a program's requirements in this regard and its approach to variables 1 and 2 above.

4. *The problem areas that are studied.* While all programs deal with technology and public policy, the specific problems they choose to work on are dictated by their approach to the previous three issues, by the interests of their faculty, and by their institutional history. Further, the way in which two programs approach the same problem may be quite different. Some programs include a concern with problems of the developing world; some do not. Some programs are concerned primarily with policy research; others place greater emphasis on issues of implementation and management. The student can get a sense of the interests and orientations of a specific program by requesting lists of faculty publications and past thesis topics.

5. *The way skills are learned.* Because of the different educational objectives and philosophies of these programs, there is a substantial variation between the relative weight that they place on traditional course work, case study–oriented course work, independent study and research, group research projects, and internships or other on-the-job training. Programs that are oriented primarily toward training practitioners who will hold

Technology and Public Policy (continued)

policy analysis positions in organizations such as government operating agencies tend to place greater emphasis on case-oriented course work and on internship experience. Programs that are oriented primarily toward training people to engage in policy-oriented research tend to place greater emphasis on traditional course work, on group research projects, and on independent study and research. However, these are generalizations, and students should look closely at the specific requirements of individual programs before deciding which are most suited to their individual backgrounds and future career objectives.

Technology and public policy is an exciting new field that offers enormous intellectual challenge. Graduates are in great demand by government, by private and public policy research groups, by regulatory agencies, by industry, and by universities.

M. Granger Morgan, Professor
Head, Department of Engineering and Public Policy
Carnegie-Mellon University

ACCOUNTING
TO
ZOOLOGY:
ALPHABETICAL INDEX

Accounting to Zoology: Alphabetical Index

Have You Seen These Other Publications from Peterson's Guides?

Peterson's Graduate Education Directory
Editors: Paul Miers, Ph.D., and Amy J.
Goldstein
This directory is the Who's Who of graduate education in the United States and Canada. It includes over 1,400 accredited institutions offering graduate degrees. Each listing has an overview describing the type of institution and giving data on number of students and tuition. There is also a roster of the top administrative officers, such as director of sponsored research and head librarian. Separate entries outline all of the graduate and professional schools at each institution and list degrees offered right down to programs within departments. Because it contains the name, title, and phone number of each administrative head, this directory is a valuable reference for anyone who deals regularly with higher education.

8½" x 11", 641 pages   Stock no. 4459
ISBN 0-87866-445-9   **$29.95** paperback

Grants for Graduate Students 1986–88
Editor: Andrea Leskes, University of
    Massachusetts at Amherst Graduate School
Finally, there is a single, comprehensive source of information about grants and fellowships exclusively for graduate students. More than 600 such programs are described in this valuable new directory, which details the focus of the individual awards, their number and amount, the ratio of awards to applicants, eligibility requirements, application deadlines, and contact names and addresses. Compiled by the Office of Research Affairs at the Graduate School of the University of Massachusetts at Amherst.

8½" x 11", 395 pages   Stock no. 4831
ISBN 0-87866-483-1   **$29.95** paperback

Graduate and Professional Programs: An Overview 1987
TWENTY-FIRST EDITION
Series Editor: Amy J. Goldstein
Data Editor: Raymond D. Sacchetti

Covers the spectrum of U.S. and Canadian graduate programs in a single reliable volume. The organizational structure and heads at each level are shown for every institution, together with details on facilities, enrollment, faculty, and research. Includes a complete list of over 1,400 schools with all graduate and professional degrees they offer.

8½" x 11", 1,065 pages   Stock no. 4718
ISBN 0-87866-471-8   **$17.95** paperback

Graduate Programs in the Humanities and Social Sciences 1987
TWENTY-FIRST EDITION
Series Editor: Amy J. Goldstein
Data Editor: Raymond D. Sacchetti
The only annually updated comprehensive guide to graduate and professional degree offerings in 151 academic areas in the humanities and social sciences, including business, architecture, law, and international affairs.

8½" x 11", 2,095 pages   Stock no. 4726
ISBN 0-87866-472-6   **$27.95** paperback

Graduate Programs in the Biological, Agricultural, and Health Sciences 1987
TWENTY-FIRST EDITION
Series Editor: Amy J. Goldstein
Data Editor: Raymond D. Sacchetti
The only annually updated comprehensive guide to graduate and professional degree offerings in 78 academic areas in the biological sciences, including medicine, nursing, pharmacology, and veterinary medicine.

8½" x 11", 2,442 pages   Stock no. 4734
ISBN 0-87866-473-4   **$29.95** paperback

Graduate Programs in the Physical Sciences and Mathematics 1987
TWENTY-FIRST EDITION
Series Editor: Amy J. Goldstein
Data Editor: Raymond D. Sacchetti
The only annually updated comprehensive guide to graduate and professional degree offerings in 22 academic areas in the physical sciences and mathematics, including astronomy, chemistry, earth sciences, and statistics.

8½" x 11", 700 pages   Stock no. 4742
ISBN 0-87866-474-2   **$24.95** paperback

Graduate Programs in Engineering and Applied Sciences 1987
TWENTY-FIRST EDITION
Series Editor: Amy J. Goldstein
Data Editor: Raymond D. Sacchetti
The only annually updated comprehensive guide to graduate and professional degree offerings in 44 academic areas in engineering and the applied sciences, including biomedical engineering, computer science, and mechanical engineering.

8½" x 11", 1,090 pages   Stock no. 4254
ISBN 0-87866-425-4   **$26.95** paperback

How to Order

These publications are available from booksellers, or you may order direct from **Peterson's Guides, Dept. 7702, P.O. Box 2123, Princeton, New Jersey 08543-2123.** Please note that prices are subject to change without notice.

- Enclose full payment for each book, plus postage and handling charges as follows:

Amount of Order	4th-Class Postage and Handling Charges
$1–$10	$1.75
$10.01–$20	$2.75
$20.01–$40	$3.75
$40.01 +	Add $1.00 shipping and handling for every additional $20 worth of books ordered.

Place your order TOLL-FREE by calling 800-225-0261 between 8:30 A.M. and 4:30 P.M. Eastern time, Monday through Friday. From New Jersey, Alaska, Hawaii, and outside the United States, call 609-924-5338. Telephone orders over $15 may be charged to your charge card. Institutional and trade orders over $20 may be billed (use your institutional ordering process). You may also use the order form below. After completing the form, just tear out this page and send it to us along with your check or charge card information.

- For faster shipment via United Parcel Service (UPS), add $2.00 over and above the appropriate fourth-class book-rate charge listed.

- Bookstores and tax-exempt organizations should contact us for appropriate discounts.

- You may charge your order to VISA, MasterCard, or American Express. Minimum charge order: $15. Please include the name, account number, and validation and expiration dates for charge orders.

- New Jersey residents should add 6% sales tax to the cost of the books, excluding the postage and handling charge.

- Write for a free catalog describing all of our latest publications.

ORDER FORM

Name _____

Address _____

City _____ State _____ Zip _____

Telephone (___) _____

Quantity	Stock No.	Book Title	Cost Each	Total

Subtotal _____

Sales tax (NJ residents add 6%) _____

Shipping and handling _____

Grand total _____

METHOD OF PAYMENT

☐ Check or money order enclosed.
☐ Charge to MasterCard, VISA, or American Express (minimum order $15).

CHARGE CARD INFORMATION
(Minimum charge order $15)

☐ MasterCard   ☐ VISA   ☐ American Express

Name _____

Account No. _____

Valid from _____ Valid to _____

Signature _____

Peterson's Guides
Department 7702, 166 Bunn Drive, P.O. Box 2123, Princeton, NJ 08543-2123